汽／车／先／进／技／术／译／丛

电动汽车实用技术

ICE FREE ELECTRIC VEHICLE TECHNOLOGY FOR BUILDERS AND CONVERTERS

（双语版）

（英）约翰·哈代 著
徐永 杨斐翡 译

机械工业出版社

本书提供了将一辆传统的由内燃机为动力的汽车改装为电动汽车所需的知识和原则，包括电动机及其控制器、电池及管理系统以及车内辅助设备等。这些基本知识和原则既可帮助您深入地了解电动汽车各个部分的工作原理，又可应用于未来几年将会出现的产品，也适用于电动汽车的使用者和爱好者，为您挑选和使用电动汽车提供指导。此外，本书还详细介绍了电动汽车的优缺点，包括其超强的加速性能以及它对目前的石油和汽车行业及原材料等方面可能带来的冲击。

图书在版编目 (CIP) 数据

电动汽车实用技术：双语版：汉、英/（英）哈代（Hardy, J.）著；徐永，杨斐翡译.—北京：机械工业出版社，2013.9
（汽车先进技术译丛）
书名原文：ICE Free—Electric vehicle technology for builders and converters
ISBN 978-7-111-43591-4

Ⅰ.①实… Ⅱ.①哈… ②徐… ③杨… Ⅲ.①电动汽车-汉、英 Ⅳ.①U469.72

中国版本图书馆CIP数据核字（2013）第 180992 号

机械工业出版社（北京市百万庄大街 22 号 邮政编码100037）
策划编辑：何士娟 责任编辑：何士娟
责任校对：刘 岚 封面设计：鞠 杨
责任印制：张 楠
北京诚信伟业印刷有限公司印刷
2013 年 9 月第 1 版第 1 次印刷
169mm × 239mm •16 印张 • 382 千字
0 001— 4000 册
标准书号：ISBN 978-7-111-43591-4
定价：58.00 元

凡购本书，如有缺页、倒页、脱页，由本社发行部调换

电话服务	网络服务
社服务中心：（010）88361066	教材网：http://www.cmpedu.com
销售一部：（010）68326294	机工官网：http://www.cmpbook.com
销售二部：（010）88379649	机工官博：http://weibo.com/cmp1952
读者购书热线：（010）88379203	**封面无防伪标均为盗版**

谨将本书献给我的儿子阿舍，他在 15 岁时说出了一个五脏俱全的、完整的英文句子："爸爸，您真的应该读更多的莎士比亚"。㊀

For my son, Asher, who at the age of 15 came out with a perfectly formed and complete English sentence "Dad, you really should read more Shakespeare".

献给钴酸锂电池的发明者、德州大学奥斯汀分校的约翰·B·古迪纳夫教授（Professor John B.Goodenough）。他所领导的小组在该电池之后还发明了磷酸铁锂电池以便做进一步的改进。

For Professor John B Goodenough of the University of Texas, Austin, credited with inventing the Lithium Cobalt cell. For good measure, the group that he leads also proposed its successor, the Lithium Iron Phosphate cell.

献给中国的电池制造商，他们为我们提供了私营散户能够买得起并足以驱动一辆电动汽车的锂离子电池。

For the battery makers of China who gave us Lithium ion batteries that a private individual could buy with money and which were big enough to power an EV.

"我们曾经是燃料的供应者，现在我们正日益成为一个燃料的吞噬者。这些外国液体燃料的供应商毫无疑问对我们的工业至关重要，但我们对他们日益增加的依赖应该引起严重的且及时的关切。"

——温斯顿·斯潘塞·丘吉尔（1928 年 4 月 24 日国会辩论）

We used to be a source of fuel; we are increasingly becoming a sink. These supplies of foreign liquid fuel are no doubt vital to our industry, but our ever-increasing dependence upon them ought to arouse serious and timely reflection.

——Winston Spencer Churchill (Parliamentary Debate 24 Apr 1928)

"作为历史上最伟大的技术进步之一的内燃机有一个不幸的缺点，即空气污染。这种污染是如此的严重，以至于 64 个内燃机很快就可将天空染成棕褐色。"

——卡斯伯特·苏珀，一个完整的诺特尔故事

"The internal combustion engine, one of the greatest technological advancements in history, has an unfortunate downside, namely air pollution so thick that, very soon, sixty-four packs of crayons will include the colour Sky Brown".

——Cuthbert Soup, A Whole Nother Story

注：本书中的任何内容都不应被看作是对特定产品或它们之用法的推荐。本书中所提及的产品仅用于说明，并且书中对产品的描述和说明如有出入将以制造商的产品使用说明为准。

㊀ 译注：引用这句话体现了作者的幽默。因为世界上只有一个莎士比亚，并没有更多的莎士比亚，但英国人通常都是这样说的。这句话较好的译法应该是"爸爸，你真的应该多读些莎士比亚"。但为了体现作者的原意，我们采用了上面的译法。本书中还有许多类似的表达法体现了作者的睿智和幽默，读者在阅读中英文对照时可认真体会作者的意思。

Acknowledgement

Many people have contributed to this book, giving their time and their knowledge with great generosity. Some have read sections of the book in draft form and commented on them. Some have shared general information pertinent to the book. Some have agreed to my using their intellectual property. I am grateful to them all: any errors that remain are my fault, not theirs.

I'd like in particular to thank the following:

- Janet Coley and colleagues in the National Grid, for reviewing the section on the impact of EVs on the generation of electrical power.
- Professor Derek Fray FRS, FREng for sharing some insights into developments in Lithium Ion electrode materials, and reading and commenting on the text.
- Huw Hampson-Jones, Daniel Ugbo and Scott Lilley of Oxis Energy for taking time out of their busy work schedule to improve my understanding of advanced batteries.
- Dr Austin Hughes, formerly Department of Electrical and Electronic Engineering, University of Leeds, UK for reading and commenting on the motor and controller chapters.
- Professor Willett Kempton of University of Delaware for reviewing the section on Vehicle-to-Grid.
- Clive Lingard for reading and commenting on sections of the text.
- Chris Rogers of Network Operations at the National Grid for supplying the data underlying Figure 9-10 and 9-11.
- Andrew Vallance of Protean Electric for contributing most of the section on wheel motors and for input on other motor-related areas.
- Dr Alan Ward (former Chairman of the Battery Vehicle Society) for wading through the entire book in draft form and suggesting a number of improvements.

致 谢

很多人都对本书有所贡献，他们非常慷慨地奉献了他们的时间和知识。有些人阅读了本书的部分手稿并予以评论；有些人为本书提供了相关的信息；有些人同意我使用他们的知识产权。我对所有这些人心存感激，但如果本书中有任何的错误都是我的过错，而不是他们的。

我特别要感谢以下这些人：

- 珍妮特•科利以及她在国家电网工作的同事，他们帮助审阅了电动汽车对发电的影响这部分。
- 英国皇家学会院士及皇家工程院院士德里克•弗赖教授，分享了对锂离子电池电极材料研究进展的一些看法并阅读和评论本书的相应部分。
- 奥克斯能源的休•汉普森 - 琼斯，丹尼尔•阿格伯和斯科特•利利，他们在繁忙的工作日程中抽出时间来帮助我对先进电池的理解。
- 原英国利兹大学电气与电子工程系的奥斯汀•休斯博士，他阅读和评论了有关电动机和控制器的章节。
- 德拉瓦大学的威利特•肯普顿教授，他帮助审阅了汽车电网的部分。
- 克莱夫•林加德，他阅读和评论了本书的部分章节。
- 国家电网网络运营部的克里斯•罗杰斯，他提供了图 9-10 和图 9-11 所需的数据。
- 普洛廷电器的安德鲁•瓦兰斯，他对轮毂电动机以及与电动机相关的其他领域作出了贡献。
- 艾伦•沃德博士（前电动汽车协会主席），他阅读了本书的全部手稿，并提出了一些改进意见。

I owe a great debt to the scores of kindly individuals and a number of commercial organisations[1] who have supplied photographs or given me permission to use photographs that they have published elsewhere.

我还要对许多好心的个人和一些商业组织表示感谢。他们为本书提供了照片，或允许我使用他们在其他地方发表的照片。

I have attributed these photos in the text. I believe I have done this accurately but if you spot an error I would be most grateful if you would let me know so that I can make a correction in future editions. If I have wrongly attributed your photo to someone else I would in addition crave your forgiveness.

对于这些照片的来源我都在书中进行了说明[⊖]。我相信我已经准确地做到了这点。但如果您发现了错误并能让我知道，我将不胜感激，这样我可以在以后的版本中加以改正。如果我错误地将您的照片说成是别人的，我渴望得到您的宽恕。

Finally I'd like to salute Jack Rickard. Jack is a wealthy American who conceals a brilliant mind and a good heart behind a bumbling and mildly abrasive down-home demeanour. He spends his time and money converting cars to electric drive and producing a free-to-view weekly web-only TV show (http://www.evtv.me/) which is a mixture of electric vehicle news, a documentary of his conversions, and primary research on batteries. Some of the battery tests that he has done (noting his data on the backs of old envelopes) have come up with results I've seen nowhere else.

最后，我想向杰克•里卡德致敬。杰克是一个富裕的美国人，他将睿智的头脑和善良的心隐藏在笨手笨脚的、温和的且经过磨练的田园风范之后。他花费了许多的时间和金钱将传统汽车改装为电动汽车，并每周制作一部可在网站上免费观看的电视节目（http://www.evtv.me/），节目涵盖了电动汽车的新闻、他改装车的过程及电池研究的主要进展。他所做的一些电池测试的结果（在旧信封背面记录了他的实验数据）是独一无二的，我在其他地方都未见过。

1 Figure 7-10 is provided by Tecumseh Products Company, contact Tony Carstensen, Masterflux Business Unit Director, Tecumseh Products Company, 1136 Oak Valley Drive, Ann Arbor, MI 48108; (734) 584-9475, http://www.masteflux.com, tc@masterflux.com "By giving permission for the use of product photographs, Tecumseh Products Company makes no representations or warranties whatsoever regarding use of Masterflux® compressor products for the purposes discussed in this work."

⊖ 例如，图 7-10 由蒂卡姆西产品公司提供，请联系托尼•卡斯滕森，地址 Masterflux Business Unit Director, Tecumseh Products Company, 1136 Oak Valley Drive, Ann Arbor, MI 48108; 电话：(734) 584-9475, http://www.masteflux.com, tc@masterflux.com "通过给予产品照片的使用许可，对本书中所讨论的有关玛斯特富鲁克斯压缩机产品，蒂卡姆西产品公司没有任何责任或作任何保证。"

译者序

Perface

2012年3月，科技部公布的《电动汽车科技发展"十二五"专项规划》（以后简称为《规划》）明确地将"纯电驱动"电动汽车作为我国新能源汽车技术发展方向的重中之重，并将其列为我国提高汽车产业竞争力、保障能源安全和发展低碳经济的重要途径之一。

可以预见，在未来的几年内，电动汽车将成为我国经济的新的增长点，也必将成为城市中产阶层人士的首选。这不仅是我国经济发展的一个目标，也是世界各国经济发展的一个趋势。译者在英国及欧洲各个国家明显地看到了这一远景。但电动汽车目前的状况与任何高科技产品在发展初期的经历十分相似。任何一个40岁以上的人，当我们回顾手机、个人电脑、DVD、电子表及互联网的初期阶段时，无论是从价格还是技术的成熟度上看，我们在当时大都会认为那些产品根本不可能普及，人们也没有那样的需求。但这些高科技产品在近20年间的发展速度之快则是大大出乎我们的意料。

目前电动汽车发展正处于当初那样的时期。但国内大多数人还没有感受到一个新时代的到来，他们还没有从目前国内各大城市的雾霾中看到空气污染的严重性和传统内燃机汽车发展的不可持续性，也没有从目前大幅增长的油价中去感知新一轮石油危机爆发的危险。这一方面是由于长期的惯性思维在短期内很难改变，另一方面也是由于对电动汽车缺乏应有的了解。本书的及时出版有助于帮助读者对电动汽车的技术和发展有一个更加全面的了解，以弥补目前国内读者在这方面信息的欠缺，并帮助他们及时地赶上世界的新潮流。

本书的作者John Hardy先生在20世纪70年代初毕业于英国剑桥大学的机械工程专业，他对各种汽车技术情有独钟，并于最近自己建造了一辆福特GT40跑车。他对电动汽车的兴趣已经持续了很多年。50年前在学生时代时，他就一直认为我们那种开发石油的速度是不可持续的。当他看到他所处的时代对北海石油的挖掘和燃烧时，他的担忧日益加重。除此之外，他还认为目前的纯活塞式发动机及其由几十个运动部件的列阵所组成的支持系统在工程上看很不优雅而且笨拙，并与他所追求的设计风格相左。因此，他决定将他多年的研究成果和心得汇集在本书中，献给读者。

虽然作者本身在传统的活塞式发动机及电动汽车方面均有所研究，但本着严谨治学的态度和对读者负责的精神，他在写作本书时还是咨询了该领域里各个方面的顶级专家和学者，包括前电动汽车协会主席艾伦·沃德博士及钴酸锂电池的发明者约翰B.古迪纳夫教授等。这就保证了本书在各个方面都能引领该领域的新潮流，也确保了各个技术细节的论述准确无误。因此，这是一本在电动汽车领域值得拥有并珍藏的好书。

本书提供了将一辆传统的由内燃机为动力的汽车改装为电动汽车所需的知识和原则，包括电动机及其控制器、电池及管理系统，以及车内的辅助设备等。这些基本知识和原则既可帮助您深入地了解电动汽车各个部分的工作原理，又可应用于未来几年将会出现的产品，也适用于电动汽车的使用者和爱好者，为您挑选和使用电动汽车提供指导。此外，本书还详细介绍了电动汽车的优缺点，包括其超强的加速性能以及它对目前的石油和汽车行业及原材料等方面可能带来的冲击。

无论您是对电动汽车有兴趣，还是仅仅想了解一下这方面的知识，本书都非常适用于您。本书也适用于电动汽车使用者、爱好者、组装者，以及各类学校相应专业的学生和科研人员。甚至如果您对与汽车有关的任何领域都不感兴趣，而仅仅是为了学习英语的话，本书也值得您拥有。因此，本书也适合于作为高校学生的课外英语读物，因为本书的语言风格很有特色，英语纯正、优雅、地道，反映了 20 世纪 70 年代剑桥人的严谨、睿智和幽默的风格，对您学习英语肯定受益匪浅。

在翻译本书时我们尽量忠实于原文，以体现作者的语言风格。对于人名或公司名字我们在文中也给出了中文的翻译，以便读者对照原文在网上找到他们。对于书中所涉及的英国俚语及风土人情等，我们在适当的地方都加了注释，以帮助读者理解。另外，在翻译本书时我们也将书中所使用的英制单位全部转换为米制的，以适应我国读者的习惯。

虽然在翻译时我们对照原稿进行了多次反复的校对，也以我们在英国生活 10 年之久的经历尽量反应出作者语言的原貌。限于译者的水平，错译和误译之处在所难免，垦请读者在阅读时不吝指出，也可将你们的感想发到译者的电子信箱：emailyxu@gmail.com，以便再版时修订。

本书在翻译过程中还得到原作者的大力支持，在此对他表示衷心感谢。

徐永，杨斐翡

2013 年 3 月

Contents

目录

1 Introducing Electric Vehicles
电动汽车简介

Electric vehicles (EVs) have a lot going for them: little noise apart from the rush of air and the whine of tyres. No urban air pollution. Little dependence on dwindling global oil supplies. Negligible fuel costs. No need for a network of fuel stations. Low speed acceleration that humbles the mightiest supercar. And (if it matters to you) lower carbon emissions.

电动汽车（简称 EV）有很多优点：除了气流声和轮胎的“呼噜”声外没有其他噪声；没有市区的空气污染；对正在日益减少的全球石油供应的依赖性很小；燃料成本可以忽略不计；不需要加油站网络；低速时的加速性能令最强大的超级跑车也显得相形见绌；减少碳排放量（如果这对您很重要的话）。它并不在乎电力的来源（图 1-1）。

Of course EVs have their problems too-primarily poor electric-only range, expensive batteries and time-consuming recharge. These problems meant electric vehicles were only just reaching mass-market early adoption in 2012, but the price of EVs from mainstream manufacturers is high, availability restricted and the choice limited; so if you want one, you may want to consider building or converting a vehicle yourself. This book will give you the knowledge you need to decide how to go about just such a build or conversion.

当然，电动汽车也有自己的问题——主要是纯电动驱动续驶里程较短，电池昂贵及充电较费时。这些问题意味着电动汽车才刚刚在 2012 年达到大规模市场应用的早期阶段，但来自主流厂商的电动汽车的价格很高，产量很小，型号有限。所以如果您想要一辆电动汽车，您可能要考虑为您自己建造或改装一辆。本书将会向您提供必要的知识，以帮助您确定如何着手进行这样的建造或改装。

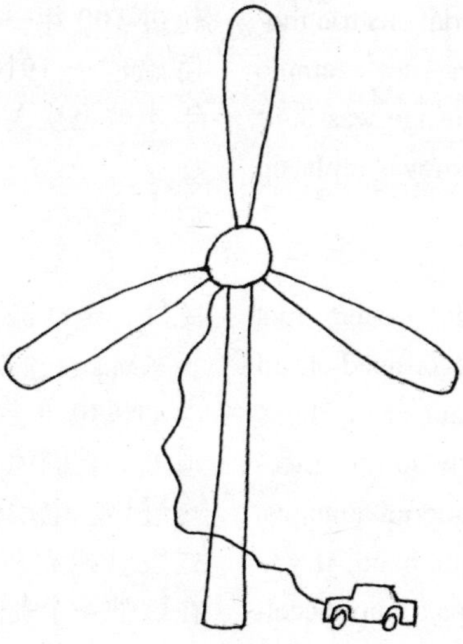

Figure 1–1 EVs are not fussy about where the electricity comes from

图 1–1 电动汽车并不在乎电力的来源

But first what do we mean by an electric vehicle (EV)? A pure EV is simple enough – a road vehicle propelled by an electric motor rather than an Internal Combustion Engine (I.C.E. - i.e. a conventional petrol or diesel engine). It is usually assumed that the electric power to run the motor comes from onboard batteries (rather than fuel cells, or overhead wires like an old-style trolley bus). Such electric vehicles are sometimes referred to as “BEVs” (Battery Electric Vehicles).

但首先要说明的是我们所说的电动汽车（EV）是什么意思？简单来说就是一辆纯电动汽车。它是一辆由电动机而不是由内燃机（简称ICE，即传统的汽油或柴油发动机）驱动的道路车辆。人们通常认为电动机的电力来自于车载电池（而不是燃料电池，或像一辆老式的无轨电车上的架空电线）。这种电动汽车有时被称为“BEVs”（电池电动汽车）。

Then there are Hybrid Electric Vehicles (HEVs). Hybrids use two sorts of power – an IC engine plus an electric motor in one of four basic configurations. HEVs are discussed in more detail later.

此外，还有一种混合动力电动汽车（简称HEVs，即混合动力汽车）。混合动力汽车使用两种动力——内燃机＋电动机，并有四种不同的基本配置。有关混合动力汽车将在后面详细讨论。

➢ Strengths and weaknesses

➢ 优点与缺点

The best part of an electric vehicle is the motor. A cheap electric motor is superior to the mostly highly developed conventional internal combustion (IC) engine in almost every respect: for similar output, electric motors are smaller, lighter, have far fewer moving parts, are much quieter and need far less maintenance (there are some industrial electric motors that have run for over 100 years – for example the Middlesbrough’s Transporter Bridge was built in 1910 and the electric drive system was replaced in 2011).

电动汽车最优越的部分是电动机。一个廉价的电动机几乎在每一个方面都优于大多数精心设计的传统内燃机（IC）的发动机。对于类似的功率输出，电动机的体积更小，重量更轻，运动部件更少，噪声更小，且需要的维护少得多（有一些工业电动机已经运行了超过100年——例如英国米德尔斯堡的转运桥始建于1910年，其电力驱动系统在2011年才被更换）。

Electric motors don’t need an ignition system, fuel system or exhaust system. They never need an oil change. Old ones don’t drip on your drive. They are very efficient so don’t get nearly so hot. Electric motors have several more subtle advantages. Piston engines have a narrow torque band: if you are driving a hot hatch and want maximum acceleration from a standing start you need to anticipate the need for power, wind up the rpm and slip the

此外，电动机不需要点火系统、供油系统或排气系统。它们从来不需要更换机油。用旧了的电动机也不会将机油滴落在您家门口的停车道上。它们运转效率非常高，因此几乎不会运转过热。电动机还有一些更微妙的优势。活塞式发动机有一个狭窄的转矩范围：如果您正在驾驶一个炙热的铁笼子，并希望从静止开始获得最大的加速度，您必须预见到对动力的需求，适时增加发动机的转速并且恰到好处地使

clutch off the line. The typical EV electric motor on the other hand is set up to provide maximum torque at or near zero rpm, so a maximum-effort standing start is simply a matter of pushing the accelerator to the floor. This is part of what makes a good EV fun: you are never caught in the wrong gear, because the torque curve looks like Table Mountain rather than Mount Fuji.

用离合器。然而，典型电动汽车的电动机是专为提供在接近或达到零转速时的最大转矩而设计的，所以那种费尽周折的由静止起步在此只是一个简单地将加速踏板一推到底的问题。这也是使得一辆很好的电动汽车能成为乐趣的部分原因：您永远不会陷入错误的档位，因为转矩曲线看起来像桌山（译注：桌山是位于南非的一个平顶的山，表明转矩曲线很平缓），而不是像富士山。

Some EVs don't even have a gearbox at all. None need automatic transmissions, flappy paddle gearboxes, lightweight flywheels and all the other paraphernalia invented to get round the limitations of IC engines.

有些电动汽车甚至没有任何变速器，更不需要自动变速器、半自动变速器、轻量化飞轮和所有其他用于消除内燃机的局限性而发明的各种玩意儿。

Electric motors tend to be high-torque devices. For example, an 11″ (28cm) diameter series wound electric motor is a monster that is quite capable of snapping a driveshaft if it is fed enough amps (Figure 1-2).

电动机往往有较高的转矩。例如：一个直径为 11in（28cm）的直流串励电动机就像一个力大无比的怪兽，如果给它喂饱电流，它就有足够大的力量来扯断传动轴（图 1-2）。

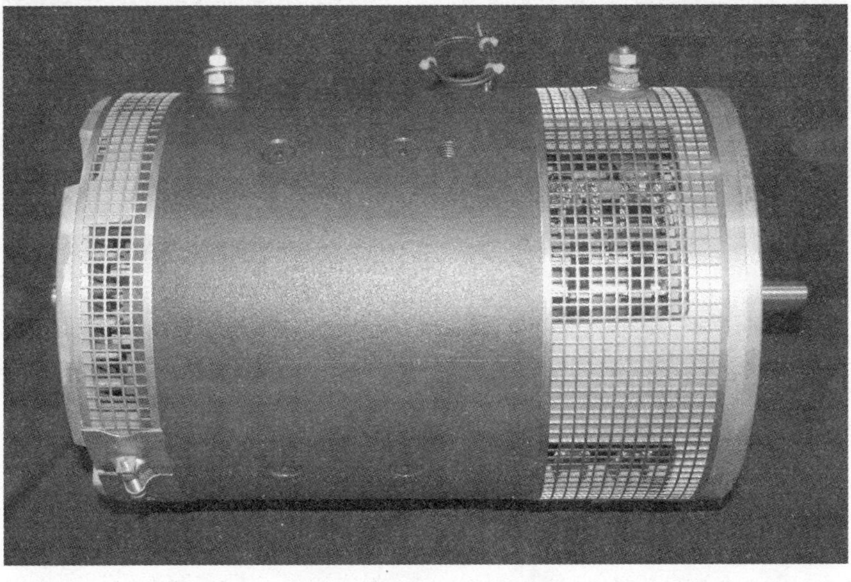

Figure 1–2 Warp 11 motor - capable of generating huge torque from zero rpm with the right controller. Photo courtesy of Netgain Motors (http://www.go-ev.com)

图 1–2 沃普 28cm 电动机 – 配上适当的控制器后能在零转速时产生大转矩。照片由那特根发动机公司提供 (http://www.go-ev.com)

That kind of motor doesn't need help from a puny little four-banger in accelerating you away from the lights. Moreover it manages to combine neck-snapping acceleration off the line with good economy in cruise. A big powerful IC engine is hopelessly inefficient around town. A big powerful electric motor isn't.

这种电动机不需要 4 个像小香肠一样的内燃机来帮您在红灯之后快速加速。此外，它能有效地将好到能扭断脖子的起步加速性能与巡航时的良好节能相结合。一辆带有高功率内燃机的汽车在市内挪动时是无可救药的低效，但一个具有大功率电动机的电动汽车则完全不同。

There is however a moment when the puny little four banger can cough modestly and take a step forward. That's when somebody mentions that there are five adults and their luggage to be taken from London to Glasgow. The 11" motor (or even a 7" motor) would have no trouble with such a trip. The issue is batteries. No one has yet marketed a battery that is anywhere close to doing the job. Compared with a tank of fuel, even the best batteries store a pitiful amount of energy and (in practice) take a long time to charge. The all-electric Tesla Roadster is said to have a range of 250 miles on a charge – that is phenomenal by EV standards (20 – 90 miles is more common) – but the Tesla has only two seats and a set of batteries that cost as much as many complete cars. When it comes to load carrying over long distances, the best EV in the world is totally outclassed by an early VW Beetle or a Fiat Panda.

然而对内燃机汽车而言，有时这 4 个“小香肠一样的活塞”会气喘吁吁地向前一步步地迈出。这就像有人提到的用车将 5 个彪形大汉连同他们的行李从伦敦拉到格拉斯哥斯时的情形。28cm 电动机（或者甚至是 18cm 电动机）在这样的行程中就没有任何麻烦。电动汽车的问题在于电池。现今所销售的电池中没有一款是能够胜任这一工作的（译注：指从伦敦到格拉斯哥斯）。与一箱油相比，即使是最好的电池也只能存储少得可怜的能量，并在实践中需要很长的充电时间。全电动特斯拉跑车据说一次充电能跑上 400km。从电动汽车的标准来看这是十分惊人的（30~150km 则是较常见的）——但特斯拉只有两个座位和一个成本高于许多整车的电池组。如果要用电动汽车来进行远距离运输，世界上最好的电动汽车也完全比不上一个早期的大众甲壳虫或菲亚特熊猫。

So is that it then?Are EVs are so seriously,er, range-challenged sa to be useless?Well,not quite. The statisticians tell us that for most people most

那么我们就没有办法了吗？电动汽车如此严重地，或者说在运行里程方面（图 1-3），受到挑战，难道它就一无用处吗？其实不然。

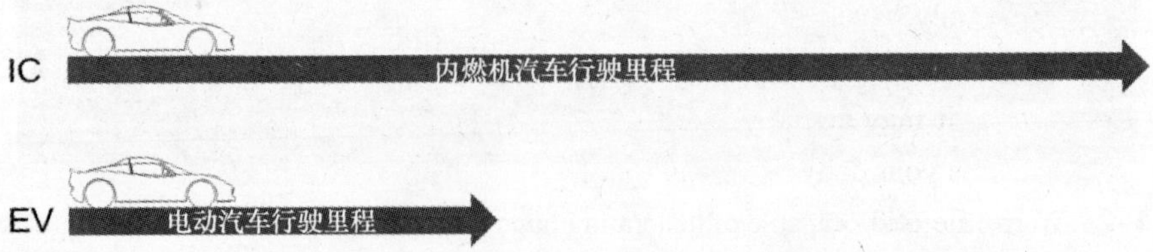

Figure 1–3 Short range is the Achilles heel of EVs

图 1–3 里程数过短是电动汽车的软肋

of the time driving distances are short. How short? Less than 40 miles a day. A 40 miles range is right in the sweet spot for an EV. If you commute 40 miles a day and can persuade your employer to put a charging post in the car park at the office, you only need a 20 – 30 mile range.

统计学家告诉我们，对于大多数人来说在大部分时间里他们的行程是很短的。有多短？每天不到 60km。60km 正是电动汽车的最佳里程范围。如果您每天上下班要开 60km，并能说服您的老板在办公室的停车场内设置一个充电插座，那么您的电动汽车只需要 30~40km 的里程范围（图 1-4）。

So whether EVs are for you depends on your needs. If you are an Account Manager covering a large territory, then an EV wouldn't work for you. If on the other hand most of your driving is moderate-distance commutes and shopping trips, then an EV may be well-suited to your needs.

所以，电动汽车是不是适合您取决于您的需要。如果您是一个客户经理，每天需要远程奔跑，那么电动汽车就不适合您。但是，如果您大部分的驾驶距离只是中等的上下班往返和购物之旅，那么一辆电动汽车可能非常符合您的需求。

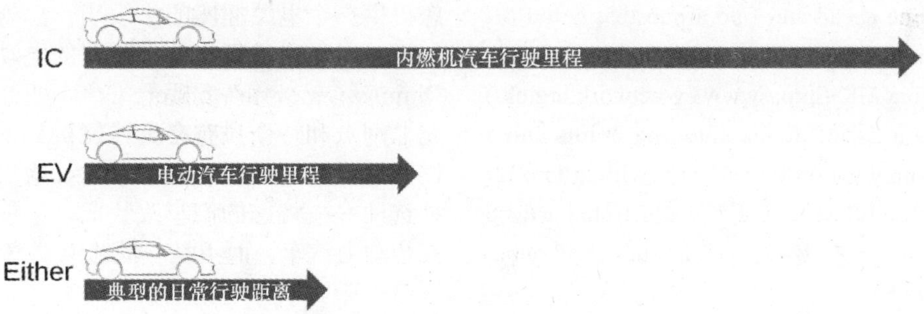

Figure 1–4 Most people don't need long range most of the time

图 1–4 大多数人在大部分时间里并不需要长的行程

So how do you cope with the occasional long journey? If you are a two-car household, one EV and one conventional car may be a good mix, with the choice of who gets which car decided over the breakfast table. If you only have one car, but you go and visit granny on the other side of the country a few times a year, it may actually work out cheaper to have an EV as your daily drive and rent a conventional car for the odd occasions that you need it. Check it out. A forty-mile commute five days a week is 200 miles a week – maybe 6 gallons of petrol a week, or 24 gallons a month. At the

那么，如何应付您偶尔的长途旅行的需要呢？如果您是有两辆车的家庭，一辆电动汽车和一辆传统的汽车可能会是一个很好的组合，可以在早餐桌上决定谁使用哪辆汽车。如果您只拥有一辆汽车，但如果您一年要去住在本国另一端的奶奶家看望几次，拥有一辆电动汽车作为您的日常驾座并在偶尔需要的时候租一辆传统汽车可能更为划算（译注：在英国人的眼中，从本国一端到另一端也就是 500~600km，因此，本方案是可行的。但由于中国的幅员辽阔，您也许可以考虑不同的方案）。我们

time of writing, petrol is about £6.00 a gallon in the UK, so 24 gallons is £120. Weekend hire of a full size car might be around £50. Even when you factor in the cost of electricity (perhaps 200 kW-[1] hours at 10p/kW hour = £20) it still looks feasible. If you are in the US the numbers will be different, but the conclusions much the same.

可以算算看。每天 60km 的里程，每周 5 天的工作日，算起来就是每周 300km，也许是每周 30 升的汽油，或每月 120L。在写作本书时，中国国内的汽油价格约为 8 块钱一升，120L 就是 960 块钱。周末租用一辆商务用车可能是 500 块钱。甚至当您算上电价成本的因素（也许是 200kW•h ㊀ × 0.70 元 /kW•h=140 元），它看起来还是可行的。如果您在美国，这一数字也许会有所不同，但结论大致相同。

Another approach is the leisurely one. A long distance drive in an EV is perfectly possible if you are prepared to take long breaks. If for example you have a 150 mile journey to do and an EV with a range of 100 miles, then you may find that you could phone ahead and find a pub that could offer you an electrical outlet whilst you have lunch. EV Network UK (http://www.ev-network.org.uk/) maintains a list of public charging points and a members-only list of fellow-EVers willing to offer charging facilities. Figure 1–5 illustrated a third option – convert your car to a plug-in hybrid rather than a pure EV.

另外一种方法是休闲式的。如果您计划在途中作较长时间的休息的话，用电动汽车进行长途旅行也是完全可能的。例如：如果您的旅程是 250km 而您只有一辆 150km 行程的电动汽车，您可以提前打电话找一家愿意为您提供一个电源插座的小饭店，您就可在吃午饭时对电池进行充电。英国的电动汽车网（http://www.ev-network.org.uk/）列出了公共充电网点和一个只有会员才能得到的愿意提供充电设施的成员名单。图 1-5 给出了第三种选项——将您的汽车改装成一辆能充电的混合动力汽车，而不是一辆纯电动汽车。

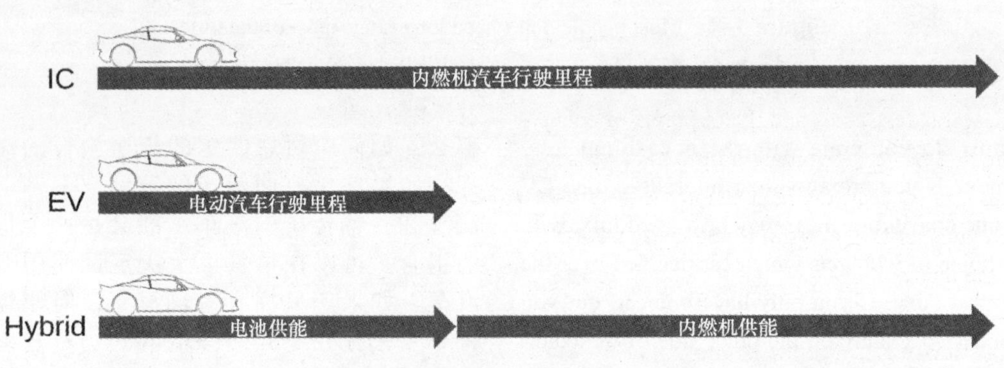

Figure 1–5 Plug in Hybrids combine the best of both worlds (at some cost)

图 1–5 插电式混合动力汽车结合了两者的优点（但要多些费用）

1 "kW" is used throughout this book as an abbreviation for "kilowatt" (1000 Watts).

㊀ 在本书中我们将用 kW（千瓦）作为功率的单位。

Most of the time, leave the IC engine switched off and use the car like an ordinary EV. When you are going on a longer trip start with charged batteries but use both sources of power to stretch the range. Hybrids are not all sweetness and light however. They need a complete electrical drivetrain, plus all or most of the elements of an IC drivetrain. Hybrids are therefore more expensive than either an equivalent IC-engined car or an equivalent EV. Furthermore (all other things being equal) they are heavier and have less room for people and luggage.

在大部分时间里您可关闭内燃机并像一辆普通的电动汽车那样使用，当您需要进行一个较长的行程时，开始将电池充满，然后使用两种动力来扩展里程范围。然而混合动力汽车并不都是令人振奋和轻松愉快的，它们需要一个完整的电气传动系统，加上全部或大部分的内燃机传动系统。因此，混合动力汽车比同等的内燃机汽车或电动汽车都要贵。此外（在所有其他方面都相同的情况下），它们更重，并有较小的乘坐和行李空间。

➢ The shape of this book

➢ 本书的结构

This book is intended to be a foundation. It introduces you to the background knowledge and principles that you need in order to build an electric car, or (more likely) to convert a car originally powered by a petrol or diesel IC engine to electric drive. It is not a detailed "how to" book, neither is it a substitute for researching what is out there: the field is moving too quickly for that. What it will give you though is enduring principles that can be applied to products that will appear in the coming years. We'll minimise the maths, but to get the best out of the book it will help to understand volts, amps, watts, resistance and the concepts of energy, torque and power. If you are a little hazy on some of these, never fear: the next chapter is a refresher which you can skip or skim if you are comfortable with the theory.

本书的目的是提供一个奠基石。它向您介绍了为建造一辆电动汽车，或者（更可能）将一辆由汽油或柴油内燃机为动力的汽车改装为电动汽车所需的背景知识和原则。它不是一本详细介绍"如何做"的书，也不是一本研究该领域最新进展的替代读物，因为这一领域的发展实在是太快了。然而，它能给您的是一些根本的原则，可应用于未来几年会出现的产品。我们将尽量少用数学，但为发挥本书的最佳效果，了解一些关于伏特、安培、瓦特、电阻以及能量、转矩和功率等概念是有益处的。如果您对这些感到有点懵懂，不必担心，下一章就对这些概念进行复习，如果您熟悉这些理论，您可以跳过或简单浏览一下。

Thereafter, we'll start with motors. There are several types of motor that could be actively considered for EV conversions (see Figure 1-6). By the time you have read the chapter on motors you should understand the principles behind all these motor types.

然后，我们将介绍电动机。可以实际用来作为改装电动汽车用的电动机有好几种（图 1 - 6）。当您读完有关电动机的这一章后，您应该明白所有这些类型电动机的工作原理。

Next we'll look at controllers (Figure 1-7). Controllers are to EVs what carburettors are to petrol engines. In an EV, the throttle pedal is connected to the controller. The type of controller is governed by the type of motor, but a poor choice of controller can either waste a lot of money or turn your car into a gutless wonder.

接下来我们将介绍控制器（图 1-7）。控制器之于电动汽车就像化油器（译注：现在用电子喷射装置）之于汽油发动机那么重要。在一辆电动汽车中，加速踏板是连接到控制器上的。控制器的类型是由电动机的类型决定的，控制器选择不当既会浪费很多钱，又可能将您的爱车变成中看不中用的东西。

Brushed Permanent Magnet DC 有刷直流永磁电动机

Series wound and Separately-excited DC 直流串励及他励电动机

Brushless DC 无刷直流电动机

AC Induction 交流感应电动机

Figure 1–6 Various Motor Types, Photos courtesy of the following - left to right: Bruce Roberts, Netgain Motors, Guangdong M&C Electric Power Co., MES-DEA.

图 1–6 各种电动机类型，从左到右照片提供者为：布鲁斯 • 罗伯茨、那特根发动机公司、广东麦科尔电力设备有限公司、MES-DEA

Low power DC controller 低功率直流控制器

High power DC Controller 高功率直流控制器

Controller for AC motors 交流电动机控制器

Figure 1–7 Typical Controllers. Photos courtesy of the following - left to right: Curtis Instruments, Kurt Clayton, BRUSA Elektronik AG

图 1–7 典型的控制器，从左到右照片提供者为：柯蒂斯仪器公司、库尔特 • 克莱顿、布鲁萨电器公司

After that we will move on to batteries (Figure 1-8). Batteries are probably the largest, heaviest and most expensive element in a conversion.

接着我们将引入电池（图 1-8）。电池也许是改装过程中最大、最重和最昂贵的部分。

The section on batteries is in two parts. The first will focus on the principles of operation of the batteries themselves. The second will look at the thorny issue of managing long strings of batteries in an EV, including how to charge them.

对电池的叙述有两部分：第一部分将注重于电池本身的工作原理；第二部分将着眼于用于电动汽车的长串电池的管理，包括如何充电等棘手的问题。

AGM Lead Acid

AGM 铅酸蓄电池

Flooded Lead Acid

富液式铅酸蓄电池

Prismatic Lithium Ion

棱柱形锂离子电池

Nickel Metal Hydride

镍氢电池

Lithium Sulphur

锂硫电池

Lithium Ion Polymer

锂离子聚合物电池

Figure 1–8 Battery Types. Photos courtesy of the following (top row, left to right) OPTIMA Batteries, Trojan Battery, Greg Sievert (bottom row) Randy Hsieh, Andrej Pecjak

图 1–8 电池的类型。照片提供者（上排从左至右）为欧帕提玛电池公司、特洛伊电池公司、格雷格•西弗特，（下排从左至右）兰迪•霍斯、安德烈•皮科克

When we have concluded the section on batteries we'll move on to the other things that you need to consider if you are going to have an EV that you can live with summer and winter. These include heating, air conditioning, power steering and power brakes.

在结束了对电池的描述之后，如果您打算拥有一辆电动汽车使您能舒适地度过夏冬二季，我们将接着谈您需要考虑的一些其他问题，如取暖、空调、动力转向系统和动力制动器等。

Next we will look briefly at some of the other technologies that have been discussed as alternatives to IC engines for powering road vehicles. These include ultra-capacitors and even hyper-flywheels and compressed air. We'll also look at fuel cells and outline why, in the short term anyway, this technology is a monstrous red herring. In this section, we will look in more detail at the four classes of hybrid, ranging from machines that are little more than an IC engined car with an electrically-augmented transmission, to EVs with a range-extender.

下一步我们将简要地讨论一些技术，这些技术已经作为内燃机的替代品为道路车辆供能。这些技术包括超级电容器，甚至还包括超级飞轮和压缩空气。我们也将讨论燃料电池并简要地说明为什么至少在短期内这项技术是不可行的。在本节中，我们将更详细地探讨四种类型的混合动力，从带有电动增强传输系统的、比内燃机发动机略为复杂的汽车到带有增程器的电动汽车。

Widespread adoption of EVs could be expected to have positive benefits in unexpected ways. We'll discuss the evidence for the likely impact on such diverse areas as childhood stress, and the severity of asthma attacks in urban areas. The CO_2 emissions associated with EVs will be covered, but there will be no preaching about climate change. We'll also talk about the risks. Oil and the automotive sector constitute a large chunk of world economic activity. Changing it radically is risky. Also a widespread move to EVs might just exchange one materials shortage (oil) for another (battery or motor raw materials).

NB where prices or price ranges are quoted in this book, they are approximate, illustrative and at the time of writing.

我们期望，电动汽车的广泛应用会带来令人意想不到的正面效益。我们将探讨一些证据，说明电动汽车在广泛的领域内对诸如儿童压力及市区内哮喘发作的严重性等方面可能产生的影响。与电动汽车相关的二氧化碳排放量也将是我们讨论的范围，但我们不会进行有关气候变化方面的说教。我们还将讨论有关的风险。石油和汽车行业构成了世界经济活动很大的一部分，从根本上改变目前的布局是有风险的。大规模地发展电动汽车也许仅仅是将一种材料（石油）的短缺换成另一种材料（电池或电动机的原材料）的短缺。

注：在本书中所引述的价格或价格范围都是近似的，说明性的，而且是在写作期间得到的。

2 Refresher course
复习课程

I promised to minimise the maths, but if the rest of this book is to make sense, you need to be equipped with a few concepts, so we will start with a refresher on these. If you know all about this kind of thing then feel free to skip the chapter. The topics we will cover include:

我将尽量少用数学。但如果您想读懂本书的其余部分，您需要理解几个概念。所以我们将从复习这些概念开始。如果您已经熟悉这些概念，您可以跳过本章。我们将讨论的主题包括：

- Volts amps and ohms
- Series and Parallel circuits
- AC and DC power
- Back EMF
- Electricity and Magnetism
- Force, Torque, Energy and Power

- 伏特、安培和欧姆
- 串联和并联电路
- 交流和直流
- 反电动势
- 电和磁
- 力、转矩、能量与功率

➢ Volts, Amps and Ohms

➢ 伏特、安培和欧姆

One of the most helpful ways of visualising electricity is to think of it like the flow of water in a pipe. Water flow has two principle characteristics:

理解电力最有用的方法之一是将它想象为管道中的水流。水流有两个主要特点：

- Pressure (measured in bar or pounds per square inch)
- Volume or mass flow (in litres per hour or gallons per minute)

压力（单位是 bar 或 Pa，即 N/m^2）

体积或质量流量（单位是 m3/h 或 kg/min）

To take an example, a pressure washer is a high pressure/low volume device. It pushes out relatively little water but does so with great force. On the other hand a culvert or drain pipe buried under a road may pass a vast amount of water but at relatively low pressure. A fire hose is somewhere in between: it produces quite a lot of water at a fairly high pressure.

举个例子，高压清洗机是一个高压低容量设备。它喷出的水量较少，但有很大的压力。另一方面，地下涵洞或排水管可以通过大量的水，但压力相对较低。消防软管则介于两者之间，它在一个相当高的压力下会喷出相当大量的水。

Voltage in an electrical circuit is a bit like water pressure: it is what makes the current flow. Electri-

电路中的电压有点像水压，它迫使电流流过。另一方面，电流则像在管道中流动的水量。

cal current on the other hand is like the amount of water flowing in the pipe. An automotive ignition system is a bit like that pressure washer: it delivers enormously high voltages but the current (the actual amount of electricity flowing) is tiny. An electric arc welder on the other hand is like the culvert: an enormous current at relatively low voltage (Figure 2-1).

汽车点火系统有点像高压清洗机，它提供了极高的电压，但电流（电荷流动的量）是很小的。另一方面，电弧焊机就像一个涵洞，在相对较低的电压下有一个巨大的电流（图 2-1）。

Figure 2–1 High pressure, low volume (top); low pressure, high volume (bottom).Photos courtesy of Auto Lavish (top left), Rob Clare (top right), Jen Cox (bottom left), Official US Navy images under the Creative Commons Attribution 2.0 Generic licence (bottom right)

图 2–1 高压低容量（上图）；低压高容量（下图）。照片由拉维斯汽车（左上）、罗布 • 克莱克（右上）、珍 • 考克斯（左下）、美国海军的官方图像经创作共署名 2.0 通用执照许可（右下）

So an electrical voltage corresponds to water pressure, and the electrical current measured in amperes (or “amps” for short) corresponds to the volume of water flowing. So how do the two relate? Once again, there is a useful analogy with water in a system of pipes: the more restrictive the pipes, the lower the flow. The higher the pressure, the greater the flow.

因此，电压就相当于水压，单位为安培 (A) 的电流则对应于流水量。那么，电压与电流的关系如何？我们再用一个水管道系统中有用的比喻：管道的限制越多，流量就越低；压力越高，流量就越大。

It is the same with electricity. The electrical equivalent of a restriction in a pipe is resistance. For a given resistance, doubling the voltage doubles the current, and halving the voltage halves the current.

在电力系统中也一样。管道中的限制等效于电路中的电阻。对于一个给定的电阻，电压增加一倍，电流也加倍；电压减半，电流也减半。

The other thing about electric current is that it normally needs a complete loop or circuit, and the current is the same all the way round the circuit. Once again, the analogy with water flowing in a pipe helps visualise it (Figure 2-2). Unlike a water pipe however, a break in an electrical circuit does not result in electricity spilling out onto the ground!

关于电流的另一个问题是，它通常需要一个完整的回路或电路，并且电流在整个电路都是相同的。当然，将电流与水在管道中流动作比喻有助于将其可视化（图 2-2）。然而，与水管不同，电路被切断时并不会使电荷倾倒到地上！

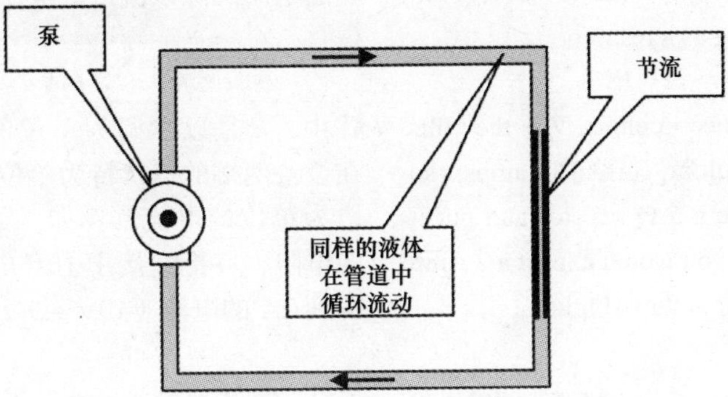

Figure 2–2 Water "circuit"

图 2–2 液压管道

Here for comparison (Figure 2-3) is a simple electrical circuit with a battery in the left hand leg and a fixed resistance in the right hand leg. As with the water, the same current flows at all points around the circuit. The concept of electrical resistance is an important one. Volts and amps can vary, but resistance is usually a fixed characteristic of an electrical device (although it may change with temperature). A motor field winding has a resistance, an electric light bulb has a resistance, even the wires that you use to connect up electrical devices will have a (small) resistance.

作为比较，图 2-3 所示为一个简单的电路，其左边有一个电池，右边有一个固定电阻。与水路一样，相同的电流流过电路中的每个部分。电阻是一个重要的概念。电压和电流可以不同，但电阻通常是一个电气设备的固有特性（虽然它可能会随温度而发生变化）。一个电动机的励磁线圈有电阻，一个电灯泡有电阻，甚至是您用于连接电气设备的导线也有一个（小的）电阻。

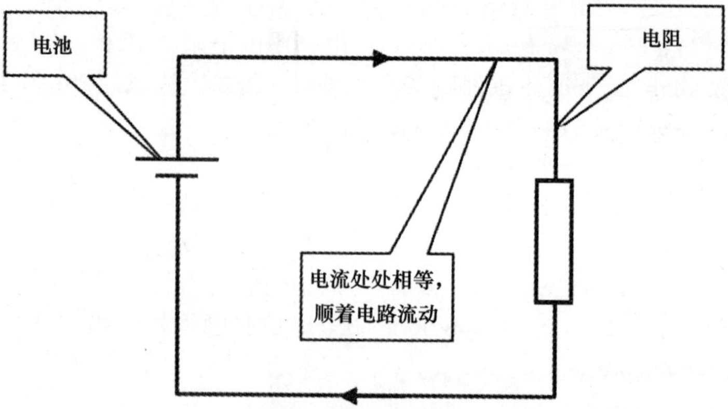

Figure 2–3 Simple electrical circuit

图 2–3 简单电路

Resistance is measured in Ohms (Symbol Ω) and is simply the voltage drop across the device divided the current flowing as a result or

$$R = U \div I \text{ or } U = I \times R$$

...where R is the resistance in ohms, V is the volts applied and I is the resulting current in amps: so for example if you have a 5 Ω resistor and put it across a 10 volt battery, you would expect a 2 Amp current (10 volts ÷ 5 Ω) to flow (Figure 2-4).

电阻的单位是欧姆（符号 Ω），它是设备两端的电压降除以流过的电流，即

$$R = U \div I \text{ 或 } U = I \times R$$

式中，R 是以欧姆为单位的电阻；U 是施加在设备两端的以伏特为单位的电压；I 是以安培为单位的电流。例如，如果您有一个 5Ω 的电阻，并把它接于 10V 电池的两端，您会得到 2A 的电流（10V ÷ 5Ω）（图 2-4）。

Alternatively if you measured the current and found that it was 5 amps, you could deduce that the battery provided 25 volts (5 Amps x 5 Ω) - Figure 2-5. Devices intended for use with mains electricity (240 Volt in the UK) have a much higher resistance than devices intended to work off (say) a 12 volt car battery. To take an example, a typical old style incandescent light bulb designed to work from UK household current will have a resistance when hot of around 1000Ω. A typical 12v volt car headlamp bulb on the other hand has a resistance of around 2.4 Ω in use. If you put mains voltage across the car headlamp bulb, the current would be 240/2.4 i.e. 100 amps – for a very short time before it burned out.

另外，如果您测量电流并发现它是 5A，您可以推断出该电池提供 25V 的电压（5A × 5Ω）（图 2-5）。使用市电（在英国为 240V）的设备比工作于（例如）12V 汽车电池的设备具有高得多的电阻。举个例子，工作于英国市电的一个典型的老式白炽灯泡在炙热状态下将有约 1000Ω 的电阻。另一方面，一个典型的 12V 电压汽车前照灯的灯泡在使用时的电阻约为 2.4Ω。如果您将市电电压施加于前照灯灯泡的两端，电流将为 240/2.4，即 100A，它将在很短的时间内被烧毁。

These terms are at the heart of electrics and electronics, and in truth they are not difficult concepts.

这些名词是电气和电子产品的核心部分。说实话，它们都是不难的概念。

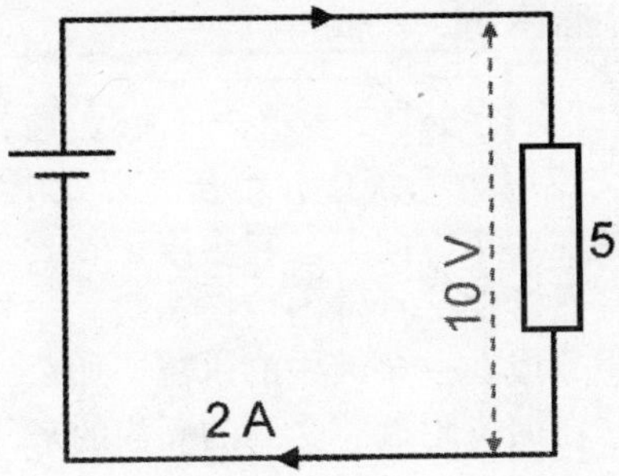

Figure 2–4 Ten volt battery, five ohm resistance = two amps

图 2–4 5Ω 的电阻连在 10V 的电池上，有 2A 的电流

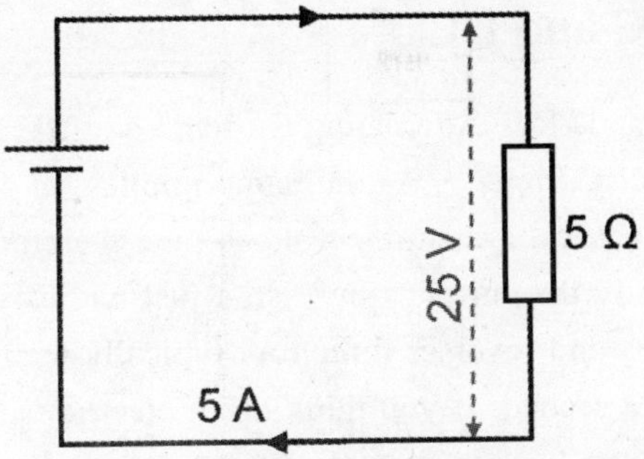

Figure 2–5 Five ohm resistor, five amps therefore twenty five volts

图 2–5 5Ω 的电阻通以 5A 的电流产生 25V 的电压

➤ Series and Parallel

If several electrical components are connected so that the current splits and a proportion of the current goes down each one independently, they are said to be "in parallel" (Figure 2-6). So for example the booths at the end of a toll road are the equivalent of parallel electrical components. On the other hand when the components are connected in a chain so that the same current is passing through them, like checkpoints on the road into a city in a war zone, they are said to be "in series" (Figure 2-7).

➤ 串联和并联

如果几个元器件连接在一起导致电流分路并且按一定的比例独立地流过每个分路，它们就被称为“并联”（图 2-6）。因此，举例来说，在收费公路端点的收费处就相当于并联的元器件。另一方面，当几个元器件连接成一串使得相同的电流流过它们，就像在战区进入城市的道路上的检查站一样，它们就被称为“串联”（图 2-7）。

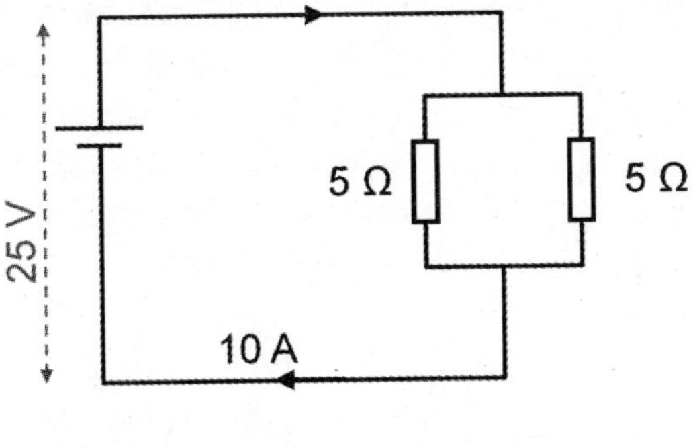

Figure 2–6 Parallel circuit (currents additive)

图 2–6 并联电路（电流相加）

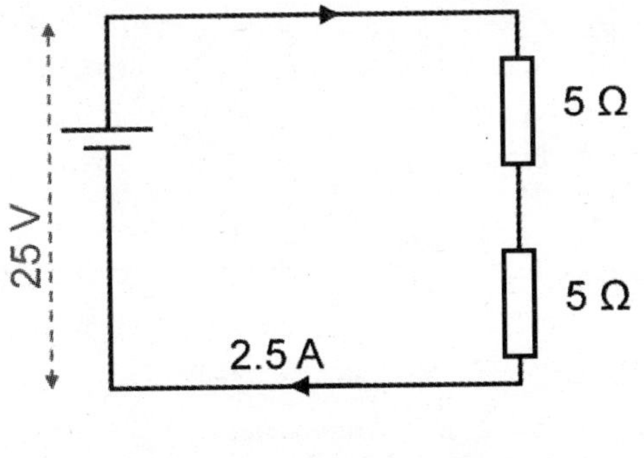

Figure 2–7 Series circuit (voltage drops additive)

图 2–7 串联电路（电压相加）

➢ AC and DC

AC stands for "Alternating Current" and DC is "Direct Current". As the name implies, in an AC electrical system the voltage (and therefore normally the current flow) isn't just one way: it stops and reverses direction, typically many times a second. If you think of an electric current being like the flow of water in a river, then AC is like the back-and-forth tidal movement you get near the mouth of the river, only immensely speeded up (Figure 2-8 shows a graph of voltage against time for a typical AC power source). DC ("Direct current") on the other hand is a one-way flow, like water in a hosepipe or a mountain stream.

For reasons that are difficult to explain in a soundbite, AC machines tend to be simpler than their DC equivalents. Critically, you can change the voltage of an AC supply using a cheap and simple transformer with no electronics and no moving parts. For this reason, if for no other, mains electricity is AC throughout the world. In the UK, it operates at 50 cycles per second, in the US at 60.

➢ 交流和直流

AC 表示“交流”，DC 表示“直流”。顾名思义，在交流电力系统中，电压（以及电流）并不只是在一个方向上。它会停止并改变方向，并且通常在一秒钟内变换多次。如果您将电流想象成在一条河中的水流，那么，交流就像您在河口附近感受到的潮汐的来回运动，但来回运动的速度要快得多（图 2-8 显示了一个典型的交流电源的电压随时间的变化）;直流（“直流电流”）是一个单向的流动，就如橡胶软管或山涧中的水流。

交流电动机往往比直流电动机简单，但用一两句话也难以解释清楚。重要的是，您可以用不含电子元件和运动部件的廉价而简单的变压器来改变交流电源的电压。如果不为别的，仅为这个原因，世界各地的市电都是交流的。在英国，它运行在每秒 50 个周期，在美国是 60 个周期（译注：在中国也为每秒 50 个周期）。

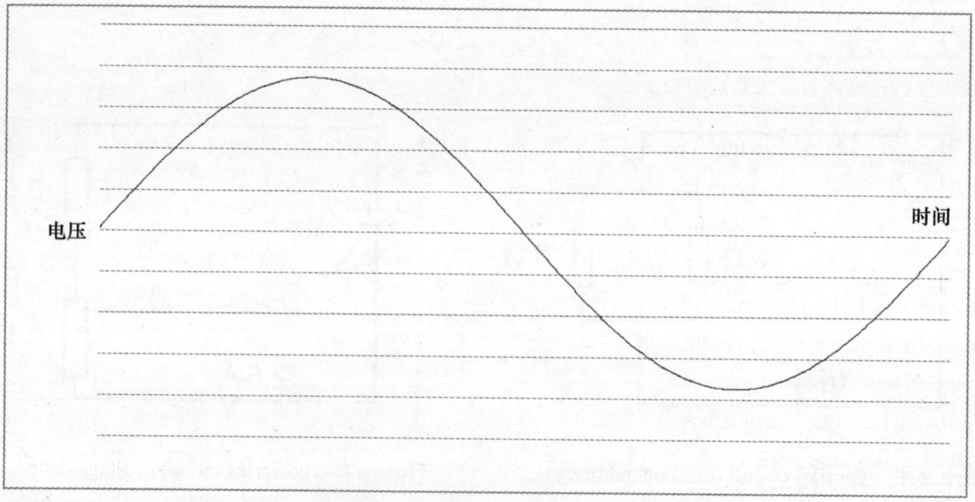

Figure 2–8 AC voltage varying with time

图 2–8 交流电压随时间的变化

Unfortunately, no one has ever produced an AC battery. Batteries are always DC. It is possible however to produce AC from a DC source using a device called an "inverter" (Figure 2-9).

不幸的是，从来没有人生产过一个交流的电池。电池输出都是直流电，但我们可以用逆变器（图 2-9）将直流电转变为交流电。

Such are the efficiency advantages of AC that it is sometimes worth going to the trouble of turning your DC into AC before you use it.

交流电的效率较高，因此有时是值得您去花费精力在使用之前将直流电变成交流电的。

Figure 2–9 - An inverter: takes in DC power from a 12 volt source and outputs mains-voltage AC. Photo courtesy of Black and Decker (http://www.blackanddecker.com/)

图 2–9 逆变器：从 12V 的直流电源中产生与电网相同的交流电压。照片由布莱克与德克尔公司（http://www.blackanddecker.com) 提供

➢ Electricity and Magnetism

There are just four things that you need to know about the interaction of electricity and magnetism to understand how electric motors work:

➢ 电和磁

为了理解电动机是如何工作的，您只要了解电和磁相互作用的四个方面：

1. Moving a wire in a magnetic field (or moving a magnetic field past a wire) creates (or "induces") a voltage in the wire.
2. A current flowing along a wire creates a magnetic field around the wire.
3. If you give a magnetic field a choice of going through air or soft iron, it will take the iron every time. You can therefore use iron to shape and focus

① 导线在磁场中运动（或将磁场移过导线）将在导线上产生（或"诱导"）电压。

② 电流在导线中流动，在导线周围产生磁场。

③ 如果您给磁场一个是通过空气还是通过软铁的选择，它每次都将选择通过软铁。因此，您可以用软铁来改变磁场的形状并聚焦磁场。

a magnetic field.

4. A current flowing in a wire in a magnetic field creates a force on the wire.

④ 在磁场中的导线通电流后，该导线将受到磁场力的作用。

Here are four experiments that you can try out in order to illustrate these principles. You can try them for real if you wish or just do the experiments in your head, or look on YouTube, or on the website for this book.

为了说明这些原理，您可以尝试以下的四个实验。如果您愿意的话，您可以真刀真枪地尝试，也可以只在您的头脑中做实验，还可以看 YouTube（视频分享网站），或上本书的网站。

➢ Experiment1-Inducing a voltage

➢ 实验 1：感应电压

Find yourself an ordinary magnet (the photo shows a powerful ring magnet) and a piece of wire. Beg or borrow a sensitive electric meter. Connect the wire to the meter. Move the wire around near the magnet. You should see the meter kick (Figure 2-10). This illustrates that moving a wire in an electric field creates a voltage. This is the basis of all electrical generators. It also happens in motors as well, as we'll see later.

找一个普通磁铁（照片显示了一个强大的环形磁铁）和一段导线，借用一个高灵敏度的电流表。然后将导线连到电流表的两端，并将导线在磁铁附近移动，您将会看到电流表的指针会摆动（图 2-10）。这表明在磁场中移动的导线会产生电压。这是所有发电机的基础。正如我们后面会看到的，它也出现在电动机上。

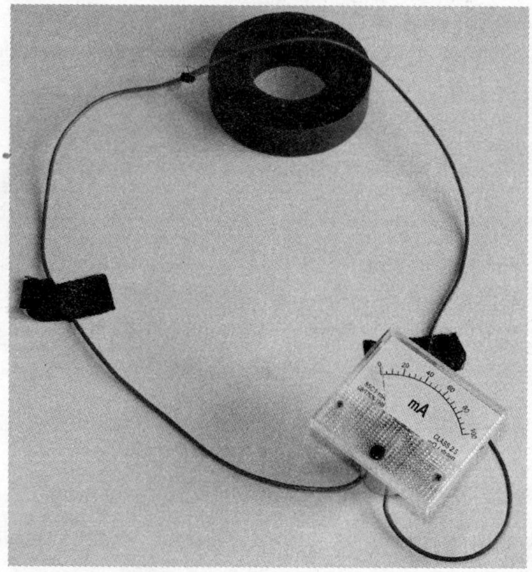

Figure 2–10 Moving a magnetic field past a wire induces a voltage in the wire

图 2–10 移动磁场通过导线时在导线中产生感应电压

➢ Experiment 2 – Magnetic field round a wire

Acquire a coil of fine wire. Connect a battery and a switch in series with the coil. Put a compass near the coil of wire. Close the switch and watch the compass react to the magnetic field created by the current flowing through the coil (Figure 2-11). Note that the magnetic effect probably won't be very strong: probably not enough to lift something like a paperclip.

This is a very simple electromagnet. All electric motors contain a magnet or magnets of some sort. They may be permanent magnets, or they may be electromagnets.

➢ 实验 2：线圈中的磁场

找一个由绝缘导线绕制的线圈，将它与一个电池和一个开关串联。把一个指南针放在线圈的附近，关闭开关并观察指南针对于由电流通过线圈而产生的磁场的反应（图 2-11）。请注意，磁场效应可能不会非常强，可能不足以吸起像一个回形针那样的东西。

这是一个非常简单的电磁铁。所有的电动机都含有某种形式的磁铁。它们可能是永久磁铁，也可能是电磁铁。

Figure 2–11 A crude electro-magnet

图 2–11 一个简易的电磁铁

➢ Experiment 3 – Add some iron

Repeat experiment 2, but this time place a big nail or any other solid iron or ordinary steel (not stainless) bar inside the coil (NB steel is just iron with a bit of carbon and sometimes other metals in it to make it stronger). I used a piece of threaded rod (Figure 2-12).

What you should see this time when you connect the battery is that the magnetic field is much stronger and focussed particularly at the ends of the bar. If you have sufficient number of turns of wire and enough current flowing, you should be able to use the metal bar like a permanent bar magnet to pick up other iron and steel objects.

This experiment illustrates why electric motors are so heavy for their (usually small) size: they have lots of iron in them. Electrical transformers are usually heavier than expected too, for much the same reason.

➢ 实验 3：添加一些铁质

重复实验 2，但这次将一个大钉子或任何其他固体铁或普通钢条（非不锈钢）放到线圈内（注：钢就是在铁内加些碳或其他金属，使其强度更高）。我用的是一根螺杆，如图 2-12 所示。

将电池连上时，您将会看到磁场加强很大且更为集中，尤其是在杆的两端。如果您有足够多圈的导线和足够大的电流，您就可以像使用一个永久磁棒一样使用这个金属条来吸起其他的铁或钢质物质。

这个实验说明了为什么电动机（通常很小）是如此沉重，因为在它们里面有大量的铁。出于这个原因，电力变压器的重量通常超过预期。

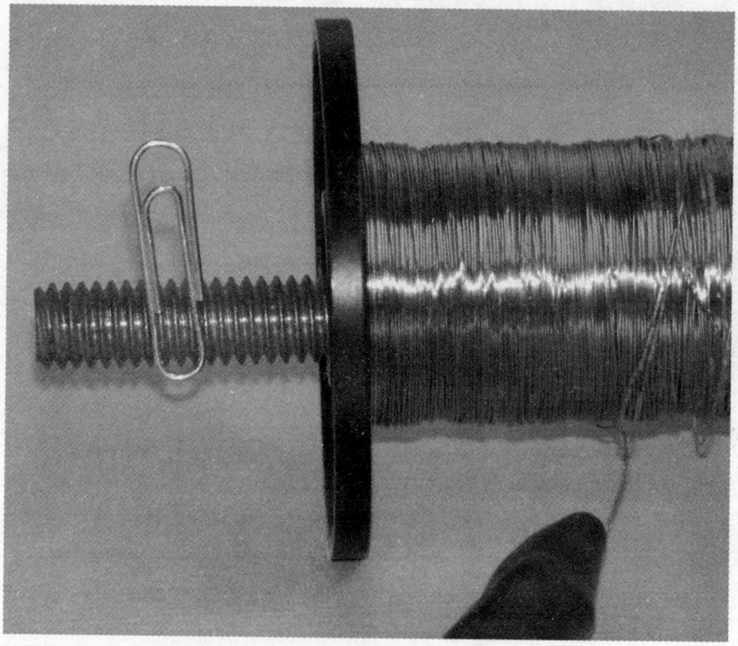

Figure 2–12 Electromagnet with Iron Core

图 2–12 拥有铁心的电磁铁

➢ Experiment 4 – the electrical kick

For this experiment drape a piece of wire loosely across the magnet you used in experiment 1 and connect it to the battery and switch that you used in experiments 2 and 3. This time when you switch on, the wire running past the magnet should twitch (Figure 2-13). The interaction between the electric current and the magnetic field applies a force to the wire. This is the principle of most electric motors as we will see later.

➢ 实验 4：电的产生

在这个实验中将一条导线松散地跨在实验 1 中使用过的磁铁上，将它连接到实验 2 和 3 中使用过的电池和开关上。接通开关时，跨在磁铁上的导线应该会抽动（图 2-13）。电流和磁场间的相互作用使导线受力。稍后我们将会看到，这是大多数电动机的原理。

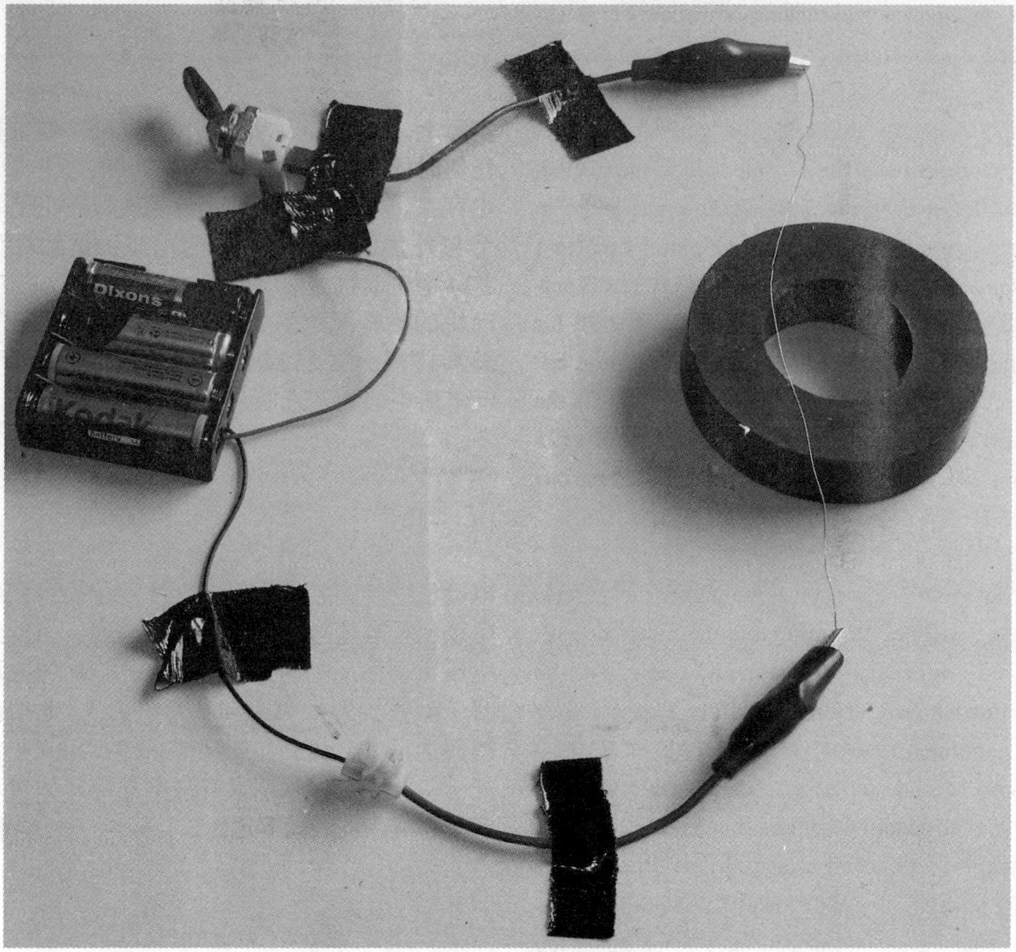

Figure 2–13 A current flowing in a wire in a magnetic field generates a force

图 2–13 在磁场中的导线通电后产生力

➤ "Back EMF"

In experiment 1 ("Inducing a voltage") we demonstrated that moving a wire in a magnetic field creates a voltage in that wire. As we shall see in more detail later, a DC motor consists of a number of wires wound around a rotor, which rotates in a magnetic field. Regardless of what else is going on, this creates a voltage in those wires. In fact if you take a DC electric motor and rotate the shaft using an external power source, you have got yourself a generator: instead of the current flow through the motor producing power, power is absorbed as a voltage is created and a current flows.

You can actually think of this "generator" effect happening all the time in electric motors, even when the electric motor is working normally: in other words the rotation of the motor creates a voltage pushing back against the externally applied voltage from the battery. In Figure 2-14 for example 25 volts is being applied to a motor, but the rotation of the motor is inducing 20 volts in the opposite direction. Net, there are just 5 volts (25 minus 20) available to drive current around the circuit.

The faster the motor spins, the higher this reverse voltage will be. Assuming that the motor doesn't exceed its mechanical limits and burst first, the maximum speed of a motor will be reached when the generated reverse voltage (or "back EMF" - Electro Motive Force) reaches the same value as the applied external voltage (minus a little bit for windage and bearing drag). So all other things being equal, we would expect EVs with the highest battery pack voltage to have the highest top speeds.

➤ 反电动势

在实验 1（“感应电压”）中，我们证明了在磁场中移动一根导线将在该导线中产生电压。正如我们将在后面详细看到的，一个直流电动机由绕在转子上并在磁场中转动的导线组成。不管将会发生其他什么事，转动的转子将在这些导线中创建一个感应电压。事实上，如果您拿一个直流电动机并用外力使转轴旋转，您就可以将它变成发电机。这时它从外界吸取能量（机械能）而产生电压和电流，而不是通过电流的流动来产生动力。

实际上，您可以认为这种“发电机”效应在任何时候都存在，甚至当电动机正常工作时也存在。换句话说，电动机的旋转产生了一个与外加电池电压相反的电压。例如在图 2-14 中电动机的两端加有 25V 的电压，但电动机的旋转产生了 20V 在相反方向的电压。总共只有 5V（25 减去 20）的净电压用来驱动电路中的电流。

电动机的转速越快，反向电压就越高。假设电动机没有超过其机械极限而爆裂，当反向电压（或称反电动势）等于外部施加的电压时（减去少量的风阻和轴承阻力），电动机的转速最大。因此，在其他条件都相同的情况下，我们可以预期具有高电池电压的电动汽车将有高的最高车速。

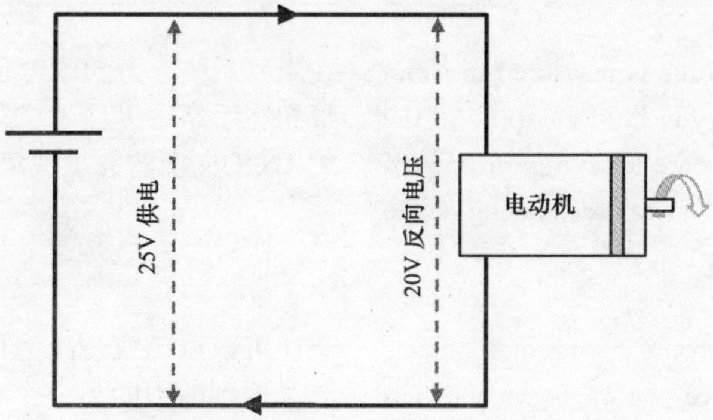

Figure 2–14 Back EMF builds up to oppose the applied voltage from the battery

图 2–14 反电动势与电池电压的方向相反

➢ Force, Torque, Energy and Power

These four terms (Force, Torque, Energy and Power) tend to be used vaguely and often interchangeably yet they have very precise meanings which it helps to understand if you are interested in the dynamics of vehicles. In particular if you are to have any hope at all of estimating the performance potential of a planned EV you need to understand them.

Motoring magazines and armchair racing drivers tend to compare the performance potential of cars using engine power output: 20 Horsepower – bad; 200 HP – good. Road tests often discuss maximum torque. On the road, torque is actually what makes a car feel lively. If you are familiar with these terms I suggest you skip to the next chapter. If not, you might want to read on...

Force

This is the easy one as most people have a feel for it. It is a push, a shove, an influence which makes a free mass move or a flexible structure change shape. Anything in earth's gravitational field experiences a force, so if you want to hold something still, you have to apply an upward force equal to

➢ 力、转矩、能量与功率

这四个术语（力、转矩、能量和功率）往往混淆不清并经常被互换，但它们有非常精确的意义。如果您对车辆动力学感兴趣的话，它将有助于您的理解。特别是如果您希望评估一辆在规划中的电动汽车的性能潜力的话，您必须要理解它们。

汽车杂志和轮椅赛车手往往用发动机的输出功率来比较汽车的性能潜力。20hp（马力）意味着性能不好；200hp 意味着性能好。在道路测试中则常常讨论最大转矩。在路上，转矩的大小实际上意味着汽车是否有力。如果您熟悉这些术语，我建议您直接跳到下一章。如果您不熟悉，您可能想继续读下去。

力

力是容易理解的，因为大多数人都能感觉到它。它是一种推力、撞力或影响，使得一个自由的物体移动或一个有弹性的结构改变形状。任何物体在地球的引力场中都能感受到力的存在。所以如果您想静止地握住某种东西，您必须施加一个向上的等于其重量的力

its weight to cancel out the effect of gravity.

来抵消重力的影响。

In the metric system, force is measured in Newtons. Appropriately, if you hold an apple in the palm of your hand you are applying an upward force to it of roughly a Newton (depending on the weight of the apple).

在米制系统，力的单位是牛顿（N）。因此如果您在手掌中握住一个苹果，您对它施加了约 1N 的向上的力（视苹果的重量而定）。

You can also measure force in pounds or kilograms (yet another unit of force you might encounter is the poundal). Unsurprisingly, a kilogram is the upward force you would have to exert if someone replaced the apple resting in your hand with a 1 kg bag of sugar. It is just less than 10 Newtons.

您还可以以磅或公斤为单位来测量力［您可能会遇到的力的另一个单位是 poundal。（译注：这是一个英制单位，在实际中不常用。1poundal=1lb（磅）× 1ft（英尺）/s^2 ≈ 0.138255 N］)。如果有人用 1kg 一袋的糖取代了搁在您手上的苹果，您就必须施加 1kgf 向上的力。它比 10N 小一点点。

Torque

Torque is a measure of how hard something is twisting. A heavy man jumping up and down on the end of a metre-long spanner can produce a lot of torque (probably more than a big V8). Torque is the rotary equivalent of a linear force: in fact it is measured as force × distance (Newton-metres or foot-pounds). So a 5 Newton force on the end of a 10 metre bar creates a torque of 5 x 10 = 50 Newton-metres. Exactly the same torque would be produced by a force of 50 Newtons at the end of a one metre bar (or a 25 Newton force on a 2 metre bar or a one Newton force on a 50 metre bar – or whatever).

转矩

转矩是用来衡量一个物体被扭曲的难易程度。一个很重的男子在 1m 长的扳手末端上下跳动可以产生很大的转矩（可能大于一个巨大的 8 缸发动机所产生的转矩）。转矩是一个与线性力相对应的旋转力，实际上它等于力 × 距离（N · m 或 lb · ft）。因此，5N 的力施加于 10m 杆的末端将产生 5 × 10 =50N · m 的转矩。相同的转矩也可以由 50N 的力施加于 1m 杆的末端而产生（或由 25N 的力施加于 2m 杆的末端而产生，或任何其他组合）。

Note that torque says nothing about speed of rotation. If you are winding a bucket of water up from an old fashioned-well the torque that you are applying is almost the same regardless of how fast you are raising the bucket (assuming that the bucket is moving at constant speed).

注意：转矩与旋转速度无关。如果您正在从一个老式的井中用轮毂提升一桶水，不管您如何快速地摇动轮毂提升水桶（假设桶以恒定的速度移动），您所施加的转矩几乎是一样的。

For most road driving, torque is more important than power. For a given gear ratio the shove in

对于大多数的道路驾驶，转矩比功率更重要。对于一个给定的变速比，当您将加速踏板踩

your back when you floor the throttle relates to the torque output of the engine. In the real world, for cars of similar weight, the maximum torque of the engine has (rather surprisingly) been found to be a better predictor of 0-60 mph acceleration time than maximum power. Electric motors are generally good at torque, so EVs often have surprisingly good acceleration.

到底时，发动机的转矩输出就加大，您就会感受到在您背部的推力。在现实世界中，对于重量相近的汽车，发动机的最大转矩（令人惊讶地）被发现是在 0 → 100km/h 的加速区，而不是在功率最大的时候。电动机的转矩一般都较大，所以电动汽车往往有好得出奇的加速性能。

Power

If you are winding up that bucket of water (Figure 2-15), you would intuitively expect that the faster you pull the bucket up, the greater the physical effort. As the physicist would put it, raising the bucket fast needs more power, even though the torque doesn't change.

功率

如果您正在摇动轮毂提升水桶（图 2-15），您会直觉地想到，越快地提升水桶，就要付出更大的体力。正如物理学家会提到的，虽然转矩不变，但快速提升水桶需要更大的功率。

Figure 2–15 High power expenditure for a short time

图 2–15 短时间内的高功率消耗

Power is torque × rotational speed or (in linear terms) force × linear speed. You come across the same kind of effect when you are push starting a car. Keeping the car rolling at a slow walking pace is no problem, but if you have to get it moving at a brisk trot to bump-start it, you get out of breath quickly. The force that you are applying hasn't changed but keeping up that force at a run demands more power than doing it at a walk.

功率等于转矩 × 转速，或者（在线性情况下）等于力 × 线速度。当您推动一辆车想让它起动时，您就可以感受到功率的意义。您让车维持在一个缓慢的行走速度是没有问题的，但如果想让它快速地移动，以便用冲击法去起动它，您很快就会累得气喘吁吁。您所施加的力并没有改变，但在小跑中维持这样的力比在慢走中需要更大的功率。

Calculating power in the metric system is easy: a force of 1 Newton at 1 metre per second is 1 Watt. So a 10 kW (10 kilowatt or 10,000 Watt) power source could in theory apply 1000 Newtons at 10 metres per second or 400 Newtons at 25 metres/second, or whatever (Figure 2-16).

在米制系统中功率的计算是很简单的。1N 的力每秒移动 1m 就是 1W。因此，一个 10kW 的功率，在理论上可以让 1000N 的力每秒移动 10m 或 400N 的力以 25m/s 的速度移动，或任何其他组合（图 2-16）。

Maximum power relates to top speed, so is very important in racing (less important on the road where cars seldom get anywhere near their maximum speed). As the speed rises, aerodynamic drag and rolling resistance are pushing against the engine. With the right gearing, maximum speed is reached when the forces trying to slow the car down multiplied by the speed of the car equal the maximum available power. At this point something quite remarkable emerges. There is a fearful symmetry in the universe; because not only is 1 watt = 1 Newton at 1 metre per second. 1 watt is also equal to a 1 volt × 1 amp. And it isn't that they just work out to be roughly similar. They are the same thing. So for example a perfectly efficient motor drawing 50 Amps at 200 volts would produce 50 × 200 = 10,000 watts. With the right gearbox and final drive it could provide a force of 400 Newtons to a car travelling at 25 metres per second as in the bottom picture in Figure 2-16.

最大功率与最高速度有关，因此功率在赛车中是非常重要的（在道路车辆中则不太重要，因为道路车辆很少接近其最高时速）。当车速增加时，空气阻力和转动阻力也随之增加。在适当的档位上，当试图减缓车速的阻力乘以车速等于可用的最大功率时，汽车达到其最高车速。这时出现一个相当奇妙的现象。在宇宙中有一个令人生畏的对称律，因为不仅 1W=1N × 1m/s，1W 也等于 1V × 1A，并且它们不只是大致相似，而是同一个物理量。因此，一个完全无损耗的电动机在 200V 时通以 50A 的电流会产生 50 × 200= 10000W 的功率。配上正确的变速器和传动系统，它可以向以 25m/s 行驶的汽车提供 400N 的力，如图 2-16 中的下图所示。

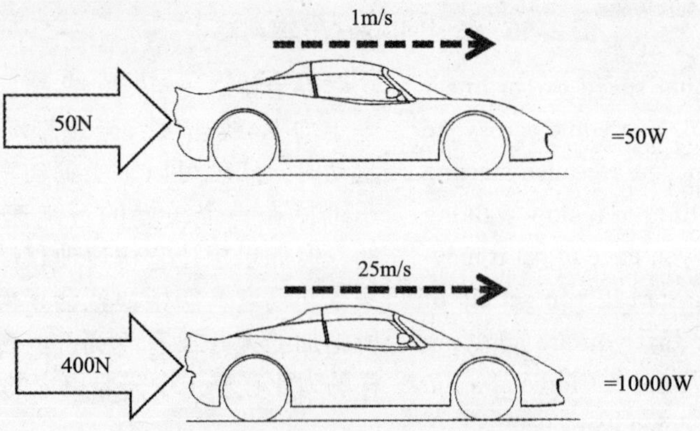

Figure 2–16 Force, speed and power

图 2–16 力、速度和功率的关系

In other words the world of moving bodies on the one hand and the world of electricity and magnetism are connected. The fact that they are exactly 1 to 1 is partly down to the cunning of the metric system, but only partly. It is enough to fill you with awe that two such different things should be so tightly bound together. It also makes the job of predicting the performance of EVs a whole lot easier. Furthermore the concept of efficiency of a drivetrain becomes meaningful. Because we measure power in to the motor as volts × amps and mechanical power out of the transmission as force × speed, we can divide one by the other to get efficiency.

换句话说，电和磁的世界与移动机构的世界相连。它们完全的 1 对 1 的事实要部分归功于米制系统，但只是部分。这样两件不同的事如此紧密地联系在一起就足以使您产生敬畏感。这也使得预测电动汽车性能的工作轻松了许多。此外，传动系统效率的概念也变得有意义。因为我们可以用电压 × 电流来衡量电动机的功率，而用力 × 速度来衡量传输系统的机械功率输出，我们可以将它们相除来获得效率。

Energy (or work done)

Energy reflects the application of a given amount of power for a given length of time (power × time). So going back to the bucket of water in the well, the total energy that you expend winding the bucket all the way up from the bottom to the top is constant regardless of whether you wind it up quickly or slowly. If you wind the bucket up very fast you need lots of power but for a short time. Conversely, if you wind it up more slowly, you will need less power, but you will need it for longer. Either way the total energy expended is the same (ignoring friction etc).

能量（或所做的功）

能量反映了一定量的功率在一个特定的时间长度内的应用（功率 × 时间）。如果回到前面井中的桶，不管您是很快或很慢地摇动，您将桶从底部一路往上摇到顶部所花费的总能量是恒定的。如果您摇得非常快，您需要在较短的时间付出很大的功率；相反，如果您慢慢地摇，您将需要较少的功率，但会用更长的时间。在这两种方法中所消耗的总能量是相同的（忽略摩擦等）。

In the metric system, energy is measured in Joules which is 1 watt for 1 second (i.e. 1 Newton being pushed along at 1 metre per second for a period of one second, or 1 Newton being pushed a metre). In electrical terms it is 1 volt × 1 amp for 1 second. That isn't much energy, so electrical energy is usually expressed in kW-hours. 1 kW-hr is 1000 watts for 3,600 seconds or 3.6 million Joules.

在米制系统中，能量的单位为焦耳（J），它等于 1W 在 1s 中内所做的功（即 1N 的力以 1m/s 的速度被移动 1s，或 1N 的力被移动 1m 的距离）。在电力方面，它是 1V × 1A 续 1s 的时间。这一能量值并不大。因此，电能通常以千瓦 · 小时（kW · h）做单位。1kW·h 等于 1000W 持持续 3600s 或 3.6×10^6J。

The distinction between energy and power will be very important when we start discussing batteries. But for now we'll take some of the electrical principles we talked about here and apply them to the kinds of motors used in EVs and HEVs. Motors are the subject of the next chapter.

当我们开始讨论电池时，能量与功率之间的区别将是非常重要的。但现在我们将采用一些我们在这里谈到的电气原理，并将它们应用在电动汽车和混合动力电动汽车用的各种电动机中。电动机将是下一章的主题。

3 Motors
电动机

Electric motors are at the heart of EVs. It is the electric motor (or motors) which turn electrical power from the batteries into mechanical power to turn the wheels. Motors are divided into two broad classes – AC and DC machines, but if you understand one class, you are well on the way to understanding the other.

电动机是电动汽车的核心。正是电动机将电池中的电能转换成机械能来转动车轮。电动机分为两大类——交流电动机和直流电动机，但如果您了解了其中的一个类，您就能很好地了解另一类。

➢ Electric Motor principles

Electric motors are much simpler than their IC counterparts. Here is a list of the moving parts in a typical 4 cylinder IC engine:

- Crankshaft
- Connecting Rods (×4)
- Pistons (×4)
- Gudgeon Pins (×4)
- Camshaft
- Cam followers (×8)
- Pushrods (×8)
- Rocker arms (×8)
- Valves (×8)
- Distributor shaft
- Oil pump

We could also mention throttles, chokes, turbo-charger turbines, waste gates, cam drive belts etc; but even this basic list is almost 50 moving parts. For a V8 it is close to 100.

Most electric motors have by contrast just two main parts of which one is fixed (Figure 3-1).

- a stator
- a rotor

➢ 电动机原理

电动机比相应的内燃机要简单得多。下面是一个典型的 4 缸内燃机中运动部件的清单：

- 曲轴
- 连杆（×4）
- 活塞（×4）
- 活塞销（×4）
- 凸轮轴
- 凸轮从动件（×8）
- 推杆（8）
- 摇臂（×8）
- 阀门（×8）
- 分布轴
- 油泵

我们还可以提到油门、阻塞器、涡轮增压器的涡轮机、排气门、凸轮传动带等等。但即使是这样一个基本的清单也近 50 个运动部件。对于一个 8 缸内燃机而言，运动部件的数量接近 100。

相比之下，大多数电动机只有两个主要部分（图 3-1 所示为交流电动机），其中一个还是固定的。

- 一个定子
- 一个转子

Figure 3–1 An AC electric motor with the stator built into the case and the rotor on the shaft. Photo courtesy of Stan Zurek

图 3–1 交流电动机的外壳为定子，内轴为转子。照片由斯坦・驻拉克提供

Regardless of type, Electric motors rely for their operation on the interplay of electricity and magnetism. Stators are usually magnets. They are often a form of electromagnet (electrical wire wound around an iron core like the wire-wound nail in the third experiment described earlier); or they may be permanent magnets. So electric motors are very simple devices. Some are low maintenance. Others are completely maintenance-free (how long has the motor in your refrigerator been running without attention?).

无论是哪一种类型，电动机依靠电和磁的相互作用而工作。通常定子是磁体。它们往往是电磁铁的形式（导线绕着铁心，就像前面所述的第三个实验中导线绕铁钉那样），也可能是永久磁铁。因此，电动机是非常简单的设备。有些电动机的维护成本很低，有些则完全免维护（想想，您是否注意过冰箱中电动机的运行？）。

One peculiarity of electric motors is that the maximum torque that they can produce tends to be related to the volume of the motor, regardless of type: so a long thin motor will have similar maximum torque to a short fat one if the volumes are the same; and (in perfectly designed and well-cooled motors) the peak torque will be much the same regardless of motor type.

电动机的一个特点是，它们能产生的最大转矩往往与电动机的体积有关，而与类型无关。因此在体积相同的情况下，一个细长的电动机与一个短胖的电动机产生的最大转矩相近，并且（在设计完美且冷却充分的电动机中）它们的峰值转矩将大致相同，并与电动机的类型无关。

Electric motors are also small when compared to an IC engine of similar output. The Netgain Impulse 9 (Figure 3-2) has, unsurprisingly, a diameter of about 9″ or roughly 22cm. This is a fairly powerful motor, quite capable of pushing a large car or small van along fast enough to keep up with the traffic. In a smaller car it is quite capable of seri-

对于相似的功率输出，电动机的体积也小于内燃机。毋庸置疑，那特根因普尔斯 23cm 电动机（图 3-2）的直径约为 9 英寸或大约 23 厘米。这是一个相当强有力的电动机，足够推动一辆大轿车或小面包车快速行驶，以跟上车流。在一个小型汽车里，它在交通信号灯转为绿灯时的起步加速性能往往令内燃

ously embarrassing IC engined cars at the traffic lights. 9" is only about the diameter of a medium sized cake tin or a small frying pan. Electric motors are usually heavy though. The Impulse 9 weighs about 60 kg. The Warp 11 illustrated in Chapter 1 weighs over 100 kg.

机为动力的汽车尴尬万分。23cm 只是一个中型蛋糕或小型煎锅的直径，但电动机通常很重。脉冲 23cm 的电动机重约 60kg。第一章所示的沃普 28cm 电动机的质量超过 100kg。

Figure 3–2 The Impulse 9 Motor. Photo courtesy of Netgain Motors (http://www.go-ev.com/)

图 3–2 因普尔斯 23cm 电动机。照片由那特根发动机公司 (http://www.go-ev.com/) 提供

➢ Types of Motor

There are many different types of electric motor but there are probably five types available for purchase today that are potential candidates for propelling an EV:

- Brushed DC Permanent Magnet
- Brushed DC Series wound
- Brushed DC Separately Excited
- AC Induction
- "Brushless DC" (really a form of AC motor despite its name)

They all have their advantages and disadvantages. The AC motors are simpler devices than the DC machines and are generally more efficient, but they need complex and expensive controllers (which, among other things) converts the DC output of the

➢ 电动机的类型

电动机的类型有多种，但现在能买到的可被作为潜在的纯电动汽车的动力有五种类型：

- 有刷永磁直流电动机
- 有刷串励直流电动机
- 有刷他励直流电动机
- 交流感应电动机
- 无刷直流电动机（尽管它名叫直流，实际上是个交流形式的电动机）

它们都有自己的优点和缺点。交流电动机比直流电动机简单且通常效率较高，但它们需要复杂和昂贵的控制器，其中（除其他事项外）电池的直流输出需要转换成电动机所需的交流电。

battery into the AC needed by the motor.

Among practical motors available today the series wound DC motors tend to be king of the hill when it comes to low speed acceleration. Electric dragsters (there are such things, honest) are often driven by Series wound motors. On the other hand brushed permanent magnet motors tend to be small, light and (relatively) cheap. Practical AC systems currently available for EVs are better at regeneration than comparable DC systems; there is no theoretical reason for this, but it appears to be so. "Regeneration" or "Regen" is slowing the car down by using the motor as a generator instead of using ordinary brakes. This puts the energy from the slowing car back into the batteries, rather than dissipating it as heat from the brakes, and thus reduces wear and tear on the brakes. In theory it also extends the range of the EV, albeit not by very much in practice under normal conditions. We discuss regen further in the section on Controllers.

在今天能买到的实用的电动机中，当涉及低速加速性能时，串励电动机往往是首选。电动高速赛车往往由串励电动机驱动（这确有其事）。另一方面，有刷永磁电动机往往体积小，重量轻，并且（相对）便宜。目前能买到的电动汽车用的交流电动机系统比同类的直流电动机系统有更好的再生性能。虽然没有理论上的原因，但事实似乎如此。"能量再生"或"再生"并不使用普通的制动装置，而是将电动机转换成发电机来使汽车减速。汽车减速时，它使能量回收到电池中，而不是从制动片中作为热量散发掉，从而降低了对制动片的磨损。在理论上它也扩展了电动汽车的行程范围，尽管实际上在正常的情况下该范围并不很大。我们将在控制器部分进一步讨论再生问题。

We'll look at the principle of each motor type starting with the simplest: the brushed DC permanent magnet motor.

我们将从最简单的有刷永磁直流电动机开始来讨论各种电动机的原理。

➢ Brushed DC Permanent Magnet motor

➢ 有刷永磁直流电动机

If you ever played with small battery-operated electric motors as a child, it is probable that the motors you were using were permanent magnet brushed DC motors. They use the principle that was illustrated in Experiment 4: a current passing through a wire in a magnetic field experiences a force. Imagine a rectangle made of wire with a pivot down the middle and a current flowing in it. The wire on one side would experience an upward force and the wire on the other a downward force

如果您在儿童时期曾经玩过用电池供电的小型电动机，那很可能就是有刷永磁直流电动机。它们应用实验 4 所示的原理来工作：在磁场中的导线通过电流后受到了力的作用。试想一下：一个由导线做成的矩形在中间有个支点，对导线通以电流，则在矩形一边的导线将有一个向上的力，在另一边的导线将有一个向下的力（图 3-3），这将使整个矩形绕其轴线旋转。

(Figure 3-3). This would turn the whole rectangle of wire on its axis.

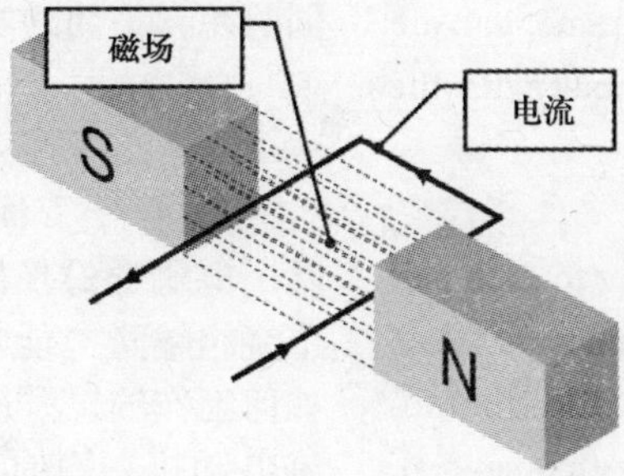

Figure 3–3 Force on a wire in a magnetic field

图 3–3 磁场对导线的作用力

That's all very well, but such a motor would have a useful life of a quarter of a turn: when the rectangle of wire was lying across the magnetic field there would be no torque on it. After half a turn, the torque would be in the opposite direction.

这很好。但这种电动机的有用寿命只有四分之一转：当矩形导线的平面与磁场垂直时，在导线上就没有转矩了。半圈后，转矩会在相反的方向。

To turn this into a usable motor, you need a commutator and brushes. A commutator is a series of conducting metal strips laid length-wise around the outside of cylinder on the axis of the motor. Each of the commutator segments is insulated from its neighbours and connected to the commutator segment on the opposite side by a wire or bundle of wires. Figure 3-4 illustrates the principle (just one winding is shown for clarity). In a real motor there would be dozens.

要将其变成一个可用的电动机，您需要一个换向器和电刷。换向器是由一系列位于电动机轴上的圆柱体外部且与轴的方向相同的导电金属条组成的。换向器上的每根导电金属条都与其临近的金属条绝缘，并用一根或一束导线将其连接到圆柱体另一端的金属条上。图 3-4 说明了其原理（为清楚起见，只显示了一个绕组）。在一个真正的电动机中会有几十个绕组。

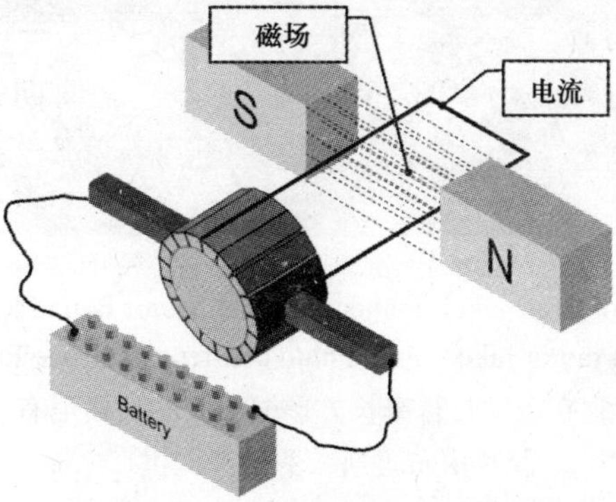

Figure 3–4 Principle of the Permanent Magnet DC Motor

图 3–4 永磁直流电动机的工作原理

A brush is a sliding electrical contact. Brushes are typically made of graphite and are mounted in a housing attached to the motor frame, and are spring loaded to keep them in contact with the commutator.

电刷是一个滑动的电接触。它们通常由石墨做成并固定在一个连接电动机架的装置里，同时用弹簧使之与换向器保持接触。

The two brushes feed electrical power to each pair of commutator segments in turn. If you want to see an animation, try searching for "DC Electric Motor" in YouTube: you will probably find several. The brushes and the commutator are an elegant idea which makes a simple DC motor feasible; but they are also a weak point. Brushes wear out and in a big motor they may be asked to carry a very high current (2000 Amps is not unheard of with series wound motors in EVs). Under these conditions you can get serious arcing which can damage the commutator and/or brushes. Brushes also limit the maximum operating speed of the motor. The best-known EV permanent magnet motors are those made by Agni motors to a design by Cedric Lynch[1] - Figure 3-5.

两个电刷通过换向器上的金属条对依次向各个绕组输送电能。如果您想动态地看看它是如何工作的，您可尝试在 YouTube 上搜索“直流电动机”，您可能会发现几个视屏。电刷和换向器是一个很精妙的想法，它使得一个简单的直流电动机变得可行。但它们也有弱点：电刷会磨损，并且在一个大型电动机中，它们可能会被通以一个非常大的电流（在电动汽车所用的串励电动机中，一个 2000A 的电流并非不常见）。在这些情况下，您可以看到很强的电弧，它可能会损坏换向器和/或电刷。电刷也限制了电动机的最高运转速度。最有名的电动汽车用的永磁电动机是由塞德里克·林奇设计、阿格尼电动机公司[⊖]制造的（图 3-5）。

Figure 3–5 Agni Brushed Permanent Magnet Motor bolted to a rectangular mount in a motor bike frame. Photo courtesy of Bruce Roberts

图 3–5 用螺栓固定在电动自行车长方形框架上的阿格尼有刷永磁电动机。照片由布鲁斯　罗伯茨提供

1 See http://www.agnimotors.com

⊖ 见 http://www.agnimotors.com。

These motors are almost unbelievably small and light; they are the size and shape of a large tin of biscuits. The largest in the range has a peak power output around 30 kW (38 HP) and weighs just 11 kg. Two of them would make a small hatchback quite frisky.

这些电动机几乎是令人难以置信的小而轻，它们的大小和形状像一个大的饼干盒。其中最大的一个有约 30 千瓦（38 马力）的峰值输出功率，但只有 11kg 重。用两个这样的电动机就可以轻松地带动一辆小的两厢车。

➢ Brushed DC series wound motor

➢ 有刷串励直流电动机

The series wound DC motor works in exactly the same way as the brushed Permanent Magnet motor. The only difference is that the magnetic field is created by an electromagnet rather than a permanent magnet. In a series wound motor, the wire creating the field (like the wire coil around the metal bar in Experiment 3 in chapter 2:) is just a few thick turns in series with the rotor (Figure 3-6).

有刷串励直流电动机的工作原理与有刷永磁电动机完全相同。唯一的区别是前者的磁场是由电磁铁而不是永久磁铁创建的。在串励电动机中，创建磁场的导线（如同第 2 章实验 3 中绕在金属棒上的导线一样）是与转子串联的多绕了几圈的绕组（图 3-6）。

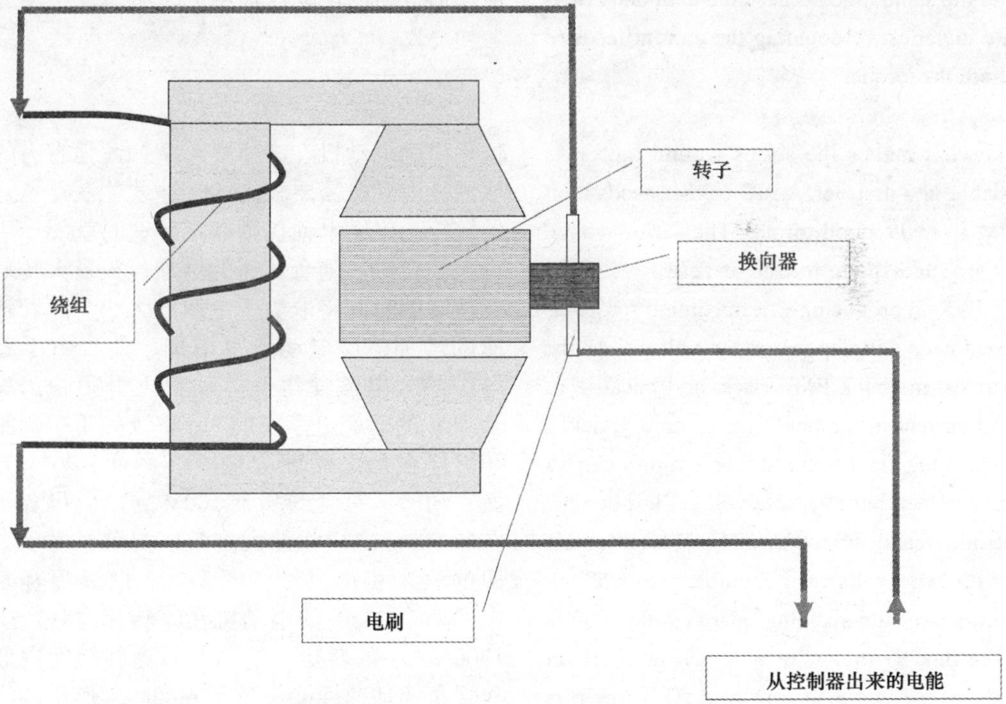

Figure 3–6 Principle of the Series-wound DC motor

图 3–6 串励直流电动机的工作原理

Neglecting losses, this means that the torque produced by a series motor goes up as the square of the current (twice the current, four times the torque, three times the current, nine times the torque).

如果不考虑损失的话，由串励电动机产生的转矩将与电流的平方成正比（电流加倍，转矩则增加 4 倍；电流为原来的 3 倍，转矩则为原来的 9 倍）。

Here is why. Suppose somehow we just doubled the current in the stator (field) windings and left the rotor (armature) current unchanged. Neglecting losses, this would double the intensity of the magnetic field which would double the torque on the rotor.

这是因为如果我们设法使定子（磁场）绕组的电流增加了一倍，但保持转子（电枢）的电流不变，若不记损失，则磁场的强度将增加一倍，这将使转子上的转矩加倍。

Now suppose instead that we kept the stator (field) current unchanged and doubled the rotor (armature) current. Doubling the rotor current also doubles the torque on the rotor. But in the real world we are doubling the current in both the rotor and the stator at the same time because the field and armature are in series: so doubling the current leads to four times the torque.

现在假设，保持定子（磁场）的电流不变，但使转子（电枢）的电流增加一倍。转子电流的加倍将使转子上的转矩也增加一倍。但实际上磁场和电枢的绕组是串联的，我们同时将转子和定子的电流增加了一倍，因此电流加倍将导致转矩增加 4 倍。

This is what makes the series wound motor so formidable in a dragster. An IC engine needs a bit of RPM to make good torque. The series-wound motor produces huge torque at zero revs. How long it goes on producing that maximum torque as the speed rises will depend on the voltage. As the speed rises, the back EMF rises: and because of the high current in the field, it rises quite quickly. A 48 volt milk float will outdrag a sports car for the first ten feet, but after that will get left behind. On the other hand, John Wayland's White Zombie racer with 300+ volts easily humbles most IC engined cars over the standing quarter mile (Figure 3-7). The dual 9″ motors in White Zombie deliver 1250 ft. lbs. of torque at zero rpm. This low rpm torque allows White Zombie to out-drag 600 HP IC engined cars. Plus you could drive your granny to the shops in it.

这是串励电动机在高速赛车中如此强有力的原因。内燃机需要较高的转速才能获得良好的转矩。串励电动机则在零转速时就能产生巨大的转矩。随着转速的增加，该最大转矩可持续的时间将取决于电压的大小。随着转速的增加，反电动势也增加，并且由于磁场中的大电流使得反电动势上升很快。一辆 48V 的运奶电车在前 3m 将领先于一辆跑车，但在那之后就会被甩在后面。另一方面，约翰·韦兰的高于 300V 的白僵尸赛车在前 500m 之内将使大多数以内燃机为动力源的汽车相形见绌（图 3-7）。白僵尸赛车中的两个 23cm 的电动机在零转速时将产生 1700N·m 的转矩。这种低转速转矩使白僵尸赛车的加速性能超过了 600hp 内燃机的汽车。此外，您还可以用这辆车带上您的外婆去逛街。

Figure 3–7 White Zombie—a road legal 1972 Datsun. Photo courtesy of Carol Brown

图 3–7 白僵尸电动汽车——1972 年由大产牌汽车首次上路。照片由卡罗尔·布朗提供

Series wound motors have a couple of drawbacks. Firstly putting over a thousand amps through a set of brushes is a bold enterprise. Brushes will always be a potential weak spot. Secondly a series wound motor will self-destruct if it is ever connected up to a power source directly without a load. This includes, for cars that are not direct drive, applying the throttle with the gearbox in neutral.

串励电动机也有几个缺点：首先，让超过千安培的电流通过一套电刷是一个大胆的设想，电刷将始终是一个潜在的弱点；其次，如果在无直接负载的情况下，将串励电动机直接连接到电源将使其自毁，如没有开动汽车时，驾驶人在变速器为空档时直接踩加速踏板。

Recall that the maximum speed of a motor is reached when the back EMF (the reverse voltage induced in the motor as it turns) is equal to the applied voltage. In an unloaded series-wound motor, the current in the rotor is very low. Because the stator windings are in series with the rotor windings, the current in the stator windings is also low. This in turn means that the magnetic field created by the stator is very weak. A weak magnetic field means lower back EMF. So the chain of events goes like this:

- Low load, low current
- Low current, weak stator magnetic field
- Weak m agnetic field, lower back EMF
- Back EMF below supply voltage, speed increases
- Repeat 1 – 4 until the motor exceeds its maximum rated mechanical speed

我们知道，当反电动势（在电动机转动时产生的反向电压）等于电源所施加的电压时，电动机的转速最大。在空载时串励电动机转子的电流非常低。因为定子绕组与转子绕组串联，定子绕组中的电流也很低。这意味着由定子产生的磁场是非常弱的。弱磁场又意味着较低的反电动势。因此，事件发生的链是这样的：

- 低负荷导致低电流
- 低电流导致弱的定子磁场
- 弱磁场导致低的反电动势
- 反电动势低于电源电压导致速度增加
- 重复上述 4 个步骤，直到电动机超过其最大额定机械速度

One other peculiarity of Series wound motors is that they will run quite happily on AC or DC – they are in fact sometimes called "Universal motors". The reason for this behaviour lies in the series arrangement. If the polarity of the supply is reversed, both the field and the armature currents are reversed at the same time and the net effect is that the motor continues to rotate in the same direction. This can actually present a bit of a challenge in a direct drive car (i.e. a car with no mechanical gearbox) if you want to allow for reverse. Some series wound motors permit you to reverse the polarity of either the stator or the rotor windings independently, which makes an electrical "reverse gear" possible. At the time of writing, three makes of series DC motor are popular with EV builders:

串励电动机的另一个特点是：它们在直流或交流上都运行得很好。因此，它们实际上有时也被称为“通用电动机”。这种现象的原因在于其串联的工作方式。如果电源的极性反转，磁场和电枢电流也同时被反转，其净效应是使电动机在同一方向上继续旋转。如果您想倒车的话，对直接驱动的汽车（即无机械变速器的汽车）而言实际上是一个挑战。有些串励电动机允许您单独反转定子或转子绕组的极性，这使得电气“倒档”成为可能。在写作本书时，电动汽车的建造者喜欢以下三种牌子的串励直流电动机：

- Netgain's Warp, Transwarp and Impulse series (the Netgain Impulse 9 is pictured in Figure 3-2)
- Advanced DC (Figure3-8)
- Kostov (Figure 3-9)

- 那特根的沃普、反式沃普和因普尔斯系列（图 3-2 给出了那特根的因普尔斯 9 系列）
- 先进的直流电动机（图 3-8）
- 科斯托夫电动机（图 3-9）

Figure 3–8 Advanced DC motor. Photo courtesy of Effran Davis SR

图 3–8 先进的直流电动机。照片由老意夫冉•戴维斯提供

Figure 3–9 Kostov Motor. Photo courtesy of Kostov motors

(http://www.kostov–motors.com)

图 3–9 科斯托夫电动机。照片由科斯托夫电动机有限公司（http://www.kostov-motors.com）提供

➢ Other types of DC motor

There are three other types of DC motors that you may come across:

- Shunt Wound
- Compound Wound
- Separately Excited (Sep Ex)

All three are very similar to the series-wound motor: the major difference being the wiring of the stator (field) windings. Shunt and compound wound motors are less applicable to EVs and there are few EVs using separately excited motors, but we will cover these types briefly for completeness.

Shunt Wound

In shunt wound motors the stator windings are connected in parallel with the rotor rather than being in series with it (Figure 3-10).

➢ 其他类型的直流电动机

您可能会遇到的其他类型的直流电动机有三种：

- 并励电动机
- 复励电动机
- 他励电动机

这三种电动机都与串励电动机非常相似，它们的主要区别在于定子绕组（磁场）的接线。并励和复励电动机不太适用于电动汽车，并且只有少数的电动汽车使用他励电动机。但为完整性起见，我们将简要介绍这些类型的电动机。

并励电动机

在并励电动机中，定子绕组与转子绕组并联而非串联（图 3-10）。

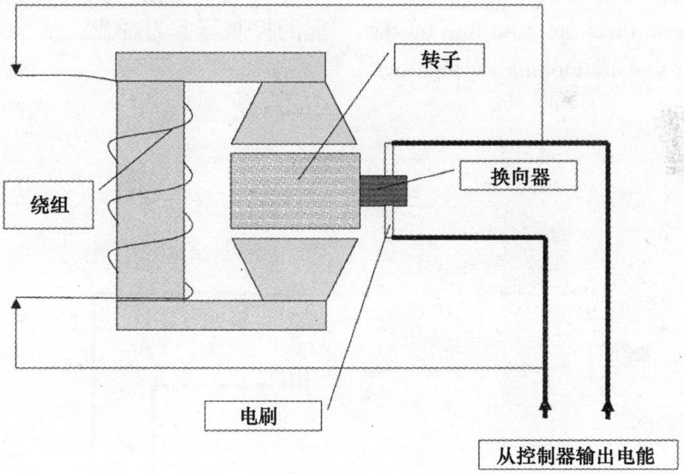

Figure 3–10 Shunt wound motor schematic

图 3–10 并励电动机原理图

In the real world, the low-speed torque of these motors is not as high as that of a similar series motor. They are probably better suited to constant speed applications such as fans and pumps.

在现实世界中，这些电动机的低速转矩不如串励电动机的大。它们可能更适合于如风扇和水泵等恒速电器使用。

Compound Wound

Compound wound motors are a bit of a throwback to the days before effective solid-state controllers, and are unlikely to be encountered new today, having been superseded by separately excited motors.

复励电动机

复励电动机是有效的固态控制器出现前的产物，并已被他励电动机所取代。因此，我们不太可能在今天见到新的此类电动机。

Separately Excited

In a "Sepex" motor, the power to the stator (field) is entirely separate from the rotor (armature) supply (Figure 3-11). With modern power electronics it is perfectly possible to control the field current to optimise performance at any combination of speed and torque. In theory, this is the best arrangement, as with a suitable controller almost any combination of "series" and "shunt" characteristics can be dialled in and adjusted by the software to optimise the motor's response. At the time of writing however, suitable controllers are a bit thin on the ground, especially if you are looking for high performance.

他励电动机

在一个"他励"电动机中，定子（磁场）的供电完全独立于转子(电枢)的供电(图3-11)。随着现代大功率电子技术的进步，我们完全可以控制磁场的电流，以便在任意速度和转矩的组合下都能最优化电动机的性能。从理论上讲，这是最好的安排。因为只要有了一个合适的控制器,几乎所有的"串励"和"并励"组合的特点都可以通过适当软件加以实现，以便优化电动机的响应。然而在写作本书时，我们还很难找到合适的控制器，高性能的控制器尤为难找。

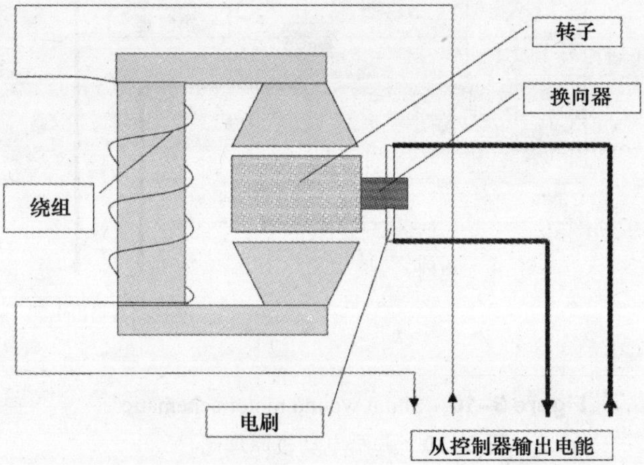

Figure 3-11 Separately-Excited ("Sepex") Motor

图 3-11 他励电动机

➢ AC motors

Both the AC motors that we are going to consider (the induction motor and the so called "Brushless DC" motor) have similar arrangements for the field: in essence a series of electromagnets (or "poles") inside the stator which are energised one after the other to produce a rotating magnetic field, in much the same way that a Mexican wave can appear to move across a stand full of spectators without anything actually changing position (Figure 3-12).

➢ 交流电动机

我们要讨论的交流电动机（感应电动机和所谓的无刷电动机）在磁场方面有类似的安排：在本质上是在定子内的一系列电磁铁（或"极"）依次通电后而产生的旋转磁场，这与墨西哥波（译注：一种人群依次站起挥动双臂再坐下所形成的波浪式场面）可以在一满场观众中出现，但观众位置没有任何实际改变的情形大致相同（图 3-12）。

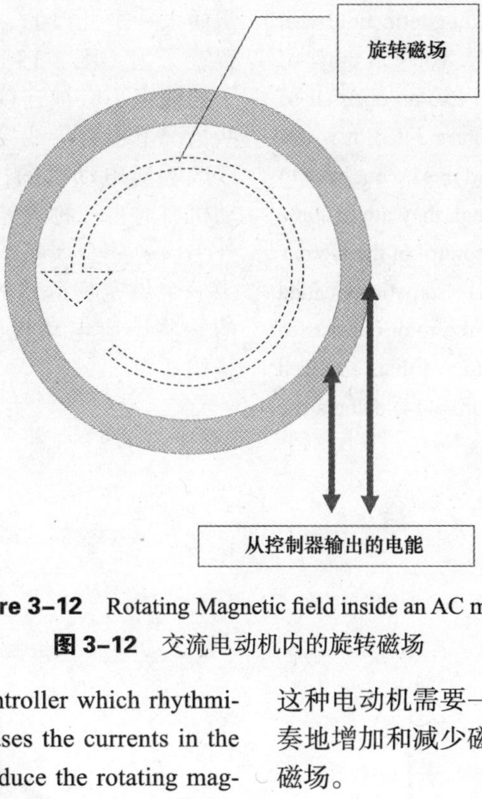

Figure 3–12 Rotating Magnetic field inside an AC motor

图 3–12 交流电动机内的旋转磁场

This requires a special controller which rhythmically increases and decreases the currents in the pole field windings to produce the rotating magnetic field.

这种电动机需要一个特殊的控制器，它有节奏地增加和减少磁极绕组的电流而产生旋转磁场。

The bulk of the electrical power is fed into the (fixed, stationary) field windings. There is usually no power supplied directly to the rotor. Note that this arrangement has a huge advantage over the DC motors that we have been looking at – no brushes.

大部分的电流都被送入（固定而静止的）励磁绕组中。通常没有电流直接提供给转子。请注意，相对于直流电动机，这样的安排具有巨大的优势，而这种优势正是我们一直在寻找的——无电刷。

➢ AC Induction motors

You will recall that in Experiment 1 in Chapter 2 we moved a wire in an electric field and it generated a current in the wire. Imagine a loop of wire inserted into the rotating magnetic field generated by the field windings described above. The movement generates a voltage in the wire which will (if the circuit is complete) cause a current to flow. Also, from Experiment 4, a current-carrying wire in a magnetic field experiences a force on it. The end result is that a simple loop of wire on a pivot placed in the rotating magnetic field will be "dragged round" electrically. You can think of it as being like dipping a spoon into an open jar of honey sitting on a turntable (Figure 3-13). It is important to note that the rotor windings do not have to be connected to anything (although they are in some cases because this can improve control of the motor). The simplest induction motors are sometimes called "squirrel cage" motors because the rotor consists of nothing more than some metal strips or bars arranged like a pet's exercise wheel (Figure 3-14). Others use more conventional wire windings.

➢ 交流感应电动机

您也许还会记得第 2 章实验 1 中我们在磁场中移动导线并在其中产生电流。现在设想有一个闭合回路的导线放入到上述励磁绕组产生的旋转磁场内。磁场的旋转将在导线内生成电压，如果电路是全闭合的，这将导致电流在其中流动。此外，从实验 4 可以知道，载有电流的导线在磁场中将受到磁力的作用。其最终的结果是一个放置在支点上的简单的闭合导线在旋转磁场中将被电力“拖着旋转”。您可以将这一过程想象为将一个调羹插入一个开口的、放在可旋转的盘上的蜂蜜罐子里（图 3-13）。重要的是要注意到转子的绕组不必被连接到任何地方（虽然在某些情况下也有导线接到转子上，因为这样可以改善对电动机的控制）。最简单的感应电动机有时也被称为笼式电动机，因为转子不外乎由一些金属条或杆构成，它们看起来就像一个供宠物运动的轮毂（图 3-14）。其他的一些感应电动机则更多地使用常规导线绕组。

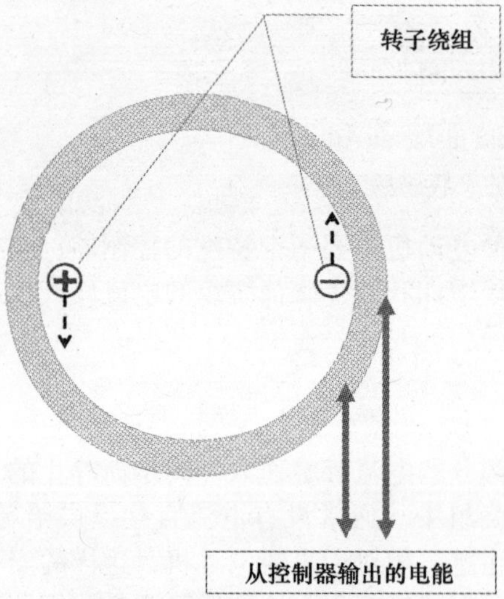

Figure 3–13 AC Induction Motor
图 3–13 交流感应电动机

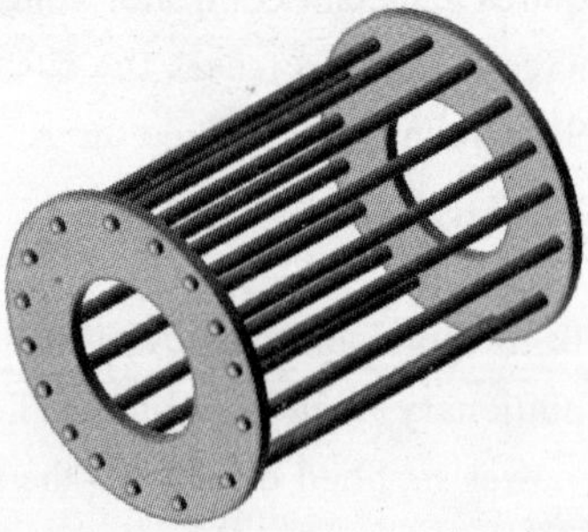

Figure 3–14 Induction "Squirrel Cage"
图 3–14 感应“鼠笼”

In any form of induction motor the rotor never quite keeps up with the rotating magnetic field. There is always a bit of "slip" i.e. a speed difference between the rotating field and the rotor. If the rotor was turning at the same speed as the magnetic field, there would of course be no relative movement, so no induced current in the rotor, so no torque. This means that the induction motor is a kind of asynchronous motor.

任何形式的感应电动机的转子都未能完全跟上旋转磁场的步伐，它们间始终有一个"转差率"，即旋转磁场与转子之间速度的差异。如果转子的转动速度与磁场的相同，它们之间就没有相对运动，在转子上就没有感应电流产生，所以没有转矩。这意味着感应电动机是一种异步电动机。

Most of the motors connected to mains electric power around the world are AC induction motors. They are about as simple and robust as you could hope to find, and for single speed use from the mains they do not need any form of controller. The Tesla Roadster (Figure 3-15) and Tzero sports cars both use induction motors manufactured by AC Propulsion.

世界各地连接到市电的电动机大部分是交流感应电动机。它们与您所希望看到的一样简单和强大，并且如果从市电中使用单一的速度，它们不需要任何形式的控制器。特斯拉跑车（图 3-15）和 Tzero 跑车（译注：一种世界上最快的电动跑车）都是使用由 AC Propulsion 制造的感应电动机作为动力。

Figure 3–15 Tesla Roadster. Photo courtesy of David Breach (http://www.flickr.com/people/davidbreach)

图 3–15 特斯拉跑车。照片由大卫・布里奇（http://www.flickr.com/people/davidbreach）提供

There are a number of other AC motors sold for use in EVs (see for example Figure 3-16, Figure 3-17 and Figure 3-18). These tend to be somewhat more expensive than their DC counterparts.

电动汽车也使用其他类型的交流电动机（例如，图 3-16、图 3-17 和图 3-18 所示的电动机）。这些往往比同类的直流电动机更贵。

Figure 3–16 MES DEA. Photo courtesy of MES s.a. (http://www.mes.ch)

图 3–16 MES DEA 电动机。照片由 MES S.A.(http://www.mes.ch) 提供

Figure 3–17 AC55 and DMOC 445. Photo courtesy of Azure Dynamics Force Drive(http://www.azuredynamics.com)

图 3–17 AC55 及 DMOC 445 电动机。照片由阿爵尔动态力驱动有限公司（http://www.azuredynamics.com) 提供

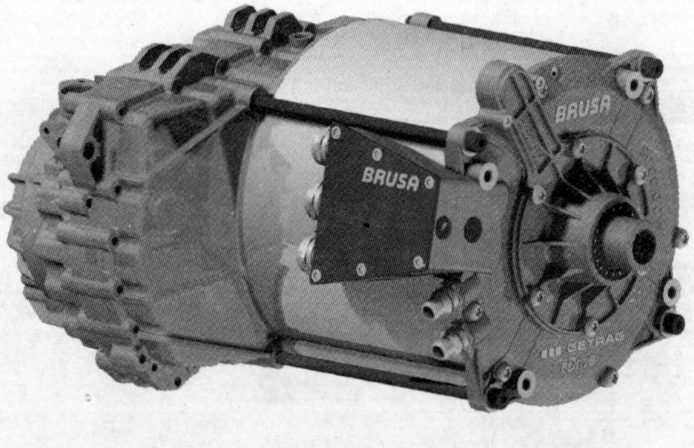

Figure 3–18 Brusa HSM 1-6.17.12 motor and transaxle gear set. Photo courtesy of BRUSA Elektronik AG(http://www.brusa.biz)

图 3–18 布鲁萨 HSM 1-6.17.12 电动机及变速器齿轮组。照片由布鲁萨电器公司（http://www.brusa.biz）提供

➤ Brushless DC (BLDC) Motors

Despite their name, these have more in common with AC motors than DC ones. They have broadly the same kind of rotating field as the induction motor, but the rotor is equipped with permanent magnets – the magnetic interaction between the permanent magnets and the rotating magnetic field is what generates the torque (Figure 3-19).

➤ 无刷直流（BLDC）电动机

尽管它们被称为直流电动机，但它们更像交流电动机。它们与异步电动机一样拥有旋转磁场，但转子是由永久磁铁组成的——转矩就是由永久磁铁和旋转磁场之间的磁相互作用而产生的（图 3-19）。

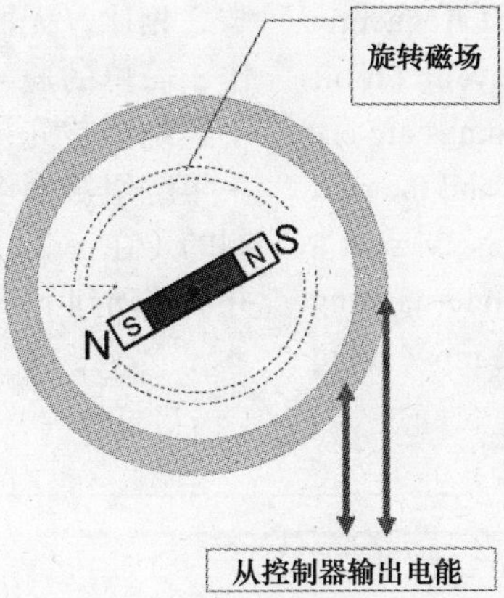

Figure 3–19 The Principle of a Brushless DC motor

图 3–19 无刷直流电动机的工作原理

The rotor in a brushless motor normally remains in lock-step with the rotating field. Brushless DC motors are therefore said to be synchronous i.e. there is no slip in normal operation.

无刷电动机的转子通常与旋转磁场步调锁定一致。无刷直流电动机因此被称为是同步的，即在正常运转时没有转差。

There is commonly (but not always) another difference between Brushless DC and AC induction motors. An AC Induction motor power supply is "sinusoidal"; that is the voltage and current rises and falls smoothly from zero to maximum positive voltage then back to zero and on to maximum negative voltage, then smoothly back to zero again (Figure 3-20).

无刷直流电动机和交流感应电动机之间通常（但并不总是）还有另一个差异。交流感应电动机的电源是“正弦的”，即电压和电流平稳地从零升到正的最大值，再返回到零和负的最大值，然后再平稳地返回到零（图 3-20）。

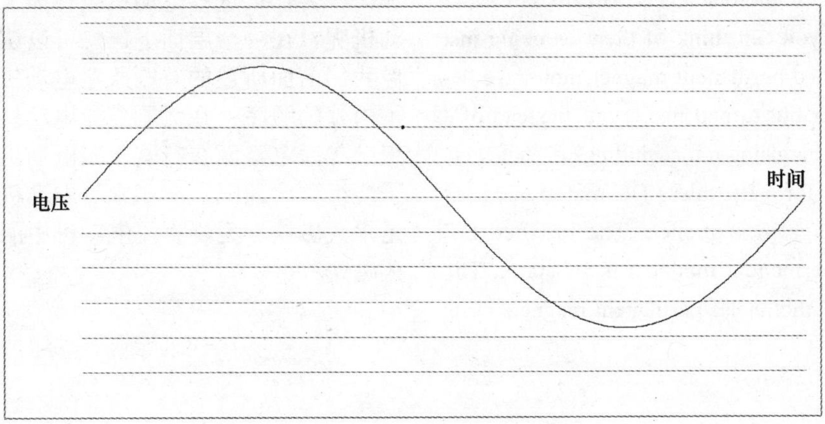

Figure 3–20 AC power supply (one pole)

图 3–20 交流电源（单相）

Brushless DC motors are by contrast frequently designed to operate with a simpler cyclic on-off switching. One part of the stator windings are energised, then that part is switched off and the next one energised. This is of course precisely what a commutator does (apply voltage to one winding segment, then switch off that one and move on to the next) - Figure 3-21.

与之相比，无刷直流电动机通常被设计成操作于简单的通 - 断开关的循环中。定子中的一组绕组首先被通电，然后被断开，接着下一组绕组被通电。这当然是由一个换向器控制的（在一个绕组段中施加电压，然后断开，并被移动到下一个绕组段中），如图 3-21 所示。

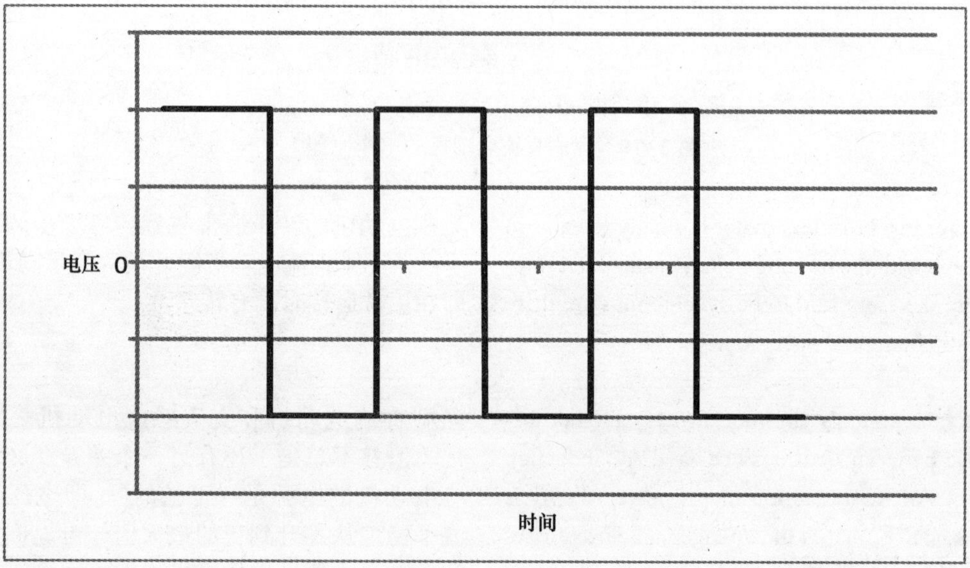

Figure 3–21 Brushless DC Power Supply (one pole)

图 3–21 无刷直流电源（单相）

So why are these motors called "Brushless DC" ? At one level you can think of them as being just like the brushed permanent magnet motor we described earlier but turned inside out: instead of a commutator energising rotor windings in sequence, the controller for a Brushless DC motor energises stator windings in sequence. The brushed DC motors has permanent magnets in its stator. The Brushless DC motor has permanent magnets in its rotor.

那么，为什么这些电动机被称为无刷直流电动机呢？在一个层面上，您可以认为它们就像我们前面所述的有刷永磁电动机，但颠倒了内外的顺序：在无刷直流电动机中定子绕组顺次通电，而在有刷永磁电动机中则是转子绕组顺次通电；有刷永磁电动机中的定子是永久磁铁，无刷直流电动机中的转子是永久磁铁。

	Brushed Permanent Magnet	Brushless DC
Stator	Permanent Magnet	Sequential switching of current in stator by the controller
Rotor	Sequential switching of current in rotor by the commutator	Permanent Magnet

	有刷永磁电动机	无刷直流电动机
定子	永磁铁	用控制器顺次切换定子电流
转子	用控制器顺次切换转子电流	永磁铁

There are a number of manufacturers building Brushless DC motors. For example M & C motors in China manufacture a range of these motors for use in everything from buses (Figure 3-22) to electric bikes (Figure 3-23).

生产无刷直流电动机的厂家有不少。例如：中国广东的麦科尔电力设备有限公司制造了可被用于从巴士（图 3-22）到电动自行车（图 3-23）的一系列这样的电动机。

Figure 3–22 M & C Brushless DC Bus motor Weight 350kg, Power 420 kW, Torque 1kN-m. Photos courtesy Guangdong M&C Electric Power

图 3–22 麦科尔无刷直流大巴用电动机，重 350kg，功率为 420kW，转矩为 1kN • m。照片由广东麦科尔电力设备有限公司提供

Figure 3–23 M&C Brushless DC Bicycle Hub Motor, Weight 2.9 kg, Power 180 Watts, Torque 6.5 N-m

图 3–23 麦科尔无刷直流电动自行车轮毂电动机，重 2.9kg，功率为 180W，转矩为 6.5N • m

➢ Other types of AC motor

➢ 其他类型的交流电动机

Reluctance motors

You may recall from chapter 2 that a magnetic field passes through iron far more easily than air. One of the side-effects of this phenomenon is that a magnetic field will exert a force on iron to minimise the amount of air that it has to pass through. This is the basis of the solenoid.

磁阻电动机

您可能还记得，在第 2 章中我们发现磁场穿过铁比穿过空气容易得多。这一现象的副作用之一是一个磁场将对铁施加一个力以尽量减少它从空气中通过的量。这就是电磁铁的基础。

There is also one form of electric motor which exploits this behaviour. The Reluctance motor offers

有一种形式的电动机就利用了这种现象。磁阻电动机为磁场提供了一个由多铁块构成的

a magnetic field a nice easy path through lots of iron rather than all that nasty air: all the magnetic field has to do is just rotate the armature a little bit until things line up nicely...

磁阻很小的路径，而不是磁阻很大的空气。磁场所需要做的就是将电枢转动一点点，直到磁场的路径能对准得很好……

Reluctance motors aren't used much, if at all, for EV propulsion but you might find them driving ancillary equipment. Stepper motors are typically a form of reluctance motor.

磁阻电动机很少用于电动汽车的动力驱动。但您会发现它们会用于驱动辅助设备。步进电动机通常是开关磁阻电动机的一种形式。

Wheel motors

Most EV conversions use an electric motor as a replacement for the IC engine and still require a mechanical transmission (gearbox, differential, half-shafts: and sometimes a propshaft).

轮毂电动机

大多数传统汽车转换为电动汽车时，除了用一个电动机去替代内燃机外，还需要机械传动，如变速器、差速器、半轴（译注：即前轮驱动轴），有时还需要一个传动轴。

It is however possible in principle to use motors which fit inside a wheel hub, eliminating the need for these mechanical components. The idea of individual in-wheel motors driving each wheel of a vehicle is not new. In 1900 at the World's Fair in Paris the 'System Lohner-Porsche' was debuted. This vehicle was designed by Ferdinand Porsche; the man who gives his name to the Porsche car company. His first job in the automotive world was with Jacob Lohner. The 'System Lohner-Porsche' was an electric vehicle driven by two in-wheel motors; this vehicle was capable of over 35mph and set several Austrian speed records. (Figure 3-24).

然而在原则上可以将电动机装进轮毂里，以便去除这些机械部件。这种用电动机驱动每个车轮的想法并不新鲜。1900 年在巴黎的世界博览会上“罗纳 - 保时捷系统”首次亮相。这款车的设计者是费迪南德 · 保时捷，保时捷汽车公司就是以他的名字命名的。他在汽车行业里的第一份工作是为雅各 · 罗纳公司工作。“罗纳 – 保时捷系统”是由两个轮毂电动机驱动的电动汽车，这辆车的车速可超过 55km/h，并打破了几个奥地利的车速纪录（图 3-24）。

Figure 3–24 Lohner Porsche of 1900 driven by in-wheel motors. Photo © Porsche AG

图 3–24 1900 年罗纳 – 保时捷由轮毂电动机驱动。照片由保时捷提供

There are organisations working on in-wheel motors today. For example Protean Electric (formerly PML Flightlink) has demonstrated their Protean Drive in-wheel motors in a variety of different vehicles and is currently working with a number of different car manufacturers and suppliers to bring this technology into volume production (Figure 3-25).

今天有不少机构致力于轮毂电动机的研发工作。例如：普洛廷电力（原 PML Flightlink）已展示了能用于各种不同车辆的、种类繁多的轮毂电动机，目前正与不同的汽车制造商和供应商合作，努力使这项技术进入批量生产（图 3-25）。

Figure 3–25 Protean Wheel Motor. Photo courtesy of Protean Electric[1]

图 3–25 普洛廷轮毂电动机。照片由普洛廷电器提供㊀

This configuration has the massive advantage that no transmission is needed. On the down side, electric power has to cross the gap between chassis and suspension. Also, if the motor is direct drive, the motor RPM is low which means that the torque has to be greater for a given power output.

这种配置具有不需要传输系统的独特优势。其不足之处在于电力必须穿过底盘和悬架之间的间隙。此外，如果用电动机直接驱动轮毂，电动机的转速更低。这意味着，在输出功率一定的条件下转矩将更大。

There is also a potential issue with unsprung weight. One of the targets of car designers is to minimise the weight of wheels, brakes, tyres and suspension components to improve ride and handling.

非簧载的重量也是一个潜在的问题。汽车设计师的目标之一是最大限度地减少车轮、制动、轮胎和悬架组件的重量，以改善平顺性和操纵。

Wheel motors do not help here, although the importance of this is often overplayed: a 2010 report

而轮毂电动机使这方面的问题变得更加严重。这方面的重要性常常被夸大，2010 年的一份报告（《簧下质量与轮毂电动机——

1 http://www.proteanelectric.com

㊀ 见 http://www.proteanelectric.com。

(Unsprung Mass with In-Wheel Motors - Myths and Realities, Anderson M, Harty D presented at AVEC 2010) concluded that "perceptible differences ... are small and unlikely to be apparent to an average driver."

神话与现实》，作者M·安德森和D·哈蒂，2010年发表在AVEC）得出的结论是"可感知的差异……都很小，并且不大可能被一般的驾驶人感觉到。"

➢ Motor ratings and motor cooling

➢ 电动机的额定值与电动机的冷却

Compared with an IC engine, electric motors are extremely efficient. But they are not 100% efficient and they are also physically small. A motor putting out 30 kW with 90% efficiency is still generating 3 kW of heat in a space little larger than a big water melon. A 3kW electric heater soon warms up a living room, so without adequate cooling, 3kW will generate high temperatures inside a motor.

与内燃机相比，电动机的效率极高，但是也达不到100%的效率，并且它们的体积也很小。一个30kW的电动机即使有90%的效率，仍然能在一个比大西瓜略大的空间里产生3kW的热量。一个3kW的电加热器很快就能使一间客厅变得暖和起来。所以没有足够的冷却，3kW将会在电动机内产生很高的温度。

Most EV motors are air cooled. An obvious solution is to put a fan on the motor shaft (most electric tools take this approach for example). This is OK, but it does mean that cooling air flow drops off at low speed which can be an issue. Brushed DC motors probably have greater cooling problems, because most of the heat is generated in the rotor deep inside the motor.

大多数电动汽车的电动机采用空气冷却。一个显而易见的解决方案是把风扇放在电动机轴上（大多数电动工具都采取这种做法）。这是可行的，但它确实意味着在低速时冷空气流量的下降，而这可能是个问题。有刷直流电动机可能有更严重的散热问题，因为大部分热量是在电动机转子内部的深处中产生的。

One thing that electric motors do have going for them is their mass. They contain a lot of metal and in consequence heat up slowly and cool down slowly. This means that they are capable of providing short bursts of higher power than they are capable of sustaining continuously.

电动机中存在的另一个问题是它们的质量。它们含有大量的金属而导致加热和冷却过程都非常缓慢。这意味着与持续不断的功率供给相比，它们更适合于在短时间内提供很高的功率。

Motors typically have a continuous rating (maximum current) and maybe one or more short-period ratings. This fits quite well with the profile of use in a car: a maximum-effort acceleration with the motor drawing (say) 1000 amps tends to last no more than 10 or 15 seconds for the simple reason

电动机通常有一个连续的评级（最大电流），或许还有一个或多个短期的评级。这很适合在汽车中的应用：在电动机吸入（例如）1000A的电流时产生的最大加速度的持续时间往往不超过10s或15s，因为如果这样大的加速度持续更长时间的话，您将会超过法

that accelerating that hard for any longer will put you over the legal speed limit and/or into a regime where back EMF will start to reduce the current anyway.

定的车速限制，并且进入到一个反电动势将开始减少正向电流的区域。

All the same heat is an important consideration, and one you ignore at your peril.

总之，发热是一个重要的考虑因素。如果您忽略的话，后果会比较严重。

➢ In Conclusion

➢ 小结

This completes our gallop through electric motors as applied to EVs. If you would like to go further with your understanding of motors, Electric Motors and Drives: Fundamentals, Types and Applications by Austin Hughes (ISBN 978-0750647182) is an excellent introduction at the next level of detail. In the meantime we'll move on to controllers: the boxes packed with power electronics which enable us to make use of electric motors.

我们现在将结束对电动汽车用的电动机的描述。如果您想进一步了解电动机，奥斯汀·休斯著的《电动机和驱动器：基本原理、类型和应用》（ISBN 9780750647182）是一本很好的、能提供更多细节的入门书。现在我们将进入到控制器，这是装有高功率电子器件，并使我们能够使用电动机的盒子。

4 Controllers
控 制 器

Controllers are linked directly to the accelerator (throttle) pedal of an EV. They occupy exactly the same niche as a carburettor or fuel injection system in an IC-engined car; that is, they allow the driver to control power and hence speed (Figure 4-1). Just like a carburettor or fuel injection system, a controller needs to be matched to the motor. A puny carburettor on a big IC engine will strangle it. A puny controller will likewise strangle a powerful motor and good batteries. Controllers also need to suit the type of motor that they are feeding: a controller designed for a DC motor for example could not even make an AC induction motor turn over under no load.

控制器直接连接到电动汽车的加速踏板（油门）。它们的地位与内燃机汽车中的化油器或燃油喷射系统完全相同。也就是说，它们能让驾驶人控制输入的功率和汽车的速度（图 4-1）。就像化油器或燃油喷射系统一样，控制器必须与电动机相匹配。一个很小的化油器装在一个大功率的内燃机上将扼杀它的功能；一个弱小的控制器同样会扼杀掉一个强大的电动机和良好的电池。控制器还需要适应它所操控的电动机类型。例如：为直流电动机设计的控制器甚至在空载情况下也无法使交流感应电动机工作。

In the context of EVs, Controllers can be placed into one of four groups as follows:

在电动汽车的情况下，控制器有如下四种类型：

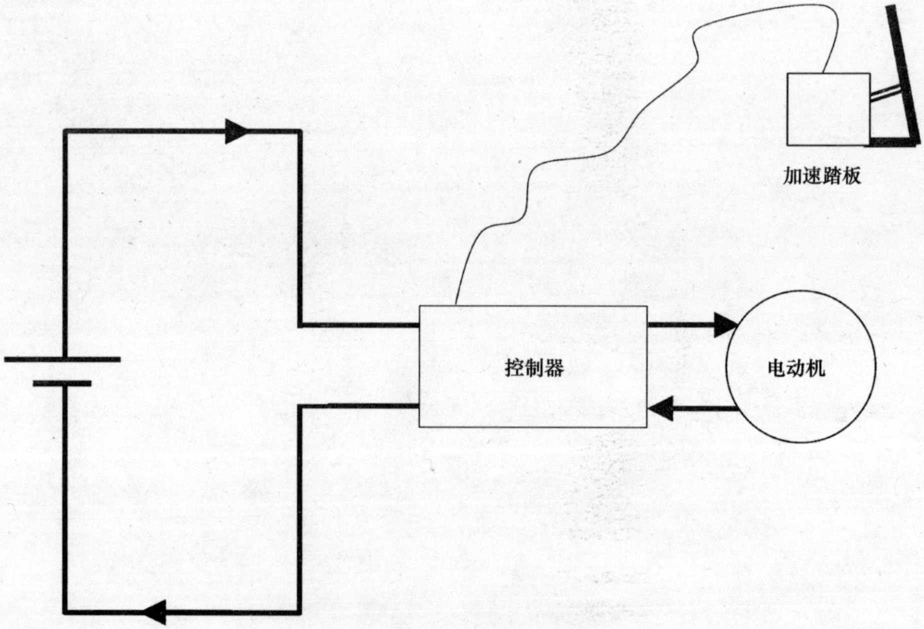

Figure 4–1 Battery, Controller and Motor
图 4–1 电池、控制器和电动机

- Controllers for Separately Excited DC motors
- Controllers for other brushed DC motors
- AC Induction Controllers
- Brushless DC (BLDC) Motor controllers

- 他励直流电动机控制器
- 其他有刷直流电动机控制器
- 交流感应电动机控制器
- 无刷直流（BLDC）电动机控制器

A controller for a separately excited motor might work with other DC motors, and an AC induction controller might work (very imperfectly) with a brushless DC motor, but none of these types of controller are otherwise interchangeable: indeed an AC Induction or Brushless DC system is best acquired as a matched motor/controller package. A controller designed for one make and model of AC Induction or BLDC motor might not work well even with another motor of the same type.

他励电动机控制器也许可以工作于其他直流电动机，交流感应电动机控制器也许可以（不是非常完美地）工作于无刷直流电动机，但其他类型的控制器都不可互换。一个交流感应或无刷直流电动机的确最好与一个匹配的电动机 / 控制器对一起工作。一个为某种牌子或型号的交流感应或无刷直流（BLDC）电动机而设计的控制器在不同牌子或型号的同种电动机上可能无法正常工作。

The simplest controller is the type typically used with a Series wound DC or a brushed Permanent magnet motor. We'll start with that.

最简单的控制器是那种用于串励直流或有刷永磁电动机的控制器。我们将由此开始。

1. The simple DC motor controller

The very simplest form of DC motor controller (never used in an EV) is a variable resistor (or rheostat) in series with the motor. Increasing the resistance reduces the current flow, which in turn reduces the power developed by the motor (Figure 4-2). It's as simple as that.

1. 简单的直流电动机控制器

最简单的直流电动机控制器（从未在电动汽车中使用过）是一个与电动机串联的可变电阻（或变阻器）。电阻的增加将使电流减少，从而减少输送到电动机的功率（图 4-2）。它就是这么简单。

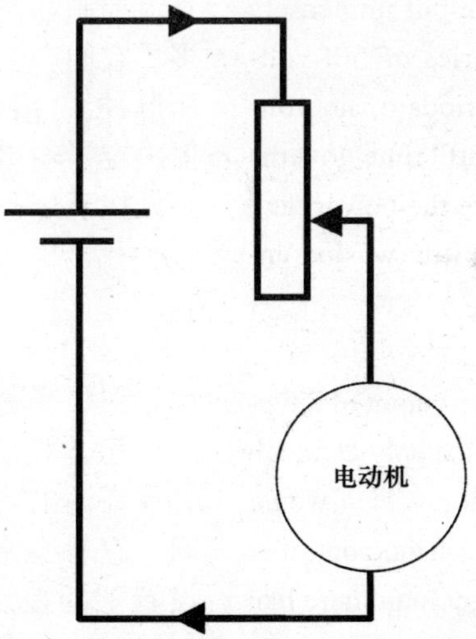

Figure 4–2 Crude Motor Control with Variable Resistor

图 4–2 由可变电阻组成的简易电动机控制器

This approach works well for tiny motors in models and toys, but it would be totally impracticable in an EV. The problem is that much of the available power is burned up in the resistor. This slashes range, and also creates a heat problem. All that waste energy has to go somewhere, so the variable resistance would need to be physically large and well-cooled or it would burn out.

这种方法可以很好地用于模型和玩具的微型电动机中，但它在电动汽车中则完全不可行。问题是很多的可用功率将被电阻消耗掉。这不仅缩短了行程范围，还导致了散热问题。所有浪费掉的能源必须有地方去，因此，可变电阻的体积必须很大且要有很好的冷却，否则就会被烧坏。

As it turns out there is a solution to the DC controller problem which is even simpler conceptually. Suppose that you were presented with an EV that had no controller – merely a big on-off switch. Could you drive it across town? Well yes you probably could, although you would be unwise to try it, and it would be an uncomfortable trip. When you wanted to move off you would switch on, wait until you had built up enough speed and then switch off and coast. As your speed dropped you would switch on again until you were back to your target speed. You would progress down the highway in a series of pulses: switch on – accelerate – switch off – coast – switch on – accelerate...

值得庆幸的是，我们有一个在概念上更为简单的直流控制器问题的解决方案。假设有人给了您一辆没有控制器的电动汽车——它仅有一个大的通断开关。您能不能开着它穿过市中心呢？虽然您尝试这种方法是不明智的，但您还是可能会去试一下。不过这将是一个不舒服的旅程。当您想让车开动时，您可以将电源接通。等到您已经建立了足够的速度，您就可以切断电源，让车滑行。当车速下降时，您可重新接通电源，直到汽车回到您的预定速度。您可以在一系列的接通—加速—切断—滑行—接通—加速……等脉冲中将车开到高速公路。

DC controllers use this principle but immensely speeded up. They generate a series of full-voltage pulses interspersed with periods of no voltage. The ratio of "on" time to "off" time governs the average voltage and therefore the power; and the beauty of it is that there is little wasted energy.

直流控制器使用了这一原理，但其过程快得多。它们产生了一系列穿插着零电压的全电压脉冲。"接通"时间和"切断"时间的比值决定了输出电压和功率的平均值。其美妙之处在于几乎没有能量被浪费掉。

If you were to measure the voltage output of a typical DC controller with a 100 Volt supply at a high power setting a little short of full power it would look like Figure 4-3. On the other hand controller output at a low power setting might look more like Figure 4-4.

如果您想要测量一个典型的直流控制器的输出电压，假设它具有 100V 的供电电源，并且在高输出功率的设置下只有短暂的切断时间，它看起来就像图 4-3。此外，在低功率设置下的控制器的输出可能看起来更像图 4-4。

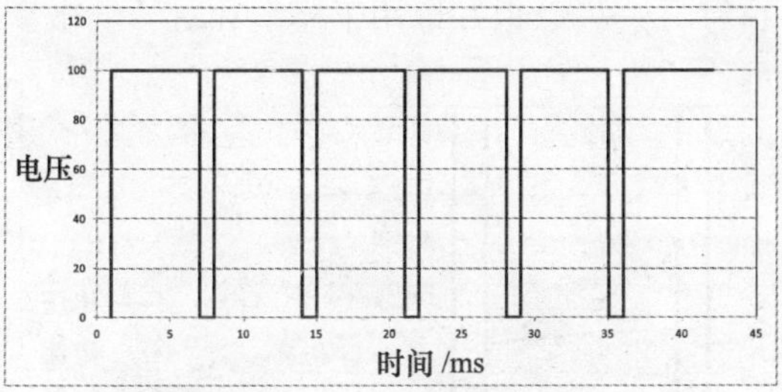

Figure 4–3 High Average Voltage

图 4–3 较高的平均电压

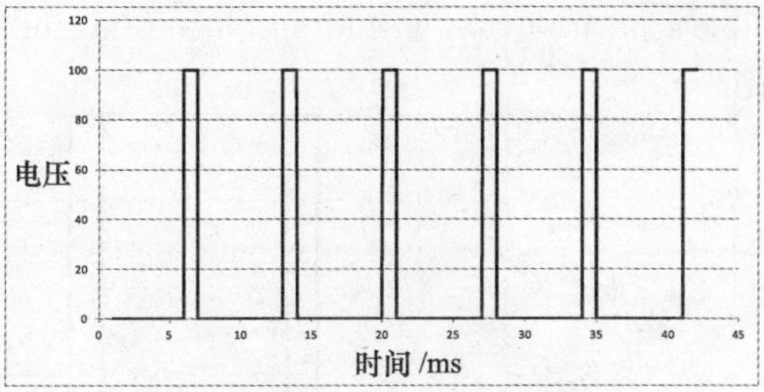

Figure 4–4 Low Average Voltage

图 4–4 较低的平均电压

This is known as Pulse Width Modulation or PWM. The frequency is typically high: thousands of pulses per second. Ideally the frequency is high enough to be beyond the range of human hearing (it isn't always that high though – some EVs emit an audible whine).

这种控制被称为脉冲宽度调制或脉宽调制。调制的频率通常很高，每秒几千个脉冲。理想的频率高到足以超出人类的听觉范围（但它并不总是那么高，有一些电动汽车会发出听得见的“呜呜”声）。

So much for the voltage. The resulting current is a bit different. One of the peculiarities of electric motors (and many other electrical devices) is that there is something like a flywheel effect on any electric current flowing through it. The current takes a little while to build up when a voltage is applied, and a little while to die away when the voltage is removed. It is as if the current has a kind of inertia and is reluctant to increase or decrease. It isn't really physical inertia but from the outside it appears to behave in a similar way. This characteristic is described as inductance and it can be measured, just as resistance can.

有关电压的问题就讲这些，但由此所产生的电流则有点不同。电动机（及许多其他电气设备）的特点之一是，电流流经它们时有一种像飞轮的效应。当施加了电压时，电流需要过一小会儿才能建立起来；而当电压被移走之后，电流也需要过一小会儿才能消失。这就好比电流有一定的惯性，不愿意被增加或减少。这不是真正的物理惯性，但从外部看来，它以类似的方式表现出来。这一特点被描述为电感，它就像电阻那样可以被测量。

One of the effects of inductance in the motor is that at these high frequencies the current through the motor varies much less than the voltage: and the higher the frequency, the less it varies. Figure 4-5 illustrates typical current variation with voltage changes.

电动机的电感效应之一，是流过电动机的电流在这些高频率的变化中远比电压要慢。频率越高，它就变得越少。图 4-5 给出了一个随电压而变的典型的电流变化。

This means that the controller has to be designed to allow for current flow continuing even during

这意味着控制器必须被设计成在一个周期中没有电源电压的部分也有电流继续流过。如

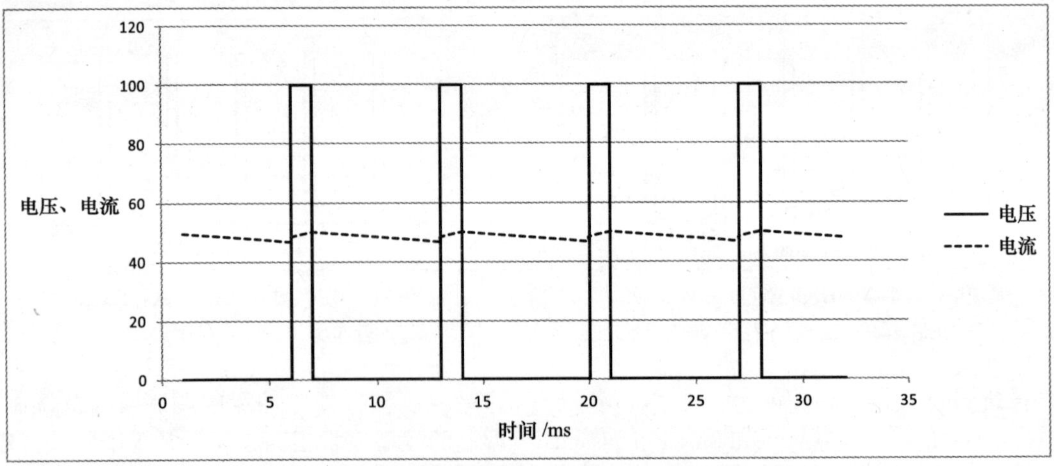

Figure 4–5 Motor current and voltage

图 4–5 电动机的电流和电压

that part of the cycle where there is no supply voltage. If it behaved like a mechanical switch and just interrupted the current on every cycle, there would be mayhem: sparks, spikes and burned out components. A path for continuing current flow is therefore created using so-called "free-wheeling diodes" . More on this later.

果它的表现就像一个机械开关，在每个周期中都要切断电流就会有点麻烦：火花、尖峰及烧坏元件。因此，可用一种所谓的"飞轮二极管"来创建一个持续电流流动的路径。我们将在以后详细讨论这一问题。

So how is the pulse width modulation achieved? You can think of a DC controller as having two halves – the brain and the brawn. The "brain" is basically a pulse generator. It translates the throttle position into a series of low-power pulses where (as in Figure 4-3 and Figure 4-4) the proportion of "on" time to "off" time depends upon the throttle position. The "brawn" switches the main drive voltage in time to the signal coming from the pulse generator (Figure 4-6).

那么，如何实现脉冲宽度调制？您可以将直流控制器想象成由两部分组成——大脑和躯体。"大脑"基本上就是一个脉冲发生器。它将加速踏板的位置转换成一系列低功率脉冲（图 4-3 和图 4-4），其"接通"时间和"切断"时间的比例取决于加速踏板的位置。"躯体"则及时将脉冲发生器送来的信号切换成主驱动电压（图 4-6）。

The "brawn" consists of one or more power transistors - solid state electronic switches. The application of a low voltage at one terminal of the "switch" turns it on: removal of the voltage turns it off (Figure 4-7).

"躯体"由一个或多个功率晶体管——固态电子开关组成。施加在这一"开关"的一个端口的低电压将它接通，该电压消失，则电路断开（图 4-7）。

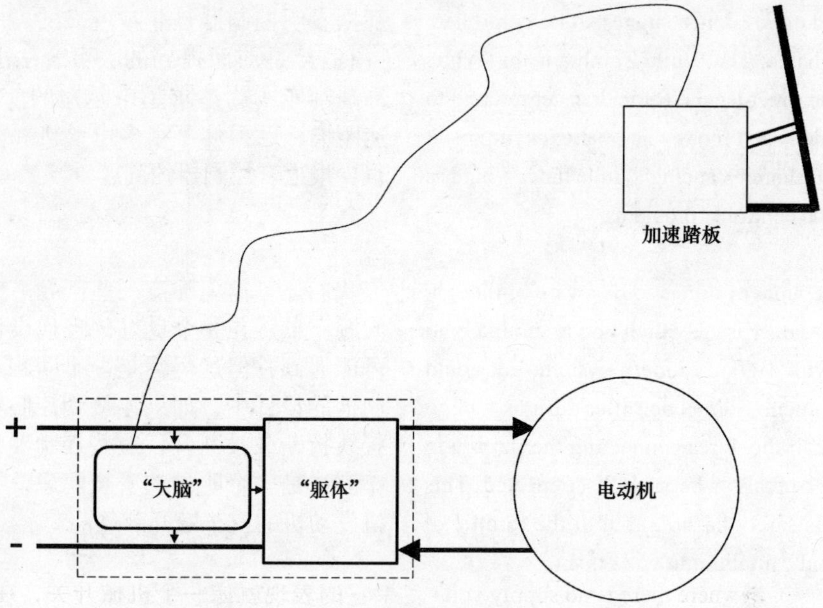

Figure 4–6 DC Controller High Level Schematic

图 4–6 直流控制器的高级方案

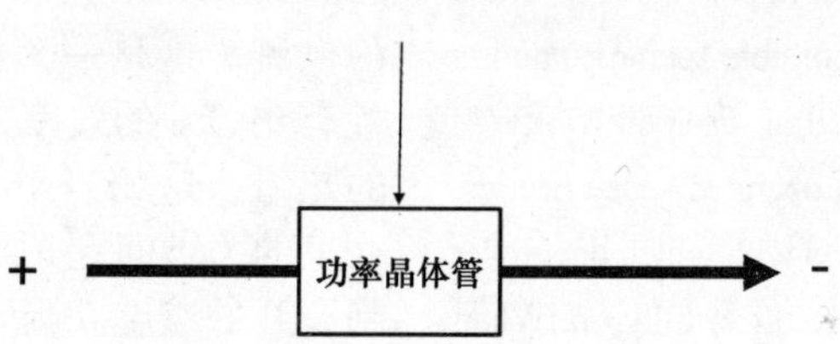

Figure 4–7 Schematic of a Power Transistor

图 4–7 功率晶体管示意图

This type of controller has only been practicable for a few decades, since the advent of "power electronics" - solid state components (primarily different forms of transistor) that can handle large currents. Even today, big power transistors are expensive in high power ratings. As a result, controllers are not cheap, and the price is linked to the maximum current and voltage ratings of the controller.

自"功率电子学"——可处理大电流的固态元件（主要是不同形式的晶体管）问世以来，这种类型的控制器只存在了几十年。即使在今天，高额定功率的大功率晶体管仍然是昂贵的。因此，控制器是不便宜的，且价格与控制器的最大电流和电压等级有关。

So what can go wrong with this kind of controller? You are entitled to assume that reputable manufac-

因此，这种控制器怎么经得起滥用呢？好在您可以认为有信誉的控制器厂家知道控制器

turers of controllers know what they are doing, and indeed anecdotal evidence suggests that controllers are pretty reliable. The White Zombie team (White Zombie is the street-legal electric dragster referred to earlier) has damaged motors and batteries in pursuit of shorter and shorter standing ¼ mile times – but has rarely reported controller problems.

的重要性和价值。实际上，确有未经证实的证据表明控制器是非常可靠的。白僵尸团队（白僵尸是前面提到的、可合法上路的电动高速赛车）为追求越来越短的前 400m 的加速距离，已损坏了很多电动机和电池——但很少报道有控制器的问题。

There are a couple of things to be aware of though. The first is a safety issue which you are unlikely to encounter with a good modern system, but could still be a problem. Some controller designs will go to full power if the wires connecting the throttle to the controller break or become disconnected. This is an obvious safety hazard, akin to the throttle of an IC engined car jamming wide open.

但我们还是需要注意一些问题。首先是安全问题，虽然在一个良好的现代设计中您不太可能遇到，但这仍然是一个问题。在有些控制器的设计中，如果连接到控制器的加速踏板线折断或被断开，这些控制器将达到满功率。这是一个明显的安全隐患，类似于内燃机发动机的汽车敞开节气门。

The second issue to be aware of is heat. The best of controllers are not quite 100% efficient and so do produce waste heat. If the controller is pulsing 1000 amps at 300 volts (an extreme, but possible scenario) and is 99.5% efficient, it will still need to dissipate 1.5kW – as much output as some mains operated space heaters. The critical issue here is the speed with which the power electronics can switch from fully off to fully on. When the switching device is fully on, there is little or no voltage drop across it, so little or no power is lost even if it is passing hundreds of amps (power = volts × amps so if either is zero, power is zero). When it is fully off the switching device itself carries no current, and once again there is little or no power lost even if there is a high voltage across the switching device. The problem is the tiny instant of time in each cycle that it is partially on. The power dissipated can be very large albeit for a very short time; and it is generated inside the large and expensive semi-conductors that do the switching. So be lavish in your cooling arrangements for a high power controller. If it is water cooled, ensure it gets what it needs. If it is air cooled, don't shove it in some corner where the air cannot circulate.

要注意的第二个问题是发热。最好的控制器也没有 100% 的效率，因此一定会产生多余的热量。如果控制器在 300V 下输入 1000A 的电流（这是一个极端的、但可能的情况）且有 99.5% 的效率，它仍然需要散发 1.5kW 的热量，这相当于一些家用加热器的输出。这里的关键问题是功率电子器件从全关切换到全开的速度。当开关设备全开时，它两端的电压降很小或为零，因此即使有数百安培的电流通过,也只有很少或没有功率消耗（功率 = 电压 × 电流，只要二者中的任意一项为零，功率就是零）。当它完全关闭时，开关本身并无电流通过，因此即使在其两端加上高电压，也只有很少或没有功率消耗。问题是在每个周期中开关部分开启的极小的瞬间。这时，在很短的时间内的功率消耗可以非常大，并且是在大型且昂贵的半导体开关内产生的。所以，对于一个高功率控制器而言，您在冷却的安排上是不能吝啬的。如果是水冷，确保它能得到它所需要的。如果是风冷，不要将它放在某些空气不能流通的角落里。

That is about it for the simplest DC controllers. We'll now move on to controllers for separately excited DC motors.

关于最简单的直流控制器就谈这些。现在，我们将讨论他励直流电动机控制器。

➢ Separately excited DC

➢ 他励直流控制器

You will perhaps recall from Chapter 3 that separately excited motors require a controller which can adjust the voltage applied to the field (stator) windings quite separately from the supply to the armature (rotor) – see Figure 4-8.

从第 3 章中您也许会记得他励电动机需要一个控制器来分别调节磁场（定子）绕组的电压和电枢（转子）的电压，如图 4-8 所示。

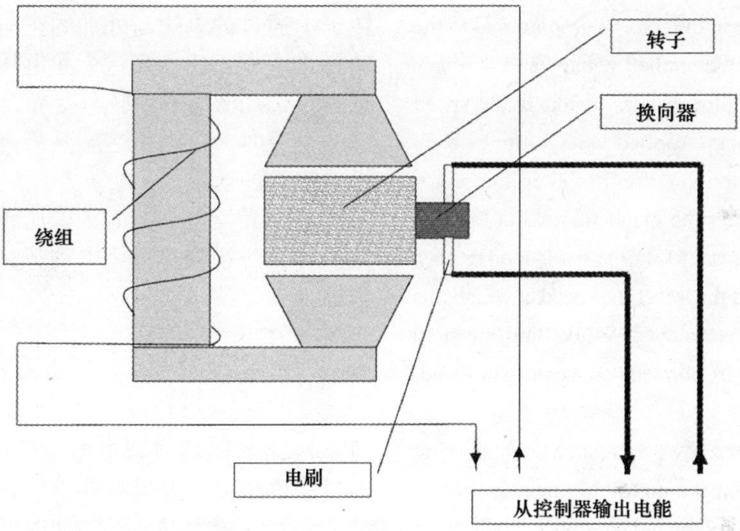

Figure 4–8 Separately Excited Motor schematic. Note separate connections for field and armature

图 4–8 他励电动机示意图，请注意磁场和电枢单独连接

The major difference between the simple DC motor controller described earlier and the controller for the separately excited motor is therefore that the latter must control two outputs – one each for the stator (field) and the rotor (armature) windings.

因此，前面描述的简单的直流电动机控制器与他励电动机控制器之间的主要差别在于，后者必须控制两个输出：一个是定子（磁场）；一个是转子（电枢）绕组。

At low speeds, the field current can be set to optimise the strength of the magnetic field in the motor to give maximum torque potential. At higher speeds however, something quite unexpected begins to happen. The

在低速时，励磁电流可设置成优化电动机的磁场强度以获得最大的转矩。然而在更高的速度，一件很意外的事开始出现。控制器实际上减少了励磁电流，以便减少电

controller actually reduces the field current, reducing the strength of the magnetic field in the motor.

动机的磁场强度。

This is counter-intuitive. Why does weakening the magnetic field allow the motor to run faster? The answer to this conundrum is related to the back EMF generated in the rotor. You will recall that there are two opposing voltages at work in a motor – the external applied voltage from the controller, and a voltage in the opposite direction resulting from the generator action that happens in any motor (see Back EMF in Chapter 2: Refresher course).

这与直觉相矛盾。为什么削弱磁场会使电动机运行得更快？这个难题的答案与转子中产生的反电动势有关。您也许会记得在电动机中有两个相反的电压在起作用——从控制器而来的外加电压，以及出现在任何电动机中的来自发电机效应的反向电压（请参阅第2章中的反电动势）。

The current flowing in the rotor is proportional to the difference between the applied voltage and the back EMF. An electric motor reaches its maximum speed when this net voltage (Applied voltage minus back EMF) gives just enough current to keep the motor spinning. The stronger the magnetic field in the motor, the higher the back EMF: or to put it another way, the stronger the field the lower the speed at which this critical back EMF is reached. Weakening the field reduces the back EMF, allowing an increase in speed.

转子中通过的电流与外加的正向电压和反电动势之差成正比。当这个净电压（外加电压减去反电动势）提供正好足够维持电动机旋转的电流时，电动机达到其最高转速。电动机内的磁场越强，反电动势就越高，或者说，在到达临界反电动势时，磁场越强，转速越低。弱化磁场将降低反电动势，从而使转速增加。

The weaker field does however reduce the maximum torque available from the motor, but therein lies the benefit of the Sepex motor and controller: high torque at low speed like the Series wound DC motor, combined with high speed albeit with lower torque.

但是较弱的磁场将减少电动机的最大转矩。不过他励电动机及其控制器的好处在于，它具有串励直流电动机低转速时的高转矩又有高转速时的低转矩。

➢ AC Induction Controllers

➢ 交流感应控制器

Controllers for AC induction motors are, as we shall see, clever gadgets. They can not only rub their tummy and pat their head at the same time, they can do this whilst simultaneously playing the Hallelujah Chorus on a mouth organ and riding a unicycle down a mountain. It is fortunately a lot easier to understand the principle of operation of an AC induction controller than it is to design one.

就像我们将要看到的那样，交流感应电动机的控制器是很巧妙的器件。它们不仅可以在搓揉自己肚子的同时拍打自己的头，它们还可以在做这些事得同时，用一个口风琴演奏哈利路亚大合唱，并且骑着独轮车下山。幸运的是，理解交流感应控制器的工作原理比设计一个这样的控制器要容易得多。

2. Mains-operated AC Induction

Probably the best place to start is to think about the AC Induction motor hooked up to a three phase mains supply. There are millions of them in factories and workshops all over the world.

2. 工作于市电的交流感应电动机

工作于市电的三相交流感应电动机也许是我们最好的开始。在世界各地的工厂和车间里有上百万台这样的电动机。

Household electricity supply consists of a single "live" delivering a straightforward AC voltage. The plot of voltage against time looks something like Figure 4-9

家庭用电由一个单一的"相线"提供一个简单的交流电压。电压与时间的关系看起来像图 4-9。

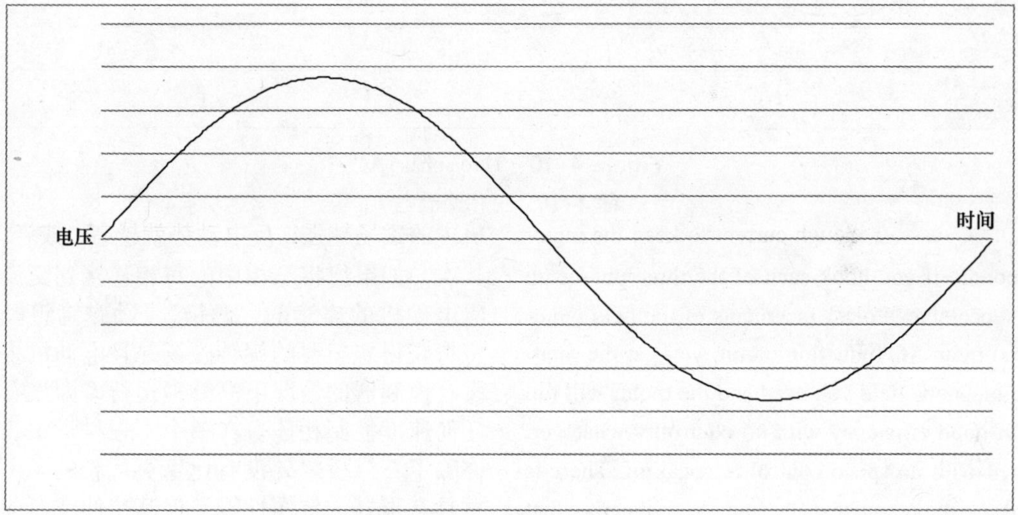

Figure 4–9 Single phase AC

图 4–9 单相交流电

On the other hand, commercial premises are usually offered three phase power – that is three "live" conductors each carrying an AC voltage. Critically, the three voltages are not in step with each other: each is shifted a third of a cycle from the previous one so that a graph of voltage against time look like Figure 4-10.

另一方面，商业楼宇通常被供以三相电源——有三个"相线"接口，每个接口提供一个交流电压。最为重要的是这三个电压并不相互同步，每个电压从上一个移动三分之一的周期。因此，这样的电压与时间的关系看起来就像图 4-10。

This has some very happy consequences. Firstly, the three phases sum to zero which means there is very little current in the common neutral or return conductor. This greatly simplifies distribution.

这样做有一些非常令人兴奋的结果。首先，三相电压的总和为零，这意味着公用的零线回路或返回导线中的电流很小，这大大简化了布线。

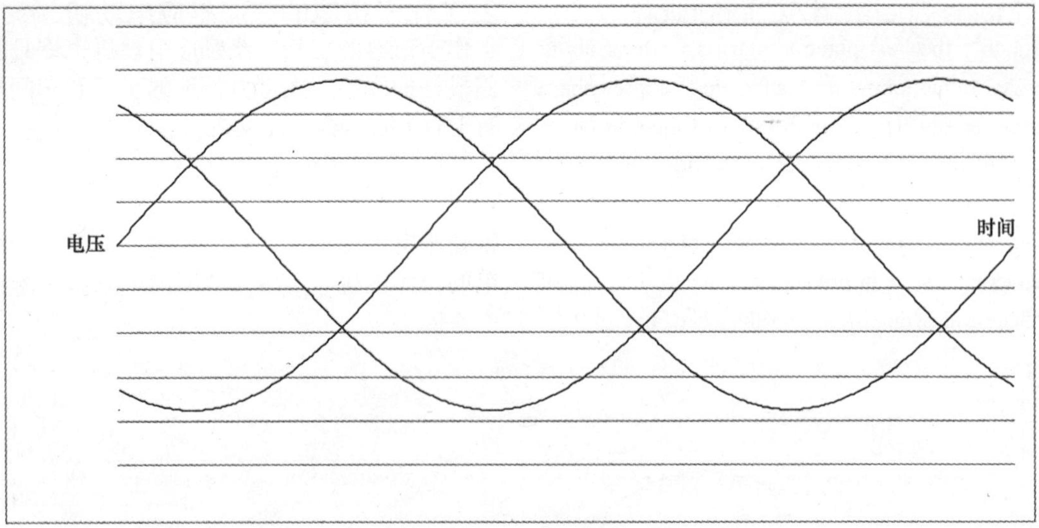

Figure 4–10 Three phase AC

图 4–10 三相交流电

Secondly if you hook each of the three phases up to successive "Poles" (segments of the field windings) in an AC Induction motor, you get the rotating magnetic field you need and the motor will run with good efficiency with no controller whatever: albeit with no speed control to speak of. There is nothing in the entire discipline of engineering that is more elegant, unless perhaps it be the stone arch (stone is good in compression, lousy in tension or bending. A stone arch bridges a wide gap using just stone in compression. Who says there is no poetry in science and technology?).

其次，如果您将三相中的每相连接到交流感应电动机的连续的"两极"（励磁绕组段），您将获得您想要的旋转磁场并且电动机将在没有控制器的情况下高效地运行，即没有与任何速度控制相连。在整个工程科学中，也许除了石拱桥之外没有比这更优雅的了（石材具有很好的抗压性能，但其拉伸或弯曲性能则很糟。石拱桥只用了石材的抗压性来跨过很大的跨距。谁说在科学和技术领域里没有诗？）。

You will recall from the section on AC induction motors that they are asynchronous – that is, the rotor rpm is always just a little lower than that of the rotating magnetic field. You might also recall that the difference is known as the slip (Figure 4-11).

您会记得在交流感应电动机部分我们称它们是异步的——也就是说，转子的转速始终比旋转磁场的速度低一点点。您可能还记得这种差别被称为转差率（图 4-11）。

As the load on the motor increases, the speed of a well-designed AC Induction motor will initially decrease but not very much. A mains-connected induction motor in its design operating range is an

随着电动机负荷的增加，一个设计良好的交流感应电动机的转速将开始下降，但不是很多。一个工作于市电的感应电动机在它的设计工作范围内几乎是一个恒速器件。随着负

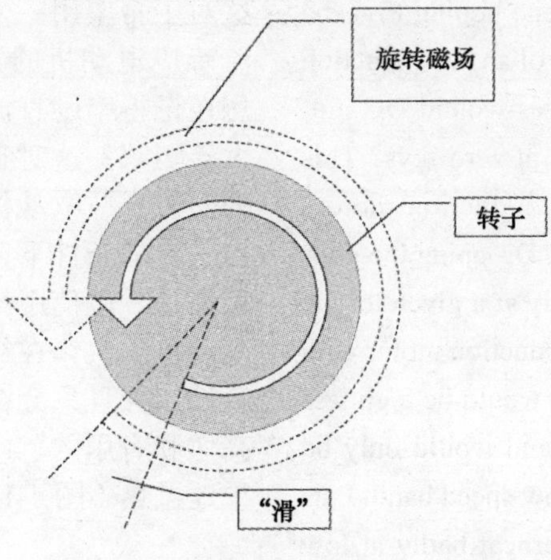

Figure 4–11 “Slip”, the difference between the speed of rotation of the field and of the rotor

图 4–11 “滑”——磁场旋转速度与转子转速之间的差异

almost constant speed device. As the load increases the speed drops very slightly, increasing the slip, and the motor just sucks more amps. Up to a point. As the load continues to rise the slip becomes so great that the torque produced by the motor peaks and starts to drop again. Unless the load drops off very rapidly as the speed drops, the motor stalls. The speed torque curve looks like Figure 4-12.

载的增加，转速只有很轻微的下降，从而增加了转差率，电动机则要吸入更多的电流。当到了一定的极限，随着负荷的继续攀升，转差率会变得如此之大，以至于电动机的转矩达到其峰值后再次开始下降。除非随着转速的下降负载也非常迅速地下降，否则电动机将停止转动。转速转矩曲线看起来像图 4-12。

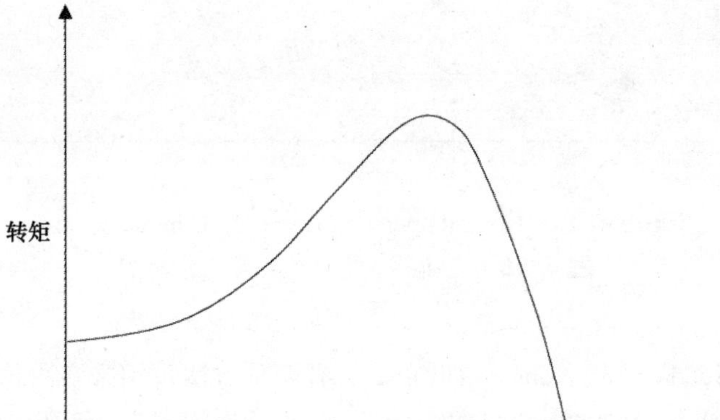

Figure 4–12 Torque/Speed Curve for AC Induction Motor at Constant Frequency

图 4–12 在固定频率下交流感应电动机的转矩 – 速度曲线

This is very bad news for anyone hoping to use a simple variable voltage to control an AC induction motor. Remember that the Series-wound DC motor produces maximum torque at zero revs? This is not the case with most AC induction motors operating at constant frequency. Dropping the voltage will increase the slip slightly at a given torque output, but a car using an AC Induction motor with a constant frequency controller would be a gutless wonder away from the lights and would only be efficient and effective in a narrow speed band. Furthermore the motor would overheat badly at low speeds (Figure 4-13).

这对于希望用一个简单的可变电压来控制交流感应电动机的人来说是非常不好的消息。您还记得串励直流电动机在零转速时产生最大转矩吗？这对于大多数工作在恒频情况下的交流感应电动机而言并非如此。在转矩输出一定的条件下，电压的减少将使转差率稍稍增加。但使用具有恒频控制器的交流感应电动机的汽车在红绿灯起步时将变得非常的笨拙，并且只会在一个狭窄的速度范围内是高效和有用的。此外，电动机在低速时将严重地过热（图 4-13）。

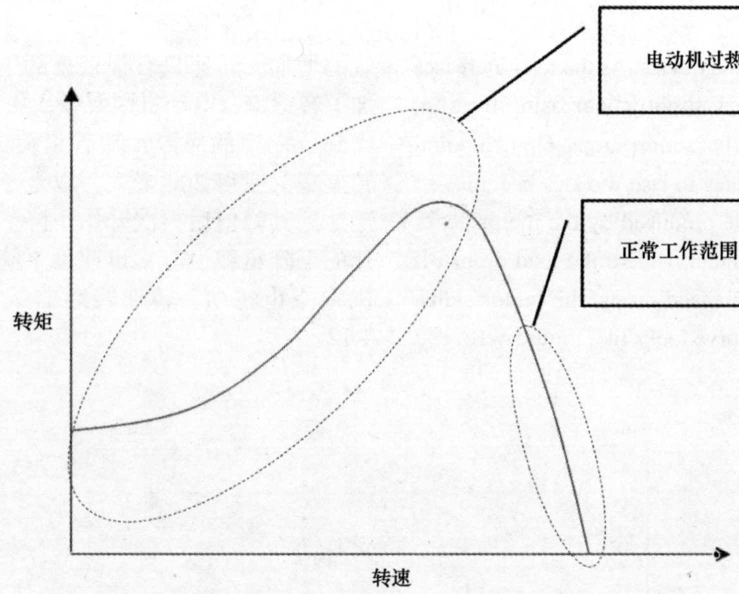

Figure 4–13 Normal operating range of AC induction motor

图 4–13 交流感应电动机正常工作范围

There are two ways to address this problem. The first is a workaround which is common in industry but which to my knowledge is never used in an EV. The second is the norm for controllers used in EVs.

有两种方法可用来解决这个问题：第一种是一个变通的方法，这在工业中是相当普遍的，但据我所知，从来没有在电动汽车中使用过；第二种是电动汽车中控制器的标准方法。

AC Induction – compromise

交流感应控制器 - 折中方案

It is possible to design an AC induction motor so

要设计出一个交流感应电动机，使其在转速

that it produces maximum torque at zero rpm, which would permit voltage control of the motor speed. Unfortunately, this is achieved by adding resistance to the stator windings! This is highly undesirable, having, as it does, at least three negative effects. It;

为零产生最大的转矩是可能的，这将允许用电压来控制电动机的转速。不幸的是，这是通过在定子绕组中加入电阻来实现的！这是极不可取的，因为它至少有三个负面效应。它将

- reduces the efficiency of the motor/controller combination, thus reducing range in an EV.
- creates additional heat which must be dissipated.
- reduces torque at higher rpm, thus reducing acceleration.

- 降低电动机 / 控制器组合的效率，从而减少了电动汽车的里程范围
- 产生额外的热量，这些热量必须被散发掉
- 降低高转速时的转矩，从而降低了加速性能

This is however the approach used in many industrial environments. The torque curve shown in Figure 4-14 is typical of a particular class of three phase industrial motors (driven from the mains without a controller) in applications that need a high starting torque.

但这是在许多工业领域中使用的方法。图 4-14 中所示的转矩曲线是实际使用中一个典型的需要大起动转矩的三相工业电动机（在没有控制器的情况下由市电驱动）的曲线。

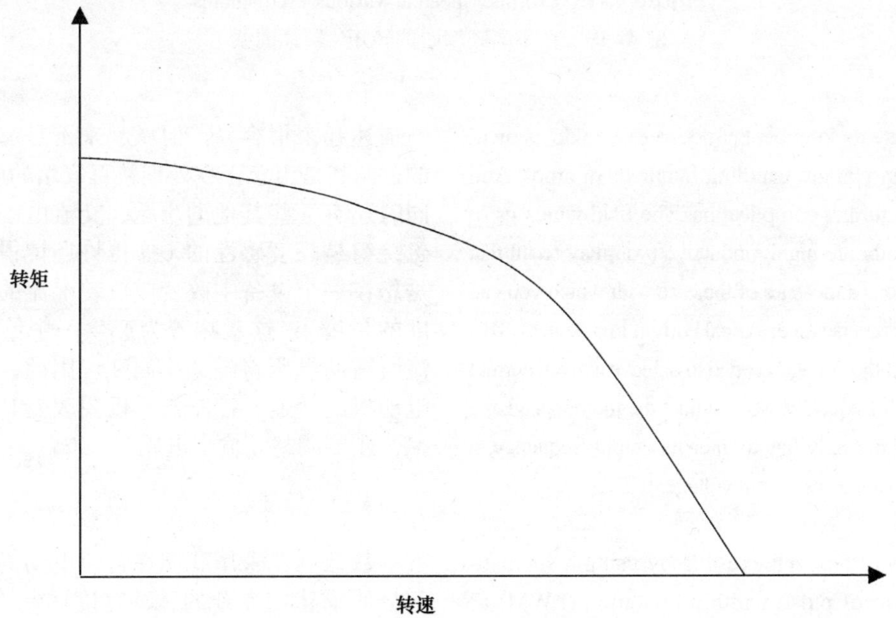

Figure 4–14 AC Induction Motor with resistive windings

图 4–14 阻性绕组交流感应电动机

Variable frequency AC

The most efficient way to control an AC induction motor is to use a variable frequency drive. Look at the constant frequency torque/speed curve depicted in Figure 4-12. Now imagine that curve replicated at a number of lower frequencies as in Figure 4-15.

变频交流

控制交流感应电动机的最有效的方式是使用变频驱动器。仔细观察图 4-12 所描绘的恒定频率的转矩－转速曲线，现在设想该曲线像图 4-15 所示的那样做一系列较低频率的复制。

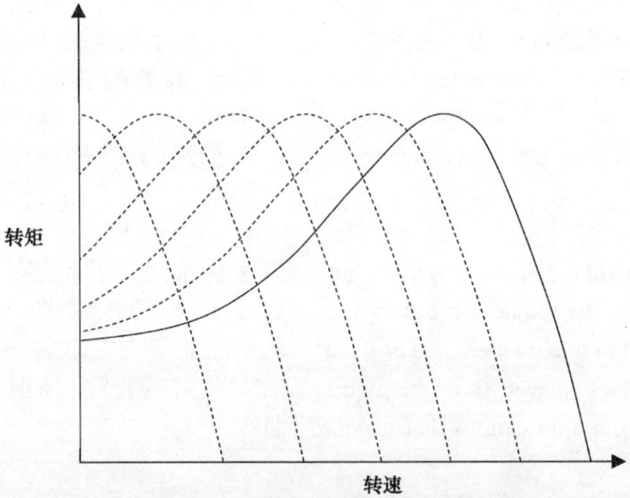

Figure 4–15 Torque/Speed at Various Frequencies

图 4–15 在不同频率时的转矩 - 转速曲线

This is easy to describe, but not so easy to do, particularly when you are handling hundreds of amps. And there is a further complication. The field windings of an AC motor are highly inductive (you may recall that inductance is a measure of the ease with which you can change or reverse an electrical current in a device). This means that the voltage needed to achieve a given current varies with frequency. So to adjust the motor speed, the controller not only has to alter its output frequency, it also has to adjust its output voltage.

这描述起来很容易，但做起来不是那么容易的，尤其是当您正在处理数百安培的电流时。同时还有一些其他的难题。交流电动机的励磁绕组是高度感性的（您也许还记得，电感是您在一个设备中改变或反转电流的容易程度的量度），这意味着为产生一个给定的电流所需的电压将随频率而变。因此，为调节电动机的转速，控制器不仅要改变其输出频率，还要调整其输出电压。

Most controllers achieve this by using a sophisticated form of pulse width modulation (PWM) as described in the section on DC motor controllers (see for example Figure 4-3 and Figure 4-4). To understand how this works, we'll conduct a mental experiment.

大多数控制器采用我们在直流电动机控制器部分所描述的复杂的脉冲宽度调制（PWM）的形式实现来这点（例如，参见图 4-3 和图 4-4）。为了理解这是如何工作的，让我们在大脑中做一个实验。

Imagine for a moment that you were driving an EV equipped with an ordinary DC motor and controller of the kind we described earlier down a straight but deserted road. Imagine that you pushed the throttle pedal slowly down to near maximum and then let it come up again. You might get an output from the controller that looked something like Figure 4-16.

想象一下，您正在驾驶一辆电动汽车沿着一条笔直的但清冷的道路上行走，车上配有前面所述的那种普通的直流电动机和控制器。试想一下，您慢慢往下踩加速踏板直至接近最大，然后让它同样缓慢地返回。您也许会得到一个看起来像图 4-16 那样的控制器的输出。

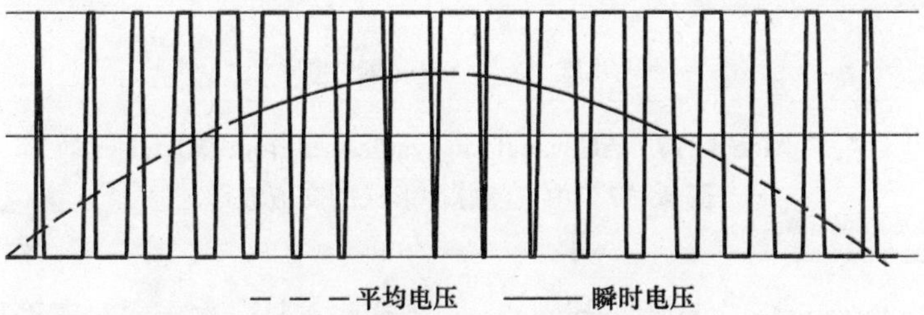

Figure 4–16 DC Controller response to opening then closing throttle

图 4–16 直流控制器对节气门开关的响应

At the start and end of your experiment, the throttle would be nearly closed and the pulses from the controller would be short. As the throttle opened, the pulses would get wider and wider until near full throttle they would almost merge. The dotted line in Figure 4-16 is the average voltage that the motor sees. Clearly, the faster you cycled the throttle the shorter and steeper the curve of resultant voltage would be.

在实验开始和结束时，节气门几乎是关闭的。因此，从控制器中发出的脉冲将是很短的。随着节气门的开启，脉冲将变得越来越宽，直到节气门全开时，脉冲的间隔几乎为零。图 4-16 所示的虚线就是电动机所得到的平均电压。显然，节气门开关的循环越快，由此产生的电压曲线将越短且越陡峭。

If this “resultant voltage” curve looks uncannily like half an AC cycle, that is because it is half an AC cycle. An AC Controller uses exactly this strategy to mimic an AC waveform (Figure 4-17).

这个“由此产生的电压”曲线看起来与交流周期的一半惊人地相像，因为它是一个交流周期的一半。一个交流控制器使用的正是这一策略来模仿一个交流波形（图 4-17）。

By varying the timing and duration of the pulses, the AC controller can produce an output waveform that is equivalent to any desired frequency and voltage.

通过改变脉冲产生的时间和持续的时间，交流控制器可产生任何所需的频率和电压输出波形。

Or rather, any three waveforms. We have been considering just a single pole in a three pole machine. A real controller has to do everything we have just

或者说任何三个波形。我们一直在考虑的只是三相发动机中的一个相。一个真正的控制器必须能够做我们刚才所描述的一切，并且

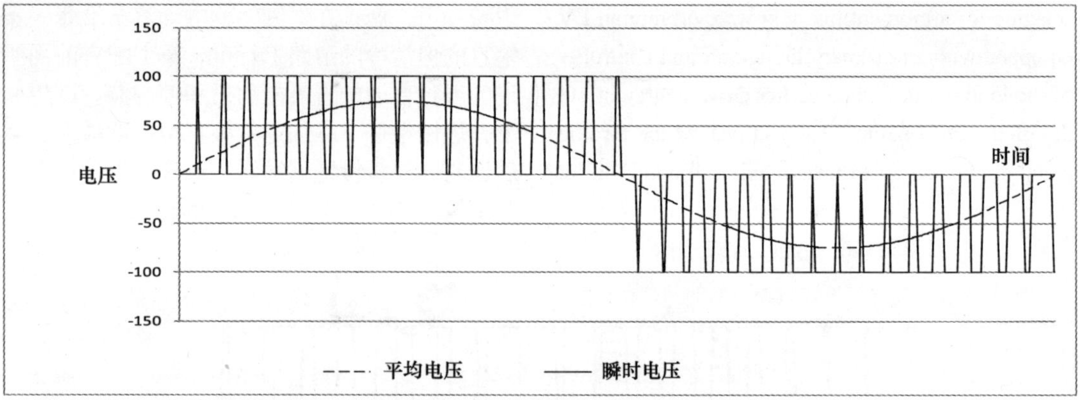

Figure 4–17 AC waveform synthesised from DC pulses

图 4–17 由直流脉冲形成的交流波形

described, but do it three times, whilst keeping the phase difference between the resulting waveforms just right (Figure 4-18).

将这些重复三次，同时正确地保持所产生的波形之间的相位差（图 4-18）。

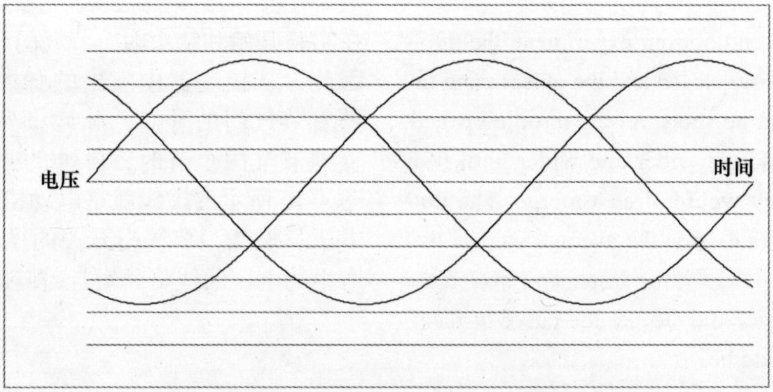

Figure 4–18 Resultant Three Phase Output

图 4–18 由此产生的三相电压输出

This brings us back to the three phase mains power where we started: but unlike the mains, the AC motor controller can adjust the frequency and voltage of all three phases at will.

这让我们回到开始时提到的三相市电。但与市电不同，交流电动机控制器可以随意调整这三相电的频率和电压。

So how does it do it? Broadly speaking the AC controller, like the DC controller, has two core modules: low power electronics that create a complex pattern of low energy pulses used to control hefty (but com-

那么它是怎样做到这一点的呢？从广义上讲，正如直流控制器，交流控制器也具有两个核心模块：产生复杂的低能量脉冲的低功耗电子器件，以便用于控制巨大（但相对简

paratively simple) electronic switches (Figure 4-19). A basic DC controller needs just one wire between these two modules, but the AC controller needs six; and there are three wires (one for each phase) running between the power electronics and the motor.

单）的电子开关（图 4-19）。一个基本的直流控制器在这两个模块之间只需要 1 根连线，但交流控制器需要 6 根,其中有 3 根导线（每相 1 根）用于功率电子器件与电动机之间的连接。

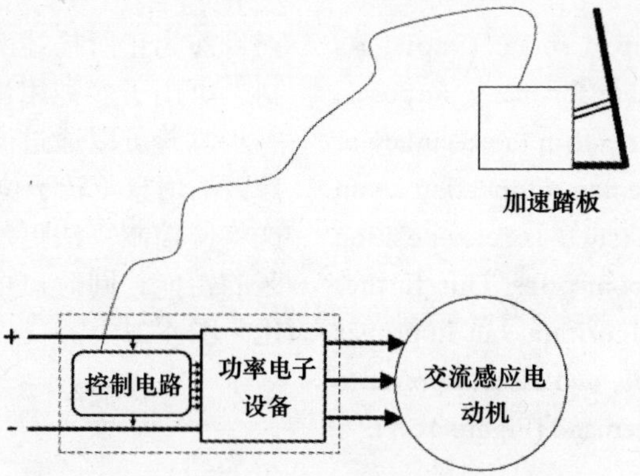

Figure 4–19 Block Diagram of an AC Controller

图 4–19 一个交流控制器框图

Similarly, the power electronics module of a DC controller need contain only one power transistor but the AC Controller needs six: two per phase. One half of each pair handles the positive half of the AC cycle, and the other one handles the negative half (Figure 4-20). As before there are freewheeling diodes (not shown).

同样，一个直流控制器的功率电子模块只需要一个功率晶体管，但交流控制器需要 6 个：每相 2 个。其中每对中的一半用来处理交流周期的正半周期，而另外一半用来处理负半周期（图 4-20）。像以前一样有飞轮二极管（未显示）。

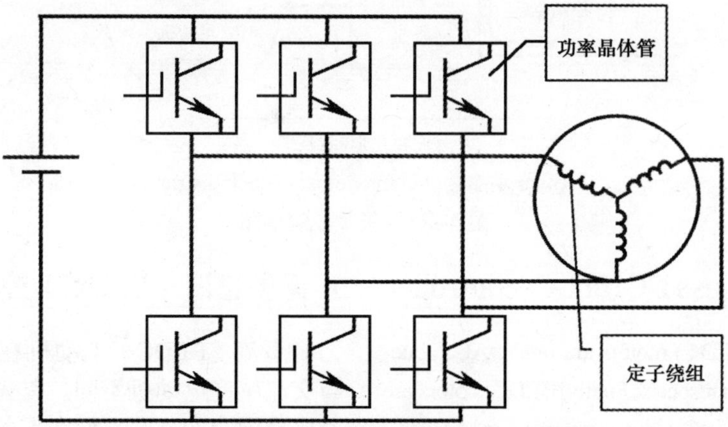

Figure 4–20 AC Induction Controller Power Module

图 4–20 交流感应电动机控制器功率模块

The control circuit is the clever bit. Whilst it would be possible to build a control circuit of this kind from discrete electronic components there are off-the-shelf integrated circuits available commercially which greatly simplify this task.

控制电路是十分巧妙的。虽然有可能从分立电子元件中组装出这样一种控制电路，但市面上有现成的商业化集成电路可供使用，从而大大简化了这一过程。

Vector Control

The arrangements described so far (known as Scalar Control) are adequate for many purposes. However, further improvements in the accuracy of control can be made by feeding information about various motor parameters (such as rotor position or field currents) to the controller. This further complicates the control algorithm, but improves the low r.p.m. performance, and also response to sudden changes in power demand (Figure 4-21).

矢量控制

到目前为止所描述的各种方案（称为标量控制）可用于多种用途。然而，控制精度的进一步改善可以通过向控制器提供各种电动机参数的信息（转子位置或磁场电流）来实现。这将使控制算法更加复杂，但提高了低转速区的性能，同时也可应对功率需求的突然变化（图 4-21）。

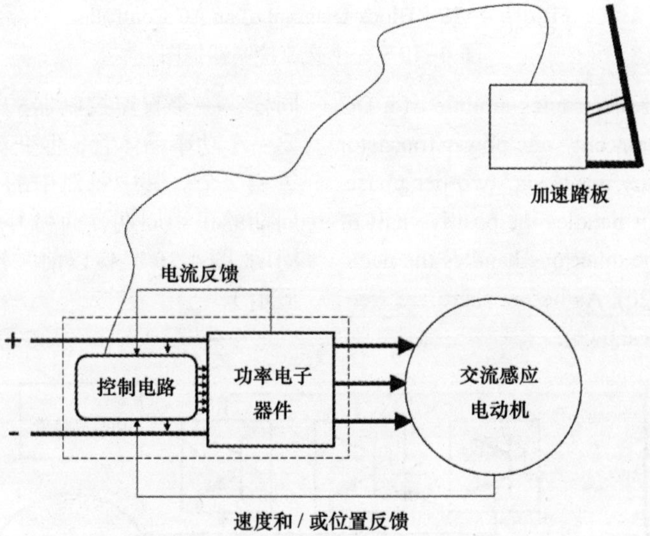

Figure 4–21 Vector Control Block diagram

图 4–21 矢量控制框图

➤ The Brushless DC (BLDC) controller

Brushless DC (BLDC) motors are unlike AC Induction motors in two respects. Firstly, BLDC motors are synchronous; that is they run with zero slip. A BLDC motor is either running at synchronous speed or it is stalled. There is no half way house. Secondly BLDC

➤ 无刷直流（BLDC）控制器

无刷直流（BLDC）电动机在以下两个方面与交流感应电动机不同。首先，无刷直流电动机是同步的，即它们在零差率下运行。无刷直流电动机要么在同步中运行要么停止（死机），没有中间过程。其次，无刷直流电

motors do not need a sine wave power supply. Power to the motor poles needs merely to be switched on and off in the correct sequence.

动机不需要正弦波电源。电动机各极间的供电只需按正确的顺序接通和关闭。

The best way to understand controllers for BLDC motors is to start by thinking about the ordinary (brushed) DC Permanent Magnet motor. You can think of the commutator in a brushed motor as being a position-sensitive switch. The commutator switches the supply current to the rotor windings in sequence so that they produce maximum torque as they interact with the field set up by the permanent magnets on the stator.

了解无刷直流电动机控制器的最佳方式是从普通（有刷）直流永磁电动机开始。您可将有刷电动机的换向器想象成一个对位置敏感的开关。换向器顺次接通转子绕组的供电电流，使得当它们与定子上的永久磁铁产生的磁场进行相互作用时能产生最大的转矩。

The BLDC motor works in just the same way but rotor and stator are the other way around, so that the controller switches the supply current to the stator windings in sequence so that they produce maximum torque as they interact with the field set up by the permanent magnets on the rotor. It would be perfectly possible in theory to use a cam-operated switch on the shaft of a BLDC motor to switch power between the stator windings (Figure 4-22).

无刷直流电动机正是采用同样的方法，但转子和定子的位子对调了一下，以便控制器顺次接通定子绕组的供电电流，使得当它们与转子上的永久磁铁产生的磁场进行相互作用时能产生最大的转矩。在理论上完全有可能使用一个无刷直流电动机轴上的凸轮操作开关切换定子绕组之间的电流（图 4-22）。

The theoretical BLDC motor pictured in Figure 4-22 could be made to work: but many of the advantages of reliability would have been lost: we would merely have substituted one mechanical device (the brushes) with another (the shaft-mounted switch).

图 4-22 所示的理论无刷直流电动机可以工作起来，但它将失去许多可靠性上的优势。我们只是用一种机械设备（轴上开关）替代了另一种机械设备（电刷）。

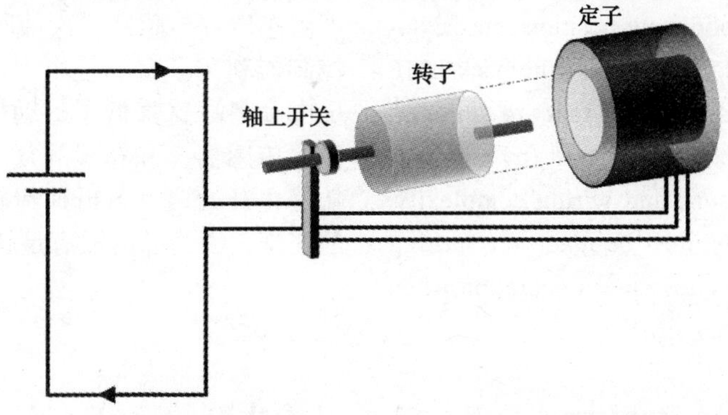

Figure 4–22 Theoretical BLDC mechanical controller

图 4–22 理论无刷直流电动机机械控制器

Real BLDC controllers use all electronic solid state components with no moving parts. The classic layout is to use a solid-state position sensor on the motor shaft to control a power electronics module of virtually the same layout as the one used by AC Induction Motor Controllers discussed earlier (Figure 4-23).

真正的无刷直流电动机控制器使用没有运动部件的全电子固态元件。经典的布局是使用电动机轴上的固态位置传感器去控制功率电子模块，其布局与前面讨论过的用于交流感应电动机的控制器几乎相同（图 4-23）。

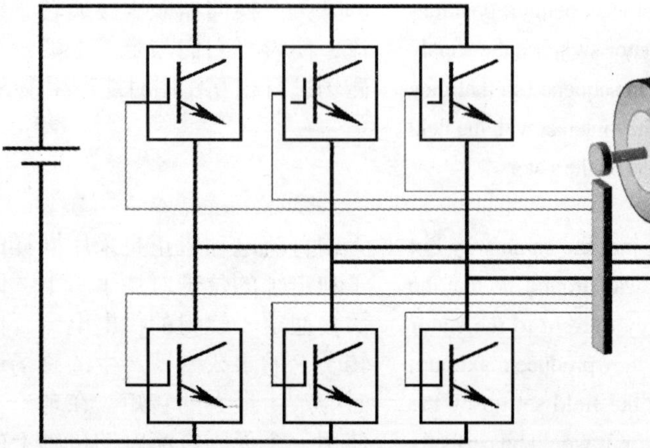

Figure 4–23 BLDC controller block diagram

图 4–23 无刷直流电动机控制器框图

Once this switching arrangement is in place, speed/torque control of a BLDC motor becomes simply a matter of using pulse width modulation of the DC in just the same way as for the brushed DC motor.

一旦这个开关安装到位，无刷直流电动机的速度 / 转矩的控制就简单地变成直流有刷电动机采用的直流脉冲宽度调制的问题。

Sensorless Control

There is a variant of the BLDC controller that even dispenses with the solid state position sensor. So-called “sensorless” controllers use the back EMF generated in the field windings that are not energised. This reduces both motor cost (by eliminating the position sensor), and wiring complexity. Special arrangements must be made for starting from rest and for very low speed operation when there is insufficient back EMF.

无传感器控制

无刷直流电动机控制器的一个变种甚至省去了固态位置传感器。这种所谓的“无传感器”控制器利用了磁场绕组中产生的未被激发的反电动势。这降低了电动机的成本（省去了位置传感器）和布线的复杂性。这种控制器从静止开始启动及低速运转时必须作出特别的安排，因为那时没有足够的反电动势。

➢ Regenerative Braking

➢ 再生制动

In most IC-engined cars when you take your foot

在大多数以内燃机为发动机的汽车中，当您

off the throttle on the move, the engine operates as a brake (this is not true of all cars – some Rovers and early Saabs among others were fitted with a freewheel to conserve fuel: when you took your foot off the throttle the engine rpm dropped to idle and the car just coasted).

的脚离开加速踏板时，发动机将起到制动的作用（并非所有的车都如此，其中包括一些路虎和早期萨博都装有飞轮，以节省燃料。当您的脚离开加速踏板时，发动机的转速下降到怠速，汽车则向前滑行）。

The simplest electrical drivetrains do not exhibit “engine braking” . When you take your foot off the throttle, the vehicle just coasts and must be slowed using conventional brakes. However with most types of motor it is possible to replicate IC engine braking behaviour. When it is done correctly, this form of braking recovers some electric power – this reduces the demands on the conventional braking system and also extends range slightly.

最简单的电气传动系统并没有表现出“发动机制动”效应。当您的脚离开加速踏板时，汽车只是向前滑行，并且必须使用传统的制动装置来减速。然而，大多数类型的电动机都可以复制内燃机发动机的制动行为。如果操作得当的话，这种制动形式可回收部分的电能——这降低了对传统制动系统的损耗，也略为扩大了行程范围。

The technique relies on the fact that an electric motor is, in most cases, electrically identical to a generator: indeed an electric motor that is being turned faster than its no-load speed IS usually a generator. If current is drawn from a motor in this state, the effect will be to create a braking torque as the energy stored in the rotating motor and load is converted into electrical power.

该技术依赖于一个事实，即在大多数情况下，一台电动机在电气上等同于一台发电机。在实际转速高于其空载转速时，一台电动机通常的确是一台发电机。如果在这种状态下从电动机中提取电流，当储存在旋转电动机中的能量被转换成电能的时候，其效果将是创建一个制动力矩。

The simplest example of this effect is short-circuiting the rotor windings in a rotating DC motor. This generates a high current in the rotor in the opposite direction to the normal motor current. This in turn creates a braking torque. The braking energy is dissipated as heat. This crude approach is effective, but the preferred technique in EV drivetrains is to use the power generated by braking to recharge the battery rather than to throw it away as heat. This recharging approach is referred to as “regenerative braking” . Controllers that allow for regenerative braking may also allow adjustment of the amount of regeneration depending upon throttle position and/or the amount of conventional braking going on.

这种效果的一个最简单的例子是将一个旋转的直流电动机的转子绕组短路。这会在转子中产生一个与正常电动机电流方向相反的大电流。这反过来又提供了一个制动力矩。制动能量以热量的形式消耗掉。这种原始的方法是有效的，但在电动汽车动力传动系统中，首选的方法是利用由制动产生的电能为电池充电，而不是当做热量“扔了”。这种充电方法被称为“再生制动”，允许再生制动系统的控制器也可以根据节气门的位置和/或常规制动量的大小来调整再生量。

Regenerative braking is not a magic bullet. Experience suggests that range improvement with "regen" may be of the order of 10% and there is even anecdotal evidence that regeneration can trigger a change in driving style which actually reduces efficiency. In some cases, a 10% increase in battery capacity may be a cheaper and simpler alternative.

再生制动不是灵丹妙药。经验表明，"再生"导致的行程范围可增加约 10%。甚至有未经证实的证据表明，再生可能引发驾驶风格的改变，这实际上降低了效率。在某些情况下，让电池的容量增加 10% 可能是一个更便宜、更简单的方法。

There are several issues associated with regenerative braking:

与再生制动相关的几个问题：

- 1, 2 and 4 quadrant operation
- Overcharging
- Battery C rating

- 第 1、2 和 4 象限运行
- 过充电
- 电池的 C 值

1, 2 and 4 quadrant operation

第 1、2 和 4 象限运行

An ideal motor/controller combination can operate as a motor or as a generator, running in either direction. This is referred to as four-quadrant operation (Figure 4-24).

一个理想的电动机 / 控制器组合运行在不同的方向时可作为电动机或发电机使用。这被称为四象限操作（图 4-24）。

	电动机	发电机
正转	Q1	Q3
反转	Q2	Q4

Figure 4–24 The four quadrants of operation of a motor/generator

图 4–24 一个电动机 / 发电机工作的 4 个象限

Some motor/controller combinations cannot manage full four-quadrant operation: they might allow just motoring in a forward direction (single quadrant) or two-quadrant (forward and reverse but no generator action).

有些电动机 / 控制器组合不能管理完整的四象限运行，它们可能只允许在前进方向（单象限）或两个象限（正向和反向，但没有发电机行为）上运行。

The simplest series wound DC motors are inherently single-quadrant devices: typically they are either incapable of regeneration, or implement it poorly. In some cases they cannot be reversed either. To reverse a DC motor, either the magnetic field in the motor

最简单的串励直流电动机本质上是单象限设备，它们通常是不能被再生的，或再生的效果不佳。在某些情况下，它们也不能被反转。为反转直流电动机，电动机的磁场或者转子（电枢）电流之一必须被反转，但不能同时

must be reversed or the current in the rotor (armature) must be reversed – but not both.

被反转。

In a series wound DC motor, the field windings are (by definition) in series with the armature so reversing the current in one reverses the current in the other. So simply reversing the polarity of the supply to such a motor makes no difference to the direction of rotation. In practice, such motors often have separately-accessible contacts for the field windings. This allows the use of a reversing contactor.

在一个串励直流电动机中，根据定义励磁绕组与电枢绕组串联，因此，反转一个绕组中的电流将同时反转另一个绕组中的电流，所以只反转这种电动机的电源极性并不改变其转动方向。在实践中，此类电动机通常有独立的磁场绕组接头，这就允许使用反向连接。

Series wound DC motors have another issue with regen. When there is no current in the motor there is no magnetic field (or very little – maybe just a weak residual field left over from the last time there was a current in the motor); no magnetic field means no voltage is generated in the rotor windings, so no current flows, so there is no braking effect. There are also potential issues with the positioning of brushes to avoid excessive sparking.

串励直流电动机的再生存在着另一个问题。当电动机中没有电流时就没有磁场（或者磁场很小，也许只是在电动机有电流通过时产生的微弱的残余磁场），没有磁场意味着在转子绕组中就没有电压产生，没有电流流过，所以也没有制动再生效应。串励直流电动机的再生还存在着为避免过大的火花而导致的电刷定位的潜在问题。

Overcharging

Normally an EV battery should have no trouble storing the energy created by regenerative braking. After all, the energy to accelerate the car came from the battery in the first place. However, there could in theory be a problem if a battery that was already fully charged was asked to absorb further energy from regeneration. This could (again hypothetically) be an issue if – say – a driver used regeneration in a long descent just after setting off. It could also be an issue with hybrids (HEVs) if such a long descent occurred just after recharge from the IC engine had completed. Note however that 30 seconds of braking at 100 Amps would represent less than 1% of the capacity of a 100 Amp-hour battery.

过充电

在通常情况下，电动汽车的电池用于存储再生制动产生的电能应该没有问题。毕竟，加速汽车的能量首先来自于电池。但如果电池在完全充满电后要进一步吸收来自再生的电能，这在理论上有可能是一个问题。又如，假设一个驾驶人在刚起步时就在一个很长的下坡中使用再生，这就可能是一个问题。在混合动力汽车中，如果刚从内燃机充电后就有一个这么长的下坡，它也可能是个问题。但是请注意，以 100A•h 的电流制动 30s 产生的能量小于 100A•h 的电池容量的 1%。

Battery C rating

In the section on batteries we discuss battery C rat-

电池的 C 值

在电池的部分我们将讨论电池的 C 值，它

ing: the ratio of maximum allowable battery current to battery amp-hour capacity. In that context we are concerned with C rating on discharge – how fast you can extract power from the battery to accelerate the vehicle. Batteries (particularly Lithium ion batteries) may also have a maximum C rate for charge. The maximum C rating for charging may be lower than the maximum discharge C rating: in other words you cannot safely push power back into the battery as quickly as you can pull it out. This means that the maximum regen current (and thus the maximum regen braking torque) may be limited by the battery.

等于电池允许的最大电流与电池安培小时容量的比。从这个意义上说，我们在放电时会关注电池的 C 值，即您能用多快的速度从电池中提取动力来加速车辆。电池（尤其是锂离子电池）在充电时也可能有一个最大 C 值。充电时最大的 C 值可能比放电时最大的 C 值要低。换句话说，您不能以从电池中提取能量一样快的速度将电能安全地放回到电池中。这意味着最大的再生电流（因而最大的再生制动力矩）也许会受到电池的限制。

➢ Some Typical Controllers

This section shows some typical controllers. These are not the only ones available, nor even necessarily the best. They do however give a flavour of the kind of thing that is available commercially at the time of writing. The specifications were current at the time of writing, but may be subject to change.

➢ 一些典型的控制器

本节展示了一些典型的控制器。这些并不是现有的全部控制器，甚至不一定是最好的。然而，它们却给出了在写作本书时可得到的一些商业化的产品。这些规格也是在写作时能得到的，但可能会有所变动。

柯蒂斯 1231C-86XX	串励或永磁直流控制器
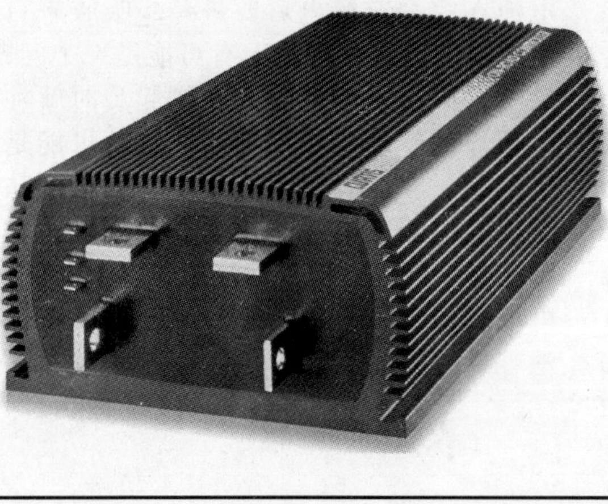	96~144V，500A（持续时间 2min），72kW
	柯蒂斯控制器很受欢迎。在写作本书时，它们都是现成的，可以从很多地方买到，价格也合理。它们的输出功率中等，所以更适合于具有变速器的轻便汽车，而不是，比方说，赛车。
	图片来源：科蒂斯仪器公司（http://curtisinstruments.com）

萨牌 SEM3	
他励直流控制器	
48~96V,400A（48V 控制器为 600A）,38kW（理论值），12kW（推荐值）	
萨牌控制器支持再生（在这张照片中，萨牌控制器安装在电动机顶部及风扇后面的椭圆形框内）	
图片来源：尼科斯·吉尔扣枚罗斯	

齐拉 Z2K	高性能直流控制器
	72~300V，2000A，600kW（理论值）
	电动赛车和其他类似车辆所选的控制器。请注意，在写作本书时，齐拉控制器的未来产品是不确定的。
	照片提供：库尔特·克莱顿（http://kurtschevys10ev.blogspot.com）

柯蒂斯 1238-75XX	
交流感应控制器	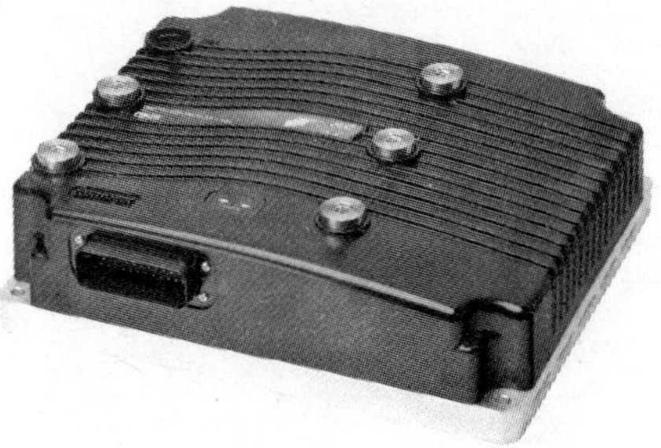
72~96V（名义值），500A（持续时间 2min），52kW（理论值）	
这个系列控制器有时与流行的 AS50 交流异步电动机在一起出售。	
照片提供：科蒂斯仪器公司（http://curtisinstruments.com）	

➢ In Conclusion

The controller is a major element in an electric drivetrain. A powerful controller may be more expensive than the motor it controls. Controller choice has a significant impact on the performance, efficiency and drivability of the finished vehicle. It is as important as the choice of battery or motor. Indeed, these three items (battery, motor, controller) should be chosen to complement each other. Using a Zilla Z2K with a low voltage, low C rating battery wastes the Zilla's prodigious capacity. Using a small Curtis controller with a 13″ DC motor is likewise pointless, as the performance potential of the big motor cannot be delivered by a controller limited to around 500 Amps.

So far we have looked at motors and controllers. In the next chapter we turn to the third main element in the EV drivetrain: the propulsion batteries.

➢ 小结

控制器是电力传动系统的主要元素。一个大功率的控制器可能比它控制的电动机还要昂贵。控制器的选择对成品车的性能、效率和可驾性有显著的影响，它与电池或电动机的选择一样重要。事实上，这三个部件（电池、电动机、控制器）的选择必须相互匹配。用一个齐拉 Z2K 控制器去与一个低电压、低 C 值的电池相配将浪费齐拉的巨大的潜力。用一个很小的柯蒂斯控制器去与一个 33cm 的直流电动机相配同样是毫无意义的，因为这个大电动机的性能潜力不能被一个限于约 500A 的控制器充分挖掘出来。

到目前为止我们已经讨论了电动机和控制器。在下一章中，我们将转向电动汽车动力传动系统的第三个主要部件：动力电池。

5 Batteries 电池

If the motor is the heart of an EV or HEV then the batteries are its Achilles heel. The limitations of batteries are the main reason for the tiny proportion of EVs on the road. You have to address at least the following issues when specifying the batteries for your car:

如果电动机是电动汽车或混合动力汽车的心脏，那么电池就是它的软肋。电池的局限性是路上电动汽车数量少的主要原因。当您想为您的汽车选择电池时，您必须至少考虑以下几个问题：

Energy Density

Batteries store a pitiful amount of energy per unit of volume (energy density) and per unit of mass (specific energy) compared with petrol or diesel fuel. One consequence of this limitation is that you need a lot of batteries to get further than the end of your road. The battery pack is usually the heaviest, bulkiest and most expensive element in a conversion. Inevitably the best batteries in terms of specific energy also tend to be the most expensive. More on this later.

能量密度

与汽油或柴油相比，每单位体积（能量密度）和单位质量（比能量）中电池存储的能量少得可怜。这种限制的一个后果是，您需要很多的电池，以便使您跑得足够远。电池组通常是在汽车改装过程中最重、体积最大且最昂贵的部件。在比能量方面的性能最好的电池往往也不可避免地是最昂贵的。我们以后将对此进行详细讨论。

Charge rate

Some batteries can only be recharged at a limited rate, so you cannot always get back on the road as rapidly as you might like after a trip which largely discharges the batteries.

充电速度

有些电池只能以有限的速度充电，所以当您在一个旅行中几乎放光了电池中的电能时，不能总是像您希望的那样很快地回到路上。

Power Density

Power density is the rate that you can draw energy (measured in kilowatts or horsepower) from the batteries per unit of volume. Specific power is the equivalent per unit of mass. Batteries have limits on the maximum discharge rate, i.e. a limit on the current (and thus power) that you should attempt to draw. This can limit acceleration: even if your motor and controller could handle more amps, your batteries may not be able to provide them. We touch on specific power later.

功率密度

功率密度是您可以从单位体积的电池中提取能量的速度（单位为 kW 或 hp）。比功率则是您可以从单位质量的电池中提取能量的速度。电池的最大放电速度有一定的限制，即对您能获得的电流（因而功率）的限制，这将限制加速性能。即使您的电动机和控制器可以处理更大的电流，电池也可能无法提供这样的电流。我们将在后面讨论比功率。

Depth of discharge

If you routinely run your batteries completely flat, you

放电深度

如果您经常将电池中的电全部放完，（对于

may (with some chemistries) shorten their life. Discharging down to 70% or 80% of maximum capacity is probably a good compromise with many types of cell.

Cell imbalance

A vehicle battery pack is made up of (typically) 24 – 150 individual cells. Particularly with some battery chemistries, these cells may get out of step with each other so that if you charge the pack as a whole, some cells may be overcharged and others undercharged.

Maintenance

Some types of battery need routine maintenance such as watering. This can be time consuming and messy.

Safety

Conventional fuels can cause fire and explosion, but a high voltage battery pack can kill you just as dead (albeit with a lot less drama). Some battery types catch fire when abused and even the humble lead-acid battery can explode if overcharging causes venting of hydrogen and there is a source of ignition in the vicinity.

Cycle life

Batteries have a limit on the number of times they can be charged and discharged. Beyond this limit either their performance will have degraded to unacceptable levels or they will be liable to sudden failure – or both. This means that you should factor in the cost of batteries when calculating the cost of electric motoring. If your batteries are good for (say) 400 cycles, cost -2000, take you 50 miles on a charge and you cover 10,000 miles a year, your batteries can be expected to last 2 years and therefore cost you £1000 a year or 10 pence per mile just for the batteries themselves.

Temperature

Some batteries operate poorly or have a shorter life if they are used outside their optimum operating temperature range. Discharged lead-acid batteries

某些化学物质的电池而言）您可能会缩短其寿命。放电到最大容量的 70% 或 80%，对多种类型的电池而言可能是一个很好的折中。

电池失衡

一个（典型的）汽车电池组由 24~150 个电池组成。特别是对某些化学物质的电池组，这些电池可能不会相互同步。因此，如果您将电池组作为一个整体来充电，某些电池可能被过充电，而另一些电池则可能会欠充电。

保养

某些类型的电池需要日常维护，如同给植物浇水一样。这可能是耗时的，且很麻烦。

安全

传统燃料可引起火灾和爆炸，但高电压电池组可以很快让人死亡（虽然少了很多戏剧性）。某些种类的电池被滥用时会着火。甚至对于不起眼的铅酸电池而言，如果过充电时导致氢气释放，并在附近有一个点火源的话，它也会爆炸。

循环寿命

电池有一个充放电次数上的限制。超出此极限，它们的性能会被退化到不可接受的程度，或者有可能会突然失效，或者两者兼而有之。这意味着，您在计算电动汽车的费用时应该考虑电池的成本因素。例如：如果您的电池为 2 万元，寿命是 400 个周期，每充一次电能行使 80km，您每年行驶 16000km，那么，您的电池预计可用 2 年。因此您每年仅在电池上的花费为 1 万元，或 0.625 元 /km。

温度

如果电池在其最佳的工作温度范围以外使用，有些电池的性能会下降，有些电池的寿命会缩短。未被充电的铅酸电池将被冻结或

can freeze and split. The ZEBRA battery (of which more below) has a normal operating temperature over 270℃ (slightly above the maximum temperature of a domestic oven).

泄漏。斑马电池（后面会更详细的讨论）的最高工作温度为 270℃（略高于家用烤箱的最高温度）。

Voltage Sag

When a high current is being drawn from a battery, the voltage will almost always be reduced. This also reduces the power available (recalling that power in watts = volts × amps, so if voltage goes down, power will too).

电压下降

当电池的输出电流很大时，其输出电压几乎总会减少。这也降低了可用功率（请注意，功率 = 电压 × 电流，因此，如果电压下降，功率也将下降）。

Cost

An EV-sized pack of good quality batteries giving you (say) a 100 mile range might costs many thousands of ￡s.The other problem with batteries is that they tend not to warn you if you are mistreating them. If for example you consistently use 95% depth of discharge, or allow cell imbalance to continue undetected, the first symptoms may become visible only after you have done irreparable damage.

成本

一个质量好的电动汽车的电池组能给您提供大约 160km 的行程，但您可能要花数万元人民币。电池的另一个问题是，您滥用它们时，它们往往不提醒您。例如，如果您经常用 95% 的放电深度，或者允许电池持续失衡而未被发现，那么，只有在您已经做了不可挽回的损害时，电池初期的症状才会变得可见。

➢ Battery Principles

Most batteries use galvanic action to produce electricity. If you put two dissimilar conductors into a suitable liquid, a voltage is generated between them, and if the two conductors are connected, a current will flow. There is evidence that galvanic cells were in use in what is now Iraq a couple of millennia ago.

You can create a simple galvanic cell very easily. Take a steel pin (like a small nail, an unfolded paperclip or the core of an old pop rivet), plus a similar piece of copper (like the core of the kind of electrical cable used in wiring houses). Acquire a lemon. Push the two pins (one steel, one copper) into the lemon without allowing them to touch. You should be able to measure a voltage between them. The two pins are electrodes, and the juice in the lemon is the electrolyte (Figure 5-1).

➢ 电池的原理

大多数电池使用电化学作用来产生电力。如果你把两个相异的导体放到一个合适的液体中，在它们之间将产生一个电压。如果这两个导体被接通，将有电流产生。有证据表明，这种能产生电流的电池在数千年前就已出现在现在的伊拉克内。

您可以非常方便地创建一个简单的原电池。拿一枚钢针（如一个小钉子、一个展开的回形针或老式弹出铆钉的金属心），再加上一小块的铜（如室内布线用的电缆心），然后取一个柠檬。将这两根金属针（一钢一铜）插入到柠檬中而不让它们接触。您应该能够测出它们之间有电压。这两根金属针是电极，柠檬中的柠檬汁就是电解质（图 5-1）。

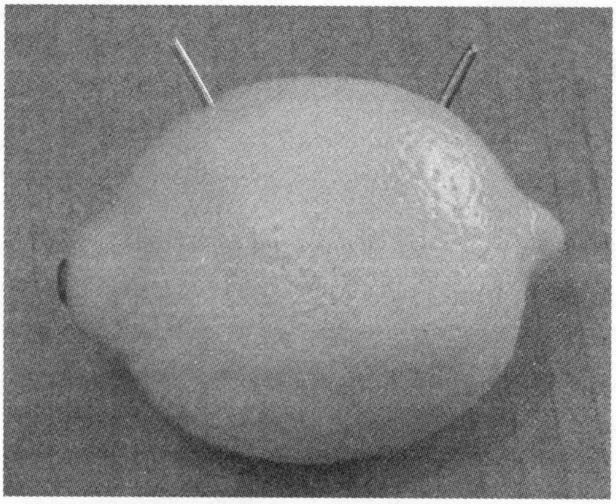

Figure5–1 “Lemon Battery”

图 5–1 一个“柠檬电池”

Just how much voltage you will see depends on the materials of which the electrodes are made. A combination of steel and copper will give you up to about 0.8 volt. In theory a lithium or sodium electrode combined with (say) a copper electrode would give you over 3 volts: at least it would do for the split second before it caught fire. Both lithium and sodium are highly reactive and not suitable for use in a battery in metallic form with an aqueous (water-based) electrolyte.

您会看到所产生电压的大小取决于电极的材料。钢和铜的组合会产生约 0.8V 的电压。从理论上说，锂或钠与（例如）铜电极相结合会产生超过 3V 的电压——至少在起火之前的几分之一秒内是这样的。锂和钠都是高活性的，并不适合于以纯金属的形式与水溶性（水性）电解质在电池中使用。

The maximum voltage of material combinations in a battery are governed by their electrode potential. Lithium has an electrode potential of -3.04 volts, copper +0.34, so in theory a lithium electrode and a copper electrode used together would give you a 3.38 volt battery (Figure 5-2). I should stress again that a lithium-copper battery is purely hypothetical.

电池材料组合产生的最大电压是由其电极电势所决定的。金属锂的电极电势为 –3.04V，铜为 +0.34V。因此从理论上讲，一个锂电极和铜电极一起使用会产生一个 3.38V 的电池（图 5-2）。我要再次强调，铜锂电池完全是虚构的。

Even with a less reactive material than lithium, there are still physical changes occurring in the electrodes of a galvanic cell as power is drawn from it. Sometimes this causes one of the electrodes to be eaten away.

甚至用比锂的活性差的物质，当电能从其中输出时，在原电池电极中仍有物理变化发生。有时，这会导致电极被蚕食。

A common example of this is the old-style zinc-carbon battery (also sometimes called a Leclanche cell - Figure

一个常见的例子是老式的碳锌电池（有时也称为勒克朗谢电池，见图 5-3），它在碱锰电

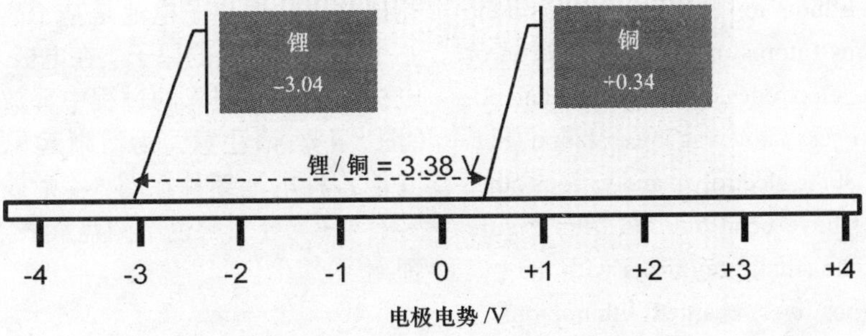

Figure 5–2 Example of Electrode potential

图 5–2 一个电极电势的例子

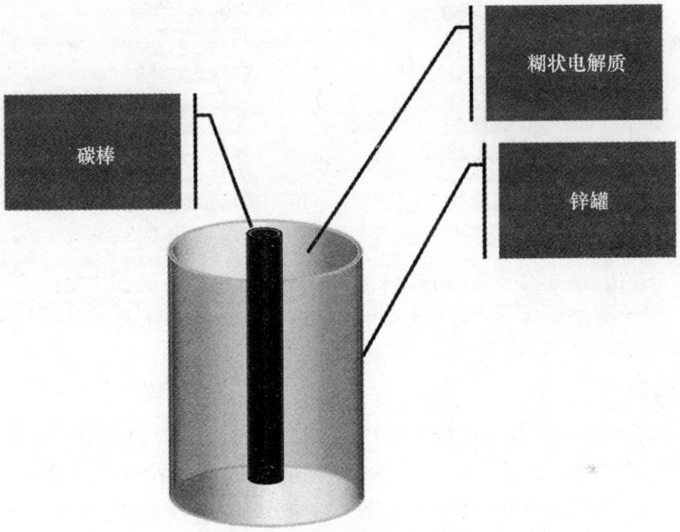

Figure 5–3 Simplified schematic of Zinc-Carbon (Leclanche) cell

图 5–3 碳锌电池（勒克朗谢电池）简化原理图

5-3) which was the normal household battery before the advent of mass-market manganese-alkali cells. Zinc-carbon cells consisted of a zinc shell or pot with a carbon cathode running up the middle surrounded by a manganese oxide paste. A paste electrolyte was sealed in to the can. As the battery was used, the zinc shell became thinner as the metal was eroded away. Such cells commonly leaked if they were left in equipment after discharge. Lithium sulphur cells are galvanic: the anode is lithium metal and the cathode a mixture of carbon and sulphur.

池大批量问世之前是常用的家用电池。碳锌电池由一个锌壳或锌罐组成，其内有糊状的氧化锰溶液，并在中央有一根碳阴极（正极）。糊状电解质被密封在罐内。随着电池的使用，由于金属被侵蚀掉，锌壳变薄。如果这些电池在放完电之后还留在设备中的话，它们通常会泄漏。锂硫电池也是电化学的，其阳极（负极）是锂金属，阴极（正极）是碳和硫的混合物。

By contrast, the lithium ion battery is based on the movement of ions (atoms missing an electron or two) between the electrodes, which release and absorb ions in a process known as intercalation (Figure 5-4). Note that the electrolyte and various other cell components have been omitted from Figure 5-4 for clarity. The small grey disks with the "+" signs represent (positively charged) lithium ions.

相比之下，锂离子电池是基于离子（失去了一个或两个电子的原子）在电极之间的运动，电极在被称为嵌入的过程中释放和吸收离子（图 5-4）。请注意，为清晰起见，电解质和其他各种电池部件在图 5-4 中被省略。图中带有"+"号的灰色小圆盘代表（带正电的）锂离子。

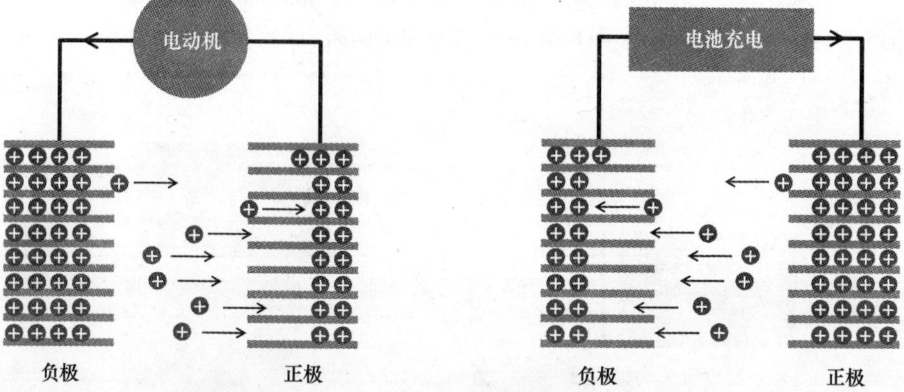

Figure 5–4 Lithium ion discharge (left) and charge (right)

图 5–4 锂离子电池的放电（左）和充电（右）

There is one other twist to the lithium ion saga. The electrolyte may be a liquid: or it may be a thin flat sheet of a suitable polymer. The latter are the so-called "lithium polymer" batteries. They still operate by intercalation of lithium ions, but the

在锂离子的传奇中还有另外一个插曲。电解液可能是液体，它也可能是一个合适的聚合物薄平板。后者就是所谓的"聚合物锂"电池。它们还是用锂离子的嵌入来工作的，但电解液的形式不同。图 5-5 显示了一个卡马聚合

Figure 5–5 Left: Lithium polymer. Right: Lithium ion prismatic Photos courtesy of Andrej Pecjak (left) and Jem Freeman (right)

图 5–5 左：锂聚合物电池，右：锂离子方形电池。照片由安德烈·皮科克（左）和杰姆·弗里曼（右）提供

electrolyte is in a different form. Figure 5-5 shows a Kokam lithium polymer cell (left) alongside a Thundersky prismatic lithium ion cell (right). Lithium polymer cells are often (but not always) thin flat pouch style cells.

➢ Terminology

The "batteries" discussed above should not, strictly speaking, be called "batteries". A battery is a collection of things – in this context, a collection of cells, just as in warfare, a battery refers to a collection of guns or missile launchers.

So an ordinary 12 volt car battery is very properly called a battery, because it consists of six cells, each of 2 volts (if you have ever topped up a car battery, you will know that you had six caps or ports where you checked the electrolyte level).

Ordinary mass-market 12 volt car batteries are commonly referred to as SLI (Starter, Lighting, Ignition) batteries. For reasons we will discuss later they are not generally suited for use as propulsion batteries in electric vehicles, but are instead optimised to deliver the high current (high power) demanded by starter motors; but only for short periods.

There is a degree of confusion around the terms anode and cathode. Anode is usually used to refer to the electrode which is the negative pole of the cell, and cathode to the electrode at the positive pole. This is, it must be said, somewhat counter-intuitive.

Cells are divided into two classes. Primary cells are use-once-and-throw-away (or recycle). Secondary cells can be recharged and used again. So the zinc-carbon cell is an example of a primary cell. The 12 volt automotive SLI battery is made up of secondary cells.

物锂电池（左）以及雷天的棱柱形锂离子电池（右）。聚合物锂电池往往是（但不总是）薄的扁平袋式的。

➢ 术语

上面讨论的“电池”严格来说不应该被称为“电池”。电池是指一些东西的集合，在本文中是电池单元的集合。就像在战争中，炮台（译注：battery一词在英文中也可被称为炮台）是指枪或导弹发射器的集合。

因此，一个普通的12V汽车电池可以非常恰当地被称为电池，因为它由6个单元组成，每个2V（如果您曾经为汽车电池加过水，您就会知道，您必须从6个盖子或端口去看电解质水面的高度）。

普通大众市场的12V汽车电池通常被称为SLI（起动、照明、点火）电池。由于我们将在后面讨论到的原因，它们一般不适合作为电动汽车的动力电池使用，而是被优化成能够提供起动电动机所需的大电流（高功率），但只能持续很短的时间。

阳极和阴极这两个术语则有一定程度的混乱。阳极通常用来指电池的负极，阴极指电池的正极。必须指出的是，这与直觉相反。

电池被分为两大类：原电池是使用一次就扔掉（或回收）；二次电池可被反复充电使用。因此，碳锌电池是原电池的一个例子。汽车的12V SLI电池是二次电池。

➢ Specific Energy and Specific Power

Specific Energy and Specific Power are important aspects of a battery. As noted above, the specific energy is a measure of the amount of energy (in Joules or in Watt-hours) that the battery is capable of storing per unit of mass (energy density is the volumetric equivalent – energy stored per unit of volume). This is directly linked to the range that can be expected from a certain mass or volume of batteries.

The specific power is a measure of the power that can be drawn from a battery (measured in Watts, or Joules per second) per unit of mass (volumetric equivalent – power density). This affects acceleration and hill climbing ability.

If energy was orange juice you could think of it like Figure 5-6, On the left is a large juice carton with a big straw. This delivers lots of juice at a high rate. This is analogous to a battery that stores a lot of energy and also delivers high power.

➢ 比能量和比功率

比能量和比功率是电池的重要参数。如上所述，比能量是衡量每单位质量的电池能够存储能量（单位是 J 或 W • h）的多少（能量密度是每单位体积的电池能够储存的能量）。这是从一定质量或体积的电池中可预测到的，与电动汽车的行程范围直接相关。

比功率是衡量可以从每单位质量的电池中提取的功率（单位为 W 或 J/s）的多少（功率密度则是单位体积的功率）。这会影响到电动汽车的加速和爬坡性能。

如果能量是橙汁，您可以想象为图 5-6。左边是一个插有一根大吸管的大盒橙汁。这将以一个较快的速度提供大量的橙汁。这是类似于电池存储了大量的能量，并且还提供了高功率。

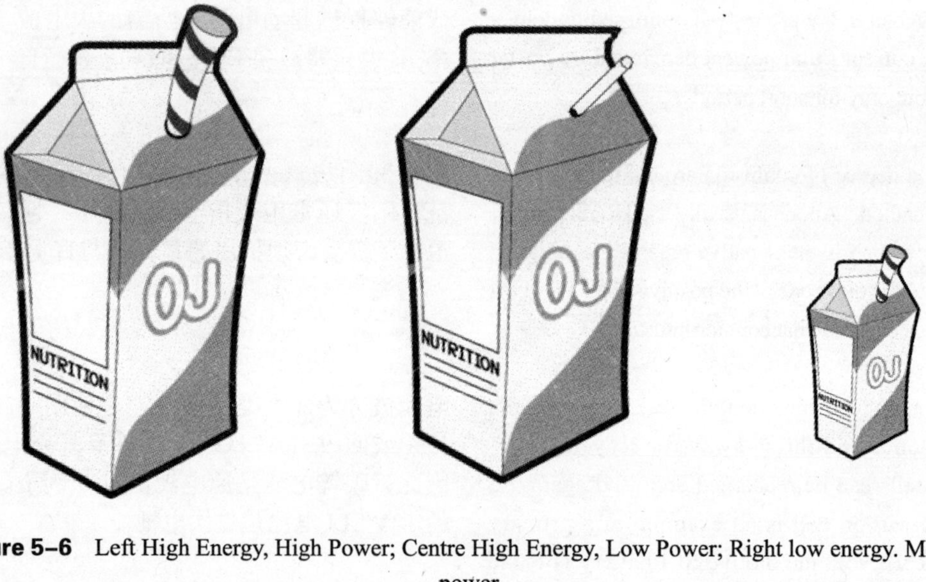

Figure 5–6 Left High Energy, High Power; Centre High Energy, Low Power; Right low energy. Medium power

图 5–6 左：高能量，高功率；中：高能量，低功率；右：低能量，中功率

The centre carton in Figure 5-6 is the same size as the previous one but has a much smaller straw. This delivers lots of juice but only at a low rate. This is analogous to a battery that stores a lot of energy but cannot deliver a lot of instantaneous power. The right hand carton is much smaller and has a medium sized straw. This delivers relatively little juice in total, but is capable of delivering a good flow rate – as long as the juice lasts. This is analogous to a battery that stores little energy but can deliver moderately high power.

图 5-6 中间的橙汁与上一个的大小相同，但吸管小得多。这也能提供大量的橙汁，但只能在很低的速度上。这是类似于电池存储了大量的能量，但不能提供很高的瞬时功率。右边的橙汁盒则小得多，它有一个中等大小的吸管。这提供了总量相对较少的橙汁，但只要盒中还有橙汁的话，它就能够提供一个很好的流量。这是类似于一个存储很少的能量，但可以提供适度高功率的电池。

Specific energy and energy density tend to be governed by battery chemistry. Lead-Acid batteries have a specific energy around 35 watt hours per kg. This means that if you want 20 kW-hrs from lead-acid batteries (typically good for 40 – 80 miles), the pack would weigh around 570 kgs. Lithium ion batteries have a specific energy around the 100 watt-hour per kg mark or better: so a 20 kW-hr pack might weigh about 200kg. Lithium Sulphur batteries promise 300 watt-hour per kg or better (the 20 kW-hr pack would weigh around 60 or 70 kgs). By contrast, petrol or diesel fuel is good for a couple of thousand watt-hours per kg, so the equivalent of a “20 kW-hr pack” would be around 10kg of fuel.

电池的比能量和能量密度往往取决于电池的化学物质。铅酸电池的比能量约为35W•h/kg。这意味着，如果您想从铅酸电池得到 20kW•h 的能量（一般为 60~120km 的行程），该电池组的重量约为 570kg。锂离子电池的比能量约为 100W•h/kg 或更高，因此，一个 20kW•h 电池组的重量约为 200kg。锂硫电池能得到 300W•h/kg 或更好的比能量（20kW•h 电池组的重量约 60 或 70kg）。相比之下，汽油或柴油燃料是每千克几千瓦时，一个相当于“20kW•h 电池组”的燃料约为 10kg。比功率和功率密度也取决于电池的化学物质，但其他因素，如电池设计，也很重要。

➢ Battery characteristics

➢ 电池的特性

Specific power and power density are also governed by cell chemistry, but other factors such as cell design are important too.There are several battery parameters which it is important to understand if you are going to do a good job of choosing batteries for your vehicle:

如果您打算为您的车辆选择电池，弄明白以下几个电池参数是很重要的：

Amp hour rating

The Amp-hour (“Amp-hours” , not “Amps per hour”) rating is the prime measure of the capacity

安时

安时（是“安培小时”，而不是“安培每小时”）是电池容量的主要量度方式。顾名思义，它

of the battery. As the term implies it is the number of Amps you can draw multiplied by the length of time that you can draw them before the battery goes flat. In a perfect world, a 20 Amp-hour battery would provide 1 amp for 20 hours or 20 amps for one hour.

等于您可以使用的安培数乘以在电池的电能耗尽前您能使用的时间长度。在理想的情况下，一个 20A•h 的电池将以 1A 的电流工作 20h 或以 20A 的电流工作 1h。

Sadly we don't live in a perfect world, so an Amp-hour rating is really only good at a certain discharge rate. A "20 Amp-hour rating at the 5 hour rate" means that the battery is capable of serving up a constant 4 amps for 5 hours; but there are no guarantees about what will happen at higher or lower discharge rate. You might for example find that drawing (say) 15 amps would flatten the battery after an hour (15 Amp-hours) or that that it could supply half an amp for 50 hours (25 Amp-hours).

可悲的是，我们不是生活在一个完美的世界里。所以安培小时数只在一定的放电率时是有用的。"在 5h 放电率时为 20A•h" 是指该电池能够提供恒定的 4A 电流持续 5h，但它不保证在较高或较低的放电率时会发生什么。您可能会发现，如果您提取 15A 的电流，1h 后该电池就放电完毕（15A•h），或者，它可以让 0.5A 的电流持续 50h（25A•h）。

Murphy's Law means that the true Amp-hour rating of a battery tends to decline as the discharge rate goes up: in other words, if you try to pull a lot of energy out of a battery quickly, you will get less out in total. Furthermore, typical EV discharge rates (30 – 90 minutes) are quite a lot shorter than the industry standard 20 hour rates, so we cannot assume that the Amp-hour rating in the brochure will necessarily apply to a typical EV application.

墨菲定律指出，一个电池的真正的安培小时数往往随着放电率的上升而下降。换句话说，如果您想要从电池中快速地提取大量的能量，您就会减少能量的总额。此外，典型电动汽车的放电率（30~90min）比工业标准的 20h 放电率短了不少，所以我们不能认为手册中给出的安时数将必定适用于一个典型的电动汽车应用。

Voltage

As we have discussed, cell voltage depends upon chemistry. Furthermore, the percentage difference in voltage between a fully-charged and a fully-discharged cell varies widely. Voltage variations with load current, temperature and even recent charge/discharge history also vary with cell type. Understanding these characteristics is important, and is discussed further both in this chapter and in the one on battery management.

电压

正如我们已经讨论过的，电池的电压取决于其内的化学物质。此外，完全充电和完全放电时电池电压变化的百分比之间的差异也很大。电压随着负载电流、温度，甚至最近的充 / 放电的历史而变化，也随着电池的类型而变化。了解这些特征是很重要的，我们将在本章和下一章的电池管理中进一步讨论这些特征。

C rate

The C Rate ("See rate" , not "crate") is an important parameter of lithium ion batteries in partic-

C 值

C 值尤其对锂离子电池是重要的参数。一个电池的最大 C 值乘以其安时数就是该电

ular. The maximum C rate of a battery multiplied by its Amp-hour rating gives the maximum current that can be drawn from the battery: so for example a 100 Amp-hour battery with a maximum C rate of 3 can safely provide 300 Amps, but a 40 Amp hour battery with the same maximum C rate can only provide 120 (40 × 3) amps safely.

池所能提供的最大电流。例如一个最大C值是3、安时数为100的电池可以安全地提供300A的电流，但具有相同最大C值且安时为40的电池只能安全地提供120（40 × 3）A的电流。

A battery may (probably will) have several C ratings: a continuous discharge rate, a continuous charge rate and 1 or more short duration charge and discharge rates.The effect of this may be felt in terms of maximum acceleration and also maximum regeneration. If you fit a big series motor and a controller capable of handling 2000 Amps, but only fit a single string of 40 Amp-hour batteries with a maximum 3C discharge you are going to be seriously disappointed, either by the lacklustre performance, or by the short battery life.

一个电池可能会（或者就是会）有几个C值：连续放电C值，连续充电C值和1个或更多的短时间充电和放电C值。不同C值的效果可能会在最大加速度和最大的再生能量中显现出来。如果您安装一个大的串励电动机和一个能够处理2000A的控制器，但只装有一个最大为3C放电率的、40A•h的电池组，那么，或者由于电动机表现平平，或者由于电池寿命短，会使您感到非常失望。

Peukert number and internal resistance

The C rate is important mostly for lithium ion batteries. For lead acid batteries, the Peukert number is critical. This is a measure of how much the capacity of the battery will drop as the current increases. The lower the Peukert[1] number the better.

帕克特数和内阻

C值的重要性主要是针对锂离子电池。对于铅酸电池，帕克特数是关键的。它是衡量随着电流的增加电池的容量会下降多少。帕克特数[㊀]越低越好。

The number is invariably greater than 1, but if it gets as high as 1.3, you have a battery that probably won't do very well in an EV. Suppose that we have four otherwise-identical batteries with different Peukert numbers between 1.0 and 1.3. Suppose that these batteries all have 20 Amp hour capacity at the 20 hour rate and we are drawing 50 Amps from each of them. The variation in time to discharge with varying Peukert numbers is as shown in Figure 5-7.

帕克特数总是大于1，但如果它高到1.3，这个电池可能不适合于电动汽车。假设我们有4个除了帕克特数在1.0和1.3之间外其他都相同的电池，并且这些电池在20h的放电率时都有20A•h的容量。现在我们正从每个电池中提取50A的电流，图5-7给出了放电时间随帕克特数的变化。

1 The “eu” in “Peukert” is pronounced like “oi” in the English word “oil”. I am indebted to Mr Wolfgang Peukert for this information

㊀ “Peukert”中的“eu”在英语中读起来像单词“oil”中的“oi”那样。感谢Wolfgang Peukert先生为我提供这一信息。

帕克特数	放电时间 /min
1.0	24
1.1	16
1.2	11
1.3	7

Figure 5–7 Discharge time for 20 Ah batteries of different Peukert number at 50 Amp discharge rate

图 5–7 20A•h 电池在不同帕克特数时在 50A•h 放电率的放电时间

So a 20 Amp hour battery with a Peukert number of 1.3 would only last 7 minutes at a 50 amp discharge rate. In other words it would in effect be a 6 Amp hour battery under these conditions. This is a pretty serious decline from the 20 Amp hours that you might have been expecting from the manufacturer's spec. sheet. It also represents a serious drop in efficiency. Over 2/3rds of the electrical energy that you put into the battery by charging it would be lost during discharge.

因此，一个帕克特数为 1.3 的 20A•h 的电池只能以 50A 的放电率维持 7min。换言之，在这些条件下，这实际上是一个 6A•h 的电池。但您从制造商的规格中也许会期望它是一个 20A•h 的电池，因而这是一个相当严重的衰退。这也代表了效率的严重下降。您的电池在放电过程中将会失去充电电能的 2/3。

It can be difficult to find Peukert values for specific batteries. However Reserve Capacity figures are sometimes published. The Reserve Capacity is a length of time that the battery will last at a higher-than normal output. For example, 12 volt battery Reserve Capacity is frequently measured at 25 Amps – so a 100 minute reserve capacity represents 100 minutes at 25 Amps.

对于特定的电池而言，要找到它的帕克特数可能是很难的。然而，储备容量的大小有时会公布。储备容量是电池在高于正常输出时，放电将持续的时间。例如，12V 电池的储备容量经常在 25A 时测得。因此，100min 的储备容量表示在 25A 时放电 100min。

➢ Batteries for EVs

➢ 用于电动汽车的电池

At the time of writing there are just two battery chemistries in common use in amateur conversions:

- Lead Acid
- Lithium Ion

在写作本书时，只有两种电池的化学物质在业余电动汽车中被普遍使用：

- 铅酸
- 锂离子

Another chemistry which is just becoming available commercially, and which could be a game-changer is:

- Lithium Sulphur

另一种刚刚上市且可能改变游戏规则的化学物质是：

- 锂硫

In addition there are three more chemistries that are or have been used by some commercial builders:

此外，还有三种化学物质已经或正在被一些专业制造商使用：

Nickel Cadmium – NiCad (Now obsolete. Was used in Citroen Berlingo Electrique and Saxo Electrique).

镍镉电池（NiCad，现已不用了，曾在雪铁龙的电动柏林阁车型和电动盛宝车型中使用）

Nickel Metal-Hydride - NiMh (Used in Toyota and Honda hybrids, and the Toyota RAV4 EV).

镍金属氢化物（NiMh，在丰田和本田混合动力车及丰田的 RAV4 电动汽车中使用）

Molten Salt (e.g. ZEBRA used in some Modec vans and a 1997 prototype electric Mercedes A class) .

熔盐（如 ZEBRA 用于 MODEC 货车和 1997 年的原型电动奔驰 A 级车型）

These latter are worth being aware of. There is a lot of battery research going on so new technologies (or new adaptations of existing technologies) may pop up at any time.

后几种是值得关注的。目前对电池研究的投入很大，因此，很多的新技术（或现有技术的更新）会随时出现。

➢ Lead Acid

➢ 铅酸电池

All lead-acid batteries use the same basic electrode materials – a lead anode and a lead dioxide cathode. This combination produces just over 2 volts per cell. In most lead-acid batteries, the electrodes are not pins or rods but flat plates. The electrolyte is sulphuric acid. There are three classes of lead acid batteries, and two (or maybe three) variants in each class.

所有铅酸电池都使用相同的基本电极材料——铅阳极和二氧化铅阴极。这种结合在每个电池单元中产生了刚好超过 2V 的电压。大多数铅酸电池的电极不是针或杆而是平板。电解液是硫酸。铅酸电池有三种类型，每种类型有两个（或三个）的变体。

The three classes of Lead Acid batteries are

这三类铅酸电池是：

- Flooded Lead Acid (sometimes “FLA” or just “Flooded”)
- Absorbed (or Absorbent) Glass Mat – AGM
- Gel

- 富液铅酸（有时简化为“FLA”或“富液”）
- 吸收（或吸水）玻璃纤维毡铅酸电池，简称 AGM
- 凝胶铅酸电池

AGM and Gel batteries are sometimes referred to as “Sealed”, “Valve Regulated Lead Acid” (VRLA) or “Starved Electrolyte” batteries. In addition, lead acid batteries are characterised by their application: SLI, Traction/Deep Cycle or Leisure:

AGM 及凝胶电池有时被称为“密封”、“阀控式密封铅酸”（VRLA）或“饥饿电解质”电池。此外，铅酸电池的特征由它们的应用所确定：SLI（起动、照明、点火），牵引 / 深循环或康乐等应用。

SLI

(Starter, Lighting, Ignition) batteries are designed to deliver lots of power but only for a short time. They are intended to be discharged just a few percent in normal operation. Regular deep discharging destroys them very quickly.

SLI 电池

（起动、照明、点火）电池被设计成用以提供大功率，但只能持续很短的时间。它们的目的是在正常运行时只放几个百分点的电。定期的深放电很快就会将它们毁坏。

Traction

Or Deep Cycle batteries on the other hand are designed for regular deep discharge. Their specific power is lower than an equivalent SLI battery, but their deep-discharge cycle life is a lot better.

牵引电池

然而，牵引电池，也叫深循环电池，被设计成定期的深放电。其比功率低于同等 SLI 电池，但其深放电循环寿命要好得很多。

Leisure

There is sometimes a third category: the Leisure battery. This is intended to be used in boats, caravans etc and is a compromise: better cycle life than the SLI battery, and better specific power than the traction battery.

康乐电池

有时还有第三类:康乐电池。这是为了在船、大篷车等使用。它是一个折中：其循环寿命优于 SLI 电池，并且比功率也好于牵引电池。

There are therefore in theory 9 types of Lead Acid battery as shown in Figure 5-8.

因此，在理论上有 9 种类型的铅酸电池，如图 5-8 所示。

	SLI	康乐	牵引
富液	X	X	X
AGM	X	X	X
凝胶	X	X	X

Figure 5–8 Taxonomy of Lead-Acid batteries

图 5–8 铅酸电池的分类

Flooded Lead Acid

The standard SLI (car) battery that most people know is usually a "Flooded Lead Acid" (FLA) battery. Each cell consists of a plastic box containing flat plate electrodes immersed in sulphuric acid. The basic principle hasn't changed since the late 1800s.

富液铅酸

大多数人都知道，标准的（汽车用）SLI 电池通常是“富液铅酸”（FLA）电池。每个电池单元由一个塑料盒及浸在硫酸中的平板电极组成。自 19 世纪后期以来其基本原理一直没变。

Each cell will have many plates interleaved with separators (anode-separator-cathode-separator-anode-separator...). The trick is to maximise the

每个电池单元都会有许多由隔离器分开的平板（阳极—隔离器—阴极—隔离器—阳极—隔离器……），关键是要最大化平板面积。

plate area. This minimises internal resistance and maximises output. Unfortunately the thinner the plates, the lower the tolerance of the battery to repeated discharge. SLI batteries have thin plates, so you can pack more plates into a given volume and as a result they can sustain high currents. Traction batteries have fewer, thicker plates, so last longer (Figure 5-9).

这可以最大限度地减少内电阻并最大限度地提高输出。不幸的是，平板越薄，电池的重复放电的耐受性就越差。SLI 电池用的是薄板，这样您就可以在一个给定的空间内放入更多的板。因此，它们可以承受大电流。牵引电池用的是较少而厚的平板，因此，它的寿命更长（图 5-9）。

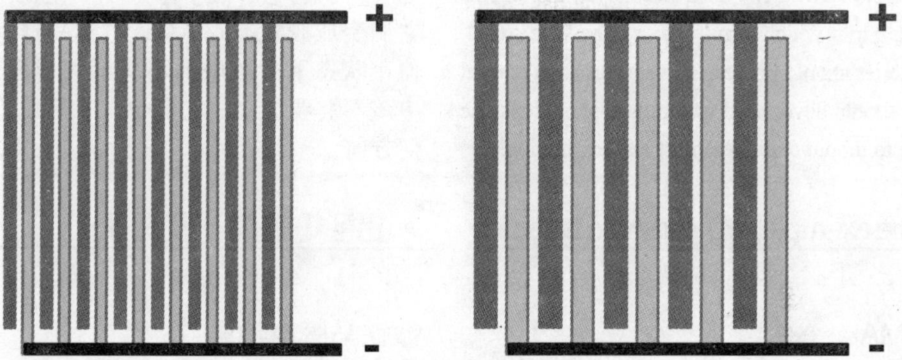

Figure 5–9 Plate Layout: SLI (Left) Traction (Right)

图 5–9 电池板的分布：启动蓄电池（左），牵引蓄电池（右）

Absorbed Glass Mat (AGM)

AGM batteries do not contain free liquid electrolyte: instead they have separators made of a form of glass fibre which holds the electrolyte. These batteries have several advantages over flooded batteries. They:

- will not give off any gas or fumes if you treat them right.
- never need watering.
- tend to have a higher specific power than flooded cells.
- are said to be much more shock and vibration resistant.
- can be mounted in almost any orientation.

They also have a reputation for low Peukert number (meaning that they retain a reasonable capacity at high discharge rates as described above). It is however im-

吸收玻璃纤维毡（AGM）

AGM 电池不包含可流动液体的电解液，它们的隔板是由含有电解液的玻璃纤维制成的。相对于富液电池，这种电池有如下几个优势：

- 如果您处理得当的话，它们不会放出任何气体或烟雾；
- 它们永远不需要浇水；
- 它们往往有比富液电池更高的比功率；
- 据说它们更耐冲击和振动；
- 它们可以在几乎任何方向被安装。

它们还有一个低的帕克特数（如上所述，这意味着在高放电率时它们会维持较高的容量）。然而重要是不能对它们过充电。如果

portant not to overcharge them. If overcharged they may start to vent. Regular venting will kill the batteries. This more or less mandates a good quality battery charger. AGM batteries are also the most expensive of the three lead acid cell types (Flooded, AGM, Gel).

过充电，它们可能会开始放气。经常性的放气会损坏电池。这就要求有一个质量好的电池充电器。AGM 电池也是三种铅酸电池类型（富液、AGM、凝胶）中最贵的。

Gel Batteries

Gel batteries are a kind of half-way house between Flooded and AGM. The acid electrolyte has chemicals added to it which turn it into a jelly. Like AGM, Gel batteries should not leak or vent fumes in normal use and should never need watering. It should also be possible to mount them in almost any orientation.

凝胶电池

凝胶电池是一种介于富液和 AGM 之间的电池。它们的电解液中添加了一些化学物质使它们变成胶状。跟 AGM 电池一样，在正常使用状态下凝胶电池不应漏气或发出烟雾，应该不需要加水。它们也几乎可以安装在任何方向。

➢ Some examples of Lead-Acid batteries

➢ 铅酸电池的一些例子

OPTIMA

OPTIMA (http://www.optimabatteries.com/) sell a range of batteries, all AGM, with an unusual design: the plates in each cell are a single long strip wound into a roll like an old-fashioned elastic bandage and inserted into a cylindrical cavity in the casing (see Figure 5-10).

傲铁马牌电池

傲铁马（http://www.optimabatteries.com/）生产和销售各式各样的 AGM 电池，它们的设计有些不寻常：每个电池单元的平板是由像一条老式的弹性绷带那样成卷长条形的单块板组成的，并将其插入在一个圆柱形的容器内（见图 5 -10）。

The batteries are colour coded by application: the

电池用不同的色码来标定不同的应用："红色

Figure 5–10 OPTIMA Batteries. Note extra terminals on one of the batteries (a "Blue Top"). Photo courtesy of OPTIMA Batteries(http://www.optimabatteries.com)

图 5–10 傲铁马牌蓄电池。请注意电池上的一个额外端子（一个"蓝顶"）。照片由傲铁马电池（http://www.optimabatteries.com）提供

"Red Tops" are SLI batteries. The "Blue Tops" have a slightly different terminal arrangement for Marine applications and are available as SLI or deep-cycle. The Yellow Tops are deep-cycle batteries. A light grey case denotes deep cycle, a dark grey case SLI.

顶盖"是SLI电池；"蓝色顶盖"在海洋应用中有略为不同终端的安排，它们可用作SLI或深循环电池；"黄色顶盖"是深循环电池；浅灰色表示深循环电池，深灰色表示SLI电池。

The OPTIMA D51 has a 38 Amp-hour capacity at the 20 hour rate, and a reserve capacity of 66 minutes. Peukert is about 1.12, so it could deliver 50 amps for about 30 minutes (equivalent to 25 Amp hours at that rate). It weighs just under 12 kg.

傲铁马牌D51电池在20h放电率下拥有38A•h的容量，并有一个66min的储备能力。其帕克特数是1.12左右，因此它可以以50A的电流工作约30min（在这一放电率下相当于25A•h的容量）。其重量不到12kg。

TrojanHaze

Trojan Battery has more than 85 years of battery engineering and manufacturing experience. The T-105 model (Figure 5-11) is the company's flagship deep-cycle flooded lead acid battery. It is 6 volts and is fairly heavy, so 24 of them weighing close to 700kg would be needed to make a typical 144 volt pack. However, it does have a high amp hour rating (225 at the 20 hour rate), so it should not be compared to the other batteries featured here which have lower amp hour ratings. Its Peukert is 1.16, and because of its large capacity it can provide 50 amps for about 3½ hours.

特洛伊牌电池

特洛伊拥有超过85年的电池工程和制造经验。T-105型电池（图5-11）是该公司的旗舰深循环富液铅酸电池。这是6V且相当沉重的电池，所以为获得一个典型的144V的电池组需要有24个这样的电池，总重量接近700kg。但它确有一个高的安时数（在20h放电率时为225），所以不应该将其与其他安时数较低的电池相比。它的帕克特数是1.16，并且由于其容量大，它可以提供50A的电流持续约3.5h。

Haze

The Haze HZY-EV12-33 (Figure 5-12) is a 12

海志牌电池

海志牌HZY-EV12-33电池（图5-12）是

Figure 5–11 Trojan T-105.Photo courtesy of Trojan Battery (http://www.trojanbattery.com)

图5–11 特洛伊T-105电池。照片由特洛伊电池（http//www.trojanbattery.com）提供

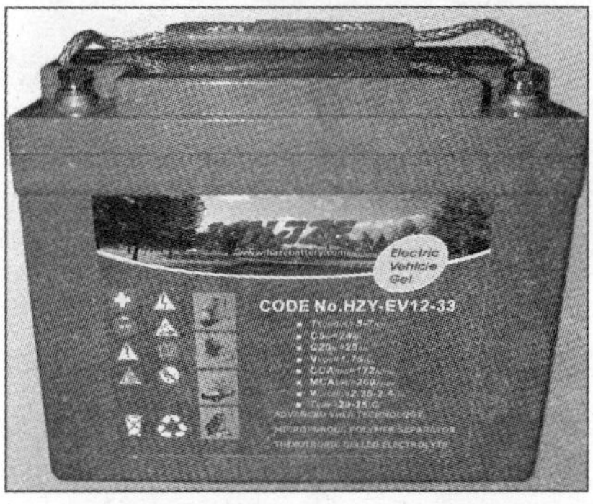

Figure 5–12 Haze Gel Battery. Photo courtesy of Haze Batteries Europe Ltd (http://www.hazebattery.com/)

图5–12 凝胶蓄电池。照片由海志电池欧洲有限公司提供（http://www.hazebattery.com）

volt gel battery with a 29 Amp hour capacity at the 20 hour rate, falling to 18 Amp hours at the 1 hour rate. This is equivalent to a Peukert value of about 1.12. It could deliver 50 amps for about 17 minutes (equivalent to 14 Amp hours at that rate). It weighs 10.4 kg.

一个 12V 的凝胶电池，在 20h 放电率时其容量为 29A•h，在 1h 放电率时其容量下降到 18A•h。这相当于一个约 1.12 的帕克特数。它可以提供 50A 的电流持续约 17min（在该放电率下相当于 14A•h）。其重量为 10.4kg。

Enersys Odyssey

Anecdotally, Enersys batteries have a good reputation in the EV world. The PC925 (Figure 5 13) is another AGM battery. It has a capacity of 28 Amp hours at the 20 hour rate and a low (= good) Peukert value of about 1.09. At 50 amps it would last about 24 minutes for an equivalent of 20 Amp hours. It weighs just under 12 kg. The PC1750 (Figure 5-14) is a larger Enersys battery. It has a capacity of 74 Amp hours at the 20 hour rate. The Peukert exponent is about 1.14. At 50 amps it would last about an hour. It weighs 26.3 kgs.

艾诺斯奥德赛牌电池

艾诺斯电池据说在电动汽车界具有良好的信誉。PC925 电池（图 5-13）是另一种 AGM 电池。它在 20h 放电率时有一个 28A•h 的容量以及一个低的（= 好的）、约 1.09 的帕克特数。在 50A 工作时，它可持续约 24min，相当于一个 20A•h 的容量。它的重量不到 12kg。PC1750 电池（图 5-14）是一种更大的艾诺斯电池。它在 20h 放电率时有一个 74A•h 的容量，其帕克特数是 1.14 左右。在 50A 工作时，它会持续大约 1h。它的重量为 26.3kg。

CSB

The CSB 12220-X2 is an example of a battery with a relatively high Peukert number. It is a 20 Amp-hour battery (measured at the 20 hour rate) weighing about 6.7 kg. Peukert, though, is around 1.2 so it would only maintain a 50 Amp discharge

CSB 牌电池

CSB 12220-X2 电池是一个相对高的帕克特数电池的一个例子。这是一个重约 6.7kg 的 20A•h 的电池（在 20h 放电率时测得）。但其帕克特数大约 1.2，所以在 50A 的放电率它只能维持 11min 左右，相当于约 9.5A•h，或

Figure 5–13 Enersys Odyssey PC925. Photo courtesy of Enersys(http://www.odysseyfactory.com)

图 5–13 艾诺斯奥德赛的 PC925 电池。照片由艾诺斯提供（http://www.odysseyfactory.com）

Figure 5–14 Enersys Odyssey PC1750s in a bike frame. Photo courtesy of Jason Siegel

图 5–14 在自行车架上的艾诺斯奥德赛电池。照片由詹森 • 西格尔提供

for 11 minutes or so; equivalent to about 9½ Amp hours, or less than half what you might expect from the headline Amp-hour rating.

➢ Lithium Ion Batteries

Lithium ion secondary cells have huge theoretical advantages over lead acid. They have three or four times the specific energy of lead acid and can in some cases deliver good specific power and long cycle life. On the other hand, lithium ion technology is still developing. The chemistry that was dominant as recently as 2 –3 years ago is now almost unobtainable. It is also an area where conspiracy theorists can have a field day: until quite recently, most US and European suppliers of lithium ion cells would not sell batteries for use by private individuals; they would only talk to vehicle manufacturers. This situation is changing however.

There are other issue with lithium ion batteries:

- They need to be looked after very carefully. More on this later.
- A large capacity lithium ion battery pack can easily cost tens of thousands of pounds from some suppliers.
- Neither the technology nor the market is mature and independent verification of things like cycle life does not, in many cases, exist.

This means that going with lithium ion carries great promise (100 mile + range is reported by some of those using them) but it is also risky. One respected author[1] recommends giving lithium ion a miss for the time being. Others with experience in the field consider them to be the only battery type for a usable electric vehicle rather than for experimental machines. We will look at them in a

1 Mike Boxwell: ‘Owning an Electric Car’ 2010 edition

比您可能期望从其标签值中得到的安培小时数的一半还少。

➢ 锂离子电池

锂离子二次电池相对于铅酸电池而言有巨大的理论优势。它们的比能量是铅酸电池的3~4倍，在某些情况下，可以提供良好的比功率和长的循环寿命。另一方面，锂离子电池技术仍处于发展阶段。现在几乎无法获得两三年前占主导地位那些电池的化学物质。这是一个阴谋的理论家可以大做文章的领域。直到最近，大多数美国和欧洲的锂离子电池供应商将不会出售个人使用的电池，他们只会与汽车制造商做生意，但这种状况正在发生变化。

锂离子电池还有其他的问题：

- 它们需要非常仔细的照顾。我们将在后面详细讨论这点。
- 你必须花费数十万元才能从一些供应商中买到一个大容量的锂离子电池组。
- 无论是技术还是市场都还不成熟，并且在许多情况下找不到对如循环寿命的独立核查。

这意味着使用锂离子电池是大有希望的（使用过它们的一些人曾报道超过160km的行程里程），但它也是有风险的。一个受人尊敬的作者㊀建议目前暂时避免使用锂离子电池。另外一些在该领域中有经验的人认为，它们是实用电动汽车而不是模型车应该使用的唯一一种电池类型。我们将对它们进行更详细的考察，然后您可以根据您钱包的厚度和期望的里程数进行选择。首先我

㊀ 迈克尔·波科斯维尔：拥有一辆电动汽车，2010年版。

little more detail and it is then up to you to make a choice based upon the depth of your wallet and your range aspirations. First a little more theory.

们要谈谈有关的理论。

Elements used in Lithium Ion

Lithium ion chemistries are often labelled using the standard chemical symbols for the elements used in the cathode. For example "Lithium-Cobalt" cells (denoting cells with a cathode made of lithium cobalt) are often shortened to LiCo. To add further confusion, this battery chemistry is properly referred to as "lithium cobalt oxide" or $LiCoO_2$.

锂离子电池中使用的化学元素

锂离子电池往往使用标准的化学符号来标记在阴极（正极）中使用的元素。例如,“锂钴”电池（指用钴酸锂作阴极的电池）常被缩写为 LiCo（译注：Li 和 Co 为锂和钴的元素符号）。更为混乱的是，这种电池的化学物质的正确名称应为“钴酸锂”或 $LiCoO_2$。

The main chemical symbols to be aware of are:
Fe – Iron (NB – Iron not Ion)
H - Hydrogen
Li - Lithium
Mn – Manganese
Ni – Nickel
O – Oxygen
O_2– Usually denotes an oxide in this context
P – Phosphorus
PO_4 – Phosphate
S – Sulphur (or Sulfur in American English as adopted by the International Union of Pure and Applied Chemistry - IUPAC)
Ti - Titanium
Y – Yttrium

这里要提到的一些主要化学符号是：
Fe—铁
H—氢
Li—锂
Mn—锰
Ni—镍
O—氧
O_2—这时通常是指氧化物
P—磷
PO_4—磷酸盐
S—硫
Ti—钛
Y—钇

Subscript numbers indicate the number of atoms in a molecule: so for example H_2O(water) is made up of molecules containing 2 Hydrogen atoms (H_2) and one Oxygen atom (O). Manganese Dioxide is MnO_2 (one Manganese atom, two oxygen atoms per molecule).

下标数字表示分子中的原子个数。例如 H_2O（水）表示由含有 2 个氢原子（H_2）和一个氧原子（O）所组成的分子。二氧化锰是 MnO_2（每个分子中有一个锰原子和两个氧原子）。

One of the main Lithium-Ion cell chemistry in use today is Lithium Iron Phosphate ($LiFePO_4$ – sometimes shortened further to "LFP"). There are a few further chemistries that you may encounter:

今天使用的主流锂离子电池的化学物质之一是磷酸铁锂（$LiFePO_4$，有时会进一步缩写为“LFP”）。您可能会遇到的另一些化学物质，如

- Lithium Cobalt Oxide ($LiCoO_2$ – dominant until recently)
- Lithium Manganese Oxide ($LiMn_2O_4$)
- Lithium Nickel Oxide ($LiNiO_2$)
- Lithium Nickel Manganese Cobalt Oxide ($LiNiMnO_2$ – or “NMC”)

All of these refer to the material used for the cathode. Normally the anode of a lithium ion cell is graphite, but some batteries use other materials. If you encounter a “lithium titanate” cell, this is a reference to the anode material which is (confusingly) also a lithium compound – lithium titanate or Li_2TiO_3.

Note that the dominance of graphite as an anode material in lithium ion cells may not be permanent. It is far from the best material electrochemically, but better alternatives (such as Tin – symbol Sn- and Silicon - Si) degrade very quickly. Changes in volume on each cycle rapidly pulverise the anode. One possible approach is to encapsulate these materials in carbon nanotubes.[1]

Lithium-air cells are also the subject of research. In addition there are all manner of doping and tweaking additives which can affect the performance and characteristics of the battery. Note that different lithium ion chemistries have different specific energies and cell voltages.

Lithium Battery Performance

There are several factors of importance with lithium ion batteries:

Voltage - nominal voltages vary from about 3.3 volts per cell to 3.8 volts per cell.

Price – expressed in £ or $ per watt-hour. This can

1 For more detail see for example “Tin-based materials as advanced anode materials for lithium ion batteries: a review” by Ali Reza Kamali and Derek J. Fray

- 钴酸锂（$LiCoO_2$，直到最近它还占主导地位）
- 锰酸锂（$LiMn2O_4$）
- 镍酸锂（$LiNiO_2$）
- 锂镍锰钴氧化物（$LiNiMnO_2$ 或 “NMC”）

所有这些都是用于阴极的材料。通常情况下，锂离子电池的阳极是石墨，但有些电池使用其他材料。如果您遇到一个“钛酸锂”电池，令人感到混乱的是这是指一种锂化合物的阳极材料——钛酸锂或 Li_2TiO_3。

请注意：石墨作为锂离子电池阳极材料的优势可能不会是永久的。这远不是电化学意义上的最佳材料，但更好的替代品，如锡（Sn）和硅（Si）的性能下降很快。每个周期的体积变化迅速吞噬着阳极。一种可能的方法是将这些材料封装在碳纳米管中[㊀]。

锂 - 空气电池也是一个研究课题。此外，还有可能会影响电池的性能和特点的各种参杂和调整添加剂的方式。需要注意的是，不同的锂离子化学物质有不同的比能量和电池电压。

锂离子电池性能

锂离子电池的重要因素有以下几点：

电压——单个电池的名义电压值约为 3.3~3.8V。

价格——表示为每瓦小时多少元人民币或美

㊀ 更详细信息请参阅例如阿里•礼萨卡迈利和狄拉克·J·弗赖著的《作为先进锂离子电池阳极的锡基材料－综述》。

vary very widely between suppliers.

元。这在不同的供应商之间具有很大的不同。

Failure rate – anecdotal evidence suggests that a small proportion of any given batch of lithium ion cells may either be dead on arrival or fail after a short period of use.

故障率——未经证实的证据表明，在一批量的锂离子电池中有很小比例的电池可能在收到时就是坏的，或在短期的使用之后就坏了。

Specific Power, Specific Energy and C rating – as discussed earlier. There is quite a lot of variance here between different lithium ion cell types.

比功率、比能量和 C 值——正如前面讨论过的，不同类型的锂离子电池之间有相当大的差异。

Cycle life – again there is a lot of variance from a few hundred cycles to several thousand; but as noted above independent evaluation is hard to come by.

循环寿命——这里的差异同样很大，可以从几百周期到几千个周期。但正如前面所述的，很难对每个电池的个体进行评估。

Lithium Cobalt Oxide ($LiCoO_2$)

Lithium Cobalt Oxide cells were dominant until just a few years ago. They have rather fallen out of favour however because there were a number of cases of these batteries overheating or exploding in consumer electronics such as laptops. Compared with other lithium ion chemistries they have:

- High specific energy
- Lower C rating (i.e. low maximum discharge rate and hence poor specific power)
- Shorter cycle life

In summary they would take you a long way on a single charge, but acceleration and hill climbing ability would be mediocre. These cells had a reputation for catching fire if abused, and they would normally need replacing every year or two.

钴酸锂（$LiCoO_2$）电池

钴酸锂电池直到几年前还占主导地位。然而，它们现已失宠，因为已经有了好几个这些电池在消费类电子产品，如笔记本电脑中过热或爆炸的案例。与其他化学物质的锂离子电池相比，钴酸锂电池具有：

- 高的比能量
- 较低的 C 值（即低的最大放电率，因而较差的比功率）
- 较短的循环寿命

总之，单次充电之后它们将持续很长的行程，但它们的加速和爬坡能力则很平庸。这些电池如被滥用则可能起火，并且它们通常每一两年就需要更换。

Lithium Iron Phosphate

$LiFePO_4$ or "LFP" is dominant for new lithium ion batteries shipping today for amateur use. Compared with lithium cobalt oxide, lithium iron phosphate cells tend to have a slightly lower specific energy (although still far better than most non-lithium chemistries). Otherwise they are a winner

磷酸铁锂电池

$LiFePO_4$ 的或"LFP"是今天业余爱好者使用的主导型新型锂离子电池。与钴酸锂相比，磷酸铁锂电池的比能略低（但仍远远高于大多数非锂化学电池）。除此以外，它们在所有其他方面都是胜者：更安全，更高的 C 值及更长的寿命。今天所有的专用电池往往有

all round: safer, higher C rating and longer life. Proprietary cells shipping today often appear to be available in two forms: optimised for specific energy or optimised for specific power.

两种形式：优化比能或优化比功率。

Other Lithium ion Chemistries

I am not going to say very much about other lithium ion chemistries, mostly because at the time of writing there are few sources of such lithium ion cells or batteries using them. Lithium manganese oxide ($LiMn_2O_4$) appears to be about mid way between lithium cobalt oxide ($LiCoO_2$) and lithium iron phosphate ($LiFePO_4$) in safety, specific energy and C rating.

其他锂离子化学电池

我不打算详细介绍其他锂离子化学物质，主要是因为在写作本书时，几乎没有这样的锂离子电池或电池组的资料。锰酸锂($LiMn_2O_4$)在安全性、比能和 C 值等方面似乎介于钴酸锂（$LiCoO_2$）和磷酸铁锂（$LiFePO_4$）之间。

You may also encounter Lithium Nickel Manganese Cobalt Oxide ($LiNiMnCoO_2$) [Kokam and Panasonic] and Lithium Cobalt Nickel Aluminium Oxide (LiCoNiAlO2) [Panasonic].

您也可能会遇到锂锰镍钴氧化物（$LiNiMnCoO_2$）[卡马和松下] 及锂钴镍铝氧化物（$LiCoNiAlO_2$）[松下] 电池。

Lithium ion Battery Packs

As described earlier, lithium ion cells may have a liquid electrolyte, or they may be polymer cells. The latter are typically (but not necessarily) a thin bag or pouch. The former are typically available as either cylindrical cells (not unlike an overgrown domestic AA or D cell) or as "prismatics".

锂离子电池组

如前所述，锂离子电池可能有液态电解质，也可能是聚合物电池。后者通常（但不一定）是薄膜袋或包。前者是典型的圆柱形（很像一个国内随处可见的 5 号或 1 号电池）或"棱柱形"的。

The cylindrical cells are typically in the 2 – 8 Amp hour range, whereas prismatic cells are available in capacities of 200 Amp hour or even higher. A 100 Amp hour prismatic cell is about the size of a small but thick book or a small box of breakfast cereal. One popular 100 Amp-hour cell is 220mm (8.66″) by 179mm (7.04″) by 62mm (2.44″) and weighs about 3.5 kg.

圆柱形电池通常在 2~8A•h 范围内，而棱柱形电池的可用容量为 200A•h，甚至更高。100A•h 的棱柱形电池是一本小而厚的书，或早餐时用的麦片盒的大小。一种流行的 100A•h 的电池为 220mm × 179mm × 62mm，重约 3.5kg。

Making up a battery pack with Prismatic cells is mostly a matter of constructing a suitable battery box (or boxes) and chaining the cells together using suitable straps or cables (Figure 5-15).

用棱柱形电池构成电池组主要是构建一个或多个合适的电池盒，并用合适的导电带或电缆将各个电池连在一起（图 5-15）。

Figure 5–15 A battery pack of prismatic cells under Construction. photo Courtesy of Greg Sievert

图 5–15 一个正在组合成的棱柱形电池组。照片由格雷格·西弗特提供

Some types of Lithium cell are commonly fitted with rigid end plates to prevent swelling of the cells. Be guided by the manufacturer's recommendations.

某些类型的锂离子电池通常配有刚性端板，以防止电池肿胀。请参照制造商的建议。

Using the cylindrical cells is a little more complicated. You need to assemble clusters of cells in parallel to get the Amp-hour rating that you need, and then assemble the clusters in series until you have enough voltage (Figure 5-16). Alternatively you might be able to assemble multiple high voltage strings in parallel (Figure 5-17).

使用圆柱形电池则有点复杂。您需要将电池并联成一个电池组以便获得您所需要的安时数，然后再将这些电池组串联，直到获得足够的电压（图 5-16）。此外，您也可以将多个高压电池组并联（图 5-17）。

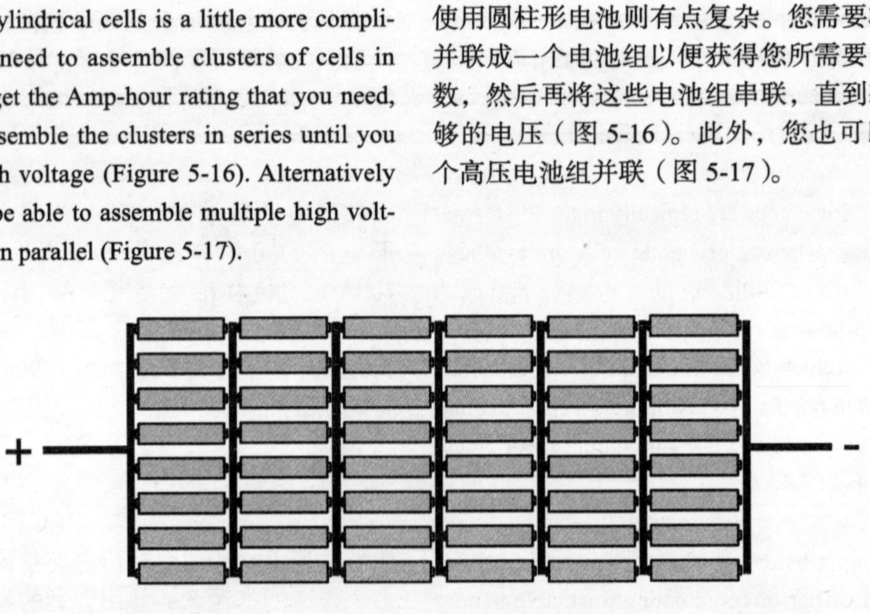

Figure 5–16 Schematic of cylindrical cell battery pack (6 clusters of 8 cells each)

图 5–16 圆柱形电池组示意图（8 个电池为一组，共 6 组）

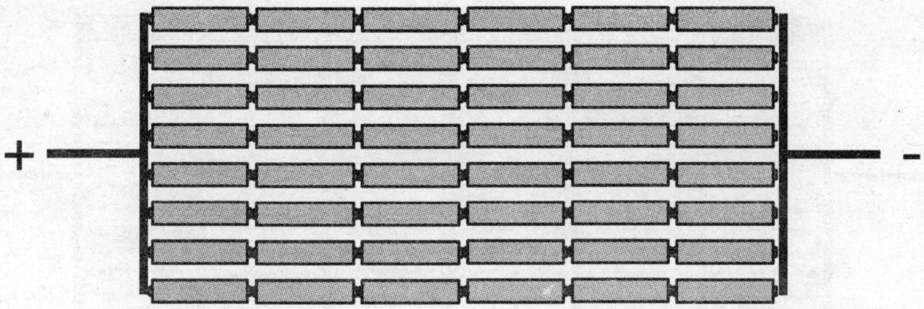

Figure 5–17　An alternative topology; multiple strings

图 5–17　另一种拓扑结构，多个串联

Some of these cylindrical cells have threaded terminals. Others have tabs that can be welded and with yet others you will need to flash-weld tabs or bus bars to the battery terminals. This sounds fiddly, but does have a couple of advantages. Firstly, if a cell fails the effect is less severe than with a single string of big prismatic cells. If you have a battery pack made up of prismatic cells in series, you have a chain that is only as strong as its weakest link.

有些圆柱形电池带有螺纹端子，有些具有可焊接的接头，还有一些您需要将接头快速焊接到电池的端子上。这听起来很繁琐，但确实有一些优势。首先，如果一个电池单元出现故障，它的影响并不像一个大的棱柱形电池那样严重。如果您有一个串联的棱柱形电池组成的电池组，您的电池组的强度是由最薄弱的电池决定的。

Suppose for example you have such a battery pack and that ordinarily it gives you a 100 mile range. Now suppose that one of your cells partially fails and reaches minimum voltage after just 30 miles. You have two choices when the weakest cell reaches its minimum voltage: stop and recharge, or carry on and almost certainly destroy the bad cell altogether – and (with some chemistries) risk wider pack damage.

举例来说，假如您有这样一个电池组，它通常能提供一个 160km 的行程范围。现在假设电池组中有一个电池单元失效了，只行驶了约 50km 就达到最低电压。当最弱的电池达到最低电压时您有两个选择：停下来充电，或者继续行驶，但几乎可以肯定这将完全毁坏那个电池，并且（对某些化学物质而言）会有更多电池损坏的危险。

With a large number of smaller cells, any degradation is more graceful. Unless you are unfortunate, a few random cell failures are only going to cut down your range by a few percent (Figure 5-18).

如果采用大量的小电池，则任何退化的影响将更小。除非您很不幸，否则少数随机的电池故障只会减少百分之几的行程范围（图 5-18）。

The second advantage of using clusters of smaller cells is that you have more flexibility in use of space. Figure 5-19 for example is a pack made up of cylindrical cells intended to fit into spaces in the frame of an electric bike:

使用较小电池构成电池组的第二个优势是，您可以更灵活地利用空间。如图 5-19 是一个打算放在电动自行车框架内的圆柱形电池组。

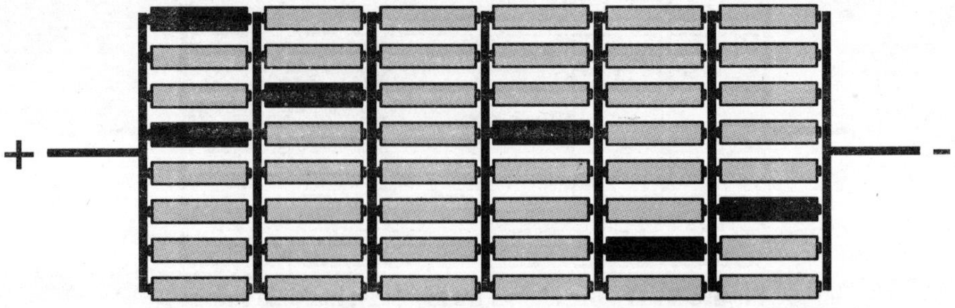

Figure 5–18 Battery pack with random failures

图 5–18 含有随机故障电池的电池组

The disadvantage with this arrangement is what can go wrong with it. Using small cylindrical cells in a full size EV implies many hundreds if not thousands of high-current connections. Every one is a potential point source of overheating.

这种安排的缺点是由此可能引发的故障。在一个全尺寸的电动汽车内使用小型圆柱形电池组意味着数以百计（如果不是千的话）大电流连接，这样每一个接头都是引起过热的潜在源。

Figure 5–19 Battery Pack for use in an electric bike. Photo courtesy of Falcon EV (http://www.falconev.com)

图 5–19 电动自行车中使用的电池。照片由福尔肯电动车有限公司提供（http://www.falconev.com）

Cylindrical Cell Sizes

Cylindrical cells are usually designated by diameter and length (albeit inconsistently). For example a “26650” cell is about 26 mm in diameter and 65 mm long (or roughly 1” diameter and 2 1/2” long). Some common sizes are listed above. Note that the diameter and length may not be exact. There are

圆柱形电池的尺寸

圆柱形电池通常由其直径和长度来标定（尽管不一致）。例如“26650”电池的直径约为26mm，长度为65mm（或大约1in直径2.5in长）。上表中列出了一些常见的尺寸。请注意，直径和长度可能不准确。有来自不同厂家之间电池的差异。“长度”也可能是电池的圆

常见圆柱形电池的尺寸

型号	名义直径 /mm	名义长度 /mm	大约相当于
10440	10	44	7 号电池
14500	14	50	5 号电池
17500	17	50	3 号电池
26460	26	46	2 号电池
26650	22	65	
32650	32	65	
33580	33	58	1 号电池
602030	60	203	

differences between cells from different manufacturers. Also, the "length" may be that of the cylindrical part of the cell and may exclude terminals on the ends. Lastly(and confusingly) a "38120" may be 120 mm rather than 12mm long.

柱部分，不包括两端的终端。最后（令人混淆的是），“38120”可能是 120mm，而不是 12mm 长。

➢ Examples of Lithium ion cells

➢ 锂离子电池的一些例子

Here are some examples of Lithium ion cells. Note that these are manufacturer's data and in some cases it's prudent to take some figures (particularly C rating and cycle life) with a large pinch of salt.

这里是一些锂离子电池的例子。请注意，这些都是制造商的数据。在某些情况下，必须审慎地、有较大保留地去使用这些数字（特别是 C 值和循环寿命）。

A123 ANR26650 M1

A123 are a US company that manufactures lithium ion cells currently regarded as amongst the best available. Probably their best known cell at the time of writing is the ANR26650M1A (Figure 5-20).

A123 ANR26650 M1 电池

A123 是一家美国公司，它所生产的锂离子电池是目前被视为最好的之一。在写作本书时，它们最知名的电池也许是 ANR26650M1A（图 5-20）。

This cell weighs 70 grams, delivers 2.3 Amp hours at 3.3 volts and astonishingly can sustain 70 Amps continuous discharge rate, or 120 Amps for 10 seconds. The latter is a C rate of over 50 (anything over 3 would until quite recently have been regarded as good). A123 claim a cycle life in excess of 1000. Plus this cell has a wide usable temperature range: it should be usable anywhere from the arctic to the

该电池重 70g，在 3.3V 时可提供 2.3A•h 的电流。令人吃惊的是它可以持续地维持 70A 的放电率，或以 120A 的放电率维持 10s。后者具有一个超过 50 的 C 值（直到最近，具有超过 3 的 C 值就已经算是不错的了）。A123 声称其循环寿命超过 1000。此外，该电池具有宽广的使用温度范围，它应该可被用于从北极到热带的任何地方。A123 最近

Figure 5–20 A123 ANR26650M1A cells. Photo courtesy of Albert Van Dalen

图 5–20 A123 ANR26650M1A 电池组。照片由艾伯特•范达伦提供

tropics. A123 have recently produced a pouch-style cell which looks interesting (albeit fairly expensive).

生产了一个看起来很有趣的袋型电池（虽然很昂贵）。

Thundersky LFP160AHA

Thundersky (aka "Winston") have been one of the most popular makers of lithium batteries amongst amateur builders and converters, although at the time of writing there was uncertainty over their future. They are based in China and specialise in large prismatic cells. Their popularity is probably explained by a combination of price and availability. A few years ago, their cells were mostly lithium cobalt oxide ($LiCoO_2$), with a relatively poor C rating (you couldn't suck power out of them too quickly) and like most cells based on this chemistry there were questions over safety. Nominal life was a few hundred cycles.

Their current generation of cells are lithium iron phosphate ($LiFePO_4$ – see Figure 5-21). Like all $LiFePO_4$ cells they have a nominal 3.2 volt output, should be fairly safe i.e. less likely than $LiCoO_2$to explode if punctured. They do have a slightly lower specific energy than other lithium ion chemistries, albeit still much better than for most non-lithium chemistries. This translates into a somewhat shorter range for a given battery pack weight than an equivalent lithium cobalt oxide pack.

雷天 LFP160AHA

雷天（又名"温斯顿"）一直是业余电动汽车的建造者和转换者们最喜欢的锂离子电池制造商之一，虽然在写作本书时还不知它将来会怎样。它的总部设在中国，并专注于大的棱柱形电池。他的知名度较大，也许可以用价格低廉和容易买到来解释。几年前，它的电池主要是钴酸锂（$LiCoO_2$），具有一个相对差的 C 值（您不可以从它们那里过快地提取能量），并且与大多数这种化学物质的电池一样拥有安全问题。其额定寿命为几百个循环。

它目前生产的电池是磷酸铁锂电池（$LiFePO_4$，参见图 5-21）。像所有的磷酸铁锂电池一样，其标称输出电压为 3.2V，也应该是相当安全的，即如果被刺破的话，不太可能像钴酸锂那样爆炸。与其他锂离子电池的化学物质相比，它们有一个较低的比能量，但仍远远好于大多数的非锂化学物质。这意味着对于一个给定电池组的重量，它要比等效的钴酸锂电池组的行程范围稍微短些。

Figure 5–21　Thundersky LFP160AHA 160 Amp-hour Cell (209 × 280 × 65 mm, 5.6 kg).Photo courtesy of Jem Freeman

图 5–21　雷天 LFP160AHA 160A•h 电池（209mm × 280mm × 65mm，5.6kg）。照片由杰姆•弗里曼提供

This cell has a maximum continuous C rating of 3 and a peak of 20. For a 160 Amp-hour cell, this translates into 480 Amps continuous and 3200 Amps peak (it is not clear for how long this peak can be maintained). Like most manufacturers of $LiFePO_4$cells Thundersky claim a cycle life in excess of 2000. If this was achieved, the cells could be charged every weekday for almost 10 years.

此电池的最大连续 C 值为 3，峰值 C 值为 20。对于一个 160A•h 的电池而言，这意味着 480A 的连续输出以及 3200A 的峰值输出（目前尚不清楚峰值可维持多久）。像大多数厂家生产的磷酸铁锂电池，雷天声称其电池的循环寿命超过 2000。如果做到这一点，这些电池每个工作日充电的话，可以工作近 10 年。

Headway

Headway are another Asian manufacturer. Like Thundersky, their current product range is dominated by Lithium Iron Phosphate ($LiFePO_4$) cells i.e. safer, longer life, higher specific power but slightly lower specific energy than Lithium Cobalt Oxide ($LiCoO_2$).

海得威电池

海得威是另一个亚洲电池制造商。像雷天一样，它目前的产品范围主要是磷酸铁锂（$LiFePO_4$）电池，具有更安全，更长的使用寿命，更高的比功率，但比能量要略低于钴酸锂（$LiCoO_2$）电池。

Unlike Thundersky however, Headway produce cylindrical cells (Figure 5-22). At the time of writing they offer a couple cell sizes. Their 38120 cells are interesting. They are all, as the name implies nominally 38 mm (about 1½ inches) in diameter and 120 mm (just under 5 inches) long. All have a nominal voltage of 3.2 and all weigh about 0.3 kg. The 38120S is optimised for specific energy (10 Amp-hours) with a maximum continuous C rating of 15 (150 Amps). The 38120P and

与雷天不同，海得威生产圆柱状电池（图 5-22）。在写作本书时，它可提供几种不同的尺寸。它的 38120 电池是有趣的。顾名思义，其名义直径都为 38mm（约 1.5in）长为 120mm（不到 5in）。所有的标称电压均为 3.2V，所有的重量约 0.3kg。38120S 电池对比能量（10A•h）进行了优化，其最大连续 C 值为 15（150A）。38120P 和 38120HP 电池则优化其他方面。其容量略低，

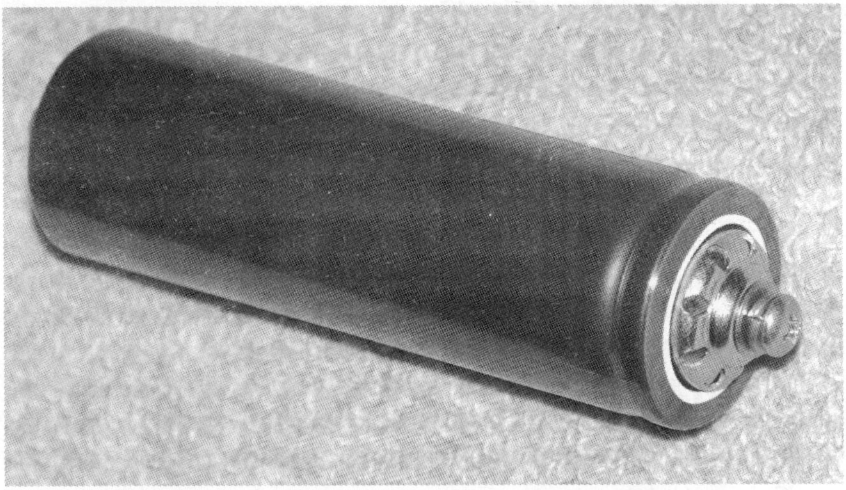

Figure 5–22 Headway 38120 Cell. Photo courtesy Tony Castley
图 5–22 海得威 38120 电池。照片由托尼·卡斯特利提供

38120HP are slanted the other way: capacity is slightly lower at 8 Amp-hours but maximum continuous C rating claimed is 25 (equivalent to 200 Amps, given the slightly reduced capacity). All other things being equal, the 38120P and HP would give you more acceleration away from the lights but 20% less range.

为 8A•h，但其所声称的最大连续 C 值是 25（相当于 200A，但能量略有减少）。在所有其他方面都相同的情况下，38120P 和 HP 在红灯后会提供更大的加速度，但其行程范围将会少 20%。

Unlike the A123 cells discussed earlier, Headway cells are available and affordable, albeit rather less capable than their A123 equivalents.

与前面讨论过的 A123 电池不同，海得威电池可以买到并且也不太贵，但与 A123 同类相比，其输出能量较少。

Sky Energy/CALB

China Aviation Lithium Battery (CALB–formerly Sky Energy) cells (Figure 5-23) are in many respects similar to their Thundersky equivalents: affordable and available lithium iron phosphate prismatics. They even look similar apart from colour. Nominally the Sky Energy/CALB cells have a slightly higher continuous C rating than the Thunderskys (4 rather than 3).

天能 / CALB

中国航空锂电池（CALB - 原天能）电池（图 5-23）在许多方面与雷天的同类相似：价格不太贵，并且有棱柱形磷酸铁锂电池。除了颜色以外，它们看起来甚至很相似。相对于雷天而言，天能 / CALB 电池有稍高的名义连续 C 值（4 而非 3）。

Kokam100216216H

Kokam Cells are lithium polymer type – thin flat

卡马 100216216H

卡马电池是锂聚合物类型——薄的扁平电

cells. The 100216216H (Figure 5-24) is a 3.7 volt 40 Amp-hour cell weighing just over 1 kg. The body of the cell (ignoring the tabs) is about 220 mm high and 215 mm wide – but only about 11mm thick.

池。100216216H（图 5-24）是 3.7V 40A•h 的电池，其重量刚超过 1kg。电池体（不包括接线）高约 220mm，宽为 215mm，但只有约 11mm 厚。

Figure 5–23 Sky Energy/CALB 130 Amp-hour cell. Photo courtesy of Greg Sievert

图 5–23 天能 CALB 130A•h 电池。照片由格雷格 • 西弗特提供

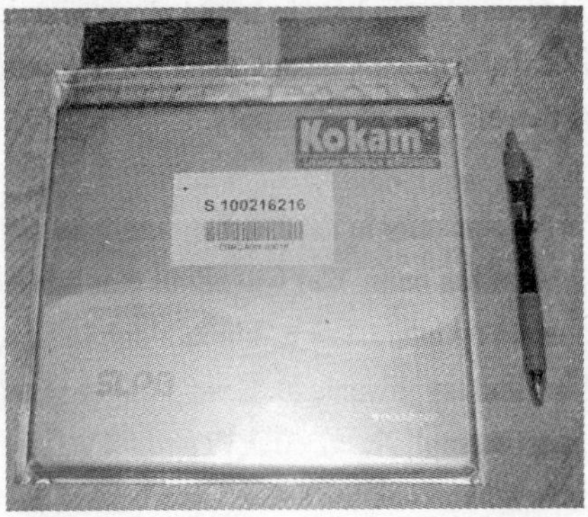

Figure 5–24 Kokam100216216H 40 Amp-hour cell. Photo courtesy of Victor Tikhonov(http://www.metricmind.com)

图 5–24 卡马 100216216H 40A•h 电池。照片由维克托 • 吉洪诺夫提供（http://www.metricmind.com）

The cathode material used in most of the latest Kokam cells is Lithium Nickel Manganese Cobalt Oxide ($LiNiMnNiCoO_2$ – often shortened to "NMC" fortunately). Anecdotally, this chemistry appears to be safer than the older Lithium Cobalt.

最新的卡马电池使用的阴极材料是锂镍锰钴氧化物（$LiNiMnNiCoO_2$，常缩写为"NMC"）。有趣的是，这种化学物质似乎比旧的钴酸锂更安全。

Battery Packs

This is a different approach. All the foregoing examples are single cells with a nominal voltage around 3.2 – 3.7. Several manufacturers offer complete battery packs containing many cells and (usually) a Battery Management System (BMS).

电池组

这是一种不同的方法。上述所有的例子都是额定电压约为 3.2~3.7V 的单个电池。有些制造商提供完整的含有许多单个电池和（通常）一个电池管理系统（BMS）的电池组。

Packs like these would appear to have advantages for use in EVs and HEVs but to date do not appear to have achieved great popularity. There are also horror

这样的电池组在电动汽车和混合动力汽车中使用有其优势，但迄今还没有得到普及。令人感到不安的是，有些电池组的管理系统很

stories circulating about poorly-constructed packs with dubious BMS systems: so it is definitely a case of caveat emptor.

差，它所造成的后果肯定是买者自负。

➢ Lithium Sulphur

➢ 锂硫电池

At the time of writing, Lithium Sulphur (Li-S) cells were only just coming onto the market in sizes, and with a cycle life, to make them practicable for EVs. Information about their performance in EVs is therefore in short supply.

在写作本书时，锂硫（Li-S）电池才刚刚批量上市场不久，并且由于其循环寿命较长，使它们能用于电动汽车。但它们在电动汽车中的表现尚不得而知。

Despite the similarity in naming they are quite different from lithium ion cells. You will recall that lithium ion cells operate by intercalation. Lithium sulphur cells on the other hand are galvanic like lead-acid cells (and like the "lemon battery" illustrated in Figure 5-1). The anode is metallic lithium and the active ingredient of the cathode is sulphur. Lithium reacts violently with water so the electrolyte is an organic solvent. The exciting thing about these cells is their potential specific energy: at least three times that of Lithium Iron Phosphate ($LiFePO_4$). Li-S cells should also turn out to be cheaper in quantity and early indications are that they are safer.

尽管有名称上的相似性，但它们与锂离子电池是相当不同的。您也许还会记得，锂离子电池通过离子的嵌入来工作，但锂硫电池是像铅酸电池那样的原电池（如图 5-1 所示的“柠檬电池”）。其阳极是金属锂，阴极的活性成分是硫。锂遇水会剧烈反应，因此其电解液是有机溶剂。令人兴奋的是，这些电池的潜在比能是磷酸铁锂（$LiFePO_4$）的至少 3 倍。Li-S 电池也应该更便宜，并且目前的迹象是，它们更安全。

➢ Nickel-based Chemistries

➢ 镍基电池

Until recently, most volume manufacturers of hybrid vehicles used either Nickel Cadmium or Nickel Metal Hydride cells. These have a better specific energy than Lead Acid, but far lower specific energy than lithium ion or lithium sulphur. Their characteristics were well known however and they were generally safer, longer lasting and more reliable than earlier generations of lithium-ion cells.

直到最近，大多数混合动力汽车的批量制造商使用的都是镍镉或镍氢电池。这些电池的比能要好于铅酸，但远远低于锂离子或锂硫电池。然而其性能是广为人知的，并且它们一般比早期的锂离子电池更安全、更持久且更可靠。

Nickel Cadmium

镍镉电池

Flooded nickel cadmium (NiCd or "Nicad") cells were used in the Citroen Berlingo Electrique and the Citroen Saxo Electrique. These cells are said to be

富液镍镉（NiCd 或 Nicad）电池被用于雪铁龙的电动柏林阁汽车和雪铁龙的电动盛宝汽车中。人们认为这些电池对“滥用”有很好

very tolerant of abuse and have long cycle life but are now obsolescent. Nickel cadmium cells are in fact banned in Europe for most purposes because cadmium is regarded as a hazardous material from a health-and-safety viewpoint. Nicads are generally robust but do have one or two potential problems. The internal resistance of a nickel cadmium cell drops as it approaches full charge and also drops as temperatures rise. With a powerful but relatively crude charging system, this can lead to thermal runaway, fire and/or explosion. When Nickel cadmium batteries were first introduced into aircraft there was some concern about this. For example in August 1971 a number of people on a Viscount aircraft had a fortunate escape when a Nickel Cadmium battery suffered thermal runaway as a result of an accidental short circuit. The heat from the battery destroyed some flight control pushrods: fortunately the aircraft had just landed. A few minutes earlier and all on board might have been killed.

The chemistry of Nickel Cadmium batteries:

- Cathode: Nickel Oxy-Hydroxide (NiOOH)
- Anode: Cadmium (Cd)
- Electrolyte: (typically) Potassium Hydroxide (KOH). This is an alkali rather than an acid.

Nickel Metal-Hydride

In a world free of patent encumbrances and commercial interest groups, it is possible that nickel metal-hydride might have been the dominant battery chemistry in EVs and HEVs. These batteries have lower specific energy and lower specific power than equivalent lithium chemistry cells but they appear to be safe, reliable, easy to manage, long-lived and (above all) much cheaper.

Nickel metal-hydride batteries have dominated in volume production EVs and HEVs. They are or were used in the following cars amongst others:

的宽容度，且循环寿命长，但现在已经过时。在欧洲，对于大多数用途而言，镍镉电池实际上是被禁止的，因为从健康和安全的角度上看镉是有害的。一般而言，镍镉电池是可靠的，但也有一两个潜在的问题。在充满电时，镍镉电池的内阻下降，并随着温度的升高而下降。如果用一个大功率但相对原始的充电系统来充电，可能会导致热失控、火灾和/或爆炸。当镍镉电池首次被用到飞机上时，相关部门对此就有些担心。例如 1971 年 8 月，在威康特飞机上，镍镉电池由于意外短路而导致热失控，一些人得以逃生。电池的热量摧毁了一些飞行控制推杆。幸运的是，飞机正好降落，使得一些人得以逃生。如果早几分钟，飞机上所有的乘客就有可能死亡。

镍镉电池的化学成分：

- 阴极：羟基氧化镍（NiOOH）
- 阳极：镉（Cd）
- 电解液：（通常）氢氧化钾（KOH）。这是一种碱，而不是一种酸。

镍氢电池

在一个没有专利负担和商业利益集团的世界里，在电动汽车和混合动力汽车领域，镍金属氢化物很可能已经是占主导地位的化学电池。与锂化学电池相比，这些电池具有较低的比能和比功率，但它们似乎更安全、可靠，更易于管理，寿命更长，且便宜得多。

在批量生产的电动汽车和混合动力汽车中，镍氢电池已占主导地位。它们正在或曾在以下汽车中使用：

- Toyota RAV4 EV
- Toyota Prius (Figure 5-25)
- Honda Civic Hybrid
- Honda Insight
- Ford Ranger EV (later versions)
- Ford Escape hybrid
- General Motors EV1 (1999 and on)
- Various Lexus hybrids

- 丰田 RAV4 电动汽车
- 丰田普锐斯（图 5-25）
- 本田思域混合动力车
- 本田 Insight
- 福特 Ranger 电动汽车（较新的车型）
- 福特 Escape 混合动力车
- 通用汽车 EV1 电动汽车（1999 年及其后的车型）
- 各种雷克萨斯混合动力车

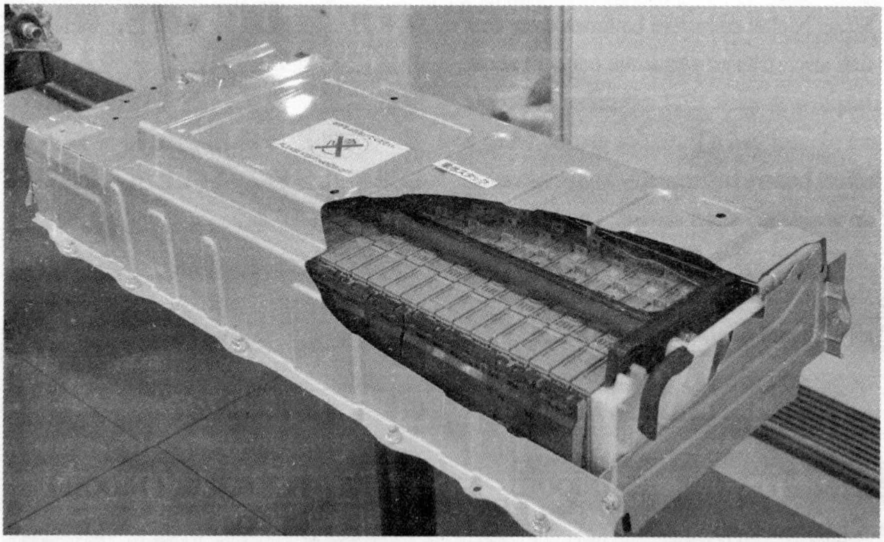

Figure 5–25 Nickel Metal Hydride Battery Pack from a Toyota Prius. Photo courtesy of Randy Hsieh(http://www.flickr.com/photos/palto243)

图 5–25 丰田普锐斯镍金属氢化物电池组。照片由兰迪 • 谢提供（http://www.flickr.com/photos/palto243）

The chemistry is similar to the nickel cadmium but without the cadmium. Cycle life of nickel metal-hydride is better than lead acid but not as good as nickel cadmium.

镍氢电池的化学物质类似于镍镉但无镉，其寿命优于铅酸电池，但不如镍镉电池。

Cathode: Nickel Oxy-Hydroxide (NiOOH)
Anode: A metal alloy capable of storing hydrogen
Electrolyte: (typically) Potassium Hydroxide (KOH)

阴极：羟基氧化镍（NiOOH）
阳极：一种能存储氢气的合金
电解液：通常是氢氧化钾（KOH）

The use of multiple small batteries in parallel as described above for lithium ion is problematic with nickel metal hydride: cell voltages drops slightly as the cell reaches full charge, so if two cells are

如果像前述锂离子电池那样将多个小的镍氢电池并联使用就会遇到下列问题：当电池被完全充满时，其电压略有下降。因此，如果两个电池单元并联充电，被完全充电的电池

charged in parallel, a fully charged cell will draw more current than its undercharged neighbour.

将比其附近的未被完全充电的电池吸入更多的电流。

Considerable controversy has however surrounded large format nickel metal hydride cells. Two things are clear:

然而对大容量的镍氢电池有着相当大的争议。两件事情是清楚的：

Firstly, until recently, nickel metal hydride patents were controlled by a large multinational oil company. Secondly, large format nickel metal-hydride batteries have been virtually unavailable for some years.

首先，直到最近，镍氢电池的专利都是被一家大型跨国石油公司控制的。其次，多年来几乎都没有出现过大容量的镍氢电池。

There have been widespread allegations that these two facts are connected and that the reason was a desire to constrain the growth of electric vehicles. As of early 2010, there have been reports[1] that suggest that the acquisition of Nickel metal-hydride patents by SB LiMotive (a Bosch-Samsung joint venture) might lead to greater availability of these batteries.

人们普遍认为这两个事实是相关联的，并且其理由是希望限制电动汽车的增长。截至 2010 年初，已有报告表明㊀，SB LiMotive（一个博世与三星的合资企业）对镍氢电池专利的收购，可能会使这些电池得到更广泛的应用。

It might not however. The main business of SB LiMotive is the production of lithium ion batteries. It is possible that they might view nickel metal-hydride as a competitor and continue to block its use in EVs. Watch this space.

但也有可能并非如此。SB LiMotive 的主要业务是生产锂离子电池，他们很可能会认为镍氢电池是其竞争对手，从而继续阻止它在电动汽车中的使用。请关注它们的动向。

➢ Molten Salt Batteries

➢ 熔盐电池

Molten Salt batteries, as their name implies, use a salt in liquid form as the electrolyte: and so (normally) operate at high temperatures.

正像其名字所示的那样，熔盐电池使用液态盐作为其电解质，因此它通常在高温下工作。

The pre-eminent molten-salt battery available today (and almost the only one available commercially) is the ZEBRA battery (Figure 5-26). This has a cathode of liquid sodium, and a nickel chloride anode. The electrolyte is Sodium Aluminium Chloride ($NaAlCl_4$). In many ways it is very attractive package; it has good specific power, fairly good specific energy (better than nickel

今天能够买到的绝大多数（几乎是唯一可以买到）的熔盐电池是斑马电池（图 5-26）。它有一个液态钠阴极和一个氯化镍阳极。其电解质是钠氯化铝（$NaAlCl_4$）。在许多方面它都是一个非常有吸引力的电池：它具有良好的比功率，相当好的比能（好于镍氢电池，但不如锂离子电池），在批量生产时是相当便宜的。它从 20 世纪八十年代就开始设计，

1 See for example http://www.sae.org/mags/AEI/7552

㊀ 例如参见 http://www.sae.org/mags/AEI/7552

Figure 5–26 ZEBRA battery.Photo courtesy of John Honniball

图 5–26 ZEBRA 电池。照片由约翰·赫尼博尔提供

metal-hydride but not as good as lithium ion), and if manufactured in quantity would be fairly cheap. The design has been around since the eighties, the active materials are cheap and plentiful, and the cycle life is both proven and good. These batteries can be recharged quite rapidly. They appear to be both safe and robust (neither overcharging nor over-discharging does them much harm).

其活性物质廉价而丰富，循环寿命稳定而良好。这些电池可以被很快地充满。它们似乎既安全又可靠（过充电和过放电对它们都没有多大的伤害）。

Sounds great, but ZEBRA batteries have one big drawback. Their normal operating temperature is around 300degrees Centigrade. This isn't hazardous – the outer surface of the battery is just warm to the touch – but it adds complexity to the control systems and means that the battery normally consumes some power when not in use just to stay at normal operating temperature. The power consumption to keep the battery warm enough to be available for immediate use is modest – about the power required by a domestic incandescent light bulb. The battery can be allowed to cool and freeze, but reheating it takes 12 – 24 hours.

听起来很不错，但 ZEBRA 电池有一个很大的缺点。它们的正常工作温度是 300℃左右。这并不具有危险性，因为电池的外表面感觉起来只是温热而已。但它增加了控制系统的复杂性，并且意味着该电池在不使用时为维持在正常的工作温度上通常也要消耗一些能量，用以维持电池的温度以便在需要时可立即使用的功耗并不太大，大约为家用白炽灯所需的功率。该电池也可以被冷却和冻结，但再加热需要 12~24h。

As mentioned above, the Zebra battery was used in some Modec vans. It has also been used in some conversions.

如上所述，ZEBRA 电池已用于某些 Modec 货车。它也被用在一些电动汽车的改造中。

➤ Batteries - in Conclusion

➤ 电池小结

If you are building an EV/HEV, or converting a car to electric power, perhaps the biggest and most

如果您正在建造一辆电动汽车或者混合动力汽车，或者将一辆汽车转换成电动的，您将

complex decision you will have to make is the choice of battery for your project. If you choose one of the more sophisticated chemistries, the batteries will probably represent the largest single element in the cost of the project. The batteries will undoubtedly be the heaviest and bulkiest component regardless of chemistry.

不得不作出的最大和最复杂的决定或许是为您的项目选择电池。如果您选择一种比较复杂的化学物质，电池可能会成为该项目的成本中花费最大的一项。无论您选择什么样的化学物质，电池无疑将成为最重的和体积最大的组件。

If you choose poorly, no amount of sophistication in the controller, the motor or other components will make up for a battery that cannot store enough energy and/or cannot deliver it fast enough to maintain an adequate speed up a long incline.

如果您选择得不好，没有复杂的控制器，电动机或其他组件会因电池不能储存足够的能量和/或不能以足够快的速度提供动力，而无法在一个长长的上坡中维持一个适当的速度。

It is also the area where you will need to do the most extensive research. For each type of motor, there are only a few manufacturers and models, but the range of potential battery suppliers is vast. There are thousands of varieties of lead acid batteries available. During the research for this book around 40 different brands of lithium ion batteries were identified: and almost all offered a range of sizes and formats.

这也是您需要研究的最广泛的领域。对于每种类型的电动机，只有少数的厂家和型号，但潜在的电池供应商的范围是很大的，有上千个品种的铅酸电池可供选用。在作者为本书做研究时，发现了约 40 种不同品牌的锂离子电池，几乎所有的品牌都提供了一定范围的大小和格式的电池。

We have now looked at the three core elements of an EV drivetrain: motors, controllers and batteries. In the next chapter we will look at the thorny topic of managing your batteries: controlling charge and discharge, monitoring their health and optimising their useful life.

到目前为止，我们已经介绍了电动汽车动力传动系统的三个核心要素：电动机、控制器和电池。在下一章中我们将介绍在电池管理中棘手的话题：控制充电和放电，监控它们的健康状况并优化其可用寿命。

6 Battery Management
电池管理

It is arguable that battery management practices, more than any other factor, determine the safety, practicality and total cost of ownership of an EV or HEV.

电池管理的方法是否比任何其他因素更能决定一辆电动汽车或混合动力汽车拥有者的安全性、实用性和总成本，这是值得商榷的。

A typical lithium ion battery pack for an EV costs thousands of £s. It is easy to destroy it in a single over-charging or over-discharging incident. If that happens after, say, 100 charging cycles, rather than the 2000 cycle design life of the individual cells, the economics of the project are just untenable: it would have been cheaper to convert the vehicle to run on single malt whiskey. Worse, if you are unfortunate, that single overcharging incident could burn out your vehicle and maybe even burn down your house.

一辆典型的电动汽车的锂离子电池组的价格为数万元人民币。它又很容易在某一次过充电或过放电的事故中被毁坏。如果这种情况发生在如100个充电周期而不是单个电池设计寿命的2000个周期之后，该转换项目的经济性就站不住脚了。如果将车辆转换成用单一的麦芽威士忌（译注：一种很贵的高度酒）来驱动也许会更便宜些。更糟糕的是，如果您很不幸的话，某一次过充电事故可能会烧毁您的车子，甚至烧掉您的房子。

Moreover, battery management is an area where there is, for some cell types, little hard research evidence, some anecdotal evidence and much heated debate. We will nevertheless attempt to pick our way through the minefield.

此外，对于某些类型的电池而言，电池管理是一个还没有过硬的研究证据的领域，有些只有零散的证据并会有很大的争论。然而，我们将尝试通过这个“地雷阵”。

Battery management comes down to three things:

- How you manage the charging process.
- How you manage the discharging process.
- How you manage long periods of inactivity.

电池管理归结为三点：

- 如何管理充电过程
- 如何管理放电过程
- 如何管理长时间的闲置

So as part of this chapter we will discuss chargers (as physical bits of kit). If your 12 volt SLI battery won't start your IC engine, you can acquire a charger for a few pounds almost anywhere, connect up and switch on and your battery will charge up. Charging the battery of an EV is sadly not so straightforward. The wrong charger, or the right charger wrongly used will kill your battery pack.

因此，作为本章的一部分，我们将讨论充电器（它是这一套件中的物理部件）。如果12V的起动电池无法起动您的内燃机，您可以（几乎在任何地方）花几十元买到一个充电器，将它连接好并打开开关后，就可以对电池充电了。可悲的是，对电动汽车电池的充电并没有那么简单。错误的充电器或不正确地使用充电器都会毁坏电池组。

In this chapter we will build up slowly

- Terminology
- General principles
- Managing single cells
- Managing entire battery packs
- Pack balancing/equalisation
- Automated battery management systems (BMSs)
- Estimating remaining charge ("fuel gauges")
- Fast charging
- Real world chargers

在本章中，我们将逐步阐述

- 术语
- 一般原则
- 管理单个电池
- 管理整个电池组
- 组内平衡 / 均衡
- 自动电池管理系统（BMS）
- 估算剩余电量（"油量计"）
- 快速充电
- 现实世界中的充电器

We will focus largely on lead acid and lithium ion cells as these are by far the most common types in EVs being built today. We'll also touch on what little is known of the latest lithium sulphur cells. Many of the same principles carry over to other cell chemistries.

我们将侧重于铅酸和锂离子电池，因为这些是目前最常见的用于建造电动汽车的电池。我们也将涉及那些鲜为人知的最新的锂硫电池。许多相同的原则也适用于其他化学物质的电池。

First of all, though a word of caution. There is real-world in-service experience with lead acid propulsion batteries in cars going back to the end of the 19th century. Experience of Nickel metal-hydride (NiMh) batteries in various mass-produced Citroen, Peugeot and Toyota EVs goes back to the mid '90s.

首先要强调的一点是谨慎。用铅酸电池驱动的汽车，其实际使用经历出现在 19 世纪末。镍氢（NiMH）电池在各种大规模生产的雪铁龙、标致、丰田电动汽车中的使用经历可以追溯到 20 世纪 90 年代中期。

Lithium ion is different. There are billions of small format lithium ion cells in laptops, mobile phones, and even model aircraft all over the world, but the use of long strings of big lithium ion cells in electric vehicles is a recent phenomenon. With few exceptions (such as Modec vans, Tesla and some Chinese manufacturers), the use of these battery packs in EVs has been pioneered by individual enthusiasts. That situation is changing with a number of volume manufacturers beginning to offer EVs powered by lithium ion cells: but most of the world's experience of large format lithium ion batteries in EVs has been accumulated since about 2005 and even by 2010 didn't amount to much. Furthermore, lithium ion cells are not all the same. As we discussed in the previous chapter, lithium

锂离子电池则有所不同。在世界各地的笔记本电脑、手机，甚至飞机模型中使用着数以十亿计的小型锂离子电池，但在电动汽车中使用长串的大型锂离子电池则是一个新的现象。除了少数例外（如 MODEC 货车、特斯拉电动车和一些中国制造商），在电动汽车中使用这些电池组率先由个人爱好者做出。随着一些批量制造商开始提供用锂离子电池供电的电动汽车，这种情况正在发生变化。但大部分大型锂离子电池在电动汽车中的实际使用经验都是在 2005 年后获得的，甚至直到 2010 年，这类经验的数量也不多。此外，锂离子电池并不都相同。正如我们在前面的章节中所讨论的那样，钴酸锂和磷酸铁锂电池也许看起来相似，但它们的工作电压不同，并且在处理不当时，它们的表现也不同（钴

cobalt and lithium iron phosphate cells may look similar but they operate at different voltages and behave differently when mistreated (lithium cobalt cells are less stable than lithium iron phosphate).

酸锂电池还不如磷酸铁锂电池稳定）。

➢ Terminology

Firstly then, a reminder of terminology. You will recall from the chapter on batteries that the fundamental unit in a battery is the cell, each cell having an anode, a cathode and some form of electrolyte. The nominal cell voltage is a factor of the chemistry: about 2 volts for a lead-acid cell, 3.2 volts for a lithium iron phosphate cell and maybe 1.2 volts for nickel metal hydride.

A battery is as a collection of cells usually connected in series, but sometimes a combination of series and parallel. A normal 12 volt automotive SLI (Starter, Lighting, Ignition) battery is 6 individual lead acid cells in series; these short strings packaged and sold as a single unit are sometimes referred to as monoblocks. Many EVs are powered by strings of monoblocks (e.g. 10 x 12 volt batteries for a nominal 120 volts). Others are powered by series strings of individual cells (e.g. 50 x 3.3 volts for a nominal 165 volts). Herein I will refer to a vehicle-scale set of monoblocks or cells as a battery pack or a traction pack.

➢ 术语

首先，我们将复习一下术语。在第 5 章中曾讲过，电池中的基本单元是电池元，每个电池元有一个阳极（负极），一个阴极（正极）和某种形式的电解质。电池元的额定电压是由其化学物质决定的：铅酸蓄电池约 2V，磷酸铁锂电池是 3.2V，镍氢电池也许是 1.2V。

一个电池通常是由电池元串联连接成为一个集合体，但有时是串联和并联的组合。一个额定电压为 12V 汽车的 SLI（起动、点火、照明）电池是由 6 个铅酸电池元串联而成的，它们被包装在一起作为一个单元销售，有时被称为一个单块。很多电动汽车都是由这种单块的电池组驱动的（如 10 个 12V 的电池的额定电压为 120V）。有些则用单个的电池串联起来驱动（如 50 个 3.3V 的电池串联起来的额定电压为 165V）。在本书中我将把车辆规模的单块或电池组直接称为电池组或驱动电池组。

➢ General Principles

The problem with managing battery packs is that each cell potentially needs treating differently, but for practical purpose a pack must be charged and discharged as a unit using the same current/time profile. The problem gets worse as the number of cells in the pack grows. As if this wasn't enough to contend with, there are a number of complicating factors.

➢ 一般原则

电池组管理所遇到的问题是，每个电池单元可能都需要区别对待。但为实用起见，一个电池组必须作为单个单元用相同的电流来充电和放电。随着电池组中电池单元数量的增加，该问题将变得更糟。如果这还不足以令您头痛的话，还有许多其他复杂的因素。

Complicating factor no 1: voltage and state of charge

Anyone who has messed around with the 12 volt

复杂因素 1：电压和荷电状态

任何研究过传统的车用 12V 电池的人都能直

electrics in a conventional car will have an intuitive understanding that open circuit voltage (voltage when there is no current flowing) varies with state of charge (SOC). Indeed the rested open circuit voltage (OCV) of a lead acid battery varies roughly linearly with state of charge (“rested” = “hasn’t been charged or discharged recently”). See for example Figure 6-1 which is based on data from a Trojan battery.

观地觉察到电池的开路电压（没有电流流过时的电压）随荷电状态（SOC）而变。事实上，铅酸电池的静态开路电压（OCV）与荷电状态大致呈线性变化（“静态”即“近期没有被充电或放电”）。例如图 6-1 是从一个特洛伊电池的数据中得出的。

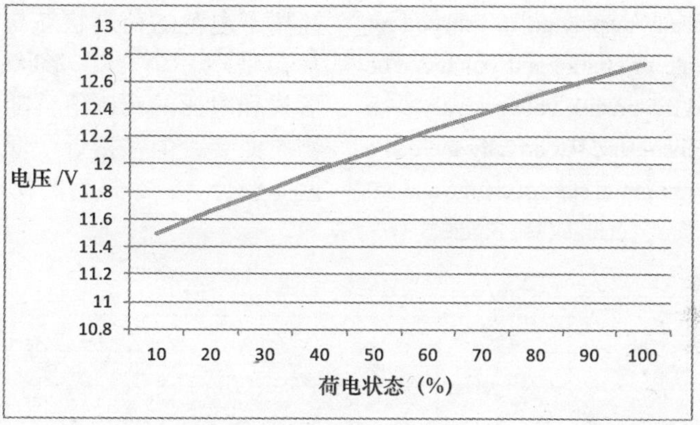

Figure 6–1 Voltage versus State of Charge for a Rested Lead Acid Cell

图 6–1 静态铅酸电池电压与荷电状态的关系曲线

Not all cell chemistries behave like this however. Nickel based cells (nickel-cadmium, nickel-metal hydride) exhibit a small voltage drop near 100% state of charge (Figure 6-2). This is seriously con-

不过，并非所有的电池化学物质都有这种关系。镍基电池（镍镉、镍金属氢化物）在接近 100% 荷电状态时表现出一个很小的电压下降（图 6-2）。这对一个曾经使用过铅酸

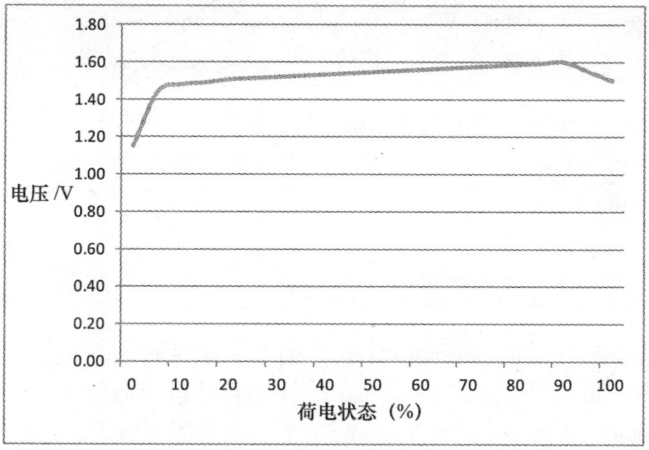

Figure 6–2 Typical Voltage versus State of Charge for Nickel Metal Hydride Cell

图 6–2 镍金属氢化物电池的典型电压与荷电状态曲线

fusing for anyone used to lead acid batteries. Note that Figure 6-1 is not directly comparable with Figure 6-2, because Figure 6-1 refers to a battery, and Figure 6-2 to a single cell.

电池的人而言是很大的困惑。请注意，图 6-1 并不直接对应于图 6-2，因为图 6-1 是指一个电池组，而图 6-2 则是指一个单一的电池单元。

With NiMh cells, once the cell voltage starts to drop at the end of the charging cycle, cell temperature and cell internal pressure start to rise rapidly.

对镍氢电池而言，一旦电池电压在充电周期结束时开始下降，则电池温度和内压将迅速上升。

Lithium ion cells typically display an "S" shaped relationship between state of charge and voltage. The exact form of this and the precise voltages vary with cell construction and chemistry, but broadly there is a pronounced knee near minimum state of charge and another near maximum state of charge (See Figure 6-3).

锂离子电池的荷电状态与电压之间的关系通常会呈现一个"S"形状。这一形状的确切形式和电压的精确值会随电池的结构和化学物质而变，但在接近最低及最高荷电状态附近一般会有一个显著的拐点（图 6-3）。

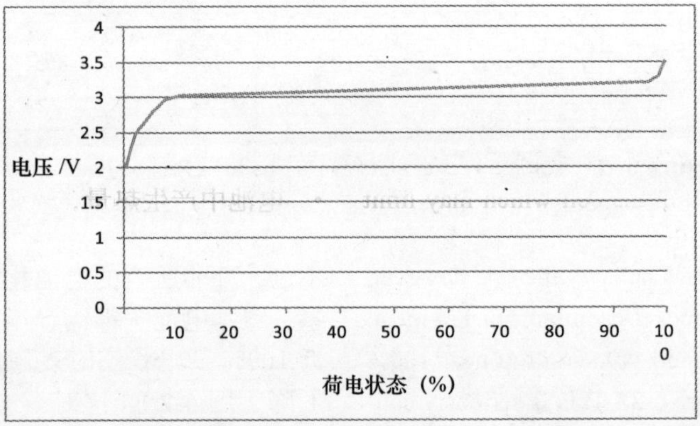

Figure 6–3 Typical Voltage versus State of Charge for Lithium Ion Cell

图 6–3 锂离子电池的典型电压与荷电状态曲线

Note that voltage versus state-of-charge curves are usually a similar shape, but not exactly the same values, for charge and discharge.

请注意，在充电和放电时，电压与荷电状态曲线通常具有相似的形状，但不完全相同。

Complicating factor no 2: Internal Resistance

复杂因素 2：内阻

All cells exhibit some degree of internal resistance. From the outside, this behaves as if you had a perfect battery connected in series with a low resistance. If the internal resistance is (say) 0.001 ohm then the terminal voltage of the cell will drop

所有的电池都表现出某种程度的内电阻。从外面看，这就像您有一个完美的电池再串联上一个低阻值电阻。如果内电阻是（比方说）0.001Ω，那么在 100A 的电流下，电池的端电压就会下降 0.1V（电压 = 电流 × 电阻：

0.1 volts at 100 amps (Volts = Amps x Resistance: 0.001 Ω x 100A = 0.1 volts: (Figure 6-4).

0.001 Ω × 100A = 0.1V，图 6-4）。

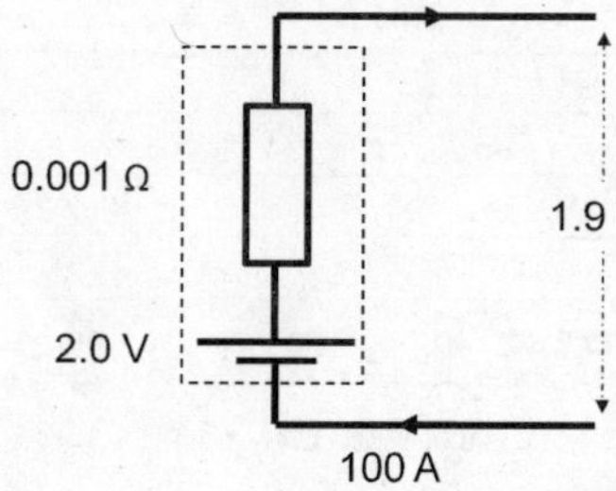

Figure 6–4 What internal resistance feels like (dotted rectangle is cell boundary)

图 6–4 内电阻的概念（虚线框是电池的边界）

Cells are not of course fitted with discrete resistors: the resistive behaviour is a side-effect of cell construction and cell parameters.

当然电池内并没有接入一个分立的电阻，电阻的表现是电池结构和电池参数的一个副产品。

This drop in voltage as the current increases has four regrettable side effects:

随着电流的增加，在内阻中会产生电压降，它有 4 个令人遗憾的副作用：

- Heat is generated in the cell which may limit the maximum continuous current.
- There is a drop in the efficiency of the cell (ratio of power out on discharge to power in on charge).
- The available pack voltage drops just when you need it: when power requirements are high.
- Cell voltage ceases to be a reliable indicator of state of charge when the battery is being charged or discharged.

- 电池中产生热量，这可能会限制最大的连续电流
- 电池的效率下降（效率为放电时的输出功率与充电时的输入功率之比）
- 当您需要大的输出功率时，可用的电池组电压反而下降
- 当对电池进行充电或放电时，电池的电压不再是一个可靠的荷电状态指示器

The last one (cell voltage useless for measuring state of charge when there is current flowing) is a major issue for battery management. Consider for example Figure 6-3. This showed the voltage versus state-of-charge curve for a specific lithium ion cell at a 1 C discharge rate (e.g. 40 Amps for a 40 Amp hour cell, 100 Amps for a 100 Amp hour cell etc).

最后一个问题是当有电流流过时，电池电压不能用于测量荷电状态，这是电池管理的一个主要问题。例如在图 6-3 中给出了一个特定的锂离子电池在 1 C 放电率（即对一个 40A • h 的电池为 40A，100A • h 的电池为 100A 等）时，电压与荷电状态的关系曲线。

Figure 6-5 is Figure 6-3 repeated with the addition of a second voltage versus state-of-charge curve

图 6-5 复制了图 6-3 并加入一个在 0.1 C 放电率时电压与荷电状态的关系曲线（对 40A • h

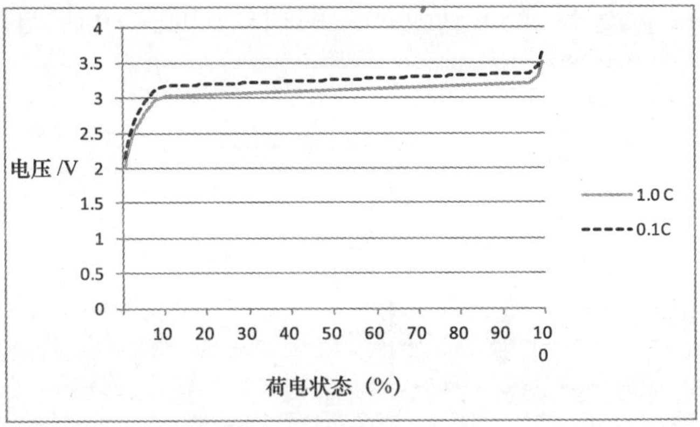

Figure 6–5 Voltage versus state of charge for a lithium cell at 0.1C & 1.0C discharge rates

图 6–5 锂电池在 0.1C 和 1.0C 放电率时电压与荷电状态的关系曲线

at 0.1 C (4 Amps for a 40 Amp hour cell, 10 Amps for a 100 Amp hour cell).

的电池为 4A，对 100A • h 的电池为 10A 等）。

Note that in this example the terminal voltage at around 95% charge with a 1 C current is almost exactly the same as the terminal voltage at 10% charge with a 0.1 C current. In other words, to a voltmeter an almost fully charged cell of this type at high current is indistinguishable from a largely-discharged cell at low current.

请注意，在本例中 1 C 电流在 95% 的荷电状态时的端电压几乎与 0.1C 电流在 10% 的荷电状态时的端电压完全一样。换言之，一个电压表无法区分哪一个是在高电流时几乎完全充满电的电池，哪一个是在低电流时几乎完全放电的电池。

Misunderstandings here have reportedly led to absurd situations where poorly-designed automated systems have unnecessarily restricted high rate discharges. A low voltage cut off is normally specified for lithium ion cells. Suppose for the sake of illustration we add to the chart of voltage versus state of charge for our typical cell, the curve for a 4 C discharge (400 Amps for a 100 amp-hour pack) - Figure 6-6.

据报道，这种误解已导致了以下荒唐的情况，即设计不良的自动化系统不必要地限制了高倍率放电。低电压时的终止放电通常适用于锂离子电池。为说明起见在典型电池中添加了一个 4 C 放电率时的电压与荷电状态的关系曲线（对 100A • h 的电池为 400A），如图 6-6 所示。

Suppose that for this cell the manufacturer specifies a cut off (minimum) voltage of 2.0, and to add a margin for error, a 2.6 volt limit is going to be enforced. If you look at Figure 6-6, you will see that the 2.6 volt limit will be reached at 50% state-of-charge under a 4 C load. Does this mean that you just cannot use the 4C capability of the cell below 50% charge?

假设这种电池的制造商规定的截止电压（最小电压）为 2.0V，并且为防止出错而增加一个余量，则一个 2.6V 的电压限制将被强制执行。如果您观察一下图 6-6，就会看到在 4C 的负载下只要 50% 的荷电状态就能达到 2.6V 的电压限制。这是否意味着在低于 50% 的荷电状态下您就不能使用 4 C 的负载？

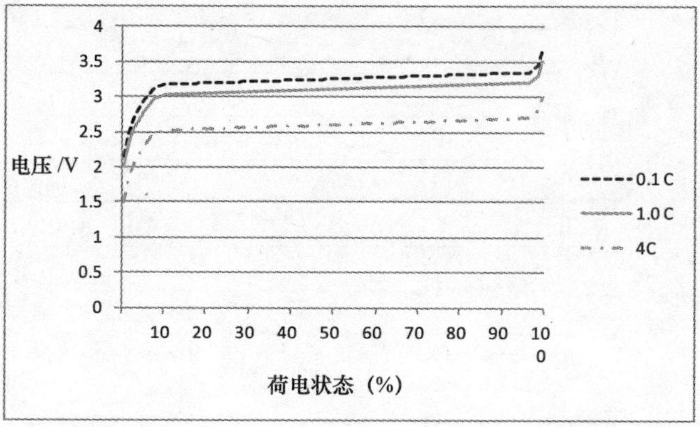

Figure 6–6 Voltage versus state of charge for a lithium cell with 4C discharge rate added

图 6–6 锂电池在 4C 放电率时电压与荷电状态的关系曲线

By no means. The cut off voltage will be specified at a given discharge rate (say 0.3 C). At other discharge rates it is meaningless. We will have to come up with another way of figuring out when the battery pack is close to exhausted.

完全不是。截止电压是在一个给定的放电率（例如 0.3C）时确定的。在其他的放电率下，它是没有意义的。我们将用另一种方式来得出在什么时候电池组将接近枯竭。

It gets worse. As discussed earlier, different cells in the same pack will have different internal resistances, so even with the same current they will exhibit different voltage drops. A voltmeter is therefore an unreliable indication even as an indication of differences in state of charge for different cells in the same pack when the pack is under load.

更糟糕的是，正如前面所讨论的，在同一个电池组中不同的电池将有不同的内电阻。因此，即使电流相同，它们也将表现出不同的电压降。所以在负载状态下，即使在显示同一个电池组中不同电池的荷电状态的差异时，电压表也不是一个可靠的指示。

Complicating factor no 3: Voltage settling

It continues to get worse. It turns out that when a charging current is shut off, the voltage may not stabilise immediately: the voltage will increase short term as the effect of internal resistance goes away, but may then drop back over a period of minutes or hours. Figure 6-7 is an example[1].

复杂因素 3：电压稳定

情况将继续恶化。事实证明，当充电电流被切断时，电压可能不会立即稳定：由于内阻效应的消失，电压在短期内会增加，但可能过了几分钟或几小时，电压又会落回。图 6-7 是一个这样例子[⊖]。

The plot starts a few seconds after the charger is disconnected (it was run for just a couple of minutes on a partially-charged battery). Even after 24 hours the

该曲线在充电器断开几秒钟后开始（它只对部分充电的电池再充了几分钟的电）。甚至在 24h 后电压也还没有完全回到静态时的值。

1 I am indebted to Compass Marine (http://www.pbase.com/mainecruising/battery_state_of_charge) for these data

⊖ 我要感谢北斗海洋公司 (http://www.pbase.com/mainecruising/battery_state_of_charge) 为我提供的这些数据。

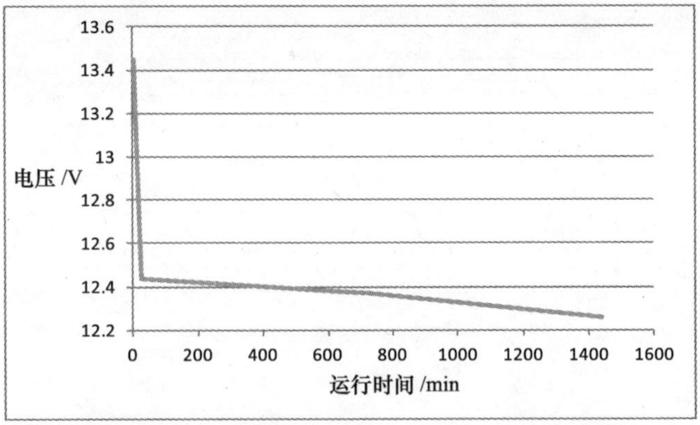

Figure 6–7 Voltage Settling in Lead Acid battery

图 6–7 铅酸电池电压的稳定过程

voltage had not quite settled back to its fully rested value. The reverse happens on discharge (the voltage bounces back a bit after a discharge current is turned off). This plot is for a lead-acid cell, but lithium ion cells also exhibit voltage changes for a period after current ceases to flow (albeit not necessarily with the same shaped recovery curve).

在放电时会出现相反的情况，即在放电电流断开后电压会小幅反弹。该图是针对铅酸蓄电池的，但锂离子电池在充电电流断开后，也在一定时间内表现出电压的变化，尽管不一定具有相同形状的恢复曲线。

You could think of charging as being analogous to the delivery of boxes at a warehouse: the charging process is like getting all the boxes offloaded and stacked in the loading bay, but the process isn't wholly complete until the boxes have been moved from the loading bay to the shelves. This is settling.

您可以将充电过程想象为在仓库中运送箱子。充电过程就像把所有的箱子卸下并在卸货区堆放，但在箱子从装卸区放到货架上之前这个过程并没有全部完成。这就是稳定过程。

Complicating factor no 4: tolerance to over-charging

复杂因素 4：对过充电的耐受性

Overcharging is leaving the charger hooked up and working after the cell is fully charged. We will discuss this in more detail later in the context of charging single cells, but tolerance to overcharge has a major effect on battery management. Some cell types (flooded lead acid for example) are fairly tolerant to the continued presence of a charging current after the cell has been fully charged. Other cell types (notably lithium ion) are destroyed by single incident of over-charging and may in the process become a fire

过充电是在电池被完全充电后还将充电器连接着并继续工作。我们将在后面阐述单个电池充电的情况下更详细地讨论这一问题。但电池对过充电的耐受性对电池管理有重大影响。电池已充满电后，某些类型的电池（例如富液铅酸电池）对充电电流的继续存在有较好的容忍性。另一些类型的电池（尤其是锂离子电池）将会由于单次的过充电而被毁，并有可能在这个过程中成为火灾隐患。还有一些电池（如阀控

hazard. Yet others (e.g. valve regulated lead acid – VRLA i.e. Gel and AGM cells) are impaired but not immediately destroyed by over-charging.

式密封铅酸电池——VRLA 即凝胶及 AGM 电池）虽然不会由于过充电而被立即摧毁，但它们的性能将被削弱。

Tolerance to overcharge is a helpful characteristic because you can charge a long string of cells together until all are fully charged, safe in the knowledge that the cells that reach full charge earlier than the others will tolerate the ongoing charge current.

耐过充电是一个非常有用的特性，因为这样的话您就可以对一长串的电池进行充电，直到所有的电池都被充满，并且这样做是安全的，因为先被完全充满的电池能够容忍对其他电池继续充电的电流。

Complicating factor no 5: Tolerance to under-charging

By “under-charging” is meant continuous partial charging, so that the cell never reaches maximum charge. Many (but, anecdotally, not all) lithium ion cell types are tolerant of under-charging. Lead acid cells of all types degrade if treated in this way due to sulphation (a build up of lead sulphate on the cell’s lead plates).

复杂因素 5：对欠充电的耐受性

所谓“欠充电”是指持续的部分充电，使该电池单元永远达不到最大荷电状态。许多(但据说不是所有）锂离子电池类型能够容忍欠充电，但所有类型的铅酸电池由于硫酸盐的产生（在电池的铅板上硫酸铅的积聚），在欠充电时其性能会下降。

Complicating factor no 6: Tolerance to over-discharging

That is, running the cell too far down. In extreme cases a weak cell in a large pack may be driven into “cell reversal” (in effect charged the wrong way) as stronger cells continue to drive a discharge current through it when it is exhausted. No cell types enjoy this kind of treatment, and some types are destroyed by it. (The particular problems of large packs are discussed in detail later).

复杂因素 6：对过放电的耐受性

过放电是指对电池放电放得太深。在极端的情况下，当一个大电池组中的强势电池持续放电时，放电电流会通过弱势电池，因此已耗尽的弱势电池可能会被放电到“电池逆转”（实际上是在反方向上充电）。没有任何类型的电池会接受这样的反充电，并且有些类型的电池将被这样的反充电摧毁（大电池组的特殊问题将在后面详细讨论）。

Complicating factor no 7: Tolerance to under-discharge

Amongst drivers of conventional IC engined cars there is a range of practice in refilling the fuel tank. Some drivers routinely run the tank as low as they dare. Others fill up at weekends, others when the tank gets down to a quarter. Some put in a fixed quantity (say £20 worth) on pay day. There is probably an actuary somewhere who never fills the tank more than ¼ full to minimise the loss of inter-

复杂因素 7：对欠放电的耐受性

对驾驶传统内燃机发动机汽车的驾驶人，他们加油的习惯并不相同。有些驾驶人经常将油用得少得不能再少。有些在周末加油，有些在油箱还有四分之一时加油。有些人在发薪水的当天加一定量的油（比如 200 块钱）。有的驾驶人也可能是个精算师，他从来不会将油箱装超过 1/4 的油量，以尽量减少油箱中油量价值的利息损失。

est on the value of the fuel in the tank.

Similarly, different users of battery-operated power tools or even mobile phones may have different battery-charging habits. Some will recharge only when the battery is exhausted, others will recharge at every opportunity.

同样，用电池供电工具的使用者（如电动汽车驾驶人），甚至是手机的用户，也有不同的电池充电习惯。有些人只有当电池电量耗尽时才会充电，有些人则会抓住每一个机会来充电。

In EVs, these charging habits can affect the health of the battery pack. In the context of batteries, "depth of discharge" (DoD) expresses the amount of electrical energy drawn from a cell as a percentage of the energy available from a fully charged cell: so for example a cell at 75% DoD has already delivered ¾ of the energy available from the fully-charged cell. This is analogous to a fuel tank that has been run down to the ¼ full mark[1].

在电动汽车中，这些充电的习惯可能会影响电池组的健康。在电池领域，"放电深度"（DOD）表示从一个电池单元中提取的电能占该电池完全充电时可用能量的百分比。例如：一个处于75%放电深度的电池，表示已从完全充电的电池提取了3/4的能量。这与油箱中仅剩下1/4的油量相似[㊀]。

Lead acid and lithium ion cells appear to thrive on under-discharging. One lithium ion cell manufacturer claims a cycle life of 5000 at 70% maximum DoD on each cycle, but only 3000 at 80% DoD. This is a difference in lifetime energy delivery of around 45%. In other words, it makes sense to buy a bigger battery pack than you need and use a smaller percentage of its capacity on each cycle. The longer life will more than pay back the higher cost. The picture is more complex for nickel-based cells. It used to be received wisdom that some types of cell should be fully discharged before recharging. The so-called "memory effect" is said to have arisen from NASA experience with nickel-cadmium cells in satellites although I

铅酸和锂离子电池似乎乐于欠放电。有一家锂离子电池制造商声称，每次都工作在70%的最大放电深度时的循环寿命为5000，但在80%的放电深度时的循环寿命只有3000。这导致了在一个生命周期中所提供的总能量有45%左右的差别。换句话说，买一个比您所需的容量更大的电池组，并且在每个周期中仅用其总能量的一个较小的比例是很有意义的。更长的使用寿命将足以补偿多付出的较高的成本，但对镍基电池而言，情况将更为复杂。一个曾被广泛认可的经验是，有些类型的电池应该在完全放电后再充电。据说这种所谓的"记忆效应"来自于美国航空航天局在卫星上

1 Confusingly 100% is sometimes considered to be "energy available when new" or the nominal capacity of the cell type, rather than the current actual capacity of the cell in question, (see for example Electric Vehicle Technology Explained by James Larminie and John Lowry) so under this convention an old cell that has suffered a 20% loss of capacity will be exhausted at 80% DoD. Not everyone appears to use the term this way however.

㊀ 令人困惑的是，100%有时被认为是"新电池所具有的能量"，或者这种类型电池的标称容量，而不是该电池现在的实际容量（如詹姆斯·拉米尼尔和约翰·洛瑞所著的《电动汽车技术说明》）。因此在这一惯例下，一部失去了20%容量的旧手机在80%的放电深度时就完全耗尽了。然而，并不是每个人都用这种方式来使用这一术语。

have not been able to find the original paper. In any case, subsequent experience suggests that whilst this effect occurs, its significance has been exaggerated. One paper for example noted that "...a regular recharge (+ 10% overcharge) restores the usual shape of the voltage-time curve and the capacity..." [1]

➢ Managing Single Cells (or Monoblocks)

This section will apply the principles we have just discussed (internal resistance, settling, tolerance to over/under charge/discharge) in the context of the management of individual cells, starting with the old familiar lead-acid cell.

Lead Acid

Most people reading this book will be familiar with the cheap and cheerful battery chargers used to charge the lead-acid SLI (Starter, Lighting, Ignition) battery in a conventional IC car. This is usually just a constant voltage source taken from the mains, courtesy of a transformer and a rectifier (Figure 6-8). The alternator charges SLI batteries on the move in much the same way; by applying a voltage just a little above the battery voltage (Figure 6-9). This causes a charging current to flow. As the difference between the battery voltage and the applied charger/alternator voltage diminishes, the current falls off to a low value.

镍镉电池的使用经验，但我一直没能找到原始文件。然而，后来的经验表明，虽然有这种效应产生，但其重要性被夸大了。例如，有篇论文指出，“……定期的充电（+10% 的过充电）可将电压－时间曲线和电池容量恢复到常态……”㊀。

➢ 管理单个（或单块）电池

本节将把我们刚才所讨论的原则（内阻、电压稳定、对过 / 欠充 / 放电的耐受性）应用于单个电池的管理。我们将从大家熟悉的铅酸电池开始。

铅酸电池

大多数阅读本书的人都会熟悉一种廉价且好用的电池充电器，它用来为传统的内燃机汽车的铅酸 SLI（起动、点火、照明）电池充电。这通常只是一个来自市电并通过变压器和整流器整流后的恒定电压源（图 6-8）。交流发电机也以大致相同的方式在运行中对起动电池充电：施加一个略高于电池电压的电压（图 6-9）。这就会使得充电电流得以流动。随着电池的电压与所施加的充电器 / 交流发电机电压之间差异的减少，电流将下降到一个较低的值。

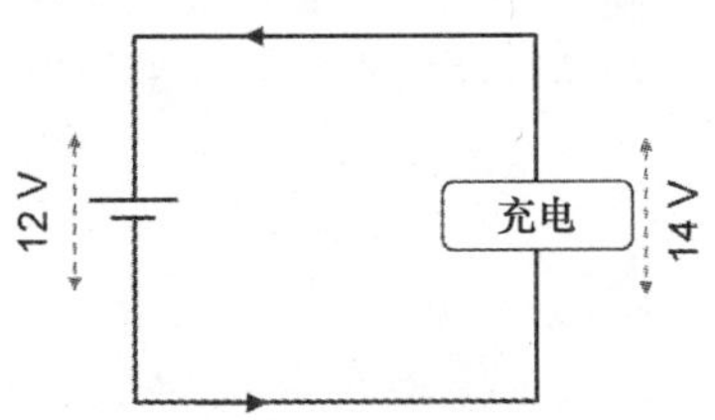

Figure 6–8 Simple Charger for lead-acid SLI battery

图 6–8 SLI（起动）铅酸电池的简易充电器

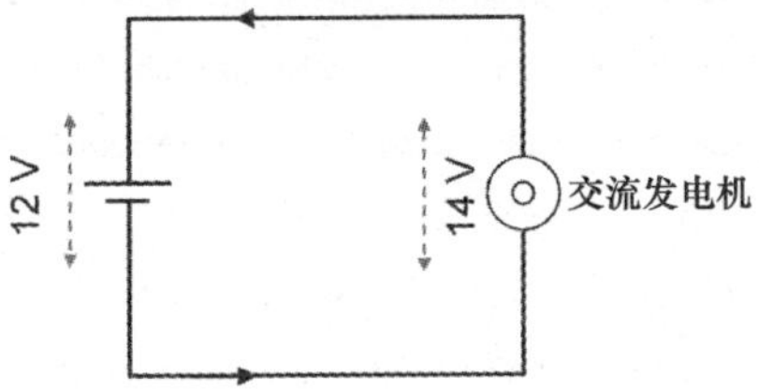

Figure 6–9 Alternator charging SLI battery

图 6–9 发动机充电的 SLI 起动电池

1 "The 'memory effect' of nickel oxide electrodes: electrochemical and mechanical aspects" G. Davolio and E. Soragni from Journal of Applied Electrochemistry Vol 28 no 12 1997.

㊀ G · 金永昌和 E · 索拉格尼，“镍氧化物电极的‘记忆效应’：从电化学和机械方面的解释”，应用电化学学报，1997 年，第 28 卷第 12 期。

You will recall from the chapter on batteries that there are three types of lead-acid battery:

第 5 章曾说过，铅酸电池主要有三种类型：

- Flooded,
- Absorbed Glass Mat (AGM),
- Gel.

- 富液
- 吸收玻璃垫（AGM）
- 凝胶

The second two (AGM and Gel) are often grouped together as "VRLA" (valve regulated lead-acid) batteries. Single lead-acid cells of all types are fairly easy to charge. Regardless of type (flooded, AGM or gel), they share some characteristics which we tend to take for granted because of long familiarity with SLI batteries. Among other things:

最后两个（AGM 和凝胶）通常被统称为"VRLA"（阀控式密封铅酸）电池。所有类型的单个铅酸电池都很容易充电。无论什么类型（富液、AGM 或凝胶），它们都拥有某些共同特征。因为长时间使用 SLI 电池，我们往往认为这些特征是理所当然的。它们包括：

- Rested open circuit voltage is a fairly good indication of state of charge (this is not true of all cell chemistries – compare for example the Lead acid battery discharge curve depicted in Figure 6-1 and the Nickel metal-hydride curve in Figure 6-2).
- They can accept high currents so are not easily charged at a dangerous rate.

- 静置开路电压是一个相当不错的荷电状态标志，但并非所有化学物质的电池都如此。例如，比较图 6-1 所示的铅酸电池和图 6-2 所示的镍氢电池的放电曲线。
- 它们可以接受大电流，因而不容易在一个危险的速度下被充电。

These two effects (increasing voltage with increasing state of charge and a high charge capacity) mean that lead-acid cells are not very prone to thermal runaway (accidental overcharging at a dangerous rate causing an accelerating temperature rise). Also, whilst different manufacturers may specify different charging profiles[1] they are tolerant of non standard profiles.

这两种效应（电压随着荷电状态的增加而增加以及高的充电容量）意味着铅酸电池并不容易出现热失控（即在一个危险的充电率下意外地过充电引起温度的加速上升）。此外，虽然不同的制造商可以指定不同的充电率[⊖]，但它们对非标准的充电方式是相当宽容的。

Lead-acid cells do exhibit several limitations though. Firstly if they are not regularly fully charged they tend to "sulphate" that is lead sulphate crystals form on the lead plates. This irreversibly reduces the capacity of a battery. Secondly they exhibit a fairly substantial rate of self-

然而，铅酸电池确实有些局限性。首先，如果它们没有经常被充满电，则它们容易生成"硫酸盐"，即在铅板上形成的硫酸铅晶体。这将不可逆地降低了电池的容量。其次，它们有可观的自放电率，即，只是将它们放在架子上，并没有连上任何负载，它们也会失

1 Charge Profiles are discussed later

⊖ 有关充电率问题将在后面讨论。

discharge; that is, they lose charge just sitting on the shelf with nothing connected to them.

去电荷。

The combination of these two means that lead-acid cells left idle for long periods will degrade. The same thing happens to cells that undergo short partial charges without ever being fully charged.

这两者结合在一起意味着长时间闲置铅酸蓄电池会降低它们的性能。同样的事情发生在经过短期部分充电但没有完全充满的电池中。

Flooded lead-acid cells exhibit another very useful characteristic: they are not seriously impaired by short periods of mild overcharging (they start gassing which in extreme cases creates risk of explosion, and they lose electrolyte, but they are not immediately and permanently damaged by overcharge like lithium ion batteries). Flooded batteries are designed to vent easily if overcharged, and there is usually provision for topping up with distilled water to compensate for any loss of electrolyte.

富液式铅酸电池表现出另一个非常有用的特性：它们并不会由于短期内温和的滥充电而严重受损。它们开始产气，在极端情况下有爆炸的危险，同时它们会失去电解质。但它们并不会像锂离子电池那样由于过充电而导致立即和永久的损坏。富液电池被设计成在过充电时很容易漏气，并且通常用蒸馏水来补足损失掉的电解质。

Valve-regulated (VRLA, i.e. AGM and Gel) cells on the other hand are a bit more picky. Most of them degrade somewhat as a result of overcharging and the effect is cumulative. Even so, one or two mild overcharging incidents in the life of a cell will not destroy it. As a result, charging a single lead-acid cell is not complex so long as it is fully charged fairly regularly, and so long as VRLA cells are not routinely overcharged.

另外，阀控式（VRLA，即 AGM 和凝胶）电池有点更为挑剔。它们中的大多数会因过充电而降低性能，且这种效果是累积的。即便如此，在整个电池寿命中一两次温和的过充电事件并不会摧毁它。因此，只要电池较为频繁地被完全充电，并且阀控式密封铅酸电池不经常被过充电，则单个铅酸电池充电就并不复杂。

Lithium ion cells

锂离子电池

As discussed in the chapter on batteries, lithium ion cells deliver far more power for a given size and weight than lead acid and have a far longer cycle life (i.e. you can charge and discharge them many more times before they fail). They are however far more expensive than lead-acid cells and are also more sensitive to mismanagement. This makes accidental damage both more likely and the consequences more severe.

正如在第 5 章所讨论的，对于给定的尺寸和重量，锂离子电池能提供比铅酸电池更大的功率，并且具有更长的循环寿命（即，您可以在它们失效之前对它们进行更多次的充放电）。然而，它们的价格远高于铅酸电池，并且对误操作也更加敏感。这使得它们更容易受到意外损坏且后果更加严重。

The fundamental problem with lithium ion cells is

锂离子电池最根本的问题是，它们很容易被

that they are easily destroyed by overcharging or over-discharging. You can turn a lithium ion cell into a very expensive paperweight in a single over-charge or over-discharge incident. In this section we'll consider the overcharge case in more detail. We'll cover over-discharge in the section on the management of whole packs.

过充电或过放电所毁坏。很容易在单次的过充电或过放电事件中将锂离子电池变成一个非常昂贵的镇纸石。在本节中，我们将详细地讨论过充电的情况。我们将在电池组管理那节中讨论过放电。

If you overcharge a lithium ion cell, the cell voltage will just keep rising beyond the allowable maximum, irreversibly damaging the cell. Figure 6-10 illustrates the results of one test. Charge continued at the 1C rate after maximum charge was reached. Voltage initially stabilised around 5 volts, and then shot up to a peak of 12 volts after just a few more minutes, at which point the cell went to open circuit. It reached a peak temperature of 160℃ (hot enough to fry an egg).

如果您对锂离子电池过度充电，电池电压将继续上升到超出所允许的最大值，从而不可逆地毁坏电池。图 6-10 示出了一个测试结果。在电池到达最大充电值后以 1C 的充电率继续充电，电压开始是稳定在 5V 左右，仅仅几分钟后就升到 12V 的高峰值，此时电池处于开路状态，且电池的温度达到峰值 160℃（热到足以煎鸡蛋）。

This particular cell failed fairly safely, but some lithium ion cells (notably lithium cobalt) are prone to a rather more abrupt termination (i.e. they explode and then burn or vice versa. Try searching

这一特定的电池损坏时还是相当安全的，但有些锂离子电池（尤其是锂钴）倾向于更为突然地损坏，即它们先爆炸，然后被烧毁，或先被烧毁，然后爆炸（请试着在 YouTube

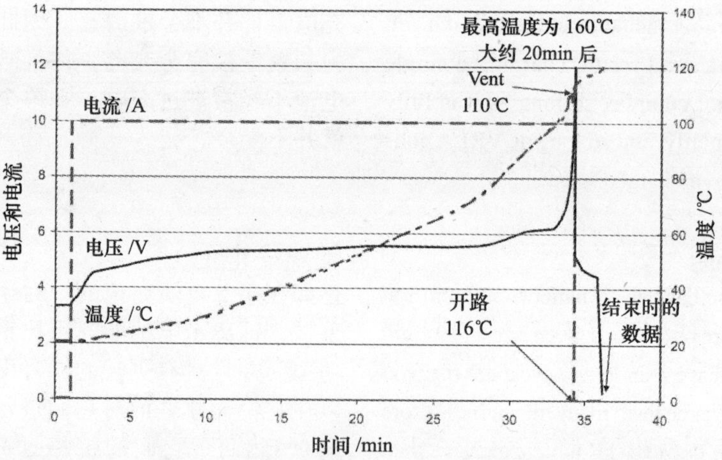

Figure 6–10 Death-rattle of an overcharged Lithium ion cell (from SAND 2008-5583 Selected Test Results from the LiFeBatt Iron Phosphate Li-ion Battery by Hund TD & Ingersoll D. Reproduced by kind permission of the Sandia National Laboratories, USA)

图 6–10 一个过充电锂离子电池的毁坏过程（桑德 2008-5583 磷酸铁锂离子电池测试结果由洪特 TD 及英格索尔 D 提供，由美国桑迪亚国家实验室许可）

YouTube for “lithium explosion”).

So much for over-charge. Some lithium ion cells are also fussy about temperature. There are issues at both high and low temperature; the cell manufacturer will probably specify temperature ranges for both charge and discharge. If you allow the batteries to operate outside these ranges you are conducting an experiment rather than managing your batteries.

High temperatures may impair or destroy a cell with the same finality as over charge or over discharge. Low temperatures are more interesting. Lithium ion cells (like most cell types) lose capacity at low temperature. The paper mentioned earlier[1] records experiments with one lithium ion cell type which indicated around 25% reduction in capacity between 25 ℃ (room temperature) and 0 ℃ (Winter’s day in the UK), and that the cell was almost useless at -40℃ (Siberian winter). Cells of this type might therefore benefit from some form of cell heating arrangements in a vehicle that was to be used in temperatures typical of a European or North American winter.

Note that this applies to a specific battery type and chemistry, and other types will have different behaviour. One more recent cell type specifies a usable temperature range of -45℃ to +85℃ .

In summary, lithium ion cells have an operational “window” bounded by temperature and state of charge as indicated by cell voltage at nominal or standard charge/discharge current. If the rested open circuit voltage of an individual cell under these standard conditions gets too high or too low the cell will be damaged. If the cell gets too hot, it will also be damaged. At lower temperatures than recommended it will at least lose efficiency (see Figure 6-11).

1 SAND 2008-5583 Selected Test Results from the LiFeBatt Iron Phosphate Li-ion Battery by Hund TD and Ingersoll D

上搜索“锂电池爆炸”)。

有关过充电就讨论这些。有些锂离子电池对温度也很敏感，在高、低温度下都有问题，因此，电池制造商可能会对充电和放电指定温度范围。如果您让电池在这些温度范围之外工作，您很可能是在做有关电池的实验而不是进行电池的管理。

高温可能会像过充电或过放电那样损害或破坏一个电池。低温则更有趣。像大多数其他类型的电池一样，锂离子电池在低温下的容量将减少。前面提到的那篇论文㊀记录了与一个锂离子电池有关的实验，它表明从 25℃（室温）到 0℃（英国冬季的一天）锂离子电池的容量降低了 25% 左右，在 -40℃时（西伯利亚的冬天），该电池几乎是无用的。因此，在典型的欧洲或北美的冬季使用的车辆中装上某种形式的电池加热装置对这种类型的电池可能有益的。

请注意，这一实验结果只适用于某个特定的电池类型和化学物质，其他类型的电池将有不同的特性。一个更新的电池类型可使用的温度范围为 -45 ~ +85℃。

综上所述，锂离子电池具有一个由温度和荷电状态所的规定操作“窗口”，该荷电状态由在名义或标准充电 / 放电电流时的电压所指定。如果在这些标准的条件下单个电池的静态开路电压变得太高或太低，该电池将被损坏。如果该电池太热，它也将被损坏。在低于指定温度时，至少会使效率降低（图 6-11）。

㊀ T · D · 洪特和 D · 英格索尔，尚德 2008-5583，LiFeBatt 磷酸铁锂离子电池测试结果选。

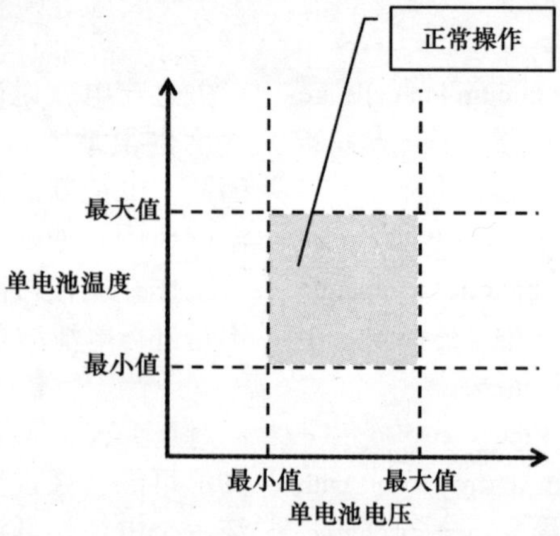

Figure 6–11 Operational window of a lithium cell

图 6–11 一个锂电池的工作区间

The final issue with lithium cells is the maximum current on charge and discharge. These limits are normally specified as C ratings: typically three different ratings, one each for:

- continuous discharge.
- short duration pulse discharge
- charge.

最后一个与锂电池有关的问题是充电和放电的最大电流。这些限制通常指定为 C 等级。一般有三种不同的等级，分别为：

- 连续放电
- 短时间脉冲放电
- 充电

So for example a 100 amp-hour cell with a 3C max charge rating implies a 300 Amp maximum charging current.

因此，例如，一个 100A・h 的电池具有 3C 的最大充电率意味着 300A 的最大充电电流。

Managing current limits on discharge is straightforward in principle (if not always in practice): the motor controller needs to know what the limits are and to be programmable to enforce them. The situation on charge is more complex. If you were to use a simple constant voltage SLI charger of the kind described earlier, you have two problems (assuming that the charger voltage is high enough to charge the cell in a reasonable length of time).

管理放电时的电流限制在原理上是简单的（如果在实践中不总是）。电动机控制器需要知道电流的极限值，并用编程来实现。充电的情况则更为复杂。如果您想要用一个前面所述的那种简单的恒压 SLI 充电器，您会遇到两个问题（假设充电器电压足够高，以便在一个合理的时间长度内对电池充电）。

Firstly, the initial charge current may exceed the allowable current limit at the start of the charging process (i.e.

首先，充电过程开始时的初始充电电流可能会超过所容许电流的限制。此时电池的

when the residual cell voltage is at its lowest, so the difference between charge voltage and cell voltage – and hence current – is at its highest). Secondly, the cell will probably be overcharged at the top end.

剩余电压处于它的最低值，所以充电电压和电池电压之差及其电流值都将处于其最高值。其次，在充电的末期电池可能会被过充电。

A modification of this process would be to shut down the charger when cell voltage reached the manufacturers specification. This would solve the top-end-overcharge problem but might (counter-intuitively) not fully charge the cell. Remember that cell voltage as a measure of state of charge is meaningless at the wrong current.

对这一过程的修正是当电池电压达到制造商的规定值时将充电器断开，这样就能解决最高端的过充电的问题，但可能（于直觉相反）会导致电池的不完全充电。请记住，作为衡量荷电状态的电池电压在错误的电流状态下是无意义的。

The normal answer to this conundrum is to use a constant-current/constant voltage (CC/CV) charge profile. For lithium ion cells this is an initial charge at constant current (voltage rising) in order to charge the cell as quickly as possible within the C rating limit, and then a "settling" period at constant (maximum) voltage with a gradually reducing current, terminated when the charging current falls to a specified level (Figure 6-12). This reduces the impact of internal resistance and charge settling on the charging process.

解决这个难题的常用方法是使用恒流 / 恒压(CC / CV)充电曲线。对锂离子电池而言，开始时采用恒流（电压上升）充电，以便在规定的 C 级内尽快对电池充电，在“稳定”期间通过逐渐减少电流以便在（最大）恒定电压下充电，当充电电流下降到某一规定值时就终止充电（图 6-12）。这样在充电过程中就减少了内阻和电荷稳定过程的影响。

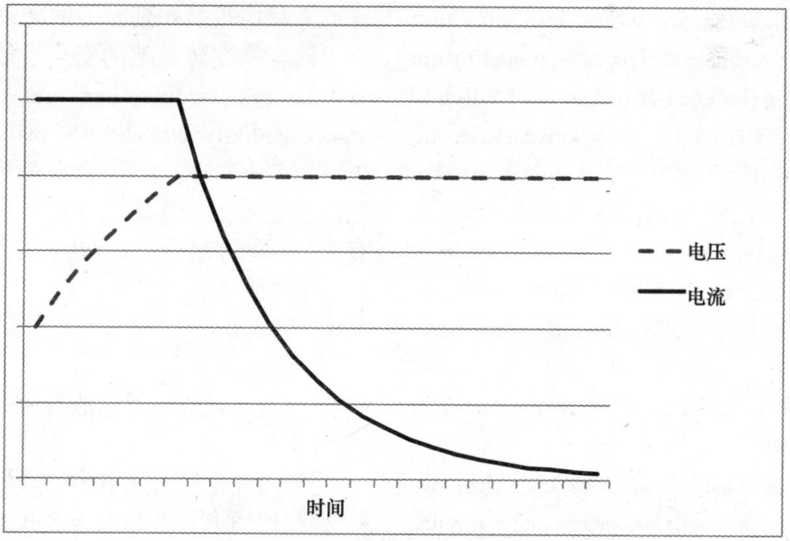

Figure 6–12 Typical lithium ion charge profile

图 6–12 典型的锂离子电池充电曲线

So the charging system for a lithium ion cell should:

- be programmable to enable it to deliver the correct charge profile, in order to keep both the maximum charging current and the maximum cell voltage within limits and also to terminate charging when the current has tapered off to a specified value.
- Ideally monitor cell temperatures and reduce charge rate or terminate charging if a cell approaches the maximum allowable figure.
- Ideally provide a backup charge termination mechanism based on elapsed charging time.

因此，锂离子电池的充电系统应该具有以下功能：

- 可编程，使其能够提供正确的充电曲线，以便在限定范围内保持最大的充电电流和电池电压，并且当电流逐渐趋近某个指定值时终止充电。
- 最好能监控电池的温度，并且当电池接近其最大允许温度时，降低充电速度或终止充电。
- 最好能提供一个基于充电时间的备用充电终止机制。

The second two (temperature monitoring and time-based charge termination) should not be necessary most of the time provided the correct charge profile is used: but cells do sometimes fail and attempting to charge a damaged cell could under some circumstances result in a conflagration.

只要能提供正确的充电曲线，后两点（温度监控和基于时间的充电终止）在大多数情况下并不是必须的。但电池有时会失效，如果试图对受损的电池进行充电，在某些情况下会导致爆燃。

Lithium Sulphur cells

There is comparatively little in the public domain about the management of these cells, although there is published work which indicates that they handle overcharge far better than lithium ion. One paper (Safety Performance of Polymer Lithium-Sulfur Cells http://www.oxisenergy.com//downloads/Safety%20Performance%20Polymer%20Li-S_IMLB_2010.pdf) reported that 24 hours of overcharging at the 1C rate caused a trivial temperature rise of under 3℃. The following do not appear to be in the public domain:

- The effect on cell life of overcharge or over discharge.
- The tolerance of the cells to routine undercharging.
- The typical state-of-charge versus voltage profile.
- Real world self-discharge rates (there is some evidence that it may be higher than lithium ion).

锂硫电池

虽然有些文献提到这类电池管理，表明它们对过充电的处理远强于锂离子电池，但在公开的文献中很难查到有关的文章。有一篇文章（聚合物锂硫电池的安全性能 http://www.oxisenergy.com/downloads/Safety%20Performance%20Polymer%20Li-S_IMLB_2010.pdf）报道，在 1C 充电率下，24h 的过充电仅仅使电池的温度上升了不到 3℃。下述议题并没有在公开的文献中讨论到：

- 过充电或过放电对电池寿命的影响
- 电池对经常性欠充电的耐受性
- 典型的荷电状态与电压之间的关系
- 现实世界中的自放电率（有些证据表明，它可能高于锂离子电池）

➤ Managing entire Battery Packs

Charging a single cell (or a 12 volt monoblock) is one thing, but charging a long string of cells is quite another. Most EV battery packs are charged as a unit by a single charger (Figure 6-13).

➤ 管理整个电池组

对单节电池（或 12V 的单块电池）充电是一回事，对一长串电池的充电又是另一回事。大多数电动汽车的电池组将作为一个单元由单个充电器充电（图 6-13）。

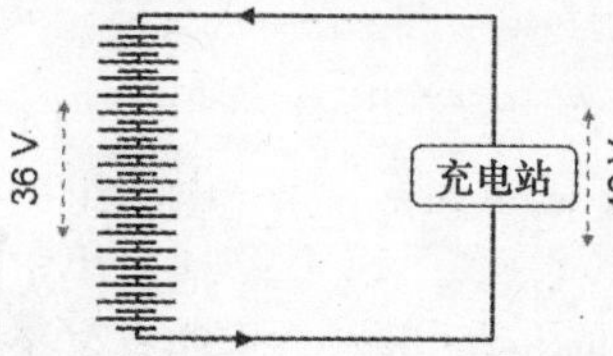

Figure 6–13 Charging a Long String of Cells

图 6–13 对一长串电池的充电

As described earlier, the fundamental problem is this: different cells in the string all get the same charging current for the same length of time (they are in series so it cannot be otherwise), but individual cells have different capacities and start with different residual charge (Figure 6-14), so will almost certainly need slightly more or less current/charge duration. The problem gets worse as the string gets longer.

如前所述，最根本的问题是电池组中不同的电池将得到相同的充电电流并持续相同的时间长度（它们是串联的，否则不会这样），但各个电池具有不同的容量，且在开始时具有不同的残余电量（图 6-14），因此不同的电池几乎肯定需要稍微多些或少些的电流 / 充电时间。随着电池组长度的增加，问题会更严重。

The outcome of this variation between cells is

电池不同导致的结果是，如果电池组被充电

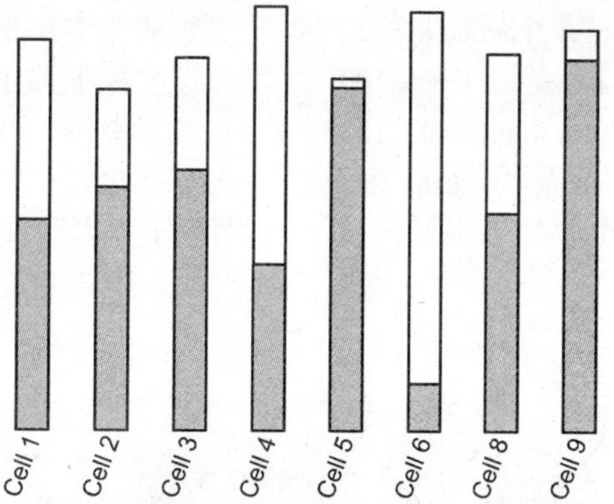

Figure 6–14 Illustration of cells in a multi-cell pack. Overall bar height represents cell capacity. Shaded area represents current state of charge for each cell

图 6–14 一个电池组中不同电池的状态。方框的高度代表电池的容量，阴影区域表示每个电池当前的荷电状态

that if the pack is charged to its nominal limit, the weaker ones (those that hold less charge, so need either lower charging current and/or shorter charge duration) will be chronically overcharged. The stronger cells will be chronically undercharged. The impact of this (and potential solutions) vary with cell chemistry, but with many cell chemistries the practical real-world outcome is that:

到其标称极限值，较弱的电池（那些能容下较少电荷，因此需要较低的充电电流和/或较短的充电时间的电池）将长时间过充电。较强的电池将长时间欠充电。它所产生的影响（及可能的解决方案）随电池的化学物质而不同，但对于许多电池的化学物质而言，现实世界中的实验结果是：

- The Amp-Hour capacity of a pack is, at best, limited to that of its weakest cell.
- If the spread of starting states of charge in the pack are too broad, the effective pack capacity will be reduced further.

- 电池组的安时容量至少是由其最薄弱的电池所决定的
- 如果各个电池在开始时的荷电状态差别太大，电池组的有效容量将进一步减少

In order to visualise why this is so, imagine a game where each contestant has a tray full of water jugs of varying sizes with varying starting amounts of water. Each jug corresponds to a single cell in a battery pack.

为了形象地说明为什么是这样，让我们来想象一下一个游戏（图 6-15）。游戏中每个选手都有一托盘，内有容量不等且起始水量不同的水杯，每个水杯对应于电池组中的一个电池单元。

The object of the game is to fill the jugs (“charge” them), carry them across the room and empty them into an urn (“discharge” them). The rules are:

比赛的目的是在水杯中装水(对它们“充电”)，将它们端到房间另一头，然后将它们全部倒入到一个缸里(对它们“放电”)。游戏规则是：

- You can add or take away as much water as you like from the jugs but you must treat them all the same: if you add 100 millilitres (ml) to one jug you must add 100 ml to them all, and if you empty 100 ml from one jug into the urn you must take 100 ml from them all. (This corresponds to charge and discharge currents. Because cells in a battery are in series, the same current necessarily flows through

- 您可以添加或从水杯中带走尽可能多的水，但您必须对它们一视同仁：如果您在一个水杯中添加 100mL 的水，您必须在所有水杯中加 100mL 的水；如果您从一个水杯中倒 100mL 的水到缸里，您必须从所有水杯中倒 100mL 的水到缸里。这对应于充电和放电电流，由于电池组中的电池是串联的，在充电和放电时相同的电

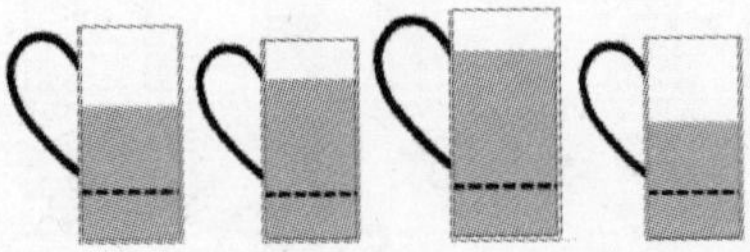

Figure 6–15 The Water Jug Game

图 6–15 水杯游戏

each of them on both charge and discharge).

- If the level of the water in any one jug gets below a dashed line marked on that jug an umpire will smash the jug. This is equivalent to going below the minimum allowable State of Charge (SOC) for a cell.
- If any of the jugs overflow (remember you are bound to add the same amount to each), that jug is smashed too (that is breaching the upper SOC limit).

流必须流过每个电池。

- 如果任何一个杯中的水位低于这个杯上标注的虚线，裁判将打碎这个杯子。这相当于有一个电池低于所允许的最低荷电状态（SOC）。
- 如果任何一个杯子溢出（请记住，您必须对每个杯子添加相同数量的水），这个杯子也将被打碎（即违反上述 SOC 的限制）。

If you were to play this game you would quickly discover two things: Firstly, you have to stop filling all the jugs when the very first jug is full, and secondly, you have to stop emptying them all when the very first jug gets down to the dashed line. So, even if everything else goes right, you are limited by the capacity of the smallest jug. Suppose for example you have nine 1000 ml jugs and just one 900 ml jug. You cannot carry any more water than another player who has ten 900 ml jugs because you have to stop filling all of them when the 900 ml jug fills up, and you have to stop emptying all of them when the 900 ml jug gets down to the dashed line.

如果您要玩这个游戏，您很快就会发现两件事情：首先，当第一杯水装满时您必须停止灌装所有的其他水杯；其次，当第一杯水位达到虚线时您必须停止倾倒所有的其他水杯。因此，即使所有一切均顺利，您的容量将被最小容量的杯所限。假如您有 9 个 1000mL、一个 900mL 的杯。您所带的水量并不比另一个只有 10 个 900mL 水杯的人所带的水多。因为当那个 900mL 的水杯被装满后您必须停止灌装所有的其他水杯，同时当 900mL 水杯的水位下降到虚线时您必须停止倾倒所有的其他水杯。

If one of your jugs starts out too full it will limit you even further: so if (in the preceding example) one of the 1000 ml jugs tops out first, you cannot even fill the 900 to the top.

如果其中的一个水杯在开始时太满，它会进一步限制您的容量。在前面的例子中，如果其中一个 1000mL 的水杯开始时是满的，您甚至不能对 900mL 的水杯添加任何的水。

➢ Pack balancing/equalisation

➢ 电池组的平衡 / 均衡

The principle of balancing is to add or remove charge from individual cells so that they end up in a similar state of charge. There are in theory several ways to achieve this:

平衡的原则是向单个电池添加或移走电荷，使它们最终处于一个类似的荷电状态。在理论上有几种方法来实现这一点：

- It can be a manual process. At its crudest, an operator can go round the pack at intervals with a voltmeter and a power supply, and when necessary adjust the state of charge to put the cells in line with each other.
- Automated "Dissipative" balancing uses cell-

- 它可以是一个手动过程。最原始的方法是，操作者可以带着一个电压表和电源，定期测量电池组中各电池的电压，并在必要时调整它们的荷电状态，使各个电池彼此一致。
- 自动“耗散”平衡，使用连接在电池单元

level modules to burn off charge from the stronger cells automatically. This necessarily involves dissipating the unwanted energy as heat: hence the term "dissipative". Comparatively low currents work fine so long as the process runs over a long enough time period.

上的模块自动耗掉较强电池的电荷。这必然涉及以热量的形式消耗掉多余的能量，因此被称为"耗散"。只要这个过程持续足够长的时间，在相对较低的电流下工作是可行的。

- A variant of dissipative balancing (using so called "shunt" balancers) divert charge current around the cell when it reaches maximum voltage during charge (Figure 6-16).

- 耗散平衡的一种变体（使用所谓的"分流"平衡器）在充电电压达到最大值时，充电电流被从电池中分流出去（图 6-16）。

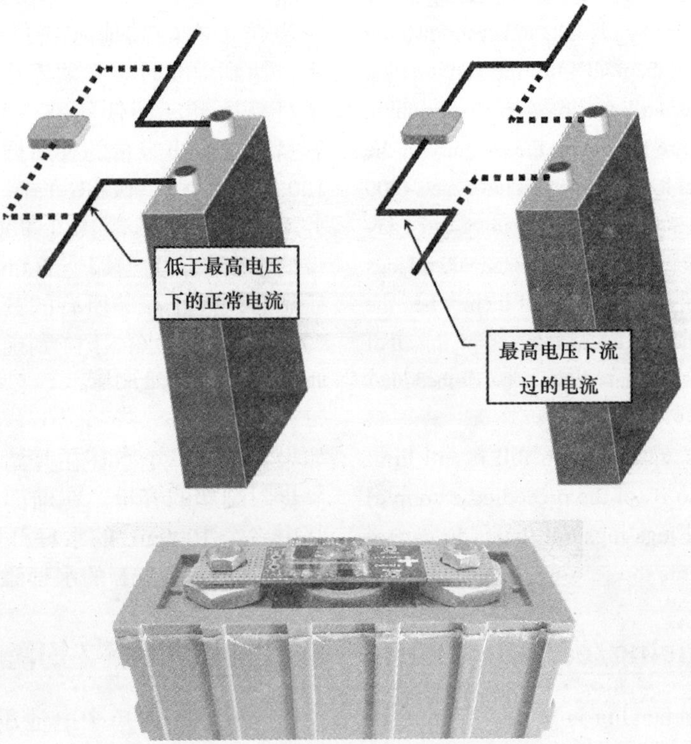

Figure 6–16 "Shunt" Balancing: top left - normal charging, top right – shunt in operation, bottom – real world Shunt Balancer. Photo courtesy of EV Power, Australia (http://www.ev-power.com.au)

图 6–16 "分流"平衡：左上——正常充电，右上——分流过程，底部——真实分流平衡器。照片由澳大利亚电动车动力提供（http://www.ev-power.com.au）

- "Non-dissipative" balancing uses electronics to shuffle power between cells so that they end up balanced.

- "非耗散"平衡使用电子线路使电能在电池之间移动，最终使它们达到平衡。

- Redistribution.

- 再分配。

Manual balancing

The principle here is to manually add or take away charge from high or low cells so that they are all at the same chosen state of charge. The rested open circuit voltage is used as the measure of state of charge. Note "rested, open circuit" : it is not enough just to go round with a voltmeter whilst the battery is charging.

手动平衡

这里的原则是从太低或太高的电池中手动添加或放掉一些电荷，使它们都具有相同的荷电状态。静态开路电压被用来衡量电池的荷电状态。请注意必须“静态、开路”，若在电池正在充电时用电压表去测量电压，是不行的。

Dissipative & Shunt balancers

The principle of dissipative balancing is to charge the entire string to suit the needs of the cell with the greatest capacity and then to provide a way to dissipate power from, or divert power around, the other cells. Figure 6-16 illustrates shunt balancing. Until the preset maximum voltage is reached, the by-pass circuit is open, so the whole charging current passes through the cell. When the maximum is reached, the by-pass circuit allows just enough current to flow through the cell to keep cell voltage at a preset maximum.

耗散及分流平衡器

耗散平衡的原理是对整个电池组充电，以适应最大容量电池的需求，然后用一种方式来消耗掉或分流掉其他电池的功率。图 6-16 说明了分流平衡。在电池达到预设的最大电压之前，旁路电路都是开路的，所以充电电流穿过整个电池。当电压达到最大时，旁路电路只允许少量的电流流过的该电池，使它的电压能维持在一个预设的最大值。

Typically this approach is implemented using small solid-state devices installed across the terminals of each individual cell (or groups of cells in parallel). Most of the time, the balancer is open circuit and inactive. If the cell voltage gets too high during charge, it starts diverting some of the charging current around the cell. These devices are sometimes self contained (no connections other than to the cell itself) and are relatively small, light and cheap. It is perfectly practicable to equip every cell in a high voltage pack with one. However there are concerns over failure modes which are discussed in more detail in the section on automated battery management systems.

通常，此方法是用安装在每个电池（或并联的电池组单元）两端的小型固态器件来实现的。平衡器在大部分时间是处于开路及非激活状态的。如果在充电过程中电池的电压变得太高，它开始将部分充电电流旁路。这些固态器件有时是自成体系的（除电池本身外并无其他连接），并且都比较小而轻，且价格便宜。在高电压的电池组中完全可以在每个电池上装一个这样的装置。但人们还是担心器件失效，有关这方面的问题将在“自动电池管理系统”这节中更详细地讨论。

"Non-dissipative" balancing

Non-dissipative balancing essentially robs Peter to pay Paul: a small amount of charge is removed from the cells that are at a higher state of charge and used to top up the other cells. This approach can only really be implemented using relatively complex elec-

“非耗散”平衡

非耗散平衡实质上采用了拆东墙补西墙的方法。少量的电荷将从较高荷电状态的电池中被移走，用于补足其他电池。这种方法只能用相对复杂的电子设备才能真正实现。无论它是如何实现的，效果都是相同的。这种方

tronics. However it is done though, the effect is the same. This approach is more expensive: and whilst in theory it is more efficient, losses in the control and "shuttling" circuits can eat into this. Furthermore, the same failure-mode issues arise here too.

法是比较昂贵的，虽然从理论上讲它更高效，但控制电路和"移动电荷"产生的附加损失足以将此抵消。此外，同样的故障模式也会在这里出现。

Redistribution

Redistribution in theory allows the maximum power to be extracted from a pack. Essentially each cell is given its own DC-DC converter. This would allow you to continue to draw power out of each individual cell until it was exhausted, using the DC-DC converter to step up from each individual cell to pack voltage (Figure 6-17).

再分配

在理论上再分配能让电池组输出最大的功率。从本质上说，每个电池都有它自己的直流 - 直流转换器。由于用了直流 - 直流转换器将每个电池提高到电池组的电压，将允许您持续从每个电池中提取能量，直到它被耗尽（图 6-17）。

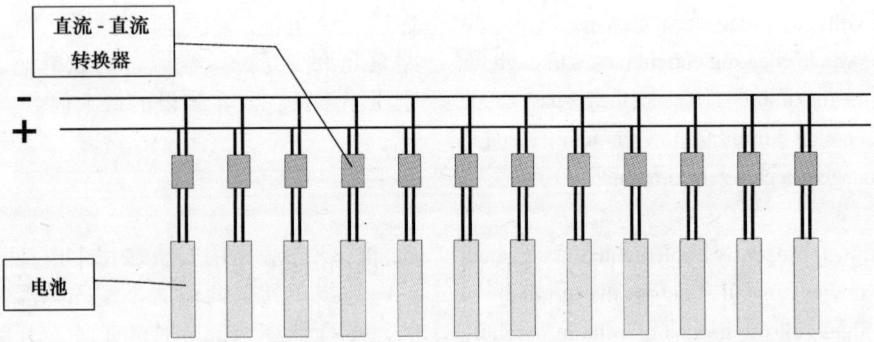

Figure 6–17 (Theoretical) Redistribution using DC-DC Converters

图 6–17 应用直流转换器的（理论）再分配

We will not be discussing redistribution further. In an EV it would demand large numbers of DC-DC converters capable of handling large currents, which would become impossibly cumbersome and expensive.

我们将不会对再分配作进一步的讨论。在电动汽车中，这将需要大量的、能够处理大电流的直流 - 直流转换器，这会使系统变得极其笨重和昂贵。

Top Versus Bottom Balancing

So far we have discussed what balancing cells in a pack means and how to do it. We next turn our attention to where to balance them. If you have a pack made up of a number of cells with varying capacities they can only be matched at one point in a charge/discharge cycle. In the real world the capacity mismatch is typically just a few percent, but to illustrate the principle suppose that you had

顶部与底部平衡

到目前为止，我们已经讨论了在一个电池组中进行电池平衡的含义以及如何做到这点。接下来，我们将把我们的注意力转移到从哪里去平衡它们上来。如果您有一个由不同容量的电池组成的电池组，在一个充 / 放电循环中它们只能在一个点中被匹配。在实际情况下容量的不匹配通常只有几个百分点，但为了便于说明平衡的原理，

a mixture of 100 Amp hour and 200 Amp hour cells in the same pack, and let's suppose that they were all exactly balanced at (say) 30% state of charge. Now take 2 Amp hours out of the pack. It is no longer balanced: the 100 Amp hour cells are at 28% (2 Amp hours is 2% of a 100 Amp hour capacity) but the 200 Amp hour cells are at 29 % (2 Amp hours is 1% of a 200 Amp hour capacity).

假设在您的电池组中有 100A • h 及 200A • h 电池的混合，并让我们假设它们全都完全平衡在（例如）30% 的荷电状态。如果从电池组中提取 2A • h，它们就不再平衡了。100A • h 的电池是 28% 的荷电状态（2A • h 为 100A • h 容量的 2%），但 200A • h 的电池是在 29%（2A • h 为 200A • h 容量的 1%）。

The most usual alternatives are top balancing (ending the charge cycle with all cells fully charged) or bottom balancing (all cells run out of power together at the bottom of the discharge cycle).

最常用的平衡方式是顶部平衡（当所有的电池完全充满时结束充电周期）或底部平衡（在放电循环结束时所有的电池同时耗尽电能）。

To illustrate this, look at Figure 6-18. Here, the individual capacity of each cell in a 9 cell pack is represented by a bar – the longer the bar, the greater the capacity. The amount of charge remaining in the cell is represented by the shaded area.

为了说明这一点请参见图 6-18。在这里，电池组由 9 个电池组成，每个电池的容量用一长方形柱来代表，方形柱越长，容量越大，电池中的剩余电量则用阴影区域来表示。

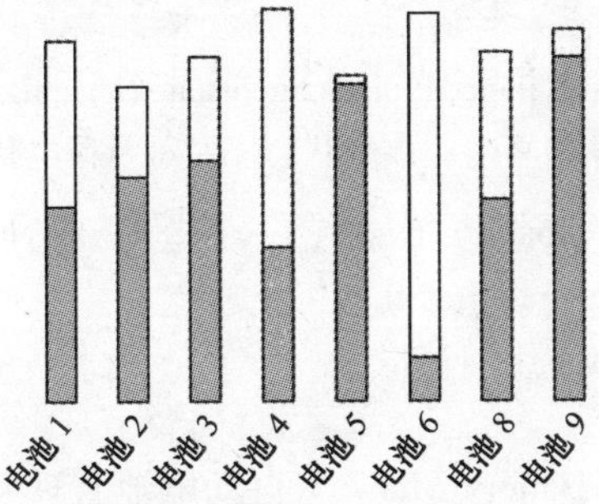

Figure 6–18 Cell Imbalance

图 6–18 电池失衡

This pack is badly out of balance. For example, cell 5 is almost fully charged and cell 6 is almost fully discharged. A short charge with no balancing on the pack as a whole will quickly top out cell 5 and leave cell 6 charged to only about 15% of its available capacity.

这个电池组是严重失衡的。例如，电池 5 几乎被完全充满，而电池 6 几乎被完全放电。在没有均衡的情况下对整个电池组进行短暂的充电后将很快把电池 5 充爆，然而电池 6 只能被充到其可用容量的 15% 左右。

Bottom balancing charges the cells so that at the end of the discharge process they all reach minimum State of Charge (SOC) together (Figure 6-19). Top balancing (Figure 6-20) is the reverse:

底部平衡是对电池进行这样的充电使得在放电过程结束时它们都达到最低荷电状态（SOC）（图 6-19）。顶部平衡（图 6-20）正相反，所有的电池都被充到最大容量。当有

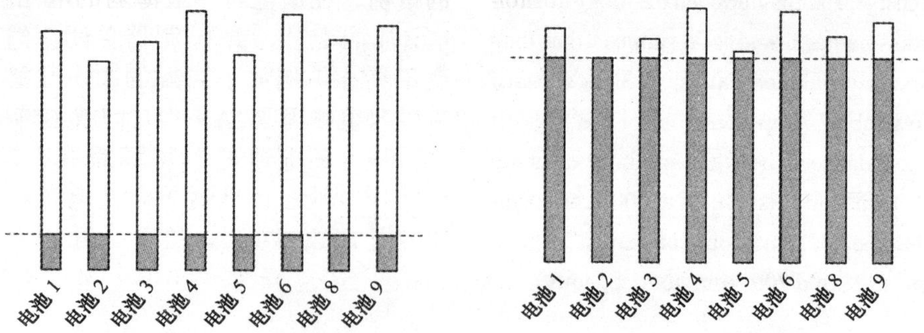

Figure 6–19 Bottom balanced: discharged state (L) and charged state (R)

图 6–19 底部平衡：放电状态（左）及荷电状态（右）

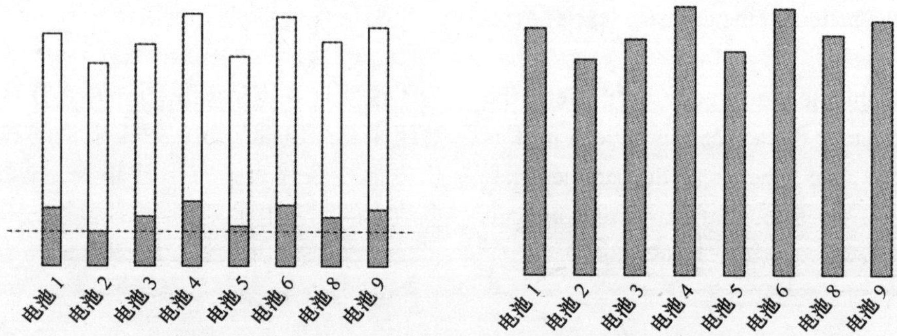

Figure 6–20 Top Balanced: discharged state (L) and charged state (R)

图 6–20 顶部平衡：放电状态（左）及荷电状态（右）

all cells are charged to maximum capacity. Discharge is stopped when the first cell reaches the maximum allowable depth of discharge.

一个电池到达所允许的最大放电深度时就停止放电。

It is easier to design an automated Battery Management System (BMS - see next section) to perform top balancing but this is arguably less desirable. Three reasons could be advanced for this:

自动电池管理系统（BMS，见下一节）的设计比较容易实现顶部平衡方案，但这个方案可以说是不太理想的，有三个原因：

Firstly the total voltage of a bottom-balanced pack will degrade more sharply near the bottom of the discharge cycle as all the cells approach minimum state of charge. This provides a strong cue that it is time to stop and recharge.

首先，一个底部平衡电池组的总电压在放电循环的底部附近，由于所有的电池都接近最小的荷电状态，而会更急剧地降低。这提供了有力的证据表明现在是停下来充电的时候。

Secondly, top balancing requires that the BMS manage both charge and discharge: it must manage top balanc-

其次，顶部平衡要求电池管理系统同时管理充电和放电。在充电时它必须管理顶部

ing during charge, and must also tell the motor controller to shut down when the weakest cell hits bottom on discharge. A bottom-balanced pack on the other hand might use a BMS to handle charge and balancing, but the motor controller can be left to handle the bottom of discharge on its own because it can (with a bottom-balanced pack) safely use low overall pack voltage as an indication of depth of discharge (DoD).

Thirdly, as discussed earlier, a cell that is routinely discharged to (say) 70% DoD will last longer than one that is routinely discharged to 80%. Top balancing routinely discharges your weakest cell to the greatest DoD, so by top balancing you are hitting your weakest cell harder than all the others. This will unbalance the pack in terms of cycle life.

Before we leave the topic of top versus bottom balancing, note again that whilst this is a live issue for lithium ion batteries, there is no choice for lead-acid batteries. If lead-acids are balanced at all they simply must be top balanced. Bottom balancing means that the strongest cells are never fully charged: this doesn't matter too much for most lithium ion cells (but do check with the manufacturer). A chronically undercharged lead-acid cell on the other hand will deteriorate due to sulphation.

The behaviour of lithium sulphur batteries in this area is not known. If they are tolerant of overcharging, there is no issue anyway. If overcharging damages them, but undercharging does not, then bottom balancing is an option for them too.

➢ Battery Management Systems (BMSs)

In this section we will look at automated battery management systems: first of all what they are, and secondly whether they are necessary (or even desirable). Note

的平衡，在放电时当最薄弱的电池触底时，它还必须让电动机控制器关闭。然而采用底部平衡的电池组可能会用电池管理系统来处理充电和平衡，但电动机控制器本身可以用来处理放电的底部情形，因为它可以（与电池组的底部平衡一起）安全地使用较低的整体电池组电压来作为放电深度（DoD）的指示。

第三，如前所述，一个经常被放电到（例如）70% 放电深度的电池的寿命将长于一个经常被放电到 80% 放电深度的电池。顶部平衡经常将您的最薄弱的电池放电到最大的放电深度，因此顶部平衡对您的最薄弱电池的冲击将大于所有其他电池。这在循环寿命方面将使整个电池组处于不平衡状态。

在我们结束顶部与底部平衡这个话题之前，值得注意的是，虽然这对锂离子电池而言是一个重要的问题，对铅酸电池而言则没有选择的余地。如果要平衡铅酸电池，它们必须是顶部平衡。底部平衡意味着最强的电池永远不会被完全充满，这对大多数锂离子电池而言关系不是太大（但请与制造商联系）。然而，由于硫酸盐化的影响，长期欠充电的铅酸电池的性能将变差。

锂硫电池在这方面的特性还不清楚。如果它们对过充电是宽容的，那就没有问题。如果过充电对它们有损害，但欠充电没有，那么底部平衡对它们来说是一个较好的选择。

➢ 电池管理系统（BMS）

本节中我们将讨论自动电池管理系统。首先要弄明白，它们是什么？其次，它们是否必要（或者是否可取）？请注意，这是一个有

that this is an area where there is much heated debate, represented on one side by Jack Rickard of EVTV[1] who hates current-generation BMSs for lithium ion packs with a passion, and BMS manufacturers on the other represented perhaps by Davide Andrea of Elithion[2].

很大争议的领域。其中的一方由 EVTV㊀的杰克·里卡德所代表，他激烈地反对当代的锂离子电池组管理系统，另一方的代表也许是电池管理系统制造商电锂㊁的大卫·安德烈。

What is a BMS?

In his book on BMSs for lithium ion packs[3], David Andrea suggests six different categories of BMS function. Simplifying this somewhat, there are broadly three types of function that could be performed by BMSs; different makes and models will provide one, two or all three of these functions:

- Monitoring individual cells (state of charge or voltage and maybe temperature) and informing the driver of any that stray outside a defined operating envelope.
- Issuing instructions to other components (such as charger or motor controller) to protect cells based on monitoring data.
- Balancing.

This necessarily involves individual wiring for each cell and/or an individual module for each cell. The exact layout varies. Some BMS's are fully centralised (Figure 6-21). Some use a master/slave topology (Figure 6-22).

电池管理系统是什么？

大卫·安德烈在关于锂离子电池组管理的书㊂中提出了 6 个不同类别的电池管理系统的功能。若稍微简化一点，由电池管理系统实现的功能大致有三种类型。不同品牌和型号的电池管理系统将提供其中的一个、两个或所有三个功能：

- 监测单个电池（荷电或电压状态，也许还有温度），并将任何超出规定的操作范围之外的电池状态通知驾驶人。
- 基于所监测的数据对其他组件（如充电器或电动机控制器）发出指令，以保护电池。
- 平衡。

这必然涉及对每个电池的单独连线，并且每个电池要有单独的模块，具体的布局则各不相同。有些电池管理系统是完全集中式的（图 6-21），有些则使用主 / 从拓扑结构（图 6-22）。

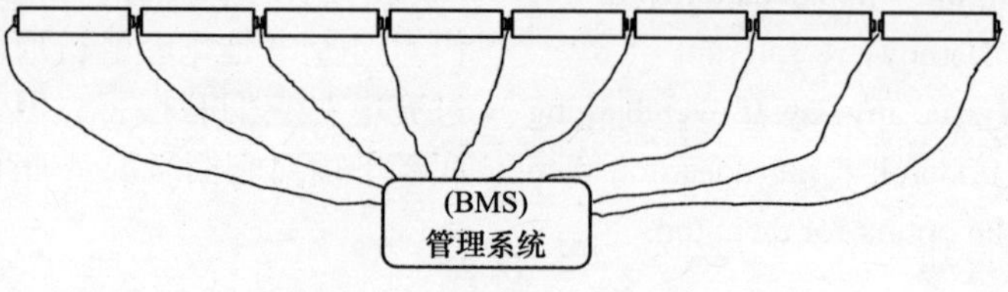

Figure 6–21 Centralised BMS

图 6–21 集中式电池管理系统

1 http://web.me.com/mjrickard/

2 http://liionbms.com/php/index.php

3 "Battery Management Systems for Large Lithium Battery Packs" Davide Andrea October 2010. ISBN 978-1608071043

㊀ http://web.me.com/mjrickard/。

㊁ http://liionbms.com/php/index.php。

㊂ 达维德·安德烈，大型锂离子电池组的电池管理系统，2010 年，ISBN：1608071049。

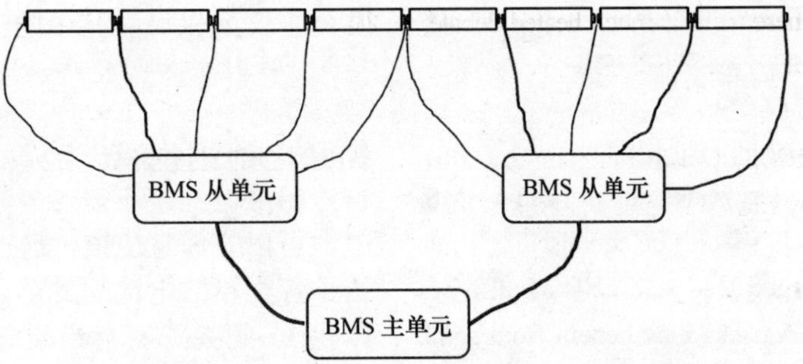

Figure 6–22 Master Slave BMS topology

图 6–22 主从电池管理系统的拓扑结构

BMS sensor wiring does not carry much power, but some wiring complexity is inevitable for either of the topologies illustrated in Figure 6-21 and Figure 6-22. Figure 6-23 shows some of the slave units and wiring of a monitoring system (this installation does no balancing and no control, merely advising the driver of cell voltage and temperature).

电池管理系统的传感器连线并没有消耗太多的能量，但在图 6-21 或图 6-22 所示的拓扑结构中布线的复杂性是不可避免的。图 6-23 显示了一些从属单元及其监测系统的布线（该装置并没有均衡和控制的功能，它只起到提示驾驶人电池电压和温度的作用。）

The shunt balancers described earlier are another form of BMS. Figure 6-24 is an example.

前面描述的分流平衡器是另一种形式的电池管理系统。图 6-24 给出了一个例子。

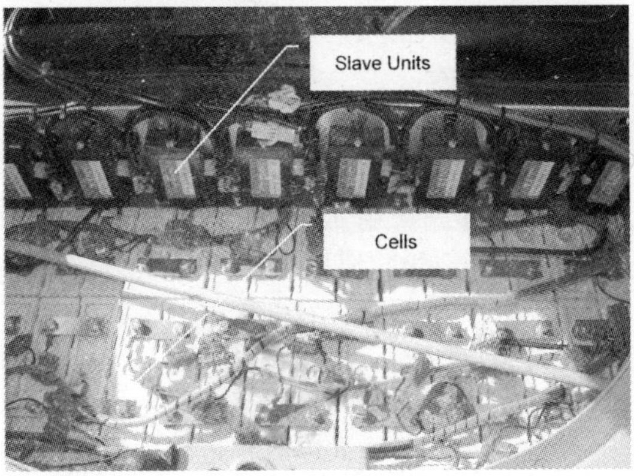

Figure 6–23 Wiring for BMS Slave units

图 6–23 电池管理系统从属单元的接线

Figure 6–24 Shunt balancers in use. This is the same battery pack shown under construction in Figure 5-1. Photo courtesy of Greg Sievert

图 6–24 实际的分流平衡器。这是图 5-1 所示的正在组成中的电池组。照片由格雷格·西弗特提供

Shunt balancers can function standalone, but are sometimes connected to a central unit.

分流平衡器可以独立发挥作用，但有时也连接到一个中央处理单元。

BMSs for lead-acid packs?

Flooded lead acid battery packs do not need a BMS. Flooded cells can (and should) be equalised by overcharging (undercharged lead acid cells of all types will sulphate). VRLA packs may benefit from some form of automated balancing. There is some evidence to suggest that VRLA packs get out of balance quite rapidly and if this is not regularly corrected the pack dies young. One study of a 48 volt string of AGM monoblocks cycled without balancing found that battery pack failure occurred at about a third of the design life of the individual cells, whilst a similar pack equipped with electronic balancers reached the design life of a single cell[1].

铅酸电池组也有电池管理系统?

富液铅酸电池组不需要电池管理系统。富液电池可以（而且应该）通过过充电来达到均衡（各类铅酸电池的欠充电将导致硫酸盐的产生）。阀控式密封铅酸电池组可能会受益于某种形式的自动平衡。有一些证据表明：阀控式密封铅酸电池组失衡得很快，而且如果不定期纠正的话，电池组很容易早损。对一个 48V 的 AGM 无均衡装置的电池组的研究发现，电池组的故障出现在单个电池设计寿命的大约三分之一处，而一个配备了电子均衡器的类似的电池组则达到了单电池的设计寿命[㊀]。

BMS's for lithium ion battery packs?

My own view is that the problem with BMS's is not what they do when they are working correctly, but what they can do if they go wrong. A BMS for a lithium ion pack is one of a small group of devices which has few safe failure modes. Consider for example the simple shunt balancer:

- If one of the units shorts out, it will melt or even start a fire, possibly damaging the cell or worse.
- If one of the units goes open circuit, that cell will almost certainly be overcharged on the next cycle; this can (as we have seen) result in fire or explosion.
- If one of the units fails to shut off fully, then even if residual resistance is high enough to prevent

锂离子电池组有电池管理系统吗?

我自己的看法是，与电池管理系统有关的问题不是当管理系统正常工作时它做了什么，而是如果管理系统出错了它会做什么。一个锂离子电池组的电池管理系统是一小组设备之一，它具有一些安全的失效模式。例如简单的分流平衡器的模式是：

- 如果其中一个单元短路，它就会融化，甚至起火，可能会损坏电池或更糟。
- 如果其中一个单元断路，与其相连的电池在下一个充电周期中将几乎肯定会被过充电，正如我们已经看到的，这将导致火灾或爆炸。
- 如果其中一个单元不能完全断开，那么即使剩余电阻足够大以防止过热，与其相连

1 Life cycle testing of series battery strings with individual battery equalizers. Kutkut N.H. Note however that although this paper has been quite widely cited, it was written by a manufacturer of equalisation devices which raises some uncertainty about its objectivity. Note also that this paper applies to AGM cells only.

㊀ Kutkut N.H.,“具有单个电池均衡器的串联电池组生命周期试验结果”。但请注意，虽然本文已被相当广泛地引用，但它是由一个均衡设备的制造商写的，这就对其客观性提出了一些不确定性。还要注意的是，这篇文章仅适用于 AGM 电池。

overheating, the malfunctioning balancer will still bleed charge from the cell and the cell will very probably be over-discharged on the next cycle. This will, at least, kill the cell.

的电池中的电荷仍会从这个出现故障的平衡器中缓慢漏掉。该电池将很可能在下一个放电周期中过度放电，这至少将损坏该电池。

Any of these scenarios is highly undesirable but there is also a statistical issue. If you have 100 cells and if (for the sake of illustration) the mean time between failure (MTBF) of the shunt balancers is 100 years then (crudely) you will lose a cell a year and maybe a car or a house every 5 – 10 years from the resulting fire.

这些情况中的任何一个都是非常不可取的，但还有一个统计的问题。如果您有 100 个电池，并且如果分流平衡器的平均故障时间（MTBF）是（为了说明起见）100 年，那么，（粗略说来）您每年将失去一个电池，并且由于其所产生的火灾，每 5 ~ 10 年也许会失去一辆汽车或一套房子。

The other aspect of this is the standard of construction. Offhand, the only other bit of electronics I can think of with so few safe failure modes is an autoland system in an aircraft. Autoland systems are built to a high standard with multiple redundancies and are consequently expensive.

其他几个方面也是设计的标准。我现在唯一能想到的具有如此低的安全失效模式的其他电子产品是飞机中的自动着陆系统。自动着陆系统是基于具有多重冗余的、非常高的标准建成的，因而很昂贵。

Cars are also aggressive environments in terms of vibration, contamination and corrosion (particularly the corrosion of electrical connections). EVs also generate a great deal of electromagnetic interference which can mess with electronic circuits: so as well as having a high specification unit with multiple redundancy, a BMS and also the BMS wiring must be designed to operate for years with no failures due to corrosion in the terminals and connectors, no conductor failures due to vibration and no errors from electrical noise. It is a tall order.

汽车将在包括振动、污染和腐蚀（特别是电连接的腐蚀）等恶劣环境中运行。电动汽车也能产生大量的电磁干扰以扰乱电子电路。因此，除了要有一个高规格的、多重冗余的器件外，电池管理系统及其系统布线的设计必须能够运行数年而不会因被腐蚀的终端及其接头而损坏，不会因振动而导致连接故障，也不会因电气噪声而出错。这是一个艰巨的任务。

Finally a monitoring system may consume some power even when the vehicle is idle, so installing one may cause the very thing that you are striving to avoid. If you forget to charge your EV before you go off on holiday and leave it parked at a low state of charge, the power consumed by the monitoring circuitry may quietly over-discharge the pack.

最后，一个监测系统即使在车辆处于闲置状态时也可能会消耗一定的功率。因此，安装一个管理系统可能会导致出现您不愿意见到或正在努力避免的事。如果您去度假之前忘记了对您的电动汽车充电，并将它停在一个低荷电状态，监控电路所消耗的功率可能会使您的电池组悄悄地过放电。

A BMS capable of handling all of these factors with

一个能够处理所有这些微小故障的电池管理

vanishingly small failure rates would be impossibly expensive. Even then, every wire and every connector in a monitoring or balancing circuit is a potential point of failure, and if you are using many cells, there are many such points of failure outside the BMS itself. Even simple cell-level voltage monitoring in a 100 cell pack is at least 200 connectors and 100 wires. A short circuit in any one of them may mean a fire. An open circuit may be trivial but it might just dupe the charger or controller into trashing the whole pack.

系统将是非常昂贵的。即使这样，监控或平衡电路中的每条线、每个接头都是一个潜在的故障点，如果您使用多个电池，在电池管理系统本身以外也有很多这样的故障点。即使是简单地在 100 个电池组成的电池组上对电池电压进行监测，也至少需要 200 个接头和 100 根连线。它们中的任何一个短路都可能意味着火灾。一个开路故障可能不太要紧，但它也有可能会欺骗充电器或控制器去摧毁整个电池组。

Alternatives to using a BMS

电池管理系统的替代方案

So is there an alternative to using a BMS? There are broadly two different schools of thought:

那么，有没有电池管理系统的替代品呢？大致有两种不同的流派：

1. The first viewpoint is that the cells in a batch are pretty close in capacity and that they can be set to similar states of charge initially; so it is quite acceptable just to use average voltages on charge and discharge, and to add a safety margin to handle the (small) variation between cells. That is, you stop charging well below the safe maximum and stop discharging well before you reach the safe minimum. This is like playing the water jug game knowing that your jugs are all between 950 and 1050 ml and stopping the filling process when they are all at about the 900 ml mark. The protagonists of this view would argue that in the real world the differences in cell capacities are quite small, and it is cheaper, easier and safer to use slightly bigger cells and charge / discharge more conservatively than to use a complex battery management system that would enable you to get the same end result from marginally smaller cells.

① 第一个观点是，同一批电池的容量是非常接近的，并且它们可以在初始时设置成相同的荷电状态。因此，在加入了用于处理电池之间小差异的一定的安全余量后，在充电和放电时只用平均电压是完全可以接受的。也就是说，您在远低于安全的最大值时停止充电，并在远低于安全的最小值时停止放电。这就像上述的水杯游戏那样，如果您知道您的水杯都在 950 ~ 1050mL 之间，您可以在它们约 900mL 时停止装水。这种观点的倡导者会说，在现实世界中电池容量的差异是相当小的，与其使用一个容量较小的电池和复杂的电池管理系统，不如使用容量稍微大一点的电池同时较为保守地充 / 放电，后者会使您得到相同的结果，并会更便宜、更方便、更安全。

2. The second viewpoint is that it is necessary to monitor the state of charge, or at least the voltage, of each cell individually and continuously. This informs a decision to stop charging when the first cell reaches its upper limit, and stop discharging when the first cell hits the lower limit. This decision can either be made by the user, or by automated control of the charger and motor controller.

② 第二个观点是，独立且持续地监测每一个电池的荷电状态或者电压是必要的。它在第一个电池达到其上限时作出停止充电的决定，并第一个电池达到其下限时作出停止放电的决定。这一决定可以由用户作出，也可以由充电器和电动机控制器的自动控制系统作出。

On the balance issue there are again two schools of thought:

在平衡问题上，仍然有两个不同流派的观点：

1. In the real world, lithium ion packs don't go out of balance quickly (if at all) so manual balancing is fine on an occasional as-required basis.

① 在现实世界中，锂离子电池组不会很快失去平衡，因此在偶尔为之的基础上手动平衡就可以了。

2. The alternative view is that lithium ion battery packs need automated active balancing or the pack will die early.

② 另一种观点是，锂离子电池组需要自动的主动平衡，否则它将被过早损坏。

It should be noted that there is little hard experimental data on the extent to which the cells in a lithium ion pack go out of balance as they age. Earlier we cited evidence that AGM packs drift out of balance and die early as a result. I have been able to find no equivalent data for any lithium chemistry. There are several possibilities:

应当指出，目前还没有过硬的实验数据来证明锂离子电池组中的电池在它们逐渐老化的过程中失去平衡的程度。前面我们列举的证据表明，AGM 电池组会逐渐失去平衡，并因此而过早损坏。我一直无法找到任何锂化学物质的相关数据。这有几种可能：

- If lithium (-ion or -sulphur) packs do not in fact drift out of balance then balancing is not required except perhaps some manual balancing when replacing cells or making up a pack from cells in different states of charge.
- If they do drift, but only very slowly, then balancing is something that could be done manually during routine servicing.
- If they drift rapidly then an automated active balancing process is required.

- 如果锂（锂离子或锂硫）电池组在实际使用中不会逐渐失去平衡，那么除了在更换电池或从不同荷电状态的电池中组成电池组时需要一些手动平衡外，不需要其他的平衡。
- 如果它们真的会逐渐失去平衡，但非常缓慢，那么可以在例行保养时手动完成平衡。
- 如果它们会很快失去平衡，则需要用自动化的平衡过程。

This is perhaps the most significant uncertainty in the management of lithium chemistry battery packs. It will only be settled by research, and we will very possibly find that different lithium cell types behave differently. The research will be difficult given the large number of variables. The long cycle lives of the latest generation of lithium ion cells (2,000 cycles or more) is good news, but it further complicates research. In an EV with a range of 100 miles, 2,000 cycles is 200,000 miles.

这也许是在锂电池组管理中最为明显的不确定性，这只能通过研究加以解决，我们可能会发现不同类型的锂电池具有不同的表现。由于众多的变化因素，这项研究将是困难的。最新一代锂离子电池的长循环寿命（2000 次或以上）是个好消息，但它使研究更加复杂。在一个 200km 行程的电动汽车中，2000 次的循环寿命就是 40 万 km。

In the meantime the arguments will rage based on opinion and anecdotal evidence. Cell manufacturers are probably the best source of data, but speaking personally I would monitor voltages manually at frequent intervals initially. I would however not install a BMS in an EV powered by the current generation of lithium ion cells: BMSs are inelegant, and in engineering, "inelegant" usually means "wrong" .

与此同时，基于个人看法和未经证实的证据基础上的争论将会很激烈。电池制造商有可能是最好的数据源，但就我个人而言，我会在最初频繁地手动监测电压。不过，我将不会在目前这一代锂离子电池供电的电动汽车中安装电池管理系统。电池管理系统是不完善的，并且在工程中，“不完善的”通常意味着“错误的”。

➢ Estimating remaining charge

➢ 估算剩余电量

For reasons that we have discussed, terminal voltage is not a very reliable indicator of state of charge. Lead acid cells have a relatively linear relationship between rested open circuit voltage and state of charge, but internal resistance and settling time distorts this under load. Nickel based chemistries confusingly exhibit a drop in voltage at full charge. Lithium ion cells have such a flat discharge curve that the change in open circuit voltage between, say, 25% discharged and 75% discharged is totally swamped by voltage changes resulting from variations in current.

由于我们前面所讨论的原因，端电压并不是荷电状态的一个非常可靠的指标。铅酸电池的静态开路电压和荷电状态之间的关系是相对线性的，但有负载时其内电阻和稳定时间将使该直线发生扭曲。镍基化学物质的电池在完全充电时其电压反而莫名其妙地下降。锂离子电池的放电曲线是如此的平坦以至于在一定范围内开路电压的变化，如在 25% 和 75% 之间放电的变化，完全被由于电流的变化而产生的电压的变化所淹没。

This is a serious issue: how are we to know how much further we can drive the car before we must recharge it? In other words, what are we going to use for a fuel gauge?

这是一个严重的问题。我们怎么知道在必须重新充电之前我们还可以把车开多远？换句话说，我们要怎样使用“燃油计”？

One approach is analogous to a fuel totaliser in an IC-engined car. A totaliser can estimate fuel used and fuel remaining (as well as providing other useful data like instantaneous fuel consumption). It typically zeros itself when the tank is full and then monitors fuel flow rate continuously, keeping a running total of fuel used and deriving fuel remaining by subtraction from the known tank capacity.

一种方法是类似于内燃机发动机汽车中的燃油累加器。累加器可以估算所用的燃料及剩余燃料（此外，它还提供如瞬时油耗等其他有用的数据）。油箱加满时它通常清零，然后持续监控燃料的流量，保存已用的燃料总和，并通过从已知的油箱容量中减去所用的燃料来计算出剩余燃料。

The electrical equivalent is sometimes known as a battery monitor and works by counting coulombs

电气上等效的方法有时也被称为电池监控器，它是靠计算库仑，而不是升或加仑来工

rather than litres or gallons. A coulomb is the charge transferred by 1 amp in 1 second (for interest, that's the charge of about 6 billion billion electrons). We have already encountered amp-hours as a measure of battery capacity (a 1 amp-hour battery will in theory sustain 1 amp for 1 hour), so you could think of an amp-hour as being 60 x 60 = 3,600 Coulombs.

作的。1C（库仑）等于1A的电流在1s内电荷的移动量（有趣的是，这相当于约600亿亿个电子的电量）。我们已经用安时来衡量电池的容量（1A • h的电池在理论上为1A的电流持续1h），所以您应该能想象得到1A • h为60 × 60= 3600库仑。

Another way to look at it is that a battery monitor measures the area under the curve of current against time (shaded area in Figure 6-25).

另一种方式是，一个电池监视器测量电流对时间曲线下的面积（图6-25中的阴影区域）。

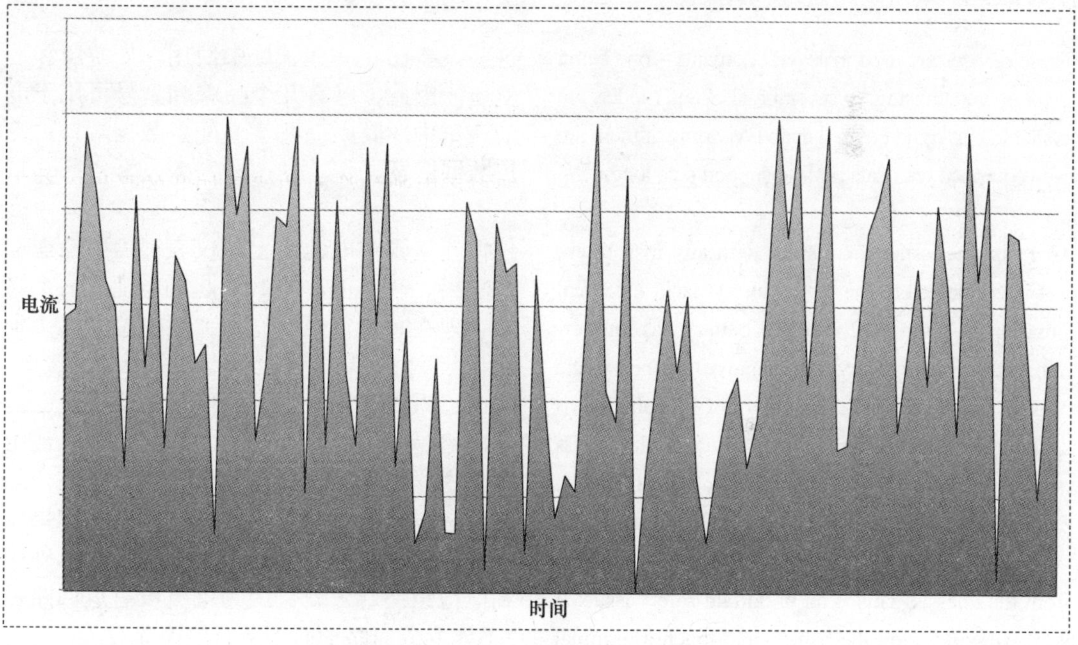

Figure 6–25 Graph of Current versus Time

图 6–25 电流随时间的变化

This is not a complex task, requiring an ammeter, a small amount of electronics and a display. In most EV applications, instead of an ammeter in series with the main power circuit, it is easier to fit a shunt in this circuit and measure the tiny voltage drop across it (Figure 6-26). This allows the use of light wiring to the instrument.

这不是一项复杂的任务，它只需要一个电流表、一些电子元器件和一个显示器。在大多数电动汽车应用中，通常在电路中装一个分流器，然后测量其两端微小的电压降，而不是将一个电流表串联在主电源电路中（图6-26）。这样就可以在仪表盘中使用细的导线。

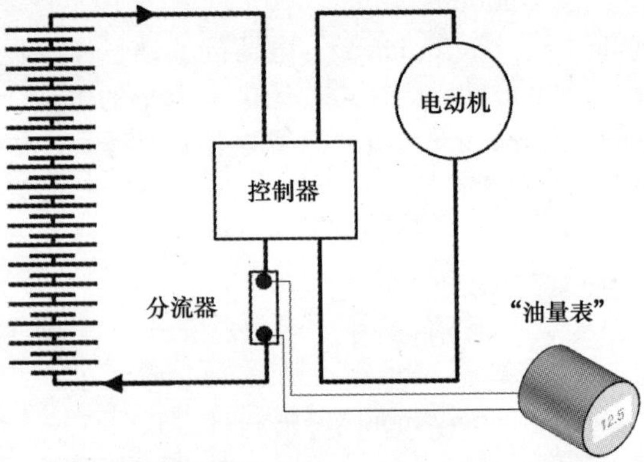

Figure 6–26 Battery Monitor Schematic

图 6–26 电池监控器原理图

These devices are used in several domains – one being yachting and cruising, so several makes and models are available that could be used in an EV. Some of them are even equipped with data ports to support data logging.

这些设备已在一些领域中使用，如游艇和巡航艇。因此，已有几个品牌和型号可用于电动汽车中。其中一些甚至配备数据端口，支持数据记录。

There is one issue to consider with any instrument that is connected to the main battery pack: electrical isolation. A normal 12 volt SLI battery has one terminal (these days always the negative) earthed to the chassis. One terminal on each item of 12 volt electrical equipment is earthed so that only a single wire is needed to supply the equipment: the current return path is through the chassis. This is not done with high voltage propulsion packs: the pack is totally isolated from the chassis. This is an important safety issue: if you are working on the battery and touch a terminal accidentally whilst also touching the chassis, no current will flow because there is no return path.

任何连接到主电池组上的仪表都需要考虑电气隔离。一个正常的 12V 起动电池有一个终端（现在总是负极）作为"地电位"连接到底盘。每个 12V 电气设备也有一个终端接地，因此，只需要用一根导线向设备供电，电流的回路是通过底盘实现的。高压驱动电池组不是这样工作的，该电池组与底盘是完全隔离的——这是一个重要的安全问题：如果您正在电池上工作，并在接触到底盘时意外碰到电池组终端，就会因为电流没有返回路径（不能形成回路）而不会有电流流过人体。

Any sort of instrument directly connected to the pack can compromise this arrangement. If there is a path to ground via the instrument case (for example) then you may be setting yourself up to get a shock from the pack (Figure 6-27).

任何直接连接到电池组的仪表都应当使用这种布局。如果有一个路径使仪器的外壳接到"地电位"，那么您可能会使自己遭受电池组的电击（图 6-27）。

This problem can be largely avoided by using an

通过使用一个绝缘的电流测量装置，如霍尔

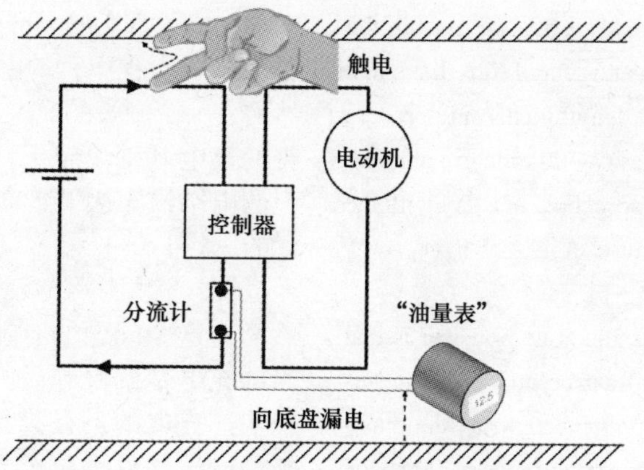

Figure 6–27 Leakage to the vehicle chassis through instrument creates a shock hazard

图 6–27 通过仪器漏电到汽车底盘而使人触电

isolated current measuring device such as a hall-effect sensor.

效应传感器，该问题可以在很大程度上得以避免。

➢ Fast charging

One of the problems with EVs is the time that they take to charge. This is at least as much an issue of mains supply infrastructure as of the batteries themselves. No charging system can deliver energy to a battery faster than it can pull it from the supply. An ordinary domestic electrical outlet in the UK is capable of delivering about 3 kW: so even if the batteries and charging system were perfect, charging a 25 kW-hour pack from 80% discharged state using such an outlet is going to take between 6 and 7 hours. Even using a 32 Amp industrial plug and socket, charging is going to take at least a couple of hours with a pack of this size. By contrast, there are around 25 kW-hours in 3 litres of petrol which can be pumped into a fuel tank in seconds. Even allowing for the lower efficiency of an IC engine, recharging an EV is clearly a couple of orders of magnitude slower than filling up an IC car.

➢ 快速充电

电动汽车的问题之一是充电需要时间。与其说这是电池本身的问题，不如说是电源基础设施的问题。没有充电系统对电池提供的能量可以快于从它那里提取的能量。英国国内一个普通的电源插座能够提供约 3kW 电能。所以，即使电池和充电系统都是完美的，对一个 25kW・h 的电池（80% 的放电状态下）用这样的电源插座充电，将要花 6 ~ 7h。即使用 32A 的工业用插头和插座，对一个这种规模的电池组充电至少也需要几个小时。作为比较，3L 的汽油具有大约 25kW・h 的能量，它可以在几秒钟之内被泵入油箱。虽然内燃机的效率较低，但是对一个电动汽车的充电显然要比对内燃机汽车的加油要慢几个数量级。

The reality is that the problem is less significant than might be imagined because most people most of the time don't drive far in a day. So most EV owners recharge at home whilst they are asleep. An EV with

现实的情况是，这个问题并不像想象的那么严重，因为大多数人在大部分时间内一天开车的里程并不长。因此，大多数电动汽车车主是睡觉时在家里充电的。开车上班、购物和送孩子

an 80 mile useful range would be fine for most of the commuting, shopping trips and school runs that make up the bulk of car usage. A lengthy charging process does mean however that (say) a 300 mile trip in an 80 mile range EV would be impractical in a day with the present charging infrastructure.

上学构成了汽车的大部分用途。对此，一辆拥有150km行程里程的电动汽车是可以应付的。然而，一个漫长的充电过程确实意味着，在现有的充电基础设施下，用例如150km行程里程的电动汽车去开500km的旅程将是不切实际的。

The interesting thing about this issue however is that with the right charging infrastructure, EV batteries could be charged rather rapidly. As I write, the maximum charge rate for two common types of Prismatic lithium ion cells is around 3C. By definition, this means that such a cell could in theory be charged in 1/3rd of an hour (i.e. 20 minutes). With a 100 Ah cell this means a current of 300 Amps. With a 250 volt pack, and assuming no losses, this would be a 75 kW load. That is about 100 hp and outside the capacity of any domestic power supply. It isn't a silly amount of power however: it is for example well within the range of an uninterruptible power supply (UPS) for a small data centre or the supply for a commercial workshop. If and when EVs become mainstream, equipment and standards will be developed to allow for fast charging on demand.

然而，这个问题的有趣之处在于，在有了适当的充电基础设施后，电动汽车的电池是可以快速充电的。在我写作本书时，两种常见类型的棱柱形锂离子电池的最大充电速率是3C左右。根据定义，这意味着，在理论上这样的电池可以在20min内被充电完毕。对于一个100A·h的电池，这意味着300A的电流。对于一个250V的电池组，并假设没有损失，这将是一个75kW的负荷。这是约100hp的负荷，并且超过了任何家用电源的供电能力。然而这不是一个很小的功率，它处于一个可以为一小型数据中心或商店供电的不间断电源（UPS）的功率范围。如果电动汽车成为主流，则设备和标准将被推出以便满足快速充电的需求。

➢ Real world chargers

➢ 现实世界中的充电器

Your choice of charger will be influenced by several factors

- Battery chemistry – charge profiles differ.
- Cell capacity (a bigger pack needs a bigger charger).
- Whether you plan to use a BMS and if so, the type of BMS.
- Whether you have high capacity industrial electrical power available.

您对充电器的选择将受到以下几个因素的影响：

- 电池的化学物质——充电曲线不同
- 电池容量（一个更大的电池组需要一个更大的充电器）
- 您是否计划使用电池管理系统，如果要的话，要确定电池管理系统的类型
- 您是否有大容量的工业电力可用

If you don't plan to use a BMS (or if you go for simple passive shunts on the cells) then you may want a charger that can be programmed to allow

如果您不打算使用电池管理系统（或如果您只用简单的在电池上的无源分流器），那么您可能需要一个可编程的充电器，使其能够

it to control the whole charging process. You will recall that different cell chemistries require different charge profiles (variation of voltage and current with time). With some chargers, these charge profiles can be manipulated by the user. Others are partially programmed at the factory, shipping with a fixed set of user-selectable charge profiles. Yet others are factory-adjusted for a particular battery pack (chemistry, voltage, amp-hour rating).

控制整个充电过程。您会记得，不同的电池化学物质需要不同的充电曲线（电压及电流随时间变化）。对于某些充电器，这些充电配置可以由用户控制；有一些充电器则在工厂时部分编程，出厂时有一组固定的、用户可选的充电曲线；还有一些在工厂时设置成为某一特定电池组（化学物质、电压、安时的评级）充电。

On the other hand you may want the BMS to call the shots, and in that case the most important feature of the charger may be that it can be controlled by the BMS. In general if you are going to use a BMS at all, then it is probably best to choose your BMS and then to seek the BMS manufacturer's advice on chargers. If you go this route however, question your BMS supplier about the way in which the charger is controlled, particularly with lithium ion cells. Look for fail-safe i.e. the charger keeps on charging only if the BMS is alive and actively calling for charging to continue, rather than the charger waiting for a shutdown signal from the BMS. If the shutdown signal does not come and the charger keeps charging a lithium ion pack after it should have shut off, then a fire is probable, and will probably occur in your garage in the middle of the night.

另一方面，您可能希望电池管理系统做主导。在这种情况下，充电器最重要的特征可能是它可以被电池管理系统所控制。一般来说，如果您要使用电池管理系统，那么最好是选择您自己的电池管理系统，然后寻求电池管理系统制造商关于充电器的意见。但是，如果您要这样做，您必须向您的电池管理系统供应商寻求充电器的控制方式，特别是对锂离子电池更应如此。检查一下它的故障安全性能，即只有当电池管理系统正常工作，且允许继续充电时，充电器才充电，而不是让充电器等待来自电池管理系统的切断信号。如果切断信号没有发出，且在充电器应该关闭时继续对锂离子电池组充电，就有可能出现火灾，并且可能会在半夜出现在您的车库里。

Some typical chargers

Here are some chargers advertised as suitable for both lead-acid and lithium chemistry battery packs when suitably configured. They are mostly about the size of a medium-to-large briefcase and can be installed in the vehicle itself (although in the UK, any onboard charger capacity over 3 kW is wasted as most electrical outlets are limited to 3 kW).

一些典型的充电器

这里列出一些在适当的配置下可以适用于铅酸和锂化学电池组的充电器。它们大多是中等到大型公文包大小，可以安装在车辆上（在英国任何容量超过 3kW 的车载充电器都是一种浪费，因为大多数电源插座被限制在 3kW）。

Brusa NLG511-xxx

3.3 kW, ~6.2 kgs

Air or water cooled

Brusa NLG511-XXX 充电器

功率 3.3kW，重约 6.2kg

风冷或水冷

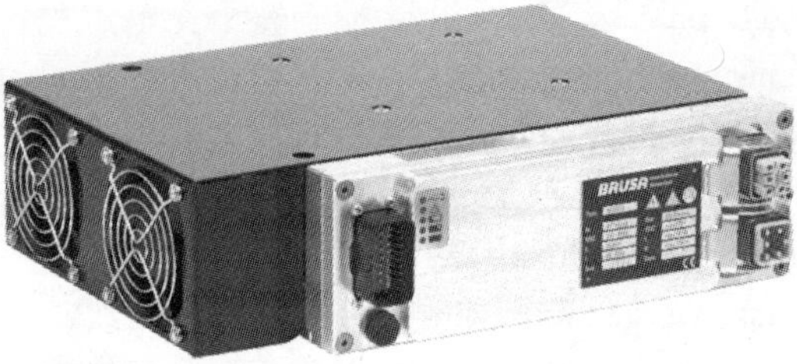

Up to 260 Volts DC
Around £2,500 - £3,000
The Brusa is expensive, but highly programmable.
Photo courtesy of BRUSA Elektronik AG (http://www.brusa.biz)

直流工作电压高达 260V
售价 2.5 ~ 3 万元人民币
Brusa 充电器很贵，但是可高度编程。
照片由 BRUSA ElektronikAG 公司提供(http://www.brusa.biz)

Manzanita Micros PFC20

4.8 kW at 240 volts input, ~ 7.2 kgs

Air cooled
Up to 360 volts DC
Around £1500 - £2000
Photo courtesy of Rich Rudman of Manzanita Micro (http://www.manzanitamicro.com)

Manzanita Micros 公司的 PFC20 充电器

在 240V 工作电压时输出功率 4.8kW，重约 7.2kg
空气冷却
直流工作电压高达 360V
售价 1.5 ~ 2 万元人民币
照片由 Manzanita Micros 公司的雷屈・拉德曼提供（ http://www.manzanitamicro.com ）

Zivan NG3

2.3 kW, ~ 6.8 kgs
Air cooled
Up to 312 Volts DC
Around £750
This charger is set up at the factory for a particular

Zivan 公司的 NG3 充电器

功率 2.3kW，重约 6.8kg
空气冷却
直流工作电压 312V
售价 7500 元人民币左右
该充电器在出厂时被设置为特定的充电曲线。

charge profile.

Photo courtesy of KTA Services (http://www.kta-ev.com/)

照片由 KTA 服务提供（http://www.kta-ev.com/）

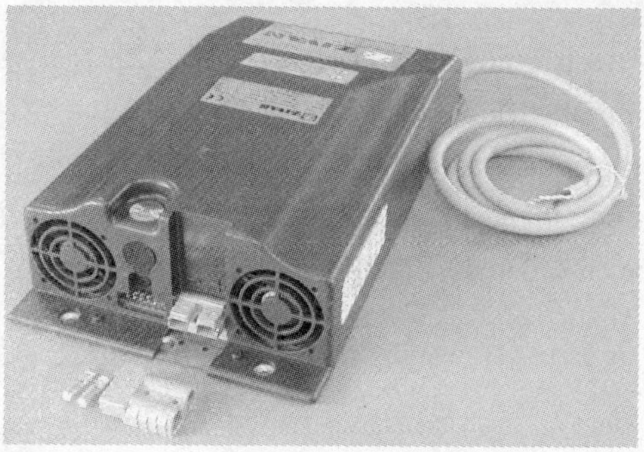

Elcon/Chennic/TCCH

Various models 1.5 - 8 kW, and up to > 400 volts are sold under several different brand names including Elcon, Chennic and TCCH

The 3 kW model weighs around 9.5 kgs. Price range is ~£300 - ~ £2,500.

These chargers ship with 10 different charge profiles preset by the factory to suit the battery chemistry and pack voltage.

ELCON/ Chennic/ TCCH 充电器

有各种型号，功率 1.5 ~ 8kW，有高达 400V 的几种不同品牌出售，包括 ELCON，Chennic 和 TCCH。

3kW 型号的重约 9.5kg。价格范围是 3000 ~ 25000 元人民币。

这些充电器带有由工厂预设的 10 种不同的充电配置，以适应不同的电池化学物质和电池组。

➢ In Conclusion

This chapter is probably the most important in the book, and also proved the most difficult to write. With new battery chemistries (such as lithium-sulphur) emerging, much of the detail may change but hopefully some of the principles (e.g. top versus bottom balancing, voltage settling etc) will be useful whatever chemistry you use. Care and thought put into the management of batteries will make a huge difference to the viability of an EV.

One final thought: the Internet is a wonderful source of information but it is also the perfect breeding ground for urban myths and disinformation. There are many armchair theoreticians out there reprocessing ideas of dubious provenance. As ever Caveat Emptor – buyer beware!

➢ 小结

本章也许是本书中最重要的，也是最难写的。随着新的电池化学物质（如锂硫）的涌现，很多细节可能会变化。但不管您使用何种化学物质，我们希望有些原则（如顶部与底部平衡、电压稳定等）将是有用的。在电池管理中谨慎行事对于一辆电动汽车的可行性将有巨大的改善。

最后还有一点感想：互联网是一个奇妙的信息来源，但它也是完美的都市神话和虚假信息的温床。有很多半桶水的理论家在那里发表一些来源不明的想法。像正常买卖一样，买者责任自负——买家要当心！

7 Ancillaries
辅助设备

Getting a car rolling under electric power is an achievement, but turning it into safe, legal, reliable and comfortable everyday transport takes more than a traction battery pack, a motor and a controller. Other items that need to be considered include:

- Cabin Heating
- Air conditioning
- Low voltage electric power (lights, horn, wipers etc)
- Power steering
- Power brakes

A major issue here is that the power consumed by these services becomes much more significant as a percentage of total power available. For example, running a 2 kW electrical cabin heater for three hours (a typical running time for a 100 mile range EV) would burn 6 kW hours and reduce the car's range by perhaps 10 – 20 miles. We therefore don't just want to provide these services; we want to provide them as efficiently as possible.

让一辆汽车在电力驱动下运行起来是一项成就，但把它变成安全、合法、可靠和舒适的日常交通工具则不是仅有牵引电池组、电机和控制器就可以的。其他需要考虑的问题包括：

- 车舱供暖
- 空调
- 低压电力设备（灯光、喇叭、刮水器等）
- 动力转向
- 助力制动

这里的主要问题是，这些附件所消耗的功率相对于总功率的百分比而言变得越来越显著。例如：一个 2kW 的电车舱加热器运行 3h（这是 160km 里程范围电动汽车的典型运行时间）将耗掉 6kW • h 的电能，有可能减少 20 ~ 30km 的里程数。因此，我们不只是要提供这些服务，还希望能够尽可能高效地提供。

➢ Cabin Heating

Until the 1960s, car heaters were regarded as optional extras. However since then an efficient arrangement for demisting has become mandatory in most jurisdictions. This requirement is usually met in modern cars by provision of warm air heating onto the windshield. The source of heat is usually the IC engine (although a few cars use electrical windshield heating). More than three quarters of the calorific value of fuel burned in a conventional IC engine ends up as heat rather than useful power. In most modern cars, this heat is normally dissipated by circulating liquid coolant (a mixture of water and anti-freeze) through a coolant radiator. Siphoning some of this heat off to the warm the cabin is trivial –

➢ 车舱供暖

20 世纪 60 年代以前，汽车供暖被视为可选部件。然而，自那时以来，有效的除雾设备在大多数辖区已成为必须的。在现代汽车中，通常将暖空气的热量吹到风窗玻璃上来满足这一要求。热源通常来自内燃机发动机（虽然有少数汽车风窗玻璃的加热使用电）。传统内燃机有超过四分之三的燃料热值变成热，而不是有用的能源。在大多数现代汽车中，这种热量通常是通过散热器中冷却液（水和防冻剂的混合物）的循环被排掉。将这些热量中的一部分拿来为车舱供暖是很容易的，这只需要让一些冷却液通过车内的加热器芯（小型二次散热器）即可（图 7-1）。

just run some of the coolant through the heater core (a small secondary radiator) inside the car (Figure 7-1).

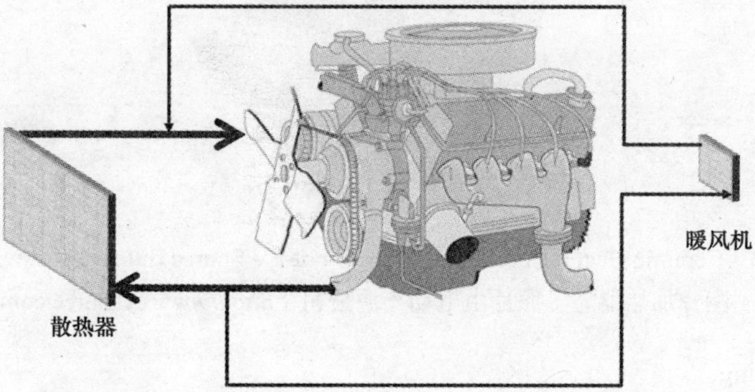

Figure 7–1 Heater in an IC car
图 7–1 在内燃机汽车中的加热器

This approach does not work with electric motors. They are just too efficient. At typical low speed cruise in an EV they don't produce enough waste heat to keep a doll's house warm. There are in practical terms six alternatives:

这种方法并不能用于电动机，因为它们的效率太高了。电动汽车在典型的低速巡航时没有产生足够的废热来维持车舱的温暖。在实践中有 6 种替代品：

1. An electrical air heater (akin to a domestic heater) powered from the traction batteries.
2. An electrical air heater powered from the 12 volt supply.
3. An electrical water heater.
4. An air heater powered by gas of the kind used in small boats.
5. A petrol or diesel powered air heater.
6. A petrol or diesel powered water heater.

① 由牵引电池供电的电空气加热器（类似于家用的加热器）
② 由 12V 电源供电的电空气加热器
③ 电热水加热器
④ 小船用的以燃气加热的空气加热器
⑤ 以汽油或柴油为动力的空气加热器
⑥ 汽油或柴油热水加热器

Each of these has its advantages and disadvantages:

每一种都有各自的优点和缺点。

Electrical Air Heating from the traction batteries

牵引电池供电的电空气加热

Most EV parts suppliers will sell you a ceramic heater core (Figure 7-2) that you can run from the traction batteries. Power output is typically around 1.5 kW – similar to a domestic electrical fan heater

大多数电动汽车零部件供应商会卖给您可以在牵引电池上运行的陶瓷加热器芯（图 7-2）。输出功率一般是 1.5kW 左右，类似于在低功率设置时的家用电暖风机。

Figure 7–2 Ceramic Heater Core. Photo courtesy of EV Source (http://www.evsource.com)

图 7–2 陶瓷加热器芯。照片由电动车源公司（http://www.evsource.com）提供

on a low power setting.

This is on the face of it a relatively low cost approach: the heater core itself might be £100 - £200 (although the cost of a suitable high voltage relay should be added to this). Furthermore, heat is available almost instantly. On the other hand, there are several drawbacks.

这是相对成本较低的方法。加热器芯本身可能是 1000 ~ 2000 元（虽然应该加入适当的高压继电器成本）。此外，热量几乎是瞬间就能得到的。然而，它也有几个缺点。

Firstly, if you are converting a car, and if you want to retain the original heater box, it will be necessary to remove the old heater core and adapt the ceramic replacement to fit in its place.

首先，如果您在转换的汽车中想要保留原有的加热箱，则需要拆除旧的加热器芯并装上陶瓷加热器芯。

Secondly, the full traction battery pack voltage must usually be brought inside the cabin. This creates a small but significant extra safety hazard

其次，牵引电池组的总电压要被送到车舱内，这将带来一个小的但重要的额外安全隐患。

Thirdly, the heater will take a significant amount of power. Assuming an average heater current draw of 1 kW for an hour in a car that uses 1kW for four miles then at an average of 40 miles per hour (all typical numbers), the heater will reduce range by up to about 10%. To the cost of the heater core itself, it would be fair to add 10% of the traction battery cost.

第三，该加热器将耗掉不少的功率。假设汽车平均每 6km 用 1kW 的电能且加热器平均每小时消耗 1kW 的电能，那么，当汽车以 60km/h（典型值）行驶时，加热器将使行程减少达到 10% 左右。除了加热器芯体本身的成本，牵引电池的成本必须增加 10% 才公平。

In a very cold environment it would be possible to use two such cores. It would also be possible to adapt a domestic ceramic heater for this application but this would not be wise unless you know

在一个非常冷的环境中，将有可能使用两个这样的加热器芯，也有可能使用家用的陶瓷加热器，但除非您确切地明白您所做的，否则是不明智的。

exactly what you are doing.

12 Volt electrical Heating

Standalone 12 volt heaters (and 12 volt hairdryers) are readily available (see Figure 7-3 for an example). They may be helpful for demisting and localised heating, but anecdotal evidence and simple arithmetic suggests that they are unlikely to be very satisfactory for heating a large space. The basic problem is that their power ratings are low: ranging from 100 watts to a maximum of about 300 watts. 300 watts is less than most electric drills and kitchen blenders. Compare this with 1500 watts for a ceramic heater core powered by the traction batteries or 2000 watts for the smallest fuel/air heaters discussed later.

12V 的电暖气

独立的 12V 加热器（及 12V 的电吹风）是很现成的（参见图 7-3 中的例子）。它们可能有助于除雾和局部加热，但未经证实的证据及简单的计算表明，它们对加热大空间不可能是非常令人满意的。这里的一个基本问题是，它们的额定功率太低，从 100W 到最大约 300W 的范围。300W 低于常用的电钻和厨房搅拌机的功率。与此相比，牵引电池组供电的陶瓷加热器芯的功率为 1500W，后面将讨论的最小的燃料 / 空气加热器的功率为 2000W。

Figure 7–3 RoadPro C3606A 12 Volt 140 watt heater/demister. Photo courtesy of RoadPro Ltd (http://www.roadpro.co.uk)

图 7–3 RoadPro C3606A 12V140W 的加热器 / 除雾器。照片由洛地泊罗有限公司（http://www.roadpro.co.uk）提供

The limitation is the massive current required at this low voltage. 300 watts at 12 volts requires 25 amps. An 1800 watt 12 volt heater would require 150 amps. This would flatten the average 12 volt starter battery in a few minutes and require heavy cabling and a very large and expensive relay.

其限制是在这样的低电压下需要大量的电流。在 12V 时 300W 的功率需要 25A 的电流。一个工作于 12V 的 1800W 的加热器将需要 150A 的电流。这将在几分钟内耗尽一个常用的 12V 起动电池，并需要很粗的电缆和一个非常大且昂贵的继电器。

An electrical water heater

As noted earlier, most IC-engined cars use liquid coolant and use the waste heat to warm the cabin. One approach therefore is to retain the existing heating system, and merely to add an in line electrical water heating element to replace the IC engine water jacket (Figure 7-4, Figure 7-5).

电热水加热器

如前所述，大多数内燃机发动机的汽车使用冷却液，并使用余热预热汽车舱。因此，一种方法是保留现有的加热系统，并只要用一个电热水加热元件去替换内燃机发动机的水套（图 7-4 和图 7-5）。

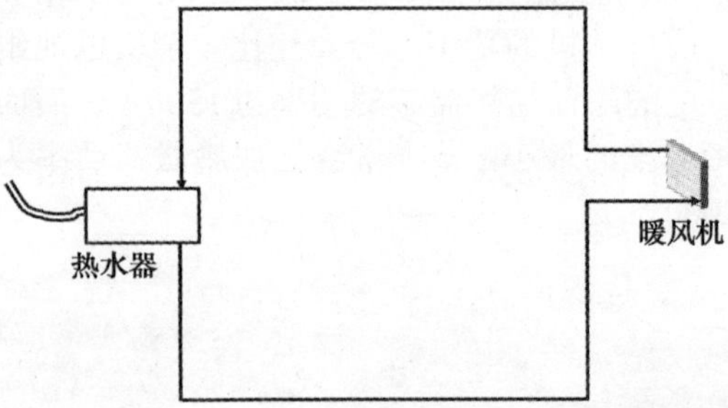

Figure 7–4 Electric Water Heater Schematic

图 7–4 电热水器原理图

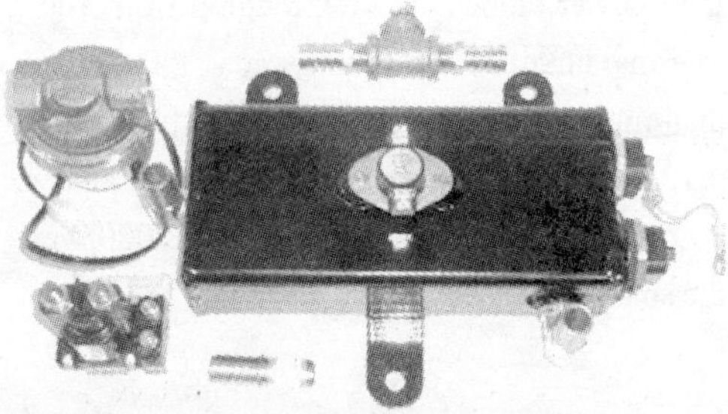

Figure 7–5 In line Water Heater. Photo courtesy of EV Source (http://www.evsource.com)

图 7–5 在线热水器。照片由电动车源公司（http://www.evsource.com）提供

As with air heaters, it is in theory possible to draw power from either the traction batteries or the 12 volt system. However the 12 volt option can be discounted on the grounds that at a practical power output the time taken to produce perceptible heat at the heater vents would be very long. Traction battery powered water heaters are a possibility however. They are easier to install than a ceramic air heater and keep high voltages out of the cabin. The high power drain will have the same negative impact on range however. A water heater is also more expensive than an equivalent air heater.

像空气加热器一样，它在理论上可以从牵引电池或 12V 的系统中吸取能量。然而，在实用的输出功率中，12V 系统将需要很长的时间才能产生可察觉到的热风，因此，该选项可被略去。然而，牵引电池供电的热水器将是一种可能。它们比陶瓷空气加热器更容易安装，且可将高电压限制在车舱外。但高电力消耗对汽车的行程将有同样的负面影响。比起同等的空气加热器，热水器也比较贵。

The biggest drawback of any water heater is the time it takes to warm up – probably longer than the heater in a conventional IC-engined car. It has to heat the water in the whole system to a temperature well above ambient before any heat will filter through to the cabin.

热水器的最大缺点是加热所需的时间，也许比传统的内燃机发动机汽车中的加热器所花的时间更长。任何热量能经过车舱之前，它必须将整个系统中的水加热到远高于室温的温度。

An air heater powered by gas

It is possible to heat your car with the kind of small gas heater that is used in boats and caravans (Figure 7-6). This of course requires a gas bottle which must be recharged or replaced periodically. This in turns adds weight and requires space. It also creates a potential safety hazard (although some IC engined cars are themselves driven by natural gas so the hazard isn't novel). Figure 7-6 shows a Propex heater with an output in the range 1.5 – 2 kW. Such a heater requires a 12 volt supply for control and ignition but draws far less power than an electric heater. Note also that it contains a heat exchanger with an external vent. A free standing self contained gas heater in a car would be an accident looking for a place to happen.

燃气空气加热器

您也可以用小船和大篷车中使用的那种小型燃气加热器来对您的汽车加热（图 7-6）。当然，这需要一个液化气瓶并要定期进行充气或更换。这又增加了重量并占用空间，同时也造成了潜在的安全隐患（由于一些内燃机发动机的汽车本身就是天然气驱动的，所以危害并不是电动汽车所特有的）。图 7-6 示出了功率输出范围为 1.5 ~ 2kW 的 Propex 加热器。这样的加热器需要 12V 的电源来控制和点火，但所用的功率比电加热器小得多。还要注意的是，它包含了一个有外部通风口的热交换器。在汽车中一个独立的燃气加热器将是一个容易发生事故的地方。

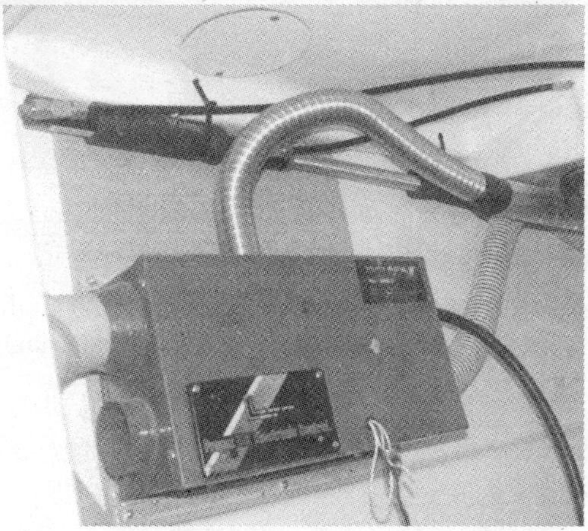

Figure 7–6 Propex Gas Heater. Photo courtesy of Björn Sjöling and "Restless"

图 7–6 Propex 燃气热水器。照片由比约恩•赫亚令及"勒斯特乐思"提供

These heaters are not cheap either – in the range £600 - £900 new at the time of writing.

这些加热器还是不便宜的。在写作本书时，一个新的燃气加热器为 6000 ~ 9000 元。

A petrol or diesel air heater

Lorry cabs sometimes include overnight accommodation for the driver and require heating. Small motor vessels also need heat when moored. Even some small twin-engined aircraft use heaters that are independent of the engines because of the difficulty of ducting hot air from the nacelles on the wings.

汽油或柴油空气加热器

货车驾驶室有时也要为驾驶人准备过夜的设备并且也需要加热。小型机动船在停泊时也需要加热。即使是一些小型的双发动机飞机也会使用独立于发动机的加热器，因为将热空气从位于机翼的发动机舱中引过来有点难度。

For these applications, several companies have developed heaters powered by petrol or diesel fuel. They obviously use some fuel, but far less than would be required by the main engine.

在这些应用中，有些公司已经开发出用汽油或柴油做燃料的加热器。很明显，它们要消耗一些燃料，但远远低于发动机所使用的。

Once again though, these heaters are not cheap, but they are expressly designed for vehicle heating. There are, at the time of writing, three main manufacturers of such units: Webasto, Mikuni and Eberspacher. Figure 7-7 is an example of a Webasto heater. Cost for this kind of unit is typically £700 upwards.

需要再次提到的是，虽然这些加热器不便宜，但它们明确设计成为车辆加热。在写作本书时，有三个主要制造商：韦巴斯特、米古尼和埃贝赫。图 7-7 是韦伯斯特加热器的一个例子。这种加热器通常在 7000 元（RMB）以上。

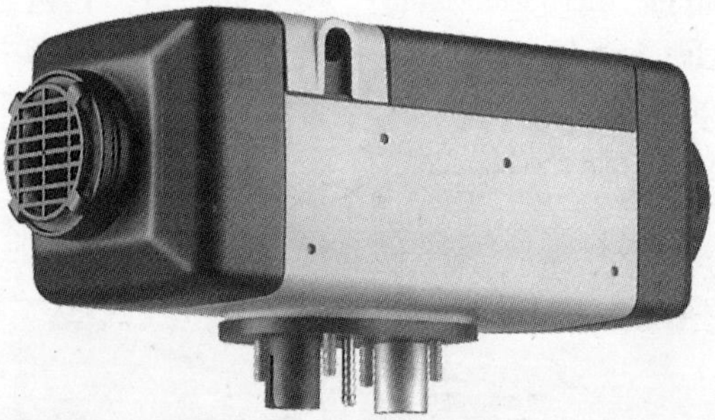

Figure 7–7 Webasto Airtop 2000 ST Air Heater. Photo courtesy of Webasto (http://www.webasto.co.uk/home/en/html/homepage.html)

图 7–7 韦伯斯特艾尔托帕 2000ST 空气加热器。照片由韦伯斯特（http://www.webasto.co.uk/home/en/html/homepage.html）提供

Clearly in a pure EV, a petrol or diesel heater has the major drawback of requiring a fuel tank and associated hardware. For some users this goes against the whole principle of EVs. For a hybrid though they look like a good fit. A hybrid will have a fuel system anyway, so tapping into it for a supply for the heater should be straightforward. Fuel consumption is of the order of 1 litre every four hours which is trivial compared with fuel consumption of a normal car engine.

显然，在纯电动汽车中，汽油或柴油加热器的主要缺点是需要一个油箱及相关的部件。对于有些用户来说，这违反了电动汽车的整体原则。然而对于混合动力汽车而言，它们看起来是一个不错的选择。无论如何，混合动力汽车具有燃料系统，因此将它输送到加热器中应该是直截了当的。4h 的燃料消耗量为 1L 左右，相对于一辆正常汽车发动机的燃料消耗量而言是微不足道的。

A petrol or diesel powered water heater

This is an alternative to an air heater. The principle is, once again, analogous to the electrical water heater. The unit is inserted into the existing heater circuit, but instead of being heated by electricity, the heat comes from burning petrol or diesel fuel. As with the electri-

汽油或柴油水加热器

这是一个空气加热器的替代品，其原理还是类似于电热水器。该加热器被插入到现有的加热器线路中，但不是由电来加热，而是由燃烧的汽油或柴油来加热。与电热水器相似，它从冷却的状态中并不能及时地获得热量，

cal water heater, heat is not instant from cold because the water in the system must be warmed up before heat becomes available (Figure 7-8).

因为在获得热量之前系统中的水必须先被加热（图 7-8）。

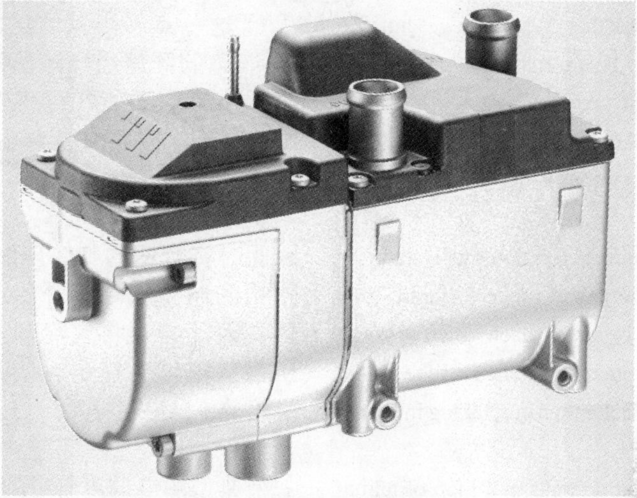

Figure 7–8 Eberspacher Hydronic Water Heater. Photo courtesy of J. Eberspaecher GmbH & Co. KG (http://www.eberspacher.com)

图 7–8 埃贝施帕赫水加热器。照片由 J. 埃贝施帕赫公司（http://www.eberspacher.com）提供

Summary

Apart from the obvious considerations of cost and safety, probably the two biggest issues are power (at least 1500 Watts for a UK winter) and speed of warm up. This tends to rule out both the 12 volt solutions and those relying on water heating (although water heating might be satisfactory with very high powered heating elements).

小结

除了明显的成本和安全方面的问题，两个最大的问题可能是功率（对于英国的冬天而言至少要 1500W）和加热的速度。这往往会将 12V 的解决方案和那些依赖于水加热的方案排除在外（虽然如果用了具有非常高功率的加热元件，水加热可能是令人满意）。

➢ Air conditioning

In the average Northern European summer, air conditioning has to be an optional extra. If you must have it, then you are probably going to need professional help, and you must accept that using air conditioning will have an impact on range.

➢ 空调

在北欧的夏季，空调只是一个可选的附件。如果您一定要在车上安装空调，那么您可能需要专业人士的帮助，同时您必须了解，使用空调会影响汽车的行程里程。

Conventional Automotive Air Conditioning

Air conditioning rests on three basic principles:

传统汽车的空调

空调基于三个基本原理：

- If you compress a gas it heats up (feel the barrel of a bicycle pump that has been used for a while).
- You can liquefy a gas by compressing it sufficiently.
- When a liquid turns into a gas it takes in heat (Sweating illustrates this. When we get hot, we sweat liquid water. This turns into water vapour by evaporation and takes in heat as it does so, cooling us down. An Aerosol can cooling down in use is another example.).

- 气体被压缩以后会变热（在自行车打气筒使用了一段时间后用手去感觉一下气筒壁）
- 如果您将气体充分压缩，它会液化
- 当液体变成气体时它要吸热（出汗说明了这一点。当我们觉得热时，我们流出液态的汗。当汗液蒸发变成水蒸气时需要吸热，这样就使我们冷却下来。还例如，气雾罐在使用中会降温。）

So the air conditioning/refrigeration cycle starts by compressing a suitable gas to make it liquid. This heats the liquid, so it is cooled back down to room temperature. Then the pressure is taken off the liquid, allowing it to expand back into a gas, taking in heat.

因此，将合适的气体压缩成液体时，空调/冰箱的制冷循环就开始了。这将使液体变热，因此必须将它冷却至室温。然后，将压强从液体中撤走，使其膨胀成气体，同时吸热。

A typical air conditioner consists of a loop of tubing with a radiator at each end, a pump between the radiators on one side and an orifice on the other. The whole is filled with a "refrigerant" . This is a gas at room temperature and low pressure but becomes a liquid relatively easily when compressed. It works as follows.

一个典型的空调由管道的环路组成，在其每一端有一个散热器，散热器的一侧和一个节流孔之间有一个泵。整个系统被“制冷剂”充满。它在室温及低压力下为气体，但被压缩时较容易变成液体。其工作原理如下。

The pump (or "compressor" – normally belt driven from the engine in an automotive context) takes in gas at around ambient temperature and compresses it, which heats it up. It is still a gas at this point, but only because it is hot. The hot gas circulates through one of the radiators (the "condenser" – outside the cabin) which cools it back down to near ambient temperature at which point it becomes a liquid. The cooled liquid then expands back to a gas as it passes through an orifice, cooling further as it does so. The cold gas is circulated through the other radiator (the "evaporator" – in the cabin). Air is blown through the evaporator by a fan, which causes cool air to circulate in the cabin. The spent gas goes back to the pump inlet and the cycle is repeated (Figure 7-9).

该液泵（或“压缩机”，在汽车的情况下通常由从发动机而来的传动带驱动）在室温下吸入气体，将其压缩，使它变热。这时它仍然是气体，但却是热的。热气体通过一个散热器（车舱外的“冷凝器”）循环，将其冷却到接近室温，并在此时变成液体。然后，冷却后的液体通过一个节流孔时膨胀回到气体，使其进一步冷却。冷却后的气体循环通过另一个散热器（车舱内的“蒸发器”）。空气通过风扇吹到蒸发器，使得冷空气在车舱内循环。用过的气体返回到泵的进气口，并重复该循环（图 7-9）。

Engine-driven compressors are normally fitted with electrically-actuated clutches. With the clutch disen-

发动机驱动的压缩机通常装有电驱动的离合器。当离合器分开时空调处于关闭状态。虽

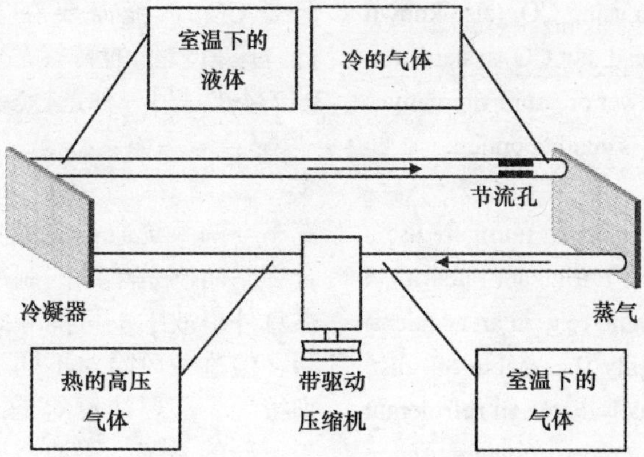

Figure 7–9 Air Conditioning in a Conventional Car

图 7–9 传统汽车中的空调

gaged the air conditioning is off; although the compressor pulley is rotating, the compressor itself is not, so nothing happens. The air conditioning is actuated simply by closing a switch which supplies power to the compressor clutch. The clutch engages, the compressor starts to rotate and the air conditioning starts to operate.

然压缩机带轮还在旋转，但压缩机本身并没有转动，所以空调不工作。简单地将一个为压缩机的离合器提供电源的开关关闭就能将空调激活。这时离合器啮合，压缩机开始旋转，空调开始工作。

The electrical power to the clutch is usually also controlled by a thermostatic switch, so when the cabin temperature gets down to a preset level the clutch disengages so that the cabin is not overcooled.

为离合器提供的电能通常也由一个恒温开关控制。因此，当车舱的温度下降到预定值时，离合器分开，使得车舱不会过冷。

Refrigerants

There are currently three types of refrigerant in common use in domestic (household) air conditioners – R22, R407c and R410a. R22 (Freon) is on its way out: R22 should not even be used for maintenance of old systems in the European Union.

制冷剂

目前家用空调中普遍使用的制冷剂有三种类型：R22、R407c 和 R410a。R22（氟利昂）逐步被淘汰，在欧盟，R22 甚至不能被用于维护旧的系统。

At the time of writing, most current automotive air conditioning systems use R134a. R12 was used in the past but has been implicated in ozone layer depletion and has not been used for a while now. Even R134a will not be permitted in brand new designs in the European Union from 2011 as there is concern about its supposed impact on global warming. Some

在写作本书时，大多数汽车空调系统使用 R134a。R12 在过去有被用过，但由于它与臭氧层的消耗有关，现在已有一段时间不用了。从 2011 年开始在新的设计中即使是 R134a 也不允许在欧盟中使用，因为人们担心它对全球变暖有影响。也有一些使用 CO_2 进行尝试（在这种使用中也被称为 R744）， investment has been put into using CO_2 (also known as R744 in this context) instead, but CO_2 systems run at very high pressures and lower pressure alternatives may be developed: R1234yf is another option.

但是 CO_2 系统需要在非常高的压力下运行。压力较低的替代品也可能被研制出来，R1234yf 是另一种选择。

Automotive air conditioning systems normally use a mixture of lubricating oil and refrigerant rather than pure refrigerant. System rupture (e.g. in an accident) can lead to release of a highly flammable oil mist, although the risk varies widely between refrigerant types. Note also that different types of oil are used in different systems and contamination of a system with the wrong kind of oil can cause rapid failure.

汽车空调系统通常使用润滑油和制冷剂的混合物，而不是单纯的制冷剂。系统破裂（如在意外事故中）可能导致高度易燃油雾的泄漏，但这一风险对不同类型的制冷剂而言差别很大。还要注意的是，不同类型的油被用于不同的系统，用油错误对系统的污染可能导致系统快速损坏。

Air conditioning systems operate at high pressures: A typical R134a system might run at 100 – 200 psi. A CO_2 system might be 10 times that. The very high pressures of CO_2 systems are sufficient to raise safety concerns. Note also that deliberately releasing refrigerant into the atmosphere is illegal in some jurisdictions including the European Union.

空调系统通常在高压力下工作。一个典型的 R134a 系统可能在 100 ~ 200Pa 的压力下工作。一个 CO_2 系统的压力可能是上述的 10 倍。CO_2 系统非常高的压力足以引起人们对安全的重视。还要注意的是，包括欧盟在内的某些地区中，故意向大气中释放制冷剂是非法的。

All of these issues strongly suggest that messing with air conditioning systems is not a DIY activity. There is nothing wrong with mounting the components yourself but selecting them and charging/discharging should be handled by properly equipped professionals.

所有这些问题都清楚地表明，空调系统是不适合自行装配的。您可以自己安装组件，但选择及灌装或排放制冷剂则应由具有专业设备的专业人士来处理。

Adapting A/C Systems to EVs

将交流 / 直流转换系统安装到电动汽车中

There are at least three ways to adapt an air conditioning system from a conventional car to an EV:

- Replace the engine driven compressor with a self-contained electrically driven one.
- Drive the existing compressor with a separate electric motor.
- Drive the existing compressor from the drive motor or transmission shaft.

至少有三种方法可以将传统汽车中的空调系统安装到电动汽车中：

- 将发动机驱动的压缩机换成一个自成一体的电驱动压缩机
- 用一个单独的电动机驱动现有的压缩机
- 用驱动电动机或传动轴驱动现有的压缩机

In addition there are in theory other options including

- An ice box
- Thermoelectric (Peltier) devices
- Doing without air conditioning altogether

These alternatives are discussed in more detail below.

Electrical compressors

At the time of writing, electrically driven compressors are not widely used in cars, although as pure electric production cars such as the Nissan Leaf enter the market they should become available.

Once again, there is an issue related to the power consumption of the compressor. A typical unit in a conventional car may require around 2 hp (roughly 1.5 kW) which at 12 volts works out at about 125 amps. As with the heater however, it is possible to use power from the traction batteries rather than running a compressor from the 12 volt system. With a 144 volt pack, current would be just over 10 Amps which is far more manageable.

There are a few manufacturers selling electrically driven compressors. Figure 7-10 shows an electrically driven compressor capable of operating from an EV traction pack (150 – 300 Volts). Models from this manufacturer are available operating at up to about 1.8 kW (6 Amps at 300 volts). They are driven by a brushless DC motor which needs its own controller: a scaled-down version of the main traction controller. Compressor and controller of this sophistication from any source will not be cheap however.

There is theoretically one lower cost source of high voltage air conditioning compressors – domestic air conditioners designed to operate off the mains. It might (I stress “might”) be possible to use one of these driven by a DC - AC inverter. However the engineering required to make something like

此外，在理论上还有其他选项，它们包括

- 一个冰盒
- 热电设备
- 完全不用空调

这些替代方案将在下面更详细地讨论。

电动压缩机

在写作本书时，电驱动压缩机还没有被广泛地用在汽车上，虽然随着纯电动产品（如日产 Leaf 车）进入市场，它们应该可以买到。

另外，有一个关于压缩机的功耗问题。在传统汽车中一个典型的压缩机可能需要大约 2hp（大约 1.5kW），即在 12V 时约 125A。但与加热器一样，它可以使用来自牵引电池的电能，而不是用 12V 系统来带动压缩机。如果使用 144V 的电池组，其电流仅仅大于 10A，这更易于管理。

有一些厂家销售电驱动压缩机。图 7-10 所示的电驱动压缩机能够在电动汽车牵引电池组（150 ~ 300V）下工作。该制造商销售的最大功率为约 1.8kW（在 300V 为 6A）。它们都是由无刷直流电动机驱动，需要自己的控制器，一个按比例缩小的主牵引控制器。这种复杂的压缩机和控制器从任何角度上看，都不便宜。

在理论上可以有低价的高压空调压缩机，即工作于市电的家用空调。有可能（我强调的是“可能”）使用由直流 – 交流逆变器来驱动这些空调压缩机。然而，要让这一压缩机能可靠地工作，需要作出的努力将是巨大的。

Figure 7–10 Masterflux® Sierra Air Conditioning Compressor (Photograph: © 2010 Tecumseh Products Company, all rights reserved. Masterflux® and Sierra ™ ® are trademarks of Tecumseh Products Company. http://www.masterflux.com/)

图 7–10 马斯特夫陆克思的西拉空调压缩机

（摄影：©2010 蒂卡姆西产品公司，版权所有，严禁翻录。Masterflux® 和 Sierra™® 是蒂卡姆西产品公司的注册商标。http://www.masterflux.com/）

this work reliably would be considerable.

There are a number of considerations. Firstly domestic goods are built to a lower specification than automotive items because they don't have to put up with constant motion and vibration. If you look at the wiring in your cooker, washing machine or refrigerator, you'll see that it is usually less well supported than the wiring under the bonnet of a car. At the least such unsupported wiring in a moving vehicle is likely to cause irritating rattles. At worst the constant chafing and flexing will result in short circuits, open circuits or both.

这里有几个顾虑。首先家用物品的建造规格都要低于汽车用品，因为它们没有处于不断的运动和振动的环境。观察一下家中灶具、洗衣机或冰箱中的布线，您会看到它们通常不像汽车发动机盖下的布线那样固定得很牢固。在移动的车辆中这类没有固定的布线至少可能会引起刺激性的摇摆。在最坏的情况下，这些不间断的磨损及弯曲会导致短路、断路或两者兼有。

Secondly there are potential compatibility issues. This includes things like hose fittings and connectors, refrigerant types and lubricant. As described above a domestic air conditioning compressor might be designed to work with, say R410 rather than R134a and/or require a different lubricant type.

其次，还存在潜在的兼容性问题。这包括软管接头和连接器、制冷剂的类型和润滑剂等。如上所述，家用空调压缩机也许被设计成工作于如 R410，而不是 R134a 和 / 或需要不同的润滑油类型。

Separate electric motor drive

This is a practicable, although slightly less elegant solution: obtain a suitable small (1 – 2 hp) electric motor and use it to drive the existing air conditioning compressor. See Figure 7-11 for a well-used example.

分立电动机驱动

虽然这一解决方案略显不雅，但这是切实可行的。拿一个较小（1 ~ 2hp）的电动机，并用它来驱动现有的空调压缩机。图 7-11 给出一个使用得较好的例子。

Figure 7–11 Compressor Powered by External Motor. Photo courtesy of Victor Tikhonov

图 7–11 由外部电动机驱动的压缩机。照片由维克托吉洪诺夫提供

This approach typically takes up a bit more space than a self-contained electric compressor and will usually involve more metal-bashing (e.g. the construction of suitable mounting brackets). But it has the advantage of leaving most of the air-conditioning system undisturbed, and should work out to be cheaper than a new compressor. The motor will however need selecting carefully, in terms of power, direction of rotation, supply voltage and r.p.m. A direct drive of the kind shown in Figure 7-11 requires a suitable coupling, although belt drive could be used instead. In addition the motor will need its own controller.

这种方法与自成一体的电动压缩机相比通常需要更多的空间，并通常会需要更多的金属连接（例如合适的支架安装）。但它具有大部分的空调系统不受干扰的优点，并且也比一个全新的压缩机更便宜。然而，电动机在功率、转向、电源电压和转速等方面要仔细挑选。图 7-11 所示的那种直接驱动压缩机需要一个合适的耦合，但它也可用带传动来代替。此外，该电动机需要有自己的控制器。

Transmission driven

Perhaps the cheapest solution is to drive the existing compressor from the traction motor or from some part of the main transmission. If your main propulsion motor has an accessible shaft at both ends then it should be fairly straightforward to belt drive the compressor from the unused shaft. The installation issues are similar in scope to those encountered when using the separate

传输驱动

也许最廉价的解决方案是用牵引电动机或主变速器的某些部分来驱动现有的压缩机。如果您的主推进电动机轴的两端都有一个可用的轴，那么用空闲的轴装上传动带来驱动压缩机应该是相当简单的。安装的问题与上述用单独的电动机驱动时所遇到的问题是相似的。寻找或制作适合的支架和

electric motor drive described above: there may be significant effort involved with sourcing or fabricating suitable brackets and couplings or pulleys.

连接器或滑轮可能需要很大努力。

The biggest disadvantage of this approach is the obvious one that the air conditioning will only operate when the car is rolling: and even then may not be very effective at low speed. This is a pity as the worst case scenario for most air conditioning systems is slow moving nose-to-tail traffic.

这种方法最大的缺点是显而易见的，即只有当汽车开动时空调才开始工作，并且在低速时甚至可能不是很有效的。这是一个遗憾，因为对大多数空调系统而言，最坏的情况是缓慢移动的交通阻塞状况。

An ice box

This is a cheap-and-cheerful solution, but one that requires additional preparation for each journey: take along a box of ice in an insulated chest and blow air through it to cool the cabin. It sounds over-simple, but anecdotal evidence suggests that it works. Domestic ice – boxes with fans are available on line for £50 or so (try e-bay or Amazon). They are going to be bulky but might do the job, especially in a temperate climate where they are only needed occasionally.

冰盒

这是一个廉价且方便的解决方案，但每次旅行都需要额外的准备。您要随身携带一个放在保温柜中的冰，并用空气吹过它来冷却车舱。这听起来太简单了，但未经证实的证据表明它确实可行。家用的冰，包括箱子与风扇可在网上用 500 元左右购得（可以尝试易趣或亚马逊购物网）。它们的体积可能很大，但能起作用，特别是在温带气候，您只是偶尔需要它们。

A possible approach which is purely theoretical (because I have not seen it implemented) would be to use a portable freezer unit (many models are available). The freezer would be filled with suitable water containers (i.e. ones that could be frozen without splitting). When the traction battery was charging, the cooling unit in the freezer would also be connected and running. Once on the move, the "stored cold" in the frozen liquid could be used to cool the cabin.

一种纯理论的可能方法（因为我还没有看到它实现）是使用一台便携式的冷冻箱（有很多型号可供选择）。该冷冻箱装满了适当的水容器（即那些可被冻结而不破裂的容器），当牵引电池在充电时，冷冻箱中的冷却设备也被连接并工作。一旦上路,在冷冻液中“被存储的冷气”可用于冷却车舱。

Thermoelectric devices

Thermoelectric cooling normally makes use of the Peltier effect: passing a current across the junction between two dissimilar metals causes one to warm up and the other to cool down - Figure 7-12. [This is the exact opposite of the Seebeck effect exploited in thermocouples]. Peltier devices are used for spot cooling in some situations but are little use for cooling large spaces.

热电装置

热电式冷却通常使用珀耳帖效应。当电流通过两种不同金属之间的交界处时，一种金属将变热，另一种变冷，见图 7-12（这与热电偶中的塞贝克效应正好相反）。珀耳帖装置在某些情况下用于局部冷却，但很少用于大空间冷却。

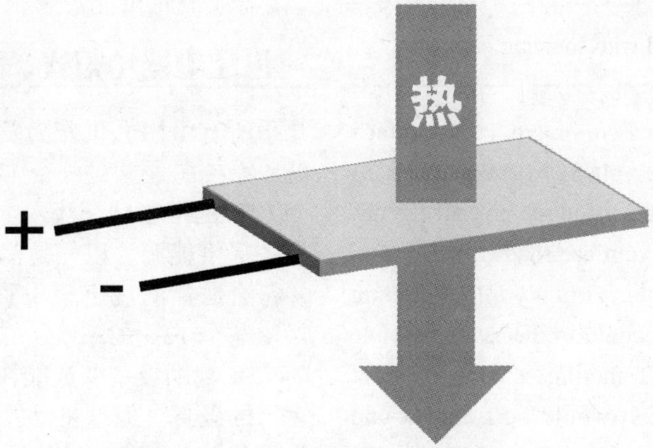

Figure 7–12 A Peltier-effect device

图 7–12 一个珀耳帖效应器件

Doing without air conditioning

In the UK, until comparatively recently, only executive barges were equipped with air conditioning. Real men (and women) driving Real cars wore shorts and tee shirts in hot weather, rolled the windows down and, if necessary, sweated. The author drove for years in Africa in air temperatures up to 45℃ without air conditioning.

不使用空调

在英国直到最近，只有豪华车才配有空调。一般人在炎热的天气驾驶汽车时都穿着短裤和T恤，如果有必要的话打开窗户，也许会汗流浃背。本书作者在非洲温度高达45℃的情况下开了多年的车都没用空调。

Open windows do increase aerodynamic drag but probably not by very much at typical EV cruising speeds. So one air conditioning option is no air conditioning at all. Strategies for keeping cool without it include the obvious one of not leaving your car to hot-soak in the sun. Park under a tree if there is one handy.

打开窗户将增加气动阻力，但在典型的电动汽车巡航速度时可能不是非常明显。因此，一种选择是完全不用空调。显然，不用空调且维持低温的策略首先包括不要将车停在阳光下吸热。如果方便的话，将它停在一棵大树下。

The other option worth investigating is window tint or film. There are strict laws in the UK about the degree of tinting permitted forward of the B pillar (i.e. the back edge of the front doors) but there are films/coatings which claim to reduce solar heating without excessive visual darkening.

值得研究的另一种选择是用有色玻璃窗或贴膜。在英国，对B柱（即前车门的后缘）前的玻璃着色深度有严格的法律规定，但有些膜/涂料声称能降低太阳热能却不会使视觉变暗太多。

So much for heating and air-conditioning. Next we will move on to the 12/14 volt supply normally provided for us in an IC engined car by a belt driven alternator.

关于暖气和空调就谈这些。下一步，我们将讨论由内燃机发动机的汽车为我们提供的带驱动交流发电机产生的12/14V电源。

➢ Low voltage electrics (lights, wipers etc)

Virtually all IC-engined cars have a low voltage system (typically a 12 volt SLI battery and a 14 volt belt-driven alternator) for running all the ancillaries needed to make a car roadworthy and to meet legal requirements. Virtually all EVs retain this 12 volt system. It would in theory be possible to swap all the 12 volt ancillaries over to run at traction pack voltage. It would be complex and expensive though: 144 volt headlamp bulbs or 300 volt rear screen heaters are not generally held in stock by your local motor factors.

There is a further complication: a "12 volt" system in an IC engined car doesn't actually operate at 12 volt when the engine is running. The alternator in such a car is normally regulated at just over 14 volts. You can see the difference between 12 and 14 volts if you leave the lights on when you shut the engine down at night; there is a noticeable drop in brightness.

As with heating and air conditioning there are several options for implementing a low voltage power supply in an EV. The two main ones are either to fit an oversize auxiliary battery and charge it up whenever you charge the traction battery, or use a DC-to-DC converter.

Fitting a larger auxiliary battery

You might recall from the chapter on batteries that ordinary SLI (Starter, Lighting, Ignition) batteries fitted to almost all conventional cars are not designed to be deeply discharged. They are quite capable of delivering short bursts of high current for engine starting, but will be destroyed quite quickly by repeated deep discharge.

If you can cope with dim headlights and sluggish wipers, there is an easy option: there are vast numbers of 12 volt "leisure" batteries on the market designed

➢ 低压电器（灯光、刮水器等）

几乎所有由内燃机作为发动机的汽车都具有低压系统（通常是一个 12V 的起动电池和一个 14V 的带驱动交流发电机）为所有的辅助设备提供能源，以便使汽车可在道路上行驶并符合法律的规定。几乎所有的电动汽车都保留这个 12V 的系统。在理论上可以将所有的 12V 辅助设备变成能在牵引电池组电压下运行的设备。但这将是复杂和昂贵的，144V 的车头灯泡或 300V 的后风窗玻璃加热器通常在汽车经销商里并没有存货。

更为复杂的是，内燃机发动机的汽车中的“12V”系统在发动机运行时实际上并不工作于 12V。这类汽车中的交流发电机通常工作在刚好超过 14V。如果您在晚上关闭发动机时让车灯亮着，您就可以看到 12V 与 14V 之间的区别，即灯的亮度明显下降。

与暖气和空调的情形相同，在电动汽车中有几个选项可以用来实现低压电源供应。两个主要的方法是：安装一个较大的辅助电池并在您为牵引电池充电时也为它充电；使用一个直流 - 直流转换器。

安装一个较大的辅助电池

在第 5 章中说过，安装在几乎所有的传统汽车中的普通 SLI（起动、照明、点火）电池并没有被设计成可供深度放电的。它们完全有能力为发动机的起动提供短脉冲的大电流，但反复的深度放电会将它很快地损坏。

如果您能适应昏暗的车灯和缓慢的刮水器，则有一个简单的选择：市场上有大量的用于船舶和大篷车的 12V “康乐”电池。一个

for use in boats and caravans. A 100 Amp-hour leisure battery should keep the headlights and wipers on for a 40 mile trip without recharging. You might not want to keep a rear screen heater or a 12 volt heater on for too long though with this kind of set up.

100A • h的康乐电池在不充电的情况下应该可以为前照灯和刮水器供电60km的路程。使用这种电池时，您不要奢望让后风窗玻璃加热器或12V加热器工作太长时间。

A variation of this idea is to use a 14 volt battery to make up for the lack of alternator output on the move. A 14 volt auxiliary battery is a little less mainstream than its 12 volt equivalent. A friend of the author used nickel-iron cells in series with an ordinary 12 volt battery; a better solution might be something like an 8 volt battery and a 6 volt battery in series. The Trojan T875 for example is an 8 volt deep cycle battery with a 170 Amp-hour rating at the 20 hour rate (see Figure 7-13). As might be expected from its capacity (2 – 3 times that of an ordinary SLI battery) it is also fairly heavy at 29 kg. In series with a 6 volt traction battery of the kind often used in golf carts, you would have a solid 14 volt battery pack.

该想法的一个变通是使用一个14V的电池，以弥补在行驶时交流发电机输出的缺乏。一个14V的辅助电池相对于12V而言较为少见。作者的一位朋友曾用镍铁电池与普通的12V电池串联。一种更好的解决方案可能是用一个8V的电池与一个6V的电池串联。例如特洛伊T875是一个在20h放电率时具有170A • h容量的8V深循环电池（图7-13）。正如人们从其功率所预期的（一个普通的SLI电池的2 ~ 3倍），它也相当重（29kg）。与在高尔夫球车中经常使用的6V牵引的电池串联后，您将得到一个实实在在的14V电池组。

Figure 7–13 Trojan T875 8 Volt Battery. Photo courtesy of Trojan Battery (http://www.trojanbattery.com)

图 7–13 特洛伊T875 8V电池。照片由特洛伊电池（http://www.trojanbattery.com）提供

Another alternative would be to build your own pack from individual cells. 7 lead acid cells at 2 Volts each would do it, 4 or 5 lithium ion cells (depending on type) would be close too – and lighter; but would present some of the same issues of battery management as for a lithium ion traction pack. In either case you may still have a charging issue: chargers for 14 volt batteries aren't very common either.

另一种方法是用单个电池来组成您自己的电池组。7个2V的铅酸电池就行了，4或5个锂离子电池（取决于类型）也很接近这一电压，并且较轻，但它会有一些与牵引锂离子电池组相同的电池管理问题。在这两种情况下，您可能还有一个充电的问题。14V电池的充电器也不是很常见。

DC – DC converter

A DC to DC converter is much like a step-down transformer, except that it works with DC rather than AC. It draws current from the propulsion battery at high voltage and delivers power to the low voltage DC circuit at 12 volts (Figure 7-14). The simplest form of DC – DC converter is a pair of resistors making up a simple dividing circuit (Figure 7-15) not unlike the crude form of variable resistance controller described in an earlier chapter.

直流 - 直流转换器

一个直流 - 直流转换器很像是一个降压变压器，不同的是它工作于直流，而不是交流。它在高电压下从驱动电池中吸入电流，并向 12V 的低压直流电路供电（图 7-14）。直流 - 直流转换器最简单的形式是用电阻建立一个简单的分压电路（图 7-15），很像前面的章节中所描述的初始形式的可变电阻控制器。

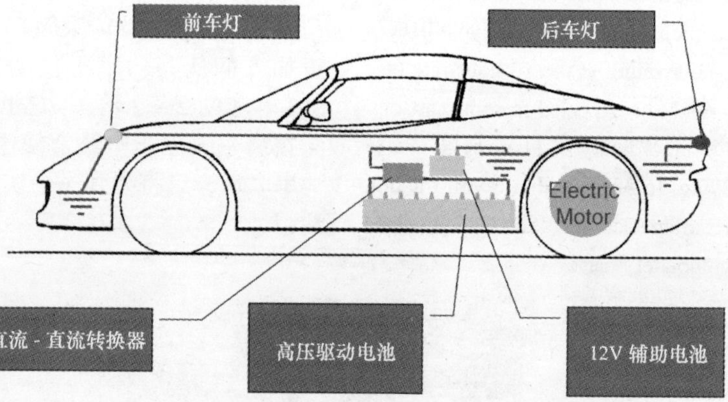

Figure 7–14 DC to DC converter Schematic

图 7–14 直流 - 直流转换器原理图

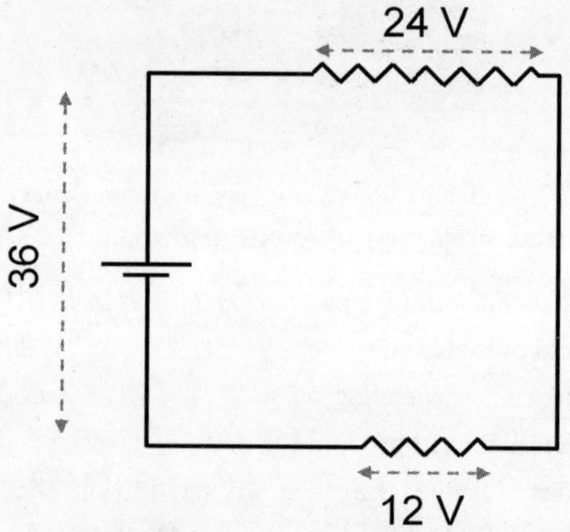

Figure 7–15 A simple voltage divider

图 7–15 一个简单的分压器

For much the same reasons as that crude controller, a simple voltage divider is impracticable in an EV. The low efficiency wastes power and generates excessive heat.

There are several different more sophisticated DC-DC converter designs that use some combination of inductors, capacitors and solid state devices. For our purposes buying a DC - DC converter from a reputable EV supplier is probably good enough.

You do have a choice to make however. Will you use a DC-DC converter on its own as the sole source of low-voltage DC power, or will you retain the 12 volt battery? Retaining the 12 volt battery has the disadvantage of extra weight and potentially adds to your battery maintenance chores. On the other hand, the battery is a buffer against failure of the DC – DC converter and may allow you to select a converter with a lower power output.

Another critical consideration is power when you are parked. Relying wholly on the DC to DC converter for 12 volt power means that if you parked in the street at night you would need to leave the traction pack live. Moreover if the DC – DC converter drains power from the traction pack even when no low voltage power is being used, then you increase the risk of damaging the traction pack if you forget to shut it down and leave the car standing for a long period.

If you decide to dispense with the 12 volt battery and rely on the DC – DC converter alone, you will need to select a converter that can handle peak power requirements – in other words, the converter must be capable of sustaining rated voltage with all electrical equipment switched on – imagine a dark, wet and cold night with the heater fan, screen demist, wipers, side, head, and fog lights, hazard warning etc all on. Table 7-1 lists typical power requirements for components. These can vary very widely, so you will

基于与初始形式的可变电阻控制器相同的原因，一个简单的分压器在电动汽车中是行不通的。它的低效率将浪费电能并产生过多的热量。

有几种不同的更复杂的直流 - 直流转换器的设计，它们使用了电感器、电容器和固态器件的一些组合。对于我们的目的，从一个有信誉的电动汽车供应商中购买一个直流 - 直流转换器可能就很好了。

但您也有一个选择。您是会用一个直流 - 直流转换器作为低电压直流电源的唯一的来源，还是会保留 12V 的电池？保留 12V 电池的缺点是具有额外的重量，并可能增加电池的维护工作。另一方面，当直流 - 直流转换器发生故障时该电池是一个备用设备，并且您可以选择一个较低输出功率的转换器。

另一个重要的考虑因素就是当您停车时的功耗。完全依靠直流 - 直流转换器的 12V 电源意味着，如果您在晚上把车停在街上，您也许需要让牵引电池组一直工作着。此外，即使在没有使用低压电源时，直流 - 直流转换器也会从牵引动力电池组中消耗功率，如果您忘记将其关闭并让汽车放置很长的一段时间，也会增加损坏牵引电池组的风险。

如果您决定不用 12V 的电池而单靠直流 - 直流转换器，则需要选择一个可以处理峰值功率需求的转换器。换句话说，当所有电气设备都开启时，该转换器还必须能够提供所需的额定电压。设想一下在一个黑暗、潮湿和寒冷的夜晚，将暖风机、屏幕除雾、刮水器、侧灯、前照灯、雾灯和危险警告灯等所有设备都启用。表 7-1 列出了一些典型组件的功率需求。这些功率可以有很大的不同，所以您必须检查汽车的

Table 7-1 Typical Power requirements [1642 watts at 12 volts is>100amps]

表 7-1 一些典型的功率需求 [1642W，在 12V 时大于 100A]

组件	典型功耗 /W	组件	典型功耗 /W
前照灯	120	仪表和车内灯	10
前侧灯 / 雾灯	100	换气扇	25
前刮水器	50	音响设备	50
后刮水器	25	座椅调节电动机	50
尾灯	10	前和 / 或后玻璃除雾器	250
制动灯	42	电动车窗	25
后雾灯	21	中控锁	10
车牌灯	20	电动助力转向泵	750
危险警告灯 / 指示灯	84	总共	1642

want to check the components in your car. This suggests that a low power (150 – 250 Watt) converter isn't going to keep the car supplied with power on that wet November night.

组件。这表明，一个低功率（150 ~ 250W）的转换器不可能为您的汽车在上述潮湿的 11 月份之夜供电。

If you decide to retain a 12 volt battery then you only have to handle average rather than peak load which should be a lot less. If you have your screen heater(s) on a time switch for example, you may be able to get away with a converter operating at a few hundred watts.

如果您决定保留一个 12V 的电池，那么您只需要处理平均而不是高峰时的负荷，这应该小得多。如果您的风窗玻璃加热器有定时开关，则可能只需要一个几百瓦的转换器。

A 1 - 2kW DC to DC converter like the one shown in Figure 7-16 might cost £1000 as opposed to £300 - £400 for a 400Watt unit. Weights for these larger converters are in the range 2.5 – 5 kgs. They are neither bulky nor heavy.

图 7-16 所示的一个 1 ~ 2kW 的直流 - 直流转换器的费用可能需要 1 万元，而一个 400W 的转换器只需 3000 ~4000 元。这些较大的转换器的重量为 2.5 ~ 5kg，它们既不大也不重。

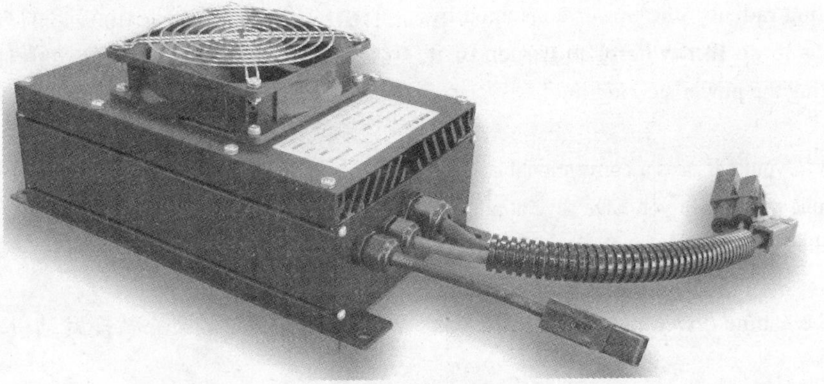

Figure 7–16 MES DC to DC Converter. Photo courtesy of MES s.a. (http://www.mes.ch)

图 7–16 MES 直流 - 直流转换器。照片由 MESS.A.(http://www.mes.ch) 提供

➢ Power steering

There are three forms of power-assisted steering in common use in IC-engined cars:

- Conventional hydraulic assistance powered by an engine-driven pump (usually via a V belt). Valves attached to the steering column direct hydraulic pressure to one or other side of a ram, which assists the driver in turning the wheels.
- Electro-hydraulic systems – similar to belt driven, but the hydraulic pump is powered by an electric motor rather than the engine.
- Pure electric systems – no hydraulics. Assistance is provided by what amounts to an electric motor controlled by sensors that read the torque being applied to the steering column.

If your car already has a pure electric or an electro-hydraulic system you will probably just want to retain it unmodified. Such systems do consume substantial power however, and the system will almost certainly be 12 volt: which means that you will have to size your DC – DC converter and/or 12 volt battery to handle the substantial extra load.

Note that some power steering systems incorporate

➢ 动力转向

内燃机发动机的汽车普遍使用的动力转向有三种形式：

- 由一个发动机驱动的泵(通常是通过 V 带)提供动力的传统的液压助动。安装在转向柱上的阀将液压送到柱塞的两侧之一，并协助驾驶人转动车轮。
- 电动液压系统。与带驱动类似，但液压泵的动力由一个电动机，而不是发动机提供。
- 纯电动系统，无液压。助力由传感器控制的电动机提供，传感器读取被施加到该转向柱的转矩的大小。

如果您的车已经配备了纯电动或电液系统，您可能只是想将它保留下来。然而，这样的系统将消耗大量的电能，并且系统将几乎可以肯定是 12V 的。这意味着您将不得不让直流 - 直流转换器和 / 或 12V 电池处理大量额外的负载。

需要注意的是，一些动力转向系统含有一

a small cooling radiator: the power consumed by the pump has to go somewhere, and much of it ends up heating the power steering fluid.

个小的冷却散热器。由泵所消耗的功率必须要有去处，其中大部分是消耗在对动力转向液加热。

If the system in your car uses a conventional engine-driven hydraulic pump then you have several alternatives (much like those associated with air-conditioning):

如果您汽车中的系统使用传统发动机驱动的液压泵，则有下述几种选择（与空调中的选择很像）：

1. Replace the engine driven pump with a 12 volt pump.
2. Use an auxiliary 12 volt motor to drive the existing pump.
3. Replace the engine driven pump with a pump powered by pack voltage.
4. Use an auxiliary motor operating directly from pack voltage to drive the existing pump.

① 用一个 12V 的泵来替换发动机驱动的泵

② 用一个 12V 的辅助电动机来驱动现有的泵

③ 用由牵引电池组电压驱动的泵来替换发动机驱动的泵

④ 用一个直接运行于牵引电池组电压的辅助电动机来驱动现有的泵

These are described in more detail below:

下面有更详细描述。

Replace the original pump

The most likely tactic here is to use an electrical power steering pump from a different car. This will, almost by definition, require a 12 volt supply. The pump from the Toyota MR2 has been used in some conversions (see Figure 7-17).

取代原来的泵

最有可能的策略是使用另外一辆汽车的电动助力转向系统泵。几乎可以肯定，这将需要一个 12V 的电源。丰田 MR2 的泵已被用于一些转换中（图 7-17）。

Figure 7–17 MR2 Power Steering Pump. Photo courtesy of EVDrive (http://www.evdrive.com/)

图 7–17 MR2 的动力转向泵。照片由电动车驱动公司（http://www.evdrive.com/）提供

One thing to watch out for here is the control system used for the pump. If the pump just runs continuously you are using electrical power from your DC-DC converter and/or your auxiliary battery to no benefit for the 99% case where you are just rolling down the highway needing negligible assistance.

需要注意的一件事是用于泵的控制系统。如果泵连续运行，您将使用从直流 - 直流转换器和 / 或辅助电池得到的电力。但在 99% 的情况下，您只是在公路上直行，助力的使用可忽略不计，因此，电力白白浪费了。

Re-use the existing pump

That is, drive the existing belt driven power steering pump with a small DC motor either directly or via a belt drive. This is more or less exactly the same principle as using a separate motor to drive the air conditioning compressor (see Figure 7-11).

重新使用现有的泵

也就是说，用一个小的直流电动机直接或通过带传动来驱动现有的带驱动的动力转向泵。这或多或少与使用单独的电动机来驱动空调压缩机的原理正好相同（参见图 7-11）。

As above though, you have a choice to make: will you leave it running all the time that your main contactor is closed, or will you only run it when it is actually needed? The former is simpler, but the latter more efficient: a 1.5 – 2 hp electric motor running continuously is going to have a significant impact on range, and will affect every journey, not just the hot or cold weather trips as would be the case with heaters and air conditioners.

但如上所述，您的选择是，当您的主连接器接通时您就会让它一直运行，还是只让它在实际需要时运行呢？前者是简单的，但后者更高效。一个 1.5 ~ 2hp 的电动机连续运行对行驶里程将有一个显著的影响，并会影响到每一个旅程，而不只是在过热或过冷的天气有使用暖气和空调的情况下的旅行。

➢ Power brakes

This one is relatively simple. Most modern cars (not all) have power assisted brakes. This usually requires a source of low pressure air (often loosely described as "vacuum" although it is nowhere near a vacuum in reality).

➢ 助力制动

这个问题是相对简单的。大多数的现代汽车（并非全部）都有动力辅助制动。这通常需要一个低压空气源（虽然它与真正的真空还有一些差别，但通常被近似地描述成“真空”）。

Almost universally, petrol engined cars use a tapping in the engine induction system as their low pressure source. However some high performance petrol engined cars and some diesel engined vehicles use an electrically driven "vacuum" pump. This means that there is a plentiful supply of pumps available for use in EVs: although once again, you will need to ensure that you take account of the power drain in your sizing of DC - DC converters, wiring etc. Figure 7-18

几乎所有的汽油机汽车都使用发动机感应系统中的真空度作为低压源。然而，有些高性能的汽油机汽车和柴油机汽车使用电力驱动的“真空”泵，这意味着电动汽车中使用的泵的来源十分充足。但必须再次指出，在考虑直流 - 直流转换器和接线等的大小时必须确保已经计入了所有设备的功耗。图 7-18 给出了由 MES DEA 制造的真空泵。这种泵是比较轻且紧凑的。这种

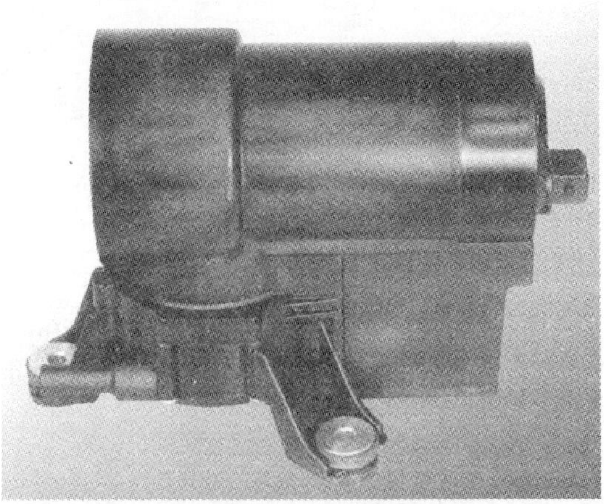

Figure 7–18 MES Vacuum Pump Photo courtesy of MES s.a. (http://www.mes.ch)

图 7–18 MES 的真空泵，照片由 MES S.A.（http://www.mes.ch）提供

illustrates a vacuum pump made by MES DEA. Such pumps are relatively light and compact: the MES pumps are around 1.3 – 1.4 kg depending on model. Be aware that some pumps used on diesel vehicles are engine driven rather than electric.

MES 泵重 1.3 ~ 1.4kg，不同的模型有所不同。请注意，有些在柴油机汽车上使用的泵是由发动机而不是电驱动的。

➢ In Conclusion

➢ 小结

Not many years ago, cars were ticklish devices. Until quite recently it was normal to come back from a long road trip with one or two things to fix. One car the author owned in the 1980s consumed three alternators, two water pumps and a range of other electrical and mechanical components over a three year period. In the 60's and 70's it was commonplace for radiators to spring leaks, cooling hoses to split, fuel tanks to rust through, handbrakes to freeze up, master cylinders to fail, starters and starter contactors to jam or fail, carburettor jets to clog up: even window winders failed, making it impossible to shut the window. Seats were often uncomfortable on long trips, heating inadequate and (in Europe at least) air conditioning was the preserve of the wealthy.

不久以前，汽车还是一个很容易出故障的设备。直到最近，在一个长途旅行回来之后，对汽车做简单维修还是很正常的。作者在 20 世纪 80 年代所拥有的一辆汽车在三年内损坏了三个交流发电机、两个水泵和其他一系列的电气和机械部件。在 60 和 70 年代，散热器泄漏、冷却软管开裂、油箱锈蚀、驻车制动不起作用、主缸损坏、起动器和起动器接触器堵塞或损坏、化油器喉阻塞，甚至车窗损坏，使它无法关闭等都是司空见惯的。在长途旅行时座位往往是不舒服的，暖气不足并且（至少在欧洲）空调只是富人才能装备的设施。

Modern production cars are by contrast very usable and very reliable: we get used to jumping into them

相比较而言，现代生产的汽车非常好用且可靠，我们习惯了甚至没有检查油量就跳上车

and driving hundreds of miles without even checking the oil. Breakdowns are rare events. Many (perhaps most) modern cars will never leave their driver stranded by the roadside in their entire working lives. This taken-for-granted reliability is not a natural state of affairs. It is the result of great attention to detail and the judicious exploitation of developments in design, materials and manufacturing techniques. It borders on a modern engineering miracle.

去驾驶数百公里，故障是较为罕见的事件。许多（也许是大多数）现代汽车在它们的整个生命周期内将永远不会让它们的驾驶人被困在路边。这种理所当然的可靠性不是一种事物的自然状态，它是对细节的高度重视和在设计、材料及制造技术等方面的发展和应用的结果，它体现了现代工程的奇迹。

This sets a high bar for conversions: if your EV has 1970's standards of comfort and reliability you will use it less than you would if it were more reliable. If it is snowing outside and you have the choice of a snug, warm and well-insulated IC car or an EV with marginal heating and a tendency to leave you stranded by the side of the road, which are you going to take? Brakes, steering, heating and cooling are important: if you convert a car that was designed and built to use servo assisted brakes and power steering, simply dispensing with them may not be an option on grounds of safety or usability. If your arrangements for heating and/or air conditioning are inadequate for your local climate you may not be able to live with it year round and it will become a fair-weather toy, or at best used for only part of the year. If the 12 volt electrics on your EV are marginal you may be nervous about taking the car out at night or in the rain.

这为车辆的转换设置了一个高的门槛。如果您的电动汽车只能达到 70 年代的舒适性和可靠性标准，则您将用得比较少。如果外面下雪的话，您有一辆舒适、温暖且隔热良好的内燃机汽车和一辆只有刚好够用的暖气并有可能将您困在路边的电动汽车，您将会选用哪辆呢？制动、转向、加热和冷却系统是很重要的。如果您要转换的是一辆专门设计和建造来使用伺服辅助制动、动力转向系统的汽车，简单地将它们撇弃基于安全性和可用性的理由可能不是一个好的选择。如果您对加热和 / 或空调系统的处理对于您当地的气候而言是不适当的，您可能无法全年都使用它，那它将成为一个天朗气清时的玩具，或者最有可能的是一年中只有一部分的时间里可以使用。如果您的电动汽车上的 12V 的电气设备较少，当汽车要在夜间或雨中行驶时，您可能会感到非常紧张。

If you want an EV that is usable everyday transport rather than a proof-of concept testbed, you need to put the same level of effort, thought and investment into these areas as you put into the drivetrain.

如果您想要一辆作为日常交通工具而不是一辆证明概念的测试平台式的电动汽车，您在这些辅助系统中所做的努力、思考和投资必须与您在动力传动系统的投入相当。

8 Other Technologies
其他技术

In Chapter 1 we promised that we would look at alternatives to batteries as a replacement for petrol or diesel fuels in vehicle drivetrains. These alternatives include

- Fuel cells
- Flywheels
- Hybrid power trains
- Ultra-capacitors
- Compressed Gas Energy Storage
- Superconducting Magnetic Energy Storage
- Inductive charging on the move
- Overhead power

In this chapter we examine some of these ideas, albeit briefly. Many of them are of purely theoretical interest either because parts are not available or because a suitable infrastructure does not exist, or both.

我们在第 1 章中承诺将讨论除电池以外的替代品来代替汽油或柴油燃料作为汽车的动力驱动系统。这些替代方案包括：

- 燃料电池
- 飞轮
- 混合动力链
- 超级电容器
- 压缩空气储能
- 超导磁储能
- 运动中的感应充电
- 架空电力线路

在这一章中，我们将简短地讨论其中的一些想法。它们中的许多想法是纯粹的理论兴趣，其原因要么是因为部件不存在，要么是因为没有一个合适的基础设施，或两者兼有。

➤ Fuel Cells

Fuel cells are an interesting technology, but are, at least in the short term, a monstrous red herring.

The concept of a fuel cell is simple. A liquid or gaseous fuel is used to create electricity directly, and this drives an electric motor. The usual fuel is hydrogen. An onboard hydrogen tank is topped up at a filling station from a special pump in much the same way as an IC engine car fuel tank is filled with petrol. On the move, the hydrogen is piped to a fuel cell which combines the hydrogen with oxygen from the air to produce water, and in the process generates electricity which is used to drive an electric motor (Figure 8-1).

➤ 燃料电池

燃料电池是一种有趣的技术，但是，至少在短期内这项技术是不可行的。

燃料电池的概念是简单的——一种液态或气态的燃料直接用于产生电力，并由此驱动电动机。氢是常用的燃料。车载氢气罐在加油站中用一个特殊的泵来加气，其过程与向内燃机汽车油箱中添加汽油的方式大致相同。在开动时，氢气被送到燃料电池中，在那里它与空气中的氧结合而产生水，并且在这个过程中产生电来驱动电动机（图 8-1）。

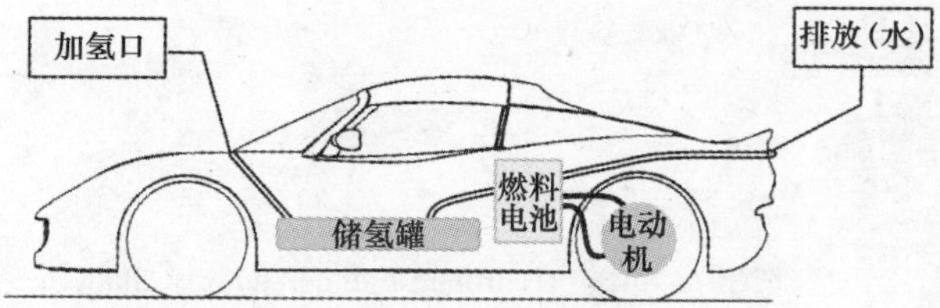

Figure 8–1 Hydrogen fuel cell propulsion

图 8–1 氢燃料电池驱动

A vehicle powered by a hydrogen fuel cell would be as quiet as one powered by batteries, and its exhaust emissions would be just water; so fuel cell cars are, like EVs, low noise, and pollution-free at the point of use. In addition, there would be none of the problems of extended recharging time or excessive weight that you can get with battery-powered vehicles.

一辆由氢燃料电池驱动的汽车与由一般电池驱动的汽车一样是很安静的，并且其排放只是水。所以像电动汽车一样，燃料电池汽车在使用时也是低噪声、无污染的。此外，它没有您在电池动力汽车中会遇到的充电时间长或车身过重等问题。

Fuel cells however have several problems. The first issue is the source of the hydrogen itself. Fuel for IC-engined cars starts as oil extracted from the ground, piped or shipped to a refinery. The refinery produces the petrol and diesel required which is then shipped again to a network of filling stations where it is bought by consumers (Figure 8-2).

然而，燃料电池也有一些问题。第一个问题是氢本身的来源。内燃机发动机汽车的燃料从地下提取的石油开始，经管道或运到炼油厂中提炼。炼油厂生产出所需的汽油和柴油，然后再运到加油站网络中供消费者购买（图 8-2）。

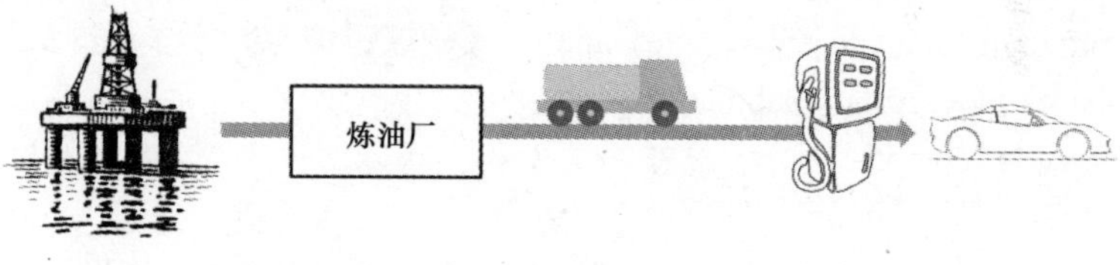

Figure 8–2 Conventional fuel supply chain

图 8–2 传统的燃料供应链

Current industrial scale production of hydrogen uses natural gas as its raw material; so the supply chain is virtually identical in principle (Figure 8-3). So, whilst fuel cells would give you the town-centre benefits of low noise and low pollution, they would do little to tackle the fossil fuel usage issues other than by a possible improvement in the "well to wheel" efficiency.

目前工业规模生产的氢使用天然气作为原料,所以其供应链在原理上几乎是相同的（图 8-3）。因此，虽然燃料电池会给城市带来低噪声、低污染的好处，但它除了有可能改善“油井到车轮”的效率外，它对于解决化石燃料使用中的其他问题则是无能为力的。

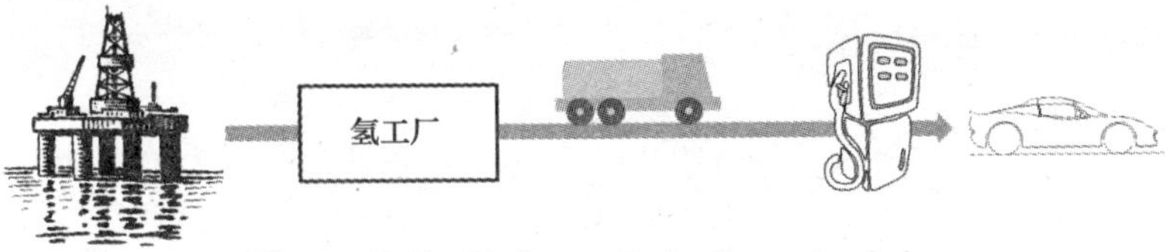

Figure 8–3 Hydrogen fuel cell supply chain

图 8–3 氢燃料电池供应链

It is true that hydrogen could be produced by electrolysis of water which might be achieved using electricity from renewable sources. This does not pass a simple sanity check for mass market application: why generate electricity, use the electricity to produce hydrogen, ship the hydrogen around the country in tankers and finally generate electricity again from the hydrogen, when you can just use the electrical energy directly in a battery electric vehicle?

氢的确可以通过电解水来产生，这也许可以用可再生能源的电力来实现，但这并没有批量生产的合理性。当您可以将电池中的电能直接用于电动汽车时，为什么要用电去产生氢气，然后将氢通过油罐车送到全国各地，最后再从氢中产生出电能呢？

Secondly, the technology is immature. There are no mass-market applications for fuel cells. By contrast, Lead-acid traction batteries have been used in things like fork lift trucks for many years, and even the newer cell chemistries like nickel metal hydride and lithium ion are widely used in consumer electronics. Fuel cells have turned up in a bunch of prototype and concept vehicles, and some in edge-cases like military submarines and spacecraft; and that is about it.

其次，技术还不够成熟，目前燃料电池还没有获得大批量的应用。相比之下，铅酸驱动电池已经在叉车等中被使用多年，甚至更新的化学成分，如镍金属氢化物电池和锂离子电池，也广泛地用于消费电子产品中。燃料电池已经在一大堆的原型车和概念车中得到使用，也用在一些如军事潜艇和航天器等边缘领域，但也差不多就这些了。

There have even been doubts expressed about the availability of the platinum used as a catalyst. One 2008 paper estimated that platinum availability might restrict fuel-cell vehicles to about 15% of the market[1]. A TIAX report for the US Department of Energy was more bullish but still concluded that "The platinum industry has the potential to meet a scenario where FCVs [Fuel cell vehicles] achieve 50% market pene-

甚至，作为催化剂的铂的可获得性也被置疑。一篇 2008 年的文章估计，铂的供应量可能会将燃料电池汽车限制在约 15% 的市场份额㊀。TIAX（译注：TIAX 是一家总部设在美国马萨诸塞州列克星敦市的、以实验室为基础的技术开发公司）给美国能源部的一份报告对此则更看好，但仍认为："铂工业具有使燃料电池汽车在 2050 年达到 50% 市场份额

1 Platinum Supply and the Growth of Fuel Cell Vehicles by Justin Boudreau, Eugene Choi, Oljora and Rezhdo, Khalid

㊀ 贾斯汀 · 布德罗，欧尔鸠拉 · 尤金财，哈立德 · 雷斯杜，铂金供应与燃料电池汽车的增长。

tration by 2050, while an 80% scenario could exceed the expansion capabilities of the industry..." .[1]

的潜力，但在 80% 的份额时可能会超过该行业的扩展能力……" ㊀

Thirdly the use of hydrogen fuel cell vehicles would require a vast new infrastructure for the large scale production, transport, storage and dispensing of hydrogen. Every filling station would need a hydrogen "pump" or refuelling point. We would need new hydrogen production plants and a new tanker fleet. Furthermore, this infrastructure has to be in place for the very first hydrogen fuel cell vehicle to be viable: if you are going to drive across the country, there have to be hydrogen filling stations across the country.

第三，氢燃料电池汽车的使用将需要大量新的基础设施来满足氢气的大规模生产、运输、储存和分装。每个加油站需要一个氢"泵"或加油点。我们将需要新的氢生产厂家和新的运输队。此外，在第一辆氢燃料电池汽车出现时基础设施就必须建好。如果您要将车开到全国各地，那么氢气加气站也要建设完善。

Battery vehicles on the other hand need no new infrastructure. The core infrastructure (the national grid) already exists. To drive an EV anywhere in the world today, all you need is an electrical extension cord (provided that you have an onboard charger, which most EVs do). EVs are also incremental. Scaling electricity production to handle mass-market EVs would be a matter of economics and planning around a well-understood industrial process.

然而，电池车辆不需要新的基础设施。核心的基础设施（国家电网）已经存在。今天在世界上的任何地方要开一辆电动汽车，您所需要的只是一条电源延长线（前提是像大多数电动汽车那样，您有一个车载充电器）。电动汽车还是增程式的。提高发电量以应付批量化的电动汽车，在这个被充分消化了的工业过程中，将只是经济和规划的问题。

There have, nevertheless, been a stream of fuel cell "concept" and "demonstrator" cars from the motor industry over the last few years, and the concept is often touted as the long term answer. A cynic might be forgiven for thinking that concept cars based on an immature technology and on a fossil-fuel supply chain might be an exercise in foot dragging: an excuse for failing to make substantive progress on usable production cars based on an imperfect but entirely practicable battery technology.

不过，过去几年在汽车行业有一串的燃料电池"概念"和"演示"汽车，并且这一概念经常被吹捧为长期的答案。一个愤世嫉俗者若认为这种基于不成熟的技术，且在化石燃料供应链基础上的概念车可以作为代步工具也许还能被原谅，因为这是一个基于这种不完美但完全可行的电池技术基础上，可用的量产车未能取得实质性进展的借口。

1 "Platinum availability and economics for PEMFC commercialization," Tiax LLC report D0034 to the US Department of Energy, Cambridge, Massachusetts, December 2003.

㊀ "作为质子交换膜燃料电池商业化的铂金的可用性和经济性"，TIAX 有限责任公司对美国能源部的报告 D0034，马萨诸塞州剑桥，2003 年 12 月。

➢ Flywheel Energy Storage (FES)

Instead of storing energy in a battery or using a liquid fuel that gives up energy, it is in theory possible to store kinetic energy (the energy of motion) in rotating mass – a flywheel. Flywheel Energy Storage (FES) is an idea that has been around a while: most men over 40 (and quite a few under 40) have used FES devices. That was the principle behind countless toy cars that were fitted with flywheels geared to the driving wheels so that the flywheel rotated very rapidly when the toy was pushed along (see Figure 8-4).

➢ 飞轮储能（FES）

除了能将能量存储在电池上，或用液体燃料提供能量外，还可将能量存储在旋转质量——飞轮的动能中（运动的能量），这在理论上是可行的。飞轮储能（FES）是一种已经存在了一段时间的想法。大多数 40 岁以上男子（也有一些 40 岁以下）都使用过飞轮储能设备。这是无数装有飞轮驱动车轮的玩具车所使用的原理，当飞轮非常迅速地旋转时，玩具车将被推向前行（图 8-4）。

Figure 8–4 Zecar Flywheel-powered toy. Photo courtesy of Justin Ketterer (http://justinketterer.com)

图 8–4 兹卡飞轮驱动的玩具。照片由贾斯廷 • 克特勒（http://justinketterer.com）提供

The same principle is used in some F1 cars: a flywheel is accelerated during braking, absorbing energy which is released to boost subsequent acceleration.

有些 F1 赛车采用的是同样的原理。在制动时飞轮被加速而吸收能量，并在随后的加速过程中被释放。

This technology is not a joke. A ring weighing 1 kg and 0.3 metres in diameter rotating at 50,000 r.p.m. would (theoretically) store about 300 Kilojoules or about 83 watt hours. The only snag is that the centrifugal force would be about 400 tones. 50,000 r.p.m. is not however absurd. Modern turbochargers run over 100,000 r.p.m. By contrast a 40 Amp hour lithium ion cell would store about 132 watt hours and weigh around 1.5 kg. The development of practical flywheel energy storage is partly a func-

这项技术不是一个玩笑。一个重 1kg、直径 0.3m、转速为 50000r/min 的环（在理论上）上可存储约 300kJ 或约 83W•h 的能量。唯一的问题是离心力的作用将是 400t 左右。然而，50000r/min 并不是荒唐的。现代涡轮增压器运行于超过 10×10^4r/min。相比之下，一个 40A•h 的锂离子电池重约 1.5kg，它将存储约 132W•h 的能量。实用飞轮储能的进一步发展源自于先进材料科学的发展。高速是必须的。因此，会有很大的离心荷载。这类飞

tion of advancing materials science. High speeds are needed, and therefore high centrifugal loads are created. Structural failure of such a flywheel is potentially catastrophic: the rim of our theoretical 300 mm diameter flywheel would be moving at over 0.75 km/second. This is the same order of magnitude as the muzzle velocity of a rifle bullet.

轮的结构故障将是潜在的灾难。上述 300mm 直径的理论飞轮的边缘速度将超过 0.75km/s。这与步枪子弹的初速是同一量级的。

An uncontained flywheel failure would be potentially lethal to anyone in the vicinity, so part of the penalty of an FES system is the weight and expense of the hardware required for containment in the event of structural failure of the flywheel.

没有保护装置的飞轮故障对任何在附近的人都会是致命的。因此，飞轮储能系统的缺点是为防止飞轮结构失效所需的硬件的重量和费用。

➤ Hybrids

➤ 混合动力

We mentioned hybrids in chapter one. A hybrid in this context is usually a vehicle with both battery electric and IC elements in its drivetrain. Like many of the concepts we have been discussing the idea is not new. In the section on wheel motors we mentioned the Lohner Porsche EV. Dr Porsche extended this idea by adding a generator to create a Hybrid (Figure 8-5).

我们在第 1 章中提到过混合动力。在这种情况下的混合动力通常是指在其动力系统中具有电池的电力和内燃机部件的车辆。像我们所讨论过的许多其他概念，这也不是一个新的概念。在轮毂电动机的部分我们提到了罗纳 - 保时捷电动汽车。波尔舍博士通过添加一个发电机来创建一个混合动力而扩展了这一想法（图 8-5）。

Hybrids have had a bad press in the EV community, perhaps because the best known and most successful commercially have been “plug free” hybrids such as the Toyota Prius which ultimately get all their power from petrol pumped into the tank. This bad press is a mistake. Unless and until battery technology gets to the point that range ceases to be an issue, a good hybrid may sometimes be worth considering for some applications.

混合动力在电动汽车领域有一个不好的印象，这也许是因为最知名且商业上最成功的“非插电式”混合动力汽车，如丰田普锐斯，它的最终动力都来自注入油箱中的汽油。这个不好的印象是错误的。除非并且直到电池技术达到这点，即行程里程不再是一个问题，否则有时候在某些应用中，一辆很好的混合动力汽车可能是值得考虑的。

Hybrids may also be a way of easing the transition from IC to EV in a commercial and emotional sense: for some buyers the security-blanket of a fill-up-and-go IC drivetrain may be necessary to encourage them to buy into electric power at all.

混合动力也可能是在商业和情感意义上能从内燃机平稳过渡到电动汽车的一种方式。对于一些购买者而言，这种加满就走的内燃机传动系统的过渡可能是必要的，以鼓励他们最终购买全电动汽车。

So what kinds of hybrid are there? There are four classes which you can think of as a 2 x 2 matrix. Some hybrids ("Plug-in" hybrids) are, at their best, ordinary EVs with an extra IC engine just to get you there on the rare occasions that your journey is greater than the EV-mode range. This sort of hybrid can be operated rather like a sailing yacht with an outboard motor – i.e. with the IC engine used as little as possible. For example, the Chinese-made BYD F3DM (Figure 8-6: not available in the West as I write) has an electric only range of around 60 miles – so could be used as an electric vehicle most of the time by many drivers whose daily commute or school/shopping trips are less than this. Such a vehicle, used most of the time in EV mode, might in practice go hundreds of EV miles for every gallon of petrol used.

那么有什么样的混合动力呢？一般有四类，您可以将它们设想为一个 2×2 的矩阵。某些混合动力汽车（“插电式”混合动力）最多只是在一辆普通的电动汽车上加一个额外的内燃机发动机，以便让您在极少数的、旅程大于电动汽车里程时使用。这种形式的混合动力汽车可以像具有舷外马达的帆船那样操作，例如尽可能少用内燃机。例如，中国制造的比亚迪 F3DM（图 8-6，在我写作本书时在西方买不到）仅有约 100km 行驶里程的电能，因此在大部分时间内可被很多驾驶人作为电动汽车使用，因为日常上下班或上学 / 购物之旅是低于这一行程里程的。这样的一辆汽车最常用的是电动汽车模式，在实际情况下，1 加仑汽油也许可以让它跑数百公里。

Figure 8–5 Replica of the Lohner Porsche Hybrid. Photo courtesy of Andreas Zarini

图 8–5 罗纳 - 保时捷混合动力车副本。照片由安德烈亚斯 • 扎伊尔提供

Figure 8–6 BYD F3DM Plug-in Hybrid. Photo courtesy of Anthony Kendall

图 8–6 比亚迪 F3DM 插电式混合动力车。照片由安东尼 • 肯德尔提供

Other hybrids (like the Toyota Prius mentioned earlier) merely use the electric motor to smooth out the power demand on the IC engine, thus making it more efficient. These vehicles are sometimes referred to as "Plug-free" hybrids (marketing speak for "you cannot charge the batteries from an external power source"). This sounds useless but curiously it does actually work. For example the second generation Toyota Prius (Figure 8-7) was a

其他的混合动力车（如前面提到的丰田普锐斯）只使用电动机去平衡对内燃机功率的需求，从而使其更加高效。这些车辆有时也被称为“非插电式”混合动力车（在营销上说成“您不能用外部电源为电池充电”）。这听起来似乎没什么用处，但奇怪的是，它的确有用。例如，第二代丰田普锐斯（图 8-7）是一个 5 座车，它可以在 10s 多一点的时间里从 0 加速到 100km/h。它有一个 1500mL

5 seater which could accelerate from 0 to 60 mph in just over 10 seconds. It had a 1500 cc petrol engine putting out 76 BHP. The contemporary Volkswagen Golf Hatchback 1.6 S FSI weighed a similar amount, accelerated to 60 in much the same time but had a 1.6 litre engine putting out 113 BHP. The official fuel consumption figure for the Prius was 65 mpg. The Golf, 41 mpg.

的汽油发动机，输出功率为76hp。当代大众高尔夫两厢1.6 S FSI汽车的重量与前者相当，在大致相同的时间里加速到100km/h，但它有一个1.6L的发动机，输出功率为113hp。普锐斯的官方油耗为3.6L/100km，高尔夫的官方油耗为5.8L/100km。

Figure 8–7 Toyota Prius Plug-Free Hybrid. Photo courtesy of Brett Cravaliat

图 8–7 丰田普锐斯非插电式混合动力车。照片由布雷特•克拉瓦利亚特提供

The reason it works is that you can use a smaller IC engine and run it closer to maximum efficiency, using the electric motor to make up the deficiency in power during hard acceleration.

它能够起作用的原因是，您可以使用一个较小的内燃机并且以接近最高的效率运行它，在急加速时可以用电动机来弥补其功率的不足。

Plug-free hybrids are better than nothing, but the improvement in efficiency over a good diesel is marginal. Many people regard them as green fashion-statements, essentially a conventional car with a transmission augmented by an auxiliary electric motor and batteries.

非插电式混合动力汽车总比没有电的好，但对于性能良好的柴油机而言，其效率的提高是微不足道的。很多人把它们当做绿色环保的时尚用语，但它本质上是一个传统汽车用的辅助电动机和电池来增强传动。

There is another way to classify hybrids apart from “Plug-in” and “Plug-Free” .

除了“插电式”和“非插电式”外，还有另一种方法可用来对混合动力汽车进行分类。

“Parallel” hybrids use both the IC engine and the electric motor to drive the wheels (Figure 8-8). By contrast in a “Series” hybrid (Figure 8-9) the IC

并联混合指同时使用内燃机和电动机来驱动车轮（图 8-8）。与其对应，在“串联”混合（图 8-9）中，内燃机并不直接驱动车轮，它

engine does not drive the wheels directly: instead it drives a generator which recharges the batteries. The batteries provide power to an electric motor which drives the wheels.

用来驱动发电机并对电池充电。电池为电动机提供电源以驱动车轮。

Indeed some EV owners have even built separate trailers with onboard generators to tow behind their cars on long journeys (Figure 8-10).

事实上，有些电动汽车车主甚至做了一个带有车载发电机的独立拖车，在长途旅行时将它们拖在汽车的后面（图 8-10）。

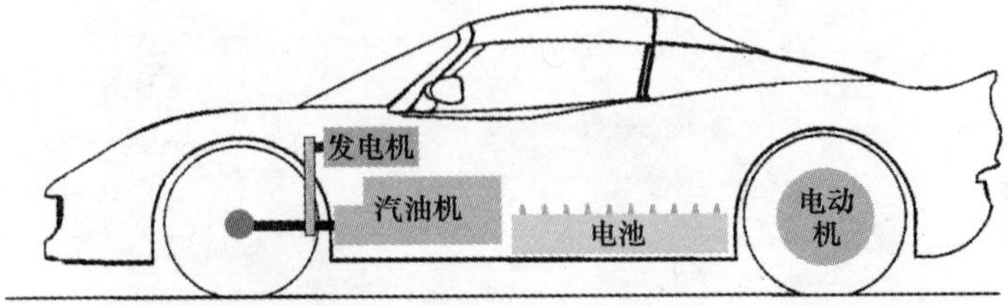

Figure 8–8 Parallel Hybrid: both the IC engine and the electric motor can drive the wheels

图 8–8 并联式混合动力：内燃机和电动机均可驱动车轮

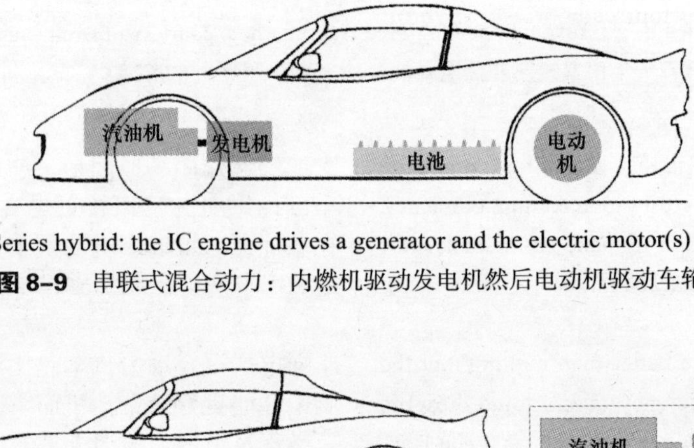

Figure 8–9 Series hybrid: the IC engine drives a generator and the electric motor(s) drive the wheels

图 8–9 串联式混合动力：内燃机驱动发电机然后电动机驱动车轮

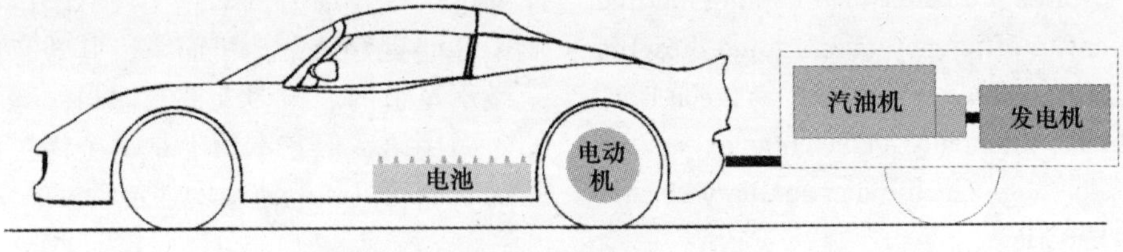

Figure 8–10 Range-extending trailer

图 8–10 用于扩充行驶里程的挂车

Parallel hybrids are more complex but in theory offer better performance. When you are accelerating hard the control systems can tell the IC engine to forget about charging the battery and help the electric motor lay some rubber. Once you are in

并联混合动力更为复杂，但在理论上却能提供更好的性能。当您正在快速加速时，控制系统可以告诉内燃机不要对电池进行充电，同时让电动机提供一些帮助。当您在巡航时，内燃机就可以对电池充电。

the cruise, the IC engine goes back to charging the batteries.

Series hybrids are simpler: conceptually they are an ordinary EV with an onboard generator to charge the batteries. A series hybrid doesn't need the complexity, weight and expense of a transmission that can mix power from two power sources. Nor does it need sophisticated control software to orchestrate the output from two power sources with very different power and torques curves.As a minimum all you need to do is crank up an onboard generator when needed. The crazy BBC Top Gear trio demonstrated the principle with an absurd EV powered by a couple of lead acid batteries supplemented by an off-the-shelf portable generator.

串联混合动力则较为简单。在概念上它们是一个普通的电动汽车加上车载发电机为电池充电。串联式混合动力并不需要一个复杂的、笨重的和昂贵的传动系统去混合来自两个能量源的功率，它也不需要复杂的控制软件，以协调两个能量源的输出功率和转矩曲线的不同。作为最低要求，您所要做的只是在需要的时候带上一个车载发电机。在英国广播公司播出的“顶级档位”（译注：英国广播公司播出的一个非常受欢迎的、收视率很高的关于汽车的电视节目）的节目中，三个疯狂的主持人用一辆荒谬的电动汽车展示了串联混合动力的原理，该电动汽车由一些铅酸电池辅以一个现成的便携式发电机作为动力。

So there are actually four categories of hybrid “Plug-in Series” “Plug-in Parallel” , “Plug-free Series” and Plug-free Parallel” (Figure 8-11).

所以，实际上有 4 类混合：插电式串联、插电式并联、非插电式串联和非插电式并联（图 8-11）。

	串联	并联
插电式	雪佛兰 Volt 	比亚迪 F3DM 
非插电式	戴尔迪克（Deltic）柴油电动 	丰田普锐斯 

Figure 8–11 The four classes of Hybrid. Photos: Chevy Volt - Mario Roberto Duran Ortiz; Deltic - Nick Drew; BYD - Anthony Kendall; Toyota Prius - Brett Cravaliat

图 8–11 4 类混合动力。照片：雪佛兰沃蓝达—由马里奥 • 罗伯托 • 杜兰 • 奥尔蒂斯提供；戴尔迪克—由尼克 • 德鲁提供；比亚迪—由安东尼 • 肯德尔提供；丰田普锐斯—由布雷特 • 克拉瓦利亚特提供

In the real world, if you want a hybrid, the series hybrid is probably the right way to go. Let the different kinds of motor play to their strengths: IC engines are at their (limited) best running at constant speed: such as when running a generator. Electric motors are just far better at propelling a car.

在现实世界中，如果您想要一辆混合汽车，串联式混合动力可能是较好的选择。它可以让不同类型的驱动装置发挥它们自己的优势。内燃机在发电时最好以（有限的）恒定速度运行。电动机用来驱动汽车则会好得多。

One possible parallel hybrid layout that might be made to work is a conversion of a four wheel drive vehicle that retains the IC engine but only driving one set of wheels and adds an electric drivetrain to power the other axle (Figure 8-12).

一种也许可以正常工作的并联式混合动力的布局是一种四轮驱动的转换模式。它保留了用内燃机来驱动一组车轮并增加了一个电力传动系统来驱动另一组车轮（图 8-12）。

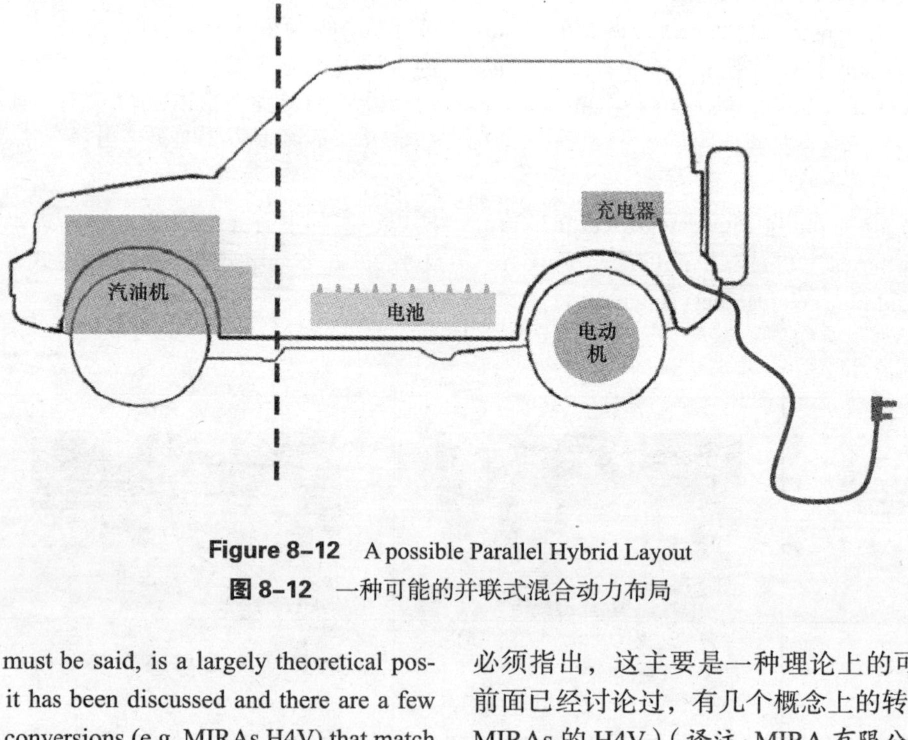

Figure 8–12 A possible Parallel Hybrid Layout

图 8–12 一种可能的并联式混合动力布局

This, it must be said, is a largely theoretical possibility: it has been discussed and there are a few concept conversions (e.g. MIRAs H4V) that match this pattern, but I am not aware of any daily-use amateur conversions. One of the issues is that you are probably limited to a direct-drive electric motor: two separate gearboxes would be unthinkable. Another intriguing possibility is the so called 'Through-The-Road-Hybrid' (TTRH) configuration. This involves adding in-wheel motors (like

必须指出，这主要是一种理论上的可能性。前面已经讨论过，有几个概念上的转换（如 MIRAs 的 H4V）（译注：MIRA 有限公司原是英国汽车工业研究协会，现在是一家汽车咨询公司，总部设在英国沃里克郡纳尼顿附近。它提供了汽车行业的产品设计、研发、测试、信息和认证服务）与此模式相匹配，但我还没有发现任何日常使用的业余转换。这里的问题之一是，您大概也仅限于直接驱动的电动机，因为两个独立的变速器将是不可想

the Protean example discussed earlier) to an existing IC-engined vehicle without modification to the existing drivetrain. This design enables the hybridisation of any existing vehicle resulting in 3 driver-selectable operating modes;

象的。另一种比较有趣的是所谓的"通路混合"(TTRH)配置。这涉及在现有内燃机汽车中加入轮毂电动机(如前面讨论过的普洛廷的例子),而无需修改现有的动力系统。这种设计使得任何现有车辆具有 3 种可供选择的混合动力操作模式:

- IC engine only,
- electric only,
- electric + IC hybrid.

- 只用内燃机
- 只用电力
- 电力 + 内燃机的组合体

Accessories like heating, power steering, air conditioning and power brakes are a concern with any form of hybrid: if the IC engine is not operating much of the time, you will have to modify these components, but then what do you do on that long road trip when the propulsion battery is discharged 50 miles from home? In the end, hybrid drivetrains will always be heavier, more complex, more expensive and higher maintenance than either an EV or an IC-engined car. You are probably better off to sell the IC drivetrain components and use the money to buy a few more batteries which you can install in the space vacated by the engine. Any money left over can be used to hire a car for the couple of occasions a year when you need more range.

任何形式的混合动力汽车中,加热、动力转向、空调和动力制动器等都是一个问题。如果内燃机大部分的时间不工作,您将不得不修改这些组件。但在长途旅行中,如果驱动电池在离家 80km 后放电完毕,您该怎么做?最后要说的是,混合动力将永远是更重、更复杂、更昂贵的,并且与纯电动汽车或内燃机汽车相比,它具有较高的维护费用。如果您能卖掉内燃机传动系统的组件,并用这些钱来多买几个电池,将它们装在发动机腾出的空间中,您的日子可能会更好过些。当您在一年中偶尔需要更大的行驶里程时,可用省下的钱来租一辆车。

➢ Ultra-capacitors

Small capacitors are commonplace in electronic equipment. Like batteries, they store electrical charge but usually in tiny amounts and in a way that is different to the typical battery. Unlike most batteries, the voltage across a capacitor tends to vary linearly with the amount of charge stored. If we re-use our earlier analogy of an electrical circuit being like the flow of water in a pipe, a capacitor is a bit like a rubber diaphragm across the flow of water: it offers little resistance at first but the resistance builds up rapidly as the flow continues (Figure 8-13). Similarly, as a capacitor is charged up its voltage rises in approximate proportion to the charge stored.

➢ 超级电容器

小电容器在电子设备中是司空见惯的。像电池一样,电容器也存储电荷,但通常只有微量的电荷,并且其方式也与典型的电池不同。与大多数电池不同,电容两端的电压与存储的电荷量具有呈线性变化的趋势。如果将电气电路比喻为管道中的水流,一个电容器就有点像一个横跨水流的橡胶膜片。首先,它最初提供很小的阻力,但随着流动的继续,阻力将迅速增加(图 8-13)。同样,当电容器被充电时,其电压的上升与存储的电荷近似成正比。

Capacitance (the “capacity of a capacitor”) is measured in Farads. The terminal voltage of a 1 farad capacitor would rise by 1 volt for every coulomb (amps x seconds) of charge stored. So a 5 farad capacitor charged to 100 volts would absorb 500 coulombs, or (say) 50 amps for ten seconds. Most capacitors used in electronic equipment are nowhere near as big as this. The range of capacitance in this kind of application would typically be from around .000005 microfarad up to 100 microfarad (a microfarad is a millionth of a farad).

电容量（“电容器的容量”）的单位是法拉第（F）。每库仑（安培 × 秒）的电荷存储在1F电容器中时，电容两端的电压会上升1V。因此，一个5F的电容器充电至100V，将吸收500C的电荷，或（例如）使50A的电流持续10s。大多数电子设备中使用的电容远不如这个大。在这种应用中，电容量的范围通常大约是0.000005~100μF（1μF等于10^{-6}F）。

It is however possible to build capacitors with ratings in the thousands of farads. For example a Maxwell BCAP3000 capacitor with a rated capacity of 3000 farad at 2.7 volts weighs around half a kilo and is about the size and shape of a big cylindrical lithium-ion cell (Figure 8-14). It could store about a bit over 3 watt-hours. By contrast a Headway 40160 lithium ion cell of similar volume and weight stores 16 Ah at 3.3 volts or around 50 watt-hours. The Maxwell capacitor is substantially more expensive than the Headway cell.

不过，数千法拉的电容器确实可以生产出来。例如麦克斯韦BCAP3000电容器在2.7V时的额定容量为3000F。该电容器重约0.5kg，大约是一个大的圆筒形锂离子电池（图8-14）的大小和形状。它可以存储超过3W•h的能量。与此相比，一个具有类似体积和重量的海得威40160锂离子电池在3.3V时可存储16A•h，或50W•h的能量。麦克斯韦电容器比海得威电池贵得多。

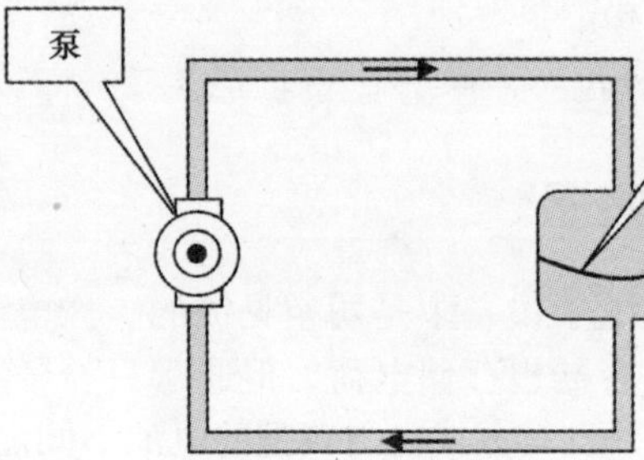

Figure 8–13 The water-pipe equivalent of a capacitor

图 8–13 与电容器等效的水管道

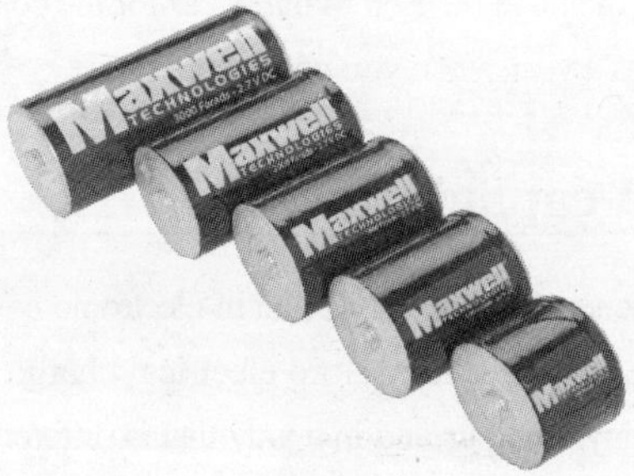

Figure 8–14 Maxwell ultracapacitors. Photo courtesy of Maxwell Technologies, Inc.(http://www.maxwell.com)

图 8–14 麦克斯韦超级电容器。照片由麦克斯韦技术有限公司 (http://www.maxwell.com) 提供

So an ultracapacitor of this type is not yet ready for prime time as the only source of power for an electric vehicle, but it might conceivably get there. In the meantime they have a niche as a way of boosting the specific power of a battery drivetrain:

因此，这种类型的超级电容器作为电动汽车唯一的动力之源还为时尚早，但它今后也许有可能。同时，它们有一个提高电池动力系统比功率的有利条件，因为电容可以提供一个短期的突发功率来加速和 / 或从再生制动

capacitors can provide a short-term burst of power for acceleration and/or accept a very high charge rate for regenerative braking.

中接受一个非常高的充电率。

Ultracapacitors have a couple of huge advantages over batteries. Firstly the specific power of these cells is staggering. The BCAP3000 can sustain almost 150 Amps continuously and over 2000 Amps for 1 second. That's equivalent to a C rating of 66 continuous and almost 900 peak.

相对于电池而言，超级电容器有一些巨大的优势。首先,这些电容器的比功率是惊人的。BCAP3000 电容器可以连续提供接近 150A 的电流，或让超过 2000A 的电流维持 1s。这相当于一个连续的 66C 值或近 900 的峰值 C 值。

The second great benefit is cycle life. Lead acid cells manage a few hundred cycles; the best lithium ion cells a few thousand. Maxwell claim over a million cycles (albeit at a 50% duty cycle) for their ultracapacitors.

第二大优势是循环寿命。铅酸电池只有几百个周期，最好的锂离子电池也只有几千个周期。麦克斯韦声称它们的超级电容器有超过一百万个周期的循环寿命（在一个放电率为 50% 的循环下测得）。

Capacitors are also more forgiving when it comes to management. They don't mind being undercharged, they don't have cell memory and they don't need watering like flooded lead-acid cells. They don't explode when overcharged or give off fumes. Long series strings of capacitors do need balancing however. The Maxwell 125 Volt BMOD0063 modules (Figure 8-15) for example have built in balancing electronics.

电容器对管理更为宽容。它们不介意被欠充电，它们没有电池的记忆，且不像富液铅酸电池那样需要浇水。它们被过充电时不爆炸，也不放气。然而，长的电容器串联是需要平衡的。例如麦克斯韦 125V BMOD0063 电容模块（图 8-15）具有内置的电子平衡器件。

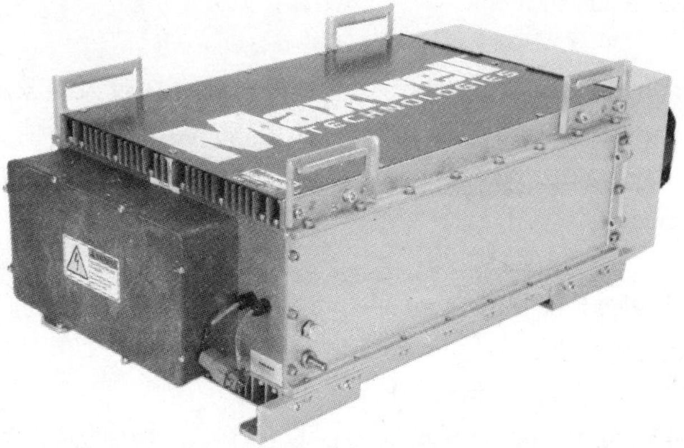

Figure 8–15 Maxwell BMOD0063 Ultracapacitor Module. Photo courtesy of Maxwell Technologies, Inc.(http://www.maxwell.com)

图 8–15 麦克斯韦 BMOD0063 超级电容器模块。照片由麦克斯韦技术有限公司 (http://www.maxwell.com) 提供

➤ Compressed Air Energy Storage

Compressed air vehicles are not complex. They use a bottle of compressed air and some kind of compressed air motor (Figure 8-16). Neither is the concept new. Whilst Queen Victoria was still on the throne Whitehead used compressed air to drive torpedoes, and the French city of Nantes had compressed air trams.

➤ 压缩空气蓄能

压缩空气汽车并不复杂，它们使用压缩空气瓶和某种压缩空气发动机（图 8 -16）。这些概念并不是新的。在维多利亚女王时代（译注：1819—1901 年，是英国最鼎盛的时期，至今还有很多英国人怀念那个时代。）怀特哈德就使用压缩空气推动鱼雷，法国的城市南特还有使用压缩空气的有轨汽车。

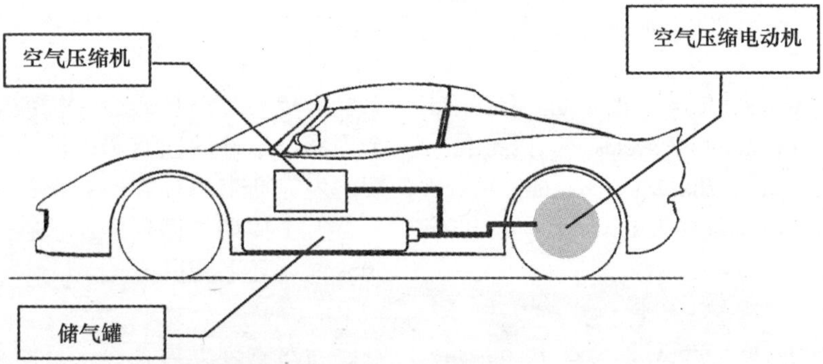

Figure 8–16 Compressed air energy storage

图 8–16 压缩空气蓄能

Compressed air drive has several problems. It tends to be relatively inefficient. The energy to drive the car is transformed many times before it reaches the wheels: there are losses in the generation and transmission of the electricity, losses in the compressor and losses in the air motor.

压缩空气驱动器有几个问题。它往往是相对低效的。用来驱动汽车的能量在到达车轮前经过了很多次的变化，有发电和输电的损失，在压缩机和空气驱动器中也有损失，等等。

There are significant thermal issues. Compressing air heats it. Releasing the pressure cools it. In extreme cases valves may ice up. There may be further sacrifices in efficiency.

此外，还存在较大的散热问题。压缩空气使其变热，释放压力后使它冷却。在极端情况下，阀门可能会结冰，并可能有更多的效率损失。

A high pressure bottle is also a liability in an accident. In July 2008 an oxygen bottle in the hold of an airliner ruptured, blowing a hole in the skin of the aircraft and projecting the bottle itself up through the floor of the cabin. Fortunately no one was injured.

高压瓶也存在潜在的危险。2008 年 7 月，一架客机中的一个氧气瓶破裂，在飞机的壁上穿了一个孔，而且瓶子穿过机舱内的地板飞了出去。幸运的是没有人受伤。

Finally, even with very high system pressures, the specific energy (amount of energy stored per unit of weight) is relatively low: anecdotally, no better than lead-acid batteries.

最后，即使它具有非常高的系统压力，比能（每单位重量的能量储存量）也是较低的，至少不会好过铅酸电池。

➢ Superconducting Magnetic Energy Storage

➢ 超导磁储能

Superconducting Magnetic Energy Storage (SMES) makes use of two phenomena

- The field generated by an electromagnet stores energy which can be recovered as electrical power.
- The electrical resistance of certain metals drops to zero at very low temperatures.

超导磁储能系统（SMES）应用了如下两种现象：

- 电磁铁产生的磁场所存储的能量可以被转换为电能。
- 在非常低的温度下某些金属的电阻下降为零。

Fundamentally an SMES is a coil of superconducting metal in a jacket of liquid helium. The SMES is “charged” by passing a current through the coil. As the magnetic field builds up, energy is absorbed.

超导磁储能系统基本上是一个在液态氦罐中的超导金属线圈。超导磁储能系统通过将电流输到线圈中来实现“充电”。随着磁场的建立，能量被吸收。

At a steady state, almost no power is required to maintain current flow. If a load is placed across the coil, the decaying magnetic field drives power through it.

在一个稳定的状态，几乎不要任何能量去维持电流。如果在线圈两端放置负载，则可通过磁场的衰减来驱动它。

Fixed SMES systems are in use in industrial environments for backup and power regulation. None are currently available for mobile use and the very low temperatures required adds a great deal of cost and complexity. Efficiency is however said to be very high and they are capable of producing very high power instantaneously.

固定的超导磁储能系统已在工业中用于储备及功率的调节。目前还没有任何可在移动中使用的系统，并且极低的温度增加了较大的成本和复杂性。然而，其效率是非常高的，并且它们也能够在瞬间产生非常高的功率。

➢ Inductive charging

➢ 感应充电

Inductive charging could conceivably be used to recharge an EV on the move thus providing infinite

可以预见，感应充电如果能被用于对移动中的电动汽车进行充电，将提供无限的行驶里

range. It is a way of transferring power to an EV (or indeed any battery powered device) without a physical connection. This sounds like magic, but isn't.If you have read earlier chapters you will be very familiar with the idea that a voltage is induced in a wire that is placed in a moving magnetic field. Indeed this is the principle of a conventional transformer: an AC current in the primary windings creates a moving magnetic field in the transformer core. The moving magnetic field induces a voltage in the secondary windings (Figure 8-17). A transformer of this kind is most efficient with a continuous iron core, but would still function (albeit with reduced efficiency) with an air gap (Figure 8-18).

程。这是一种不用物理连接对电动汽车（或由电池供电的任何设备）进行能量的传输。这听起来像变魔术一样，但并非如此。如果您已经阅读了前面的章节，您会很熟悉在移动磁场中放置一根导线就会产生感应电压的现象。事实上，这是常规变压器的原理。初级绕组中的交流电流在变压器磁芯中创建了一个移动的磁场。移动磁场诱导次级绕组中的电压（图 8-17）。这种类型的变压器中有一个连续的铁心是最有效的，但在空气间隙中仍然起作用（尽管效率较低）（图 8-18）。

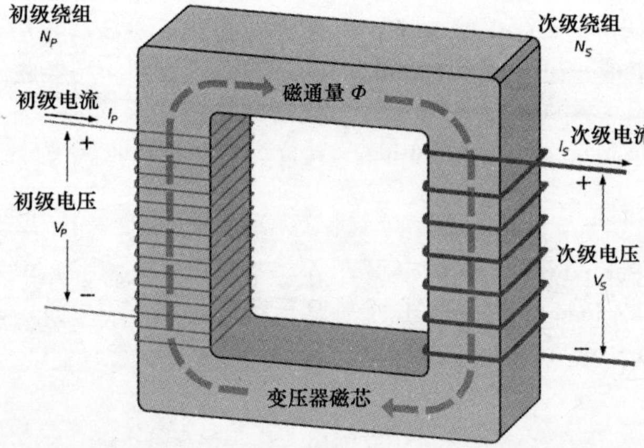

Figure 8–17 Transformer (Illustration from Daniels, A 1976.Introduction to Electrical Machines. Macmillan Publishers. ISBN 0-333-19627-9, released under the GNU Licence.)

图 8–17 变压器（插图选自 A• 丹尼尔斯 1976 由麦克米兰出版公司出版的《电动机械引论》一书。ISBN 0-333-19627-9, 根据 GNU 许可证发布。）

Now imagine the transformer in Figure 8-18 rotated through 90° with the secondary windings mounted in a vehicle and the primary windings embedded in the road (Figure 8-19). This would allow a crude form of inductive charging.

现在想象将图 8-18 的变压器旋转 90° 。将次级绕组装在车辆上，并将初级绕组嵌入道路中（图 8-19）。这将形成初始形式的感应充电。

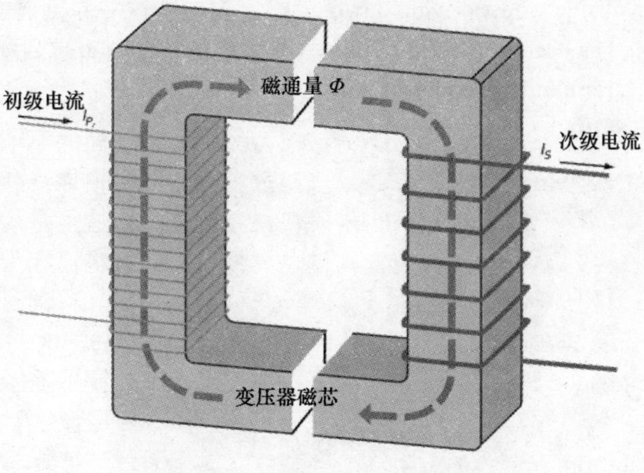

Figure 8–18 Transformer with air gap

图 8–18 具有空气隙的变压器

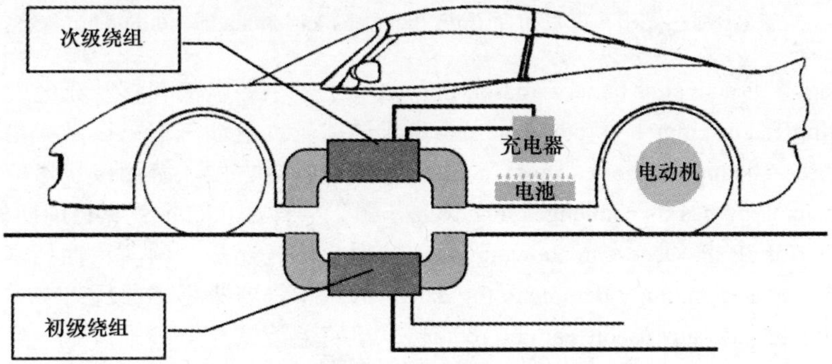

Figure 8–19 Inductive charging schematic

图 8–19 感应充电原理图

A real-world installation would use a different mechanical design, but the same electromagnetic principle. Inductive chargers are readily available for consumer electronics such as games console remotes, and there have been some forays into inductive charging for EVs.

实际中的安装采用同样的电磁原理，但不同的机械设计。感应充电器在消费型电子产品，如游戏机遥控器中是现成的，也有一些研究涉足感应电动汽车充电的领域。

A very interesting longer-term possibility is inductive charging on the move. If roads (or sections of roads such as one lane in multi-lane motorways) were modified as inductive chargers, then suitably-

一个非常有趣的长期可行性是移动中的感应充电。如果道路（或路段，如在多车道高速公路中的一个车道）被改装成感应充电器，那么配有适当设施的电动汽车就可在行驶的

equipped EVs could recharge whilst driving down the road. The principle has been illustrated by the e-quickie project at Karlsruhe University of Applied Sciences (Figure 8-20).

路上充电。这一原则已被卡尔斯鲁厄应用科学大学的 e-quickie 项目所展示（图 8-20）。

Figure 8–20 E-quickie.Photo courtesy of Hochschule Karlsruhe – University of Applied Sciences. Photographer: Uwe Krebs (http://www.hs-karlsruhe.de/en/home.html)

图 8–20 E-Quickie 感应插电式汽车。照片由卡尔斯鲁厄大学 – 应用科技大学的提供。摄影师：尤韦 • 克雷布斯 (http://www.hs-karlsruhe.de/en/home.html)

The combination of a smaller battery and on-the-move charging is enticing. EVs could be made smaller, lighter, cheaper and even more convenient. The technology has its challenges however. The e-quickie, for all its success in showing what could be done, is a technology demonstrator; far smaller and lighter than any usable car and requiring the in-road charging infrastructure which does not yet exist outside of a test track. There would be a host of problems to solve from payment to handling snow. The potential infrastructure investment is intimidating. The use of the vehicle-to-grid ideas discussed in the next chapter might be problematic.

一个较小的电池和移动充电的组合具有诱人的前景。电动汽车可以做得更小、更轻、更便宜且更方便。然而该技术有其自身的挑战性。尽管 e-quickie 就它目前所做的是成功的，但它毕竟还是一项演示性技术，比任何可用的汽车都要小得多，轻得多。并且它需要在道路上建造充电基础设施，这种设施在测试赛道之外尚不存在，但从想法到实现还有许多问题需要解决。基础设施所需的投资将是惊人的。在下一章中将讨论的汽车电网，这可能也会成问题。

➢ Overhead power

➢ 架空电力线路

The transmission of power to a moving vehicle from overhead wires (or in the case of the London underground, a third rail) has been widely used for trains and trams for over a century. (Figure 8-21).

将架空线（在伦敦地铁的情况下为第三轨道线）的电力传输到移动车辆的做法已被广泛应用于火车和电车等中长达一个多世纪（图 8-21）。

Overhead power cables are fairly easy to organise

架空电力电缆对于在固定轨道上运行的电车

with trams or trains that run on fixed rails. Overhead wires have however also been used with conventional road vehicles. Buses of this kind are normally referred to as "trolleybuses" and have been widely used around the world (Figure 8-22).

或火车而言很容易实现。然而，架空线也被用于传统的道路车辆。这种形式的大巴通常也被称作“无轨电车”，并已在世界各地广泛使用（图 8-22）。

Figure 8–21 Toronto Tram from the 1920s. Note overhead power cables. Photo courtesy of David Arthur (licensed under Creative Commons Attribution-Share Alike 3.0)

图 8–21 多伦多 1920 年代的电车。请注意其架空电缆。照片由大卫 • 阿瑟提供（由创作共署名 3.0 许可）

Figure 8–22 Trolleybus of the kind used in Newcastle-on-Tyne in the 1960s. Photo courtesy of Steve Kemp (licensed under the Creative Commons Attribution-Share Alike 3.0)

图 8–22 英国纽卡斯尔泰恩 1960 年代的无轨电车。照片由斯蒂夫 • 肯普提供（由创作共署名 3.0 许可）

The superior low-rpm torque of an electric motor makes trolleybuses attractive in hilly areas (note the twin rear axles in the Newcastle trolleybus in Figure 8-22). For example, San Francisco Municipal Transportation Authority claims to have the largest fleet of trolley buses in the USA[1]. Many modern trolleybuses are a form of hybrid with batteries or a diesel engine providing power when not connected to the overhead wires.

电动机在低转速时的超大转矩使得无轨电车在山地很有吸引力（请注意图 8-22 所示纽卡斯无轨电车后的双线）。例如，旧金山市运输管理局声称拥有全美最大的无轨电车队[㊀]。当未连接到架空电线时，许多现代的无轨电车是一种用电池和柴油机提供动力的混合动力车。

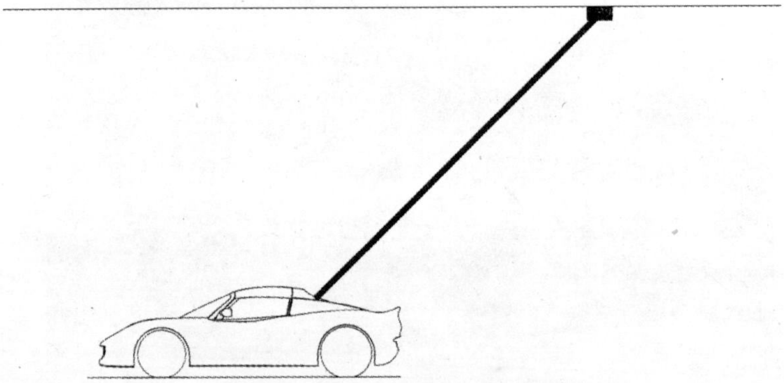

Figure 8–23 Trolleycar anyone?

图 8–23 有轨汽车，有人有吗？

Even as an adjunct to battery power, it is difficult to see the same principle being applied to private cars. Quite apart from the very long pick-up poles required with a smaller vehicle, the sheer number of cars on the road, the problem of overtaking and numerous other complications would make it difficult to implement.

即使作为电池电源的辅助手段，将同样的原理应用于私家车还是很难的。除了在较小的车辆上方需要一个很长的杆外，仅仅因为在路上的汽车数量之多，就可使超车和许多其他复杂的问题难以实现。

➢ In Conclusion

Fuel cells, flywheels, hybrids, ultra-capacitors, compressed gas, superconducting magnetic energy storage, inductive charging on the move and overhead power: someone, somewhere has demonstrated every one of these power storage methods. Some are in use in real-world applications already. The concept of inductive charging on the move is perhaps one of the strongest

➢ 小结

燃料电池、飞轮、混合动力汽车、超级电容器、压缩气体、超导磁储能装置、行驶中的感应充电和架空电力等，有人已经在某些地方证明了所有的这些蓄能方法。有些方法已在实际项目中获得应用。

1 http://www.sfmta.com/cms/mfleet/trolley.htm

㊀ 见 http://www.sfmta.com/cms/mfleet/trolley.htm。

contenders for future adoption. Existing EVs would need little modification to make use of inductive charging facilities, and would not absolutely require such facilities to be viable.

It is however difficult to see any of these technologies supplanting the pure battery EV altogether. Most either have substantially lower specific energy than Lithium-Ion cells or high cost, or both.

行驶中感应充电的技术也许是未来会被采用的最强有力的竞争者。现有的电动汽车几乎不需要任何修改就可应用感应充电设施，且并不一定需要这些设施使其变得可行。

但是，很难看到这些技术完全取代纯电池电动汽车。与锂离子电池相比，这些技术大都有较低的比能或较高的成本，或两者兼而有之。

9 Why Bother with Battery Power?

为什么要用电池供电?

Previous chapters have dealt with the technological issues surrounding EVs. In this final chapter we address an issue which for many people comes first logically. What are the motivations for making the change from our IC to EV? We have been driving IC-engined cars for nigh on 100 years. Over that time they have been transformed from nasty, noisy, unreliable devices to a level of smoothness, reliability and efficiency that is remarkable given their complexity. So why bother with EVs?

前面的章节讨论了有关电动汽车的技术问题。在这最后一章中，我们要解决对很多人来说在逻辑上摆在第一位的问题。从我们的内燃机变到电动汽车的动机是什么？在近100年的时间里，我们一直在推动内燃机汽车的发展。在这段时间里，它们从令人讨厌的、嘈杂的和不可靠的装置被改造成具有一定程度的平稳性、可靠性和高效性的代步工具。考虑到这一过程的复杂性，这是十分了不起的成就。所以何必要电动汽车呢？

Two reasons are often given –

- "peak oil" (i.e. it's running out)v
- climate change

经常被提到的两个原因包括：

- “峰值石油”（即它快被用完了）（译注：峰值石油是指石油开采达到最大速度的时刻，此后生产的速度将进入终极下降的阶段）
- 气候变化

Unfortunately both of these are contentious issues: some hold that peak oil is exaggerated and some that mankind's activities have little to do with climate change. If these were the only benefits of EVs then there would be some argument about whether the change was worth making. There are however many other powerful motives for adopting electric drive. We cover some of these, as well as addressing the "peak oil" and climate change issues.

不幸的是，这是两个有争议的问题。有些人认为峰值石油被夸大了，另一些人认为人类的活动对气候变化的影响甚微。如果这是电动汽车唯一的好处，那么会有一些质疑认为这样的变换否是值得。然而，还有许多其他强大的动机促使我们采用电力驱动。我们将介绍其中的一些，并讨论“峰值石油”和气候变化的问题。

➢ Urban air pollution

➢ 城市空气污染

Anyone who has been through a busy road tunnel knows what other people's exhaust fumes smell like. Those of us who live in big cities (i.e. most of us) spend much of our lives breathing in dilute vehicle exhaust (Figure 9-1). We would not expect

任何曾经穿过繁忙的公路隧道的人都能感受到其他汽车发出的废气闻起来的味道。我们中那些生活在大城市里的人（即我们大多数人），大部分时间都在稀释了的汽车尾气中呼吸（图9-1）。我们应该不会认为这对我们有

this to be good for us. There is evidence that diesel emissions in particular have a number of harmful effects. For example, the American Journal of Epidemiology reported an apparent link between exposure to pollutants typical of diesel engines and impaired brain development in children[1]. The New England Journal of Medicine reported a study[2] in which 60 volunteers, all asthmatics, walked down Oxford Street (diesel buses and taxis only), then Hyde Park (traffic free). There was a major difference in the level of both particulates and the aggravation of asthmatic symptoms.

好处。有证据表明，特别是柴油车的排放有许多有害的影响。例如，美国流行病学杂志上报告了典型柴油机排放物和儿童中大脑发育不全之间的明显联系[㊀]。新英格兰医学杂志报道了一项研究[㊁]，该研究让60名患哮喘病的志愿者先在牛津街（译注：牛津街是英国伦敦市中心里一条繁华的商业街）（只有柴油公交车和出租车）上走，然后到海德公园（译注：海德公园是英国伦敦市中心最大的一个公园，它毗邻牛津街，没有汽车）去。哮喘症状的严重程度与这两个地方的颗粒物的多少有很大的关系。

Figure 9–1 Exhaust fumes, especially diesel particulates, are bad for human health. Photo courtesy of Marius Zaharia (http://www.flickr.com/photos/mordax/with/3183266304)

图 9–1 汽车尾气尤其是柴油微粒对人体健康有害。照片由马里厄斯·扎哈里亚提供 (http://www.flickr.com/photos/mordax/with/3183266304)

There are many other studies suggesting links between diesel emissions and asthma, cancer, impaired brain development and other issues.

还有许多研究揭示了柴油车排放和哮喘、癌症、脑部发育受损等其他问题之间的关系。

Newer diesels are better than older ones in terms of air pollution when correctly adjusted. Allowable levels of particulates and nitrogen oxides (the main

经过适当的调整，较新的柴油机在空气污染方面比旧的要好。新车中的颗粒物和氮氧化物（主要的污染物）的允许值在美国和欧洲

1 November 2007 http://aje.oxfordjournals.org/cgi/content/abstract/kWm308v1

2 December 2008 https://content.nejm.org/cgi/content/full/357/23/2348?ck=nck

㊀ 2007 年 11 月：http://aje.oxfordjournals.org/cgi/content/abstract/kWm308v1。

㊁ 2008 年 12 月：https://content.nejm.org/cgi/content/full/357/23/2348?ck=nck。

baddies) are being steadily lowered for new cars in both the USA and Europe. The manufacturers can however only achieve the new standards by adding expensive particulate filters and/or catalytic converters. And it isn't just the basic equipment either. Extra electronics are also needed to monitor emissions to ensure that they don't drift outside the limits.

正稳步降低。然而，制造商可以通过加入昂贵的微粒过滤器和/或催化转化器来达到新的标准。但除了这些基本的装备外，还需要额外的电子设备来监测排放量，以确保它们不超出限度。

From an engineering viewpoint, making a dangerous mess, then cleaning it up on the way out of the exhaust pipe seems very inelegant. By contrast an EV charged from a renewable source (such as wind or hydro) has zero emissions, and even if electricity from a coal-fired power station is used, the indirect emissions are physically separated from population centres and are in any case more readily controlled.

从工程的角度上看，这种先制造一个危险的境况，然后在排气管内清洗的方式似乎非常不雅。相比之下，从可再生能源（如风力或水力）中充电的电动汽车为零排放，即使从燃煤电站充电，那些间接的排放物在地理上与人口聚居中心分离，并且在任何情况下它们都更容易控制。

➢ Noise pollution

➢ 噪声污染

A number of studies have suggested a link between traffic noise and hearing loss. For example an Indian study published in 2009 found very substantial hearing loss in shopkeepers working near a busy road[1].

大量的研究表明了交通噪声与听力受损之间的关系。例如，印度在2009年发表的一项研究发现，在一条繁忙的马路附近工作的店主具有非常严重的听力受损[㊀]。

Hearing loss is bad enough, but rather more seriously, a study by the Karolinska Institutet in Sweden[2] reported in the British Medical Journal suggested that people living in areas of high traffic noise have a greater risk of myocardial infarction (heart attack).

听力受损是够糟的了。然而更严重的是，英国医学杂志所刊登的瑞典卡罗林斯卡医学院的一项研究[㊁]报告表明，生活在高交通噪声领域的人具有更大的心肌梗死（心脏病发作）的危险。

Also, as long ago as 2001 an Austrian study reported that "...children living in relatively noisy neighbourhoods had raised blood pressure, heart

此外，早在2001年，奥地利的一项研究报告指出："生活在比较嘈杂街区的儿童具有较高的血压、心跳和压力荷尔蒙的分泌水

1 http://www.informaworld.com/smpp/content~content=a906346013~db=all~jumptype=rss

2 http://ki.se/ki/jsp/polopoly.jsp?l=en&d=130&a=69349&newsdep=130 and http://oem.bmj.com/cgi/content/abstract/64/2/122

㊀ http://www.informaworld.com/smpp/content~content=a906346013~db=all~jumptype=rss。

㊁ http://ki.se/ki/jsp/polopoly.jsp?l=en&d=130&a=69349&newsdep=130 以及 http://oem.bmj.com/cgi/content/abstract/64/2/122。

rates and levels of stress hormones..." . This was at sound levels far below the 85 decibels or so that are currently considered to be damaging to hearing when frequently repeated.

平……"。这是在一个远低于 85dB 左右的噪声水平下测出的结果，目前认为经常在这一噪声水平下生活时，听力会受损害。

So, conventional vehicles are implicated in hearing loss, raised incidence of heart attacks, cancer, asthmatic problems, impaired brain development and increased levels of stress in children. That ought to be enough to encourage us to look for alternatives.

因此，传统汽车与听力受损、心脏病发作率增加、癌症和哮喘问题、儿童脑部发育受损和日益增加的压力水平的发病率有关。这应该足以鼓励我们去寻找替代品。

➢ Peak oil, or the Grandkid's Aviation Fuel

➢ 峰值石油，或孙辈的航空燃油

So EVs have major benefits for our health and well being and on the health and well being of our children, but there is another issue affecting our children: the accelerating rate that we are getting through the world's oil (Figure 9-2).

所以，电动汽车对我们的健康和福祉都很有好处，对我们后代的健康和福祉也有好处。但还有另外一个问题影响到了我们的后代，就是我们正在全世界范围内日益加快的石油开采速度（图 9-2）。

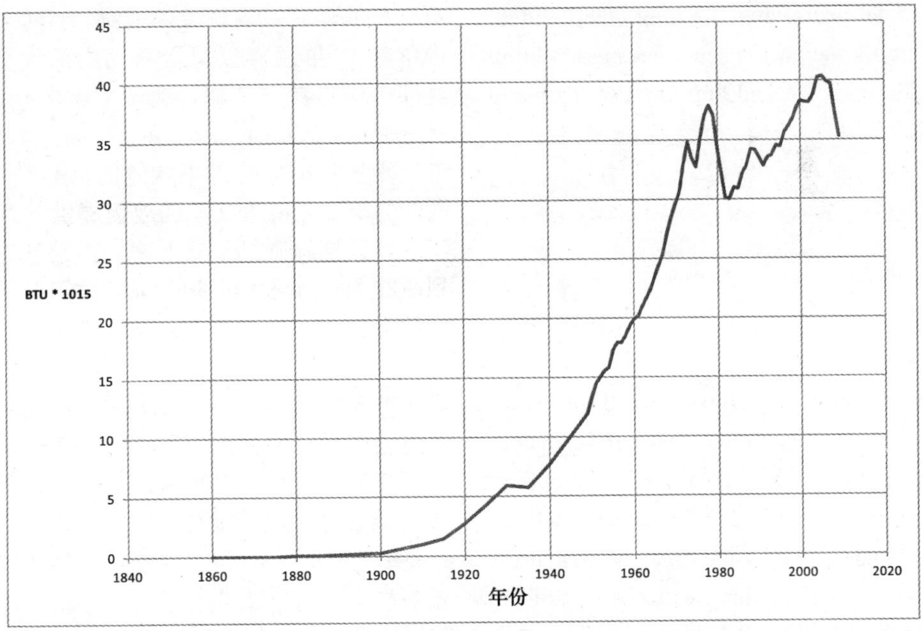

Figure 9–2 US Oil Usage 1860—2009 (Source - US Energy Information Administration)

图 9–2 1860—2009 年美国石油用量（来源：美国能源情报署）

When Stonehenge was built, what we now know as the North Sea Oil and Gas field already existed pretty much in the form in which it was discovered 4,000 years or so later. For all their exploits, the builders of Stonehenge had no idea that it was there, and could not in any case have extracted any of it.

在巨石阵建成时（译注：指在英国威尔特郡内的巨石阵，大约公元前3000年—前2000年建成），我们现在所知道的北海石油和天然气田（译注：在石油工业中，术语“北海”往往包括如挪威海和那些被称为“西设得兰群岛”、“大西洋边陲”或“大西洋边沿”等在地理上不属于北海的地区）已经存在，并与我们在约4000年以后发现它们的形式相似。对于它们的开采，巨石阵的建造者们根本不知道它们的存在，并且根本不能对它们进行开采。

It was still there nearly 2000 years later when Julius Caesar landed in what is now Kent. The Vikings crossed over it quite regularly 800 years after Caesar, again with no clue that it existed. Another 1000 years on and Admirals Jellicoe and Beatty sailed across the oil fields in their coal – powered grand fleet to the Battle of Jutland, little knowing that beneath their keels was the stuff that would power warships of the next great war. 50 years later the long sleep ended: North Sea oil was at long last detected. Within another 50 years we had dug most of it up and burned it.

2000年后的朱利叶斯·凯撒（译注：朱利叶斯·凯撒，公元前100年—前44年，是罗马将军、政治家和著名拉丁散文的作者）降落在现在称为肯特的大地上时，它仍然在那儿。凯撒之后的800年，维京人（译注：指8—11世纪中期从海上到欧洲、亚洲及北大西洋岛屿等地定居的北日耳曼人）多次穿过该地，同样不知道它的存在。1000年后，海军上将杰利科（译注：英国皇家海军上将，1859—1935年。）和贝蒂（译注：英国皇家海军上将，1871—1936年。）带领着以煤炭为动力的大舰队横渡那个油田参与日德兰战役（译注：这是第一次世界大战期间，1916年，英国海军与德国海军的一次海战），却不知他们足迹下方的东西能为下一场巨大战争的战舰提供动力。50年后，长期睡眠结束，北海石油终于被检测到。在另一个50年的时间，我们挖掘出了它的大部分，并且将它们烧掉了。

50 years in historical terms is the blink of an eye. North Sea oil is a microcosm of our whole petroleum-based culture: it's a short-term oddity, a developmental dead-end. Whether you believe that oil was laid down by the decay of animals in the Triassic or created along with the rest of the earth's crust a few thousand years ago, most of us believe that once it's gone, it's gone. You don't have to be a tree-hugger to think it unlikely that

从历史的角度上看，50年只是一眨眼的工夫。北海油田是我们整个以石油为基础的文化的一个缩影。这是一个短视的怪胎，发展的死胡同。无论石油是腐烂的动物在三叠纪（译注：三叠纪是一个地质时期，252.2±0.5~201.3±0.2万年前）时期形成的还是几千年前与地壳一起形成的，大多数人都相信，一旦它用完了，就用完了。我们的子孙后代不太可能仍然像我们现在这样可以大规模地驾驶由石油产品

our grandchildren will still be driving cars powered by petroleum products on the scale that we are. There simply isn't enough of the stuff left in the ground.

驱动的汽车。为确认这点，您不必是一个环保人士，因为在地下根本没有足够的东西留下。

If we were responsible we would use the oil we have only for activities where there is no viable alternative, such as aviation. Whilst we know several ways to power cars, commercial aircraft have always used fuels derived from petroleum. We know no other scalable way to fly people across the Atlantic. So if we really cared about our children and grand children, we would reserve oil for things like aviation where there are no alternatives. As things stand today, though, aviation accounts for just 12% of the fuel consumption of the entire transport sector, compared with 80% dedicated to road transport. We are using most of the little oil we have left in road transport where, with a little effort, we could use something else.

如果我们是负责任的，我们会将宝贵的石油用在没有可替代方案的地方，如航空中。虽然我们知道有几种方法可以为汽车提供动力，商用飞机一直都使用从石油中提炼的燃料。我们知道没有其他可扩展的方法让人们飞越大西洋。因此，如果我们真的关心子孙后代，我们应把石油留给那些没有可替代的事情，如航空。就目前情况来看，与专用于公路运输的 80% 相比，航空只占整个运输部门燃油消耗的 12%。我们将剩下的少得可怜的大部分石油都用在公路运输中，如果我们作出一点点的努力，就可以找到替代的东西。

EVs need energy but they don't need oil. You can power an EV from hydro-electric power, nuclear power stations, wind energy, tidal or wave energy, even (as costs come down) from solar panels on the roof of your house. Burning precious oil to drive cars is vandalism. We may stand accused by our grandchildren of burning the furniture because we couldn't be bothered to go out and bring in some logs.

电动汽车需要能量，但它们并不需要石油。可以用水电、核电、风能、潮汐或波浪的能量，甚至从您房顶上的太阳能电池板（如果成本下降的话）来为电动汽车提供能量。燃烧宝贵的石油来驱动汽车是蓄意破坏的行为。我们也许会被我们的子孙指控燃烧家具，因为我们不愿向前走一步去取些木材。

➢ Biofuels

First generation biofuels (broadly liquid fuels derived from foodstuffs such as corn) were described by Jean Ziegler of the UN[1] as a "crime against hu-

➢ 生物燃料

在联合国工作的让·齐格勒[⊖]将第一代生物燃料（一般是来自食品的液体燃料如玉米）描述为“危害人类的犯罪”。根据他的报告“……

1 http://www.un.org/apps/news/story.asp?NewsID=26478&Cr=food&Cr1=ziegler

⊖ http://www.un.org/apps/news/story.asp?NewsID=26478&Cr=food&Cr1=ziegler。

manity". According to his report "...232kg of corn is needed to make 50 litres of bio-ethanol....a child could live on that amount of corn for a year".

生产 50L 的生物乙醇需要 232kg 的玉米……这些玉米可让一个孩子吃一年"。

A World Bank report leaked by the Guardian newspaper opened with the startling statement: The World Bank's index of food prices increased 140 percent from January 2002 to February 2008. This increase was caused by a confluence of factors.

英国卫报披露了世界银行的一份报告，它在开篇中有令人吃惊的说法：从 2002 年 1 月到 2008 年 2 月世界银行的食品价格指数增长了 140%。这一增长是由于各种因素综合作用的结果。

Three years later, the effect of first generation biofuel production on world food prices remains a concern. It has also been realised, somewhat belatedly, that the production of the crops that go into these fuels itself consumes energy (and generates so-called "Green House Gases") in amounts that largely negate the supposed benefits. Lastly there is an issue of scalability. It takes a huge area of land to grow enough fuel to drive a car for a year, for much the same reason that it takes a large area of woodland to grow enough wood to keep a house warm using wood-burning stoves: if the US turned over its entire grain harvest to ethanol production, it would still have to find over 80% of its transport fuel from elsewhere.

三年后，第一代生物燃料的生产对世界粮食价格的影响仍令人担忧。虽然有点姗姗来迟，但人们现在已经认识到，用于生产这些燃料的作物本身所消耗的能量（并产生所谓的"温室气体"）在很大程度上抵消了原有的优点。最后，还有一个可扩展性的问题。为种植足够使汽车开动一年的燃料需要一个庞大面积的土地，它与需要大面积的林地来种植足够的木材，并燃烧木材以保持室内供暖的理由相同。如果美国将其收获的粮食全部用来生产乙醇，仍然有超过 80% 的运输用燃料需要从其他地方得到。

Second generation biofuels are produced from non-crop sources such as stalks, stems and other waste left over from food production. This reduces the impact on food prices but there are even greater concerns over scalability: think of the amount of food waste produced in your household, then think of three lanes of bumper-to-bumper traffic on the M25 on a Friday night. The numbers don't begin to work. Furthermore there is concern over the energy costs in transporting vegetable waste and by-products to biofuel production plants.

第二代生物燃料从非农作物中生产出来，如秸秆、茎和其他食品生产中遗留下来的废物。这降低了对粮食价格的影响，但对可扩展性将有更大的顾虑。想想您家里产生的食物废物量，然后再想想星期五晚上具有三个车道的 M25 高速公路（译注：英国的一条绕着伦敦的繁忙的高速公路）上首尾相接的交通量，您就会知道这些食物废物量根本不起作用。此外，人们对于运送这些蔬菜废弃物产生的能源成本以及生物燃料生产厂的副产品也有顾虑。

Another possible source of biofuels is algae. This is sometimes referred to as "2nd Generation" and sometimes as "3rd Generation" . Algae-based biofuels promise to address the scalability issue to some degree (algae are far more efficient than conventional agriculture at producing biofuels). However there are concerns over cost and the time this technology will take to reach commercial viability.

生物燃料的另一种可能的来源是藻类，它有时被称为"第二代"生物燃料，也有时被称为"第三代"。基于藻类的生物燃料承诺在一定程度上可以解决可扩展性问题（在生产生物燃料方面，藻类的效率远远高于传统的农作物），但人们对这项技术在达到商业上的可行性时所需的成本和时间也有担忧。

The widespread adoption of electric vehicles makes this problem go away. If we don't need liquid fuels at all we don't need to make biofuel. If we really want to power transport using biomass we can revert to a technology James Watt would have recognised: generate electricity from steam produced by burning wood (Figure 9-3).

电动汽车的广泛使用将使这个问题不再成为问题。如果我们完全不需要液体燃料，我们也不需要生产生物燃料。如果我们真的想要用生物质能去为运输提供动力，我们可以回到詹姆斯·瓦特（译注：1736 年 1 月 19 日—1819 年 8 月 25 日，蒸汽机的发明者）已经认识到的技术中去——通过燃烧木材产生的蒸汽来发电（图 9-3）。

Figure 9–3 The original bio fuel power plant. Photo courtesy of James Howe Photography (http://jameshowephotography.com)

图 9–3 原始生物燃料的发电厂。照片由詹姆斯•豪摄影室提供 (http://jameshowephotography.com)

➢ Climate Change

At some point in books and articles on EVs and hybrids, it is normal to go into their impact on climate change. This can be off-putting for the significant minority who are not convinced that climate change is man-made (or "anthropogenic" - i.e. caused by our activities). I do not propose to take sides in this debate as EVs are a win-win. If anthropogenic climate change is important for you then anyone who drives an EV is doing you a favour, regardless of why they are doing it. If you are keen on EVs for other reasons (such as urban air and noise pollution as described earlier), then those who are motivated by climate change are also supporting your agenda.

Briefly (for anyone who has been on silent retreat for the last 20 years) the issue is that average global temperatures have risen over the last 100 years or so, albeit with a dip between the 1940's and the 1980's and (according to the Met Office Hadley Centre) a plateau since about 2000 (Figure 9-4).

➢ 气候变化

任何关于电动汽车和混合动力汽车的书籍和文章在某个时候总要谈谈它们对气候变化的影响。这可能是令人倒胃口的，因为有不少的人不相信气候变化是人为的(或“人造的”，即我们的活动所造成的)。我不建议在这场辩论中选边站队，因为电动汽车是一个双赢的方案。如果您认为人的因素对气候变化是重要的，那么无论他们的目的是什么，任何驾驶电动汽车的人都在帮您的忙。如果您热衷于电动汽车是出于其他原因（如前文所述城市的空气和噪声污染），那么那些出于气候变化而推崇电动汽车的人也在支持您的做法。

简单说来，(对于那些在过去 20 年中已默默退休的人来说)问题是，在过去 100 年左右的时间里，全球平均气温已经上升，但在 20 世纪 40 年代和 80 年代有一个小的下降，并且(根据哈德利中心气象局)自 2000 年以来有一个峰值(图 9-4)。

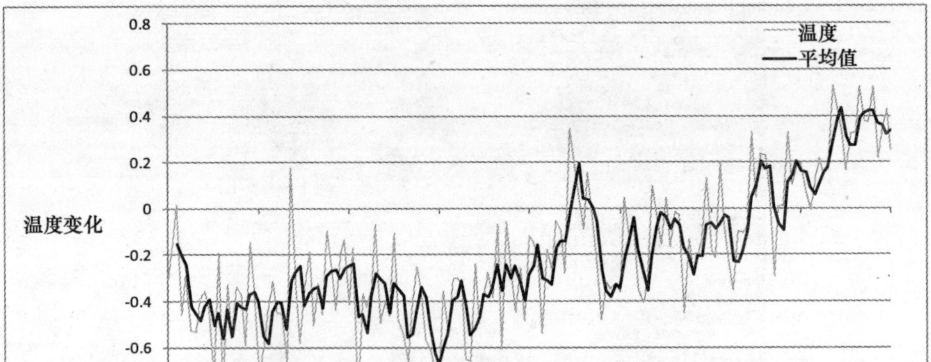

Figure 9–4 Mean Global Temperatures (HADCRUT3 data)

图 9–4 全球平均气温 (HADCRUT3 提供的数据)

The currently-dominant hypothesis is that this is due to the warming effect of the release by mankind into the atmosphere of "green house gases" (GHGs) – primarily carbon dioxide, methane, nitrous oxides and refrigerants, and that if we allow this to continue we (or our children/grandchildren) face a strong probability of dire consequences (primarily floods, crop failures, rising sea levels and some of the hotter places on earth becoming virtually uninhabitable).

目前占主导地位的假设是，这是由于人类释放到大气中的"温室气体"（GHGs）——主要是二氧化碳、甲烷、一氧化二氮和制冷剂，而产生的变暖效应。而且，如果我们允许这样的情形继续下去，我们（或我们的子孙）面临可怕后果（主要是洪涝灾害、农作物欠收、海平面上升和一些地球上较热的地方变得让人几乎无法居住）的可能性极大。

On this model, the over-riding concern is to minimise or eliminate the release of carbon dioxide into the atmosphere. For road transport the important figure is the grams of carbon dioxide produced per mile (or km) travelled.

在此模型中最重要的考虑是减少或消除二氧化碳在大气中的排放。对于公路运输而言，重要的是每公里行程产生多少克的二氧化碳。

Battery powered vehicles offer a substantial improvement to this grams-per-mile figure, but not a complete solution.

电池驱动的汽车提供了大幅改善该"克每公里"的数字，但也不是一个彻底的解决方案。

➢ Energy Efficiency and GHGs

➢ 能源效率和温室气体

It is often said that EVs have neither markedly better well-to-wheel efficiency nor better GHG numbers than the best of conventional IC engines: that they merely shift the fuel consumption and GHG production from the car to the power station. There are a number of papers by reputable organisations that purport to demonstrate this. Numerous media stories carry a similar message.

人们常说，与传统的内燃机相比，在从原始能源到终极能量的转换效率方面，电动汽车既没有明显的好转，也没有更好的温室气体排放数据，它们只能将燃料的消耗和温室气体的生产从汽车向电站转移。有些信誉良好的组织还撰文来证明这点。许多媒体的报道也传递了类似的信息。

None that I have read bear close examination. They are all based on plausible, but ultimately misleading, assumptions. Here are some of them:

然而我还没有读到过一篇能经得起仔细推敲的文章。它们都是基于合理的、但最终是误导性的假设。下面是其中的一些例子。

Ignore the power consumed extracting and refining petrol

Extracting and refining petrol itself consumes power (Figure 9-5).

忽略提取和精炼汽油消耗的能量

提取和精炼汽油本身要消耗能量（图 9-5）。

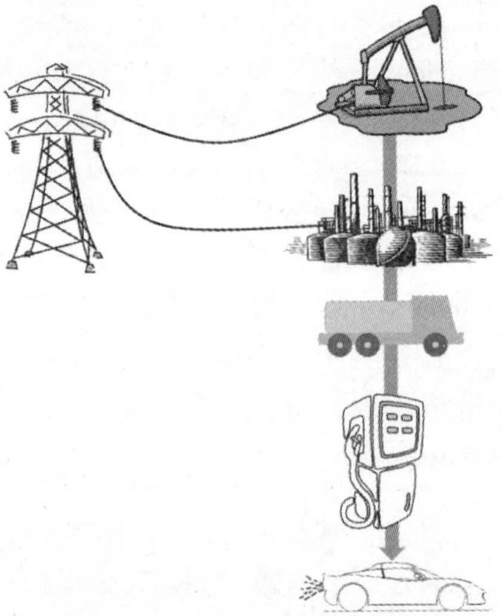

Figure 9–5 Petrol Extraction and Refining losses

图 9–5 石油提取与精炼过程中的损耗

Extraction efficiency ranges from 78% to 92%[1]. Refining efficiency is also around 90%[2]. The two added together are therefore about 80%. Energy content of a US gallon of petrol is around 32 to 34 kW-hrs[3]. Thus the energy used in extracting and refining a US gallon of petrol might be around 6 to 8 kW-hr. A typical EV achieves about 4 to 5 miles per kW-hr so if these numbers are correct, an EV could travel around 24 - 30 miles on the power required merely to extract and refine a US gallon of petrol. (Figure 9-6).

提取的效率为 78%~92%㊀，精炼的效率也是 90% 左右㊁，因此，两者加在一起的效率约为 80%。1USgal（译注：1USgal 约等于 3.8L）汽油的能量含量大约是 32~34kW•h㊂。因此，在提取和精炼 1USgal 汽油的过程中所使用的能源是 6~8kW•h。而一辆典型电动汽车可达到约 6~8km/kW•h。如果这些数字是正确的，则仅仅提取和精炼 1USgal 汽油所需的能量就可使电动汽车行驶 36~48km（图 9-6）。

1 "Fact Sheet: Energy Efficiency of Strategic Unconventional Resources" [US] DOE Office of Petroleum Reserves.

2 See "Estimation of Energy Efficiencies of U.S. Petroleum Refineries" Michael Wang, Center for Transportation Research, Argonne National Laboratory, March 2008 and "Updated Estimation of Energy Efficiencies of U.S. Petroleum Refineries" Ignasi Palou-Rivera and Michael Wang July 2010.

3 The US EPA estimate that the energy content of petrol varies between 108,000 and 117,000 BTUhttp://www.epa.gov/oms/rfgecon.htm#1

㊀ "情况报告：战略性非常规资源的能源效率"美国能源部石油储备办公室。

㊁ 参阅"美国石油精炼厂能源效率的估算"，迈克尔·王，阿贡国家实验室交通研究中心，2008 年 3 月，和"美国石油精炼厂能源效率的更新估算"，义格纳斯·帕劳 - 里维拉和迈克尔·王，2010 年 7 月。

㊂ 美国环保局估计，不同汽油的能量含量为 108000 到 117000 英热单位（译注：1 英热单位 = 1 055.05585J），http://www.epa.gov/oms/rfgecon.htm#1。

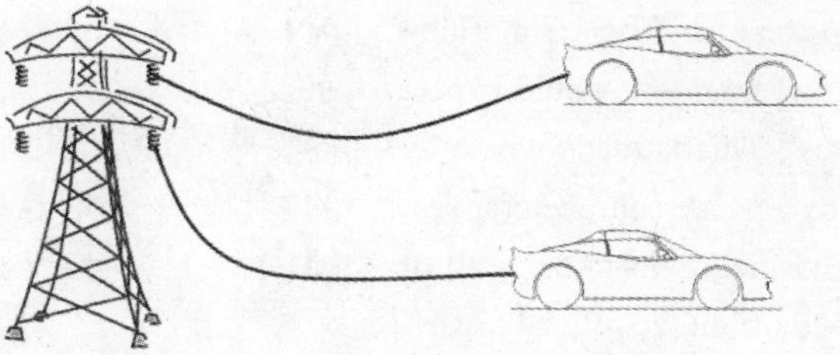

Figure 9–6 Some EVs can travel further on the energy used to extract and refine petrol than an IC engined car can drive on the petrol itself

图 9–6 有些电动汽车用提取和精炼汽油所耗的能量就能行驶得比内燃机汽车用的汽油本身更远

The average in-use fuel consumption for passenger cars in the US is only 21.5 m.p.g.[1]. It therefore seems likely that some EV drivers go further on the power needed to extract and refine a gallon of petrol than many IC engined cars go on the petrol itself: although to be fair, the typical EV is smaller and lighter than the average US passenger car.

美国乘务车的平均油耗为 10.9L/100km[⊖]。因此，有些电动汽车驾驶人用那些提取和精炼 1gallon 汽油所需的能量似乎就能比许多内燃机汽车用这 1gallon 的汽油走得更远。然而为了公平起见，必须指出典型的电动汽车比一般美国乘务车的体积更小、重量更轻。

Use official fuel consumption figures for IC engined cars

Efficiency comparisons invariably use the official fuel consumption figures published by national bodies (such as the Vehicle Certification Authority in the UK). Real world average fuel economy figures for IC-engined cars are however nowhere near these official figures (often quoted in the small print of advertisements). "Highway" fuel economy figures are measured for a car in good condition, tuned and adjusted to perfection, operated by a skilled driver in mild weather, with few ancillaries running and with the engine fully warmed up.

使用官方的内燃机汽车的耗油数字

效率的比较毫无例外地总是使用国家机构（如英国车辆认证局）公布的官方耗油数字。然而，现实世界中内燃机汽车平均燃油经济性的数字远高于这些官方数字（经常在小字体印刷的广告中被引用）。“公路”燃油经济性的数字通常是汽车在良好的条件下、调节和调整完美、由一个熟练的驾驶人在温和的天气情况下，加上一些辅助设备的运行，并且在发动机充分预热的情况下测得的。

There is much anecdotal evidence that even on long trips with a thoroughly-warm engine few people get close to the official figures. At the other end of the scale, the first mile or two of a school run or

有很多未经证实的证据表明，在长途旅行时，即使用一个充分预热的发动机，也很少有人能得到接近官方的数字。在天平的另一端，在寒冷冬天的早晨，在上学或去商店的路上，

1 http://www.epa.gov/oms/consumer/f00013.htm

⊖ http://www.epa.gov/oms/consumer/f00013.htm。

a trip down to the shops on a cold winter morning consume vastly more fuel than you would expect from the official figures[1]. This is made worse by the power consumed by rear screen heaters, seat heaters, headlights, windshield wipers etc – all of which would be switched off on the official tests.

前一两千米的油耗比您预期从官方得到的数字要大得多㊀。更糟糕的是后风窗玻璃加热器、座椅加热器、前照灯、刮水器等所消耗的能量——所有这些在官方的测试中都被关掉。

And recall that most cars are driven fewer than 40 miles a day so a high proportion of real-world driving is done with a cold engine. This has a major impact on real world fleet-wide fuel consumption.

回想一下，大部分汽车每天行驶不到 60km，因此，冷机驾驶在实际中具有很高的比例。这对现实世界中整个车队的燃油消耗有着重大的影响。

Ignore traffic jams

Another issue is nose-to-tail stop-start traffic. This has a disastrous effect on the per-mile emissions of IC engined vehicles, as anyone who has endured a traffic jam in a tunnel can testify. It has little effect on the per-mile energy consumption and no effect on direct emissions of EVs.

忽略堵车

另一个问题是拥堵的、忽开忽停的交通状况。任何在车流中忍受过交通堵塞的人都可以作证，这对内燃机汽车燃油经济性有着灾难性的影响，但这对电动汽车每公里的能源消耗及直接排放并没有影响。

Assume that the IC car is always correctly tuned

Not all cars are operating at their optimum all the time. According to figures released by VOSA[2] over 1.7 million cars in the UK failed their MOT tests in 2009/10 on the "fuel and exhaust" area. IC engined cars are, as has been noted, complex devices and the partial failure of obscure components such as lambda (oxygen) sensors can have a major impact on both fuel consumption and emissions.

假设内燃机汽车总是调配得很好

并不是所有的汽车在所有的时间内都处于最佳的操作状态。根据英国车辆和运营商服务局公布的数据㊁，2009—2010 年度在英国有超过 170 万辆的汽车在“燃料与废气”方面没有通过 MOT（译注：英国的 MOT 相当于中国的年检）的测试。正如前面所指出的那样，内燃机汽车是一个很复杂的系统，并且某些不起眼的部件［如 λ（氧）传感器］的

1 In the UK, the AA noted "...Even at relatively mild winter temperatures, the fuel consumption of a cold car leaving its driveway is 40 per cent higher than normal..." (http://www.theaa.com/motoring_advice/news/aa-fuel-for-thought-increased-cost-of-winter-motoring.html)

2 http://www.dft.gov.uk/vosa/repository/10%20180a1.pdf

㊀ 在英国，AA（译注：AA 是汽车协会的简称。英国汽车协会成立于 1905 年，1999 年进行股份化，成为一家私营有限责任公司，目前提供汽车保险、驾驶学校、故障保险、贷款和汽车咨询及其他服务。）指出，“……即使在相对温和的冬季温度下，冷车离开停车道时，油耗比正常高出 40%”。

㊁ http://www.dft.gov.uk/vosa/repository/10%20180a1.pdf。

It is reasonable to assume that a high proportion of these MOT failures will have been exhibiting higher-than expected fuel consumption and/or emissions. This will push up the real-world national fleet average for IC engined cars by an indeterminate but possibly significant amount. EVs are vastly simpler mechanically and do not suffer from this kind of generalised efficiency degradation.

部分失效对燃油经济性和排放性有重大的影响。我们可以作出如下合理的假设，这些高比例的 MOT 未通过率已表现出高于预期的燃料消耗和排放。它会将全国内燃机汽车的实际平均耗油量推向一个中等、也可能是显著的高位。电动汽车在机械方面要简单得多，并且没有这种广义的效率降低。

Ignore fuel distribution

There are energy costs associated with maintaining a network of petrol stations and keeping them all supplied with fuel. These include the energy associated with distributing thousands of tons of fuel from refinery to filling station, the additional miles driven by customers of those filling stations and the lighting and heating associated with operating those filling stations (Figure 9-7). It is difficult to quantify these losses exactly, but here are some order-of-magnitude estimates:

忽略燃料的运输

维持一个加油站网络，并使它们能提供所需的燃料，需要有能源的消耗。这包括将几千吨的燃料从炼油厂运到加油站所需的能量、客户开到加油站所需的额外的公里数，以及与加油站有关的照明和暖气所需的能量（图 9-7）。要想准确地量化这些损失是很困难的，但这里有一些数量级方面的估计。

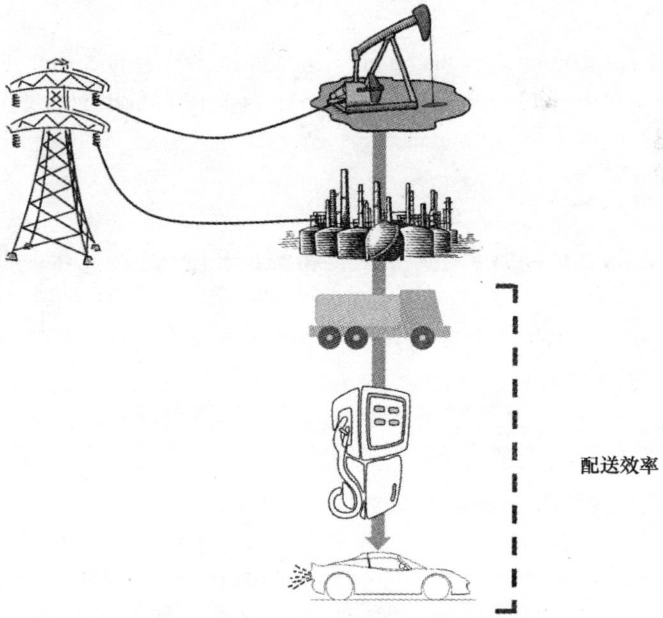

Figure 9–7 Distribution Efficiency

图 9–7 配送效率

One UK tanker operator claims to cover 6 million miles a year delivering 2000 million litres of fuel[1]. If we assume 10 m.p.g. (generous to the tanker), then road tankers in this fleet burn around 1.3% of the fuel they deliver.

一个英国油罐车运营商声称为提供20亿升的燃油，他们每年要跑10万公里㊀。如果我们假设23.5L/100km（对油罐车而言这是够少的了），那么，这个油罐车队烧掉了它们所提供燃料的约1.3%。

A 5 mile diversion by car drivers every 300 miles to get to a filling station would represent about 1.6% efficiency reduction.

假设一个驾驶人每开500km就要到一个8km远的加油站去加油，那么这将减少约1.6%的效率。

Forecourt lighting is a major energy cost for filling stations. A typical small petrol station might sell 38,000 litres/week or about 2 million litres/year. The calorific value of 2 million litres of petrol is about 70 million megajoules or (very approximately) 20,000 megawatt-hours. One study suggested an energy consumption of 40 megawatt-hours per year just on forecourt lighting – that would represent another 0.2% of the energy in the fuel sold: just to light the forecourt.

加油站前露天广场的照明是一个重要的能源成本。一个典型的小型加油站出售的燃油为38000L/周或约200万L/年。200万L汽油的热值约7千万MJ或（约）20000MW•h。一项研究表明，每年仅仅是露天广场照明的能源消耗就为40MW•h，这将是另一个在销售中仅为照亮露天广场而产生的0.2%的能源消耗。

These are relatively small numbers but they add up: just these factors alone would represent fuel consumption equivalent to over 3% of the energy content of the fuel sold.

这些都是比较小的数字，但这些因素加起来将相当于在燃料出售中的能源消耗量超过3%。

Compare the best IC car with the worst power stations

将最好的内燃机汽车与最差的发电站进行比较

Older power stations are less efficient, and coal-fired power stations produce a great deal of CO_2. For a variety of reasons, our current electricity generating infrastructure contains a lot of coal fired

旧的发电厂效率较低，并且燃煤发电厂产生大量的CO_2。由于各种各样的原因，我们目前的火力发电基础设施中包含着大量的燃煤发电站。从温室气体排放的角度来看这很糟

1 http://www.fleetdirectory.co.uk/fleet-news/index.php/2010/09/30/suckling-transport-improve-fleet-efficiency-while-recording-huge-falls-in-the-severity-and-frequency-of-crashes

㊀ http://www.fleetdirectory.co.uk/fleet-news/index.php/2010/09/30/suckling-transport-improve-fleet-efficiency-while-recording-huge-falls-in-the-severity-and-frequency-of-crashes。

power stations which can be made to look very bad from a GHG standpoint[1]. The comparison is drawn between idealised figures from the best modern diesel (ignoring the beat-up old rust-buckets and the V8 petrol 4x4s) on the one hand, and actual performance of the current generating infrastructure with present-day fuel mix on the other (Figure 9-8).

糕[⊖]。这种比较的一方面来自于现代最好的柴油机（忽略了破旧而老锈的内燃机以及 4×4 的 V8 汽油机）产生的理想数字，另一方面则来自于现时各种混合燃料的电力基础设施所达到的实际性能（图 9-8）。

Figure 9–8 An unfair comparison

图 9–8 一个不公正的比较

Back in the real world, the lifetime efficiency of a typical conventional car doing large numbers of short journeys with a cold engine in heavy traffic will be a lot less than the theoretical efficiency figure. For these and other reasons battery vehicles can be expected to bring about a significant real-world reduction in total energy use and emission of pollutants.

回到现实世界中，一个典型的传统汽车冷发动机时在交通繁忙的路上做大量短途旅行的全程效率比理论效率的数字要低很多。由于这些以及其他原因，可以预期，电池车辆在真实世界中的总能耗和污染物的排放将有一个显著的下降。

1 However, from a fuel-independence point of view, the replacement of oil with coal is a huge win: whilst our coal production is low, we have enormous reserves of the stuff left in the ground which could be exploited. Also we expect carbon capture to become possible with fixed power stations but not with cars.

⊖ 然而，从一个与燃料无关的角度来看，用煤替代燃油有很大的好处。虽然煤的产量很低，但在地下有庞大的储备可资利用。此外，我们预计固定电站中的碳捕获将成为可能，但在汽车上则不行。

➢ The impact on electricity generation

It is sometimes argued that a large fleet of battery vehicles would swamp the electricity generating infrastructure of many countries including the UK. In fact the opposite is likely; a large fleet of EVs could easily become an integral and indispensable part of that infrastructure. With the addition of some fairly simple electronics, a fleet of EVs would provide a unique opportunity to set up a scalable mechanism for buffering or smoothing electrical power.

Even in the worst case, the numbers suggest that EVs would not in fact require major additional generating capacity. The power consumption of EVs would be a small percentage of current peak demand from commercial and domestic customers. Department for Transport statistics[1] show an average UK annual mileage for cars of about 8,800 each. That is about 24 miles/day per car. If we assume between 4 and 5 miles per kW-hour, the average daily energy required by a battery vehicle at 24 miles per day is 5 - 6 kW-hours.

Even if we make the severe assumption that recharging is all done during the day (i.e. we spread the load over a 12 hour period rather than 24 hours), the power required is on average about 0.5 kW (6 kW-hours divided by 12 hours) per car or 500,000 kW for 1 million EVs. The UK generating capacity is around 80 GW i.e. 80,000,000 kW[2] - so the first million battery-powered vehicles would represent only about

1 See: http://www.dft.gov.uk/pgr/statistics/datatablespublications/vehicles/

2 2008 figures – see for example http://www.nationalgrid.com/uk/library/documents/sys05/default.asp?action=mnch3_11.htm&Node=SYS&Snode=3_11&Exp=Y#Power_Station_Capacities

➢ 对发电量的影响

有时人们会认为，一个庞大的电池车辆队伍将吞没包括英国在内的许多国家的电力基础设施。然而事实却可能正好相反。一大队的电动汽车很可能会成为基础设施中一个不可或缺的组成部分。当加上一些相当简单的电子元器件后，电动汽车的车队将提供一个独特的机会，用于建立一个可扩展的缓冲或平衡电力的机制。

数字表明，即使在最坏的情况下，电动汽车实际上不需要大量的额外发电量。电动汽车的功耗将只占当前商业及住宅客户峰值功率需求的一个很小的百分比。（英国）交通运输部的统计数据㊀显示，英国每辆汽车平均每年的行驶里程约为14000km，即每车约38km/天。如果我们假设每千瓦小时可行驶6~8km，平均每天38km的电池车一天所需的能量为5~6kW•h。

即使我们作出这样严格的假设，即所有的充电都在白天完成（将负载在12h而不是24h内平均），每辆车所需的平均功率约为0.5kW（6kW•h除以12h），或对100万电动汽车而言是50万kW。英国的发电能力为8000万kW左右㊁，因此一百万辆电动汽车将只有目前电网容量的0.6%~0.7%，这是小到几乎微不足道的。

㊀ 参阅http://www.dft.gov.uk/pgr/statistics/datatablespublications/vehicles/。

㊁ 2008年的数字，参阅http://www.nationalgrid.com/uk/library/documents/sys05/default.asp?action=mnch3_11.htm&Node=SYS&Snode=3_11&Exp=Y#Power_Station_Capacities。

0.6% - 0.7% of current grid capacity. That is so small as to be virtually insignificant.

Even if all 26 million private cars on Britain's roads were eventually replaced by battery-powered ones, we would only be talking about a 16% - 17% uplift in power requirements.

即使在英国路上所有的2千6百万辆私家车最终由电池车取代了，我们也只有16%~17%附加电能的需求。

There is another major factor. The experience of early adopters is that most charging of EVs takes place, not during the day at public charging stations, but at night. Electrical demand falls off precipitously in the late evening (Figure 9-9). If most EV charging occurred in this period substantial EV-related demand could be added without any significant increase in peak demand.

还有另外一个重要因素。早期电动汽车使用者的经验是，大部分电动汽车并非白天在公共充电站上充电，而是晚上充电。电力需求在深夜时急剧下降（图9-9）。如果大多数电动汽车的充电都发生在此期间，大量与电动汽车相关的电力需求可以在没有任何显著增加峰值需求的情况下得以满足。

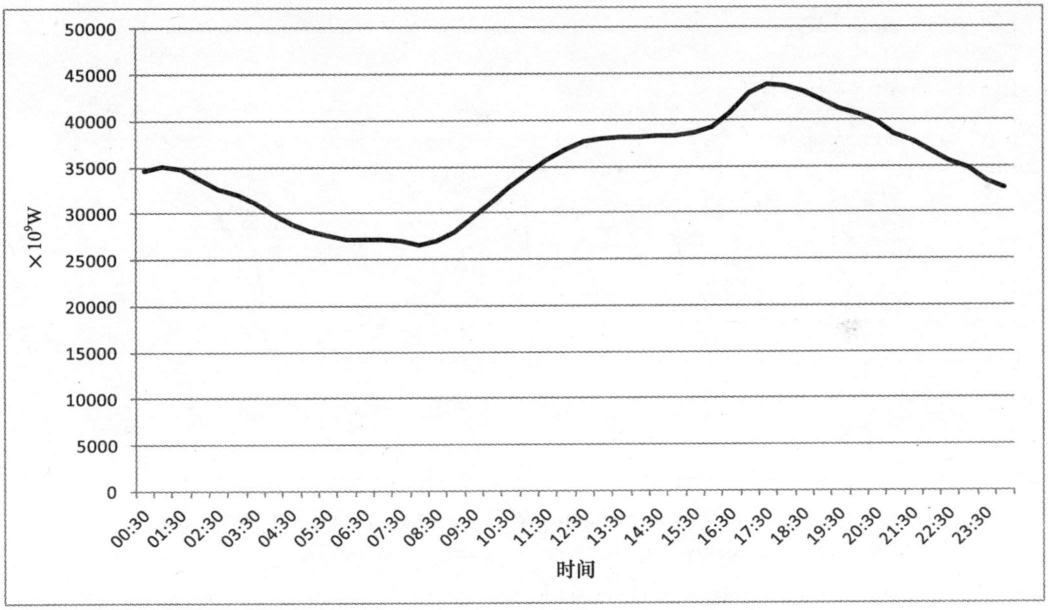

Figure 9–9 UK Power Demand on 5th January 2011

图9–9 2011年1月5日英国的电力需求

So much for the power requirements of EVs. Now for the benefits for power generation, which have the potential to be huge. The big problem for electricity generation is that (apart from expensive

关于电动汽车的电力需求就谈这些。现在谈谈对于发电站的巨大的潜在益处。电力的最大问题是，除了昂贵的抽水蓄能外，它不能被大规模地存储。它必须在需要的瞬间被产

pumped storage) electricity cannot be stored in a scalable fashion. It must be produced the instant that it is needed. This means that some generating capacity must be kept in reserve, ready to meet the huge fluctuations in demand that can occur, such as when (for example) everyone switches on their electric kettle at half time in a major nationally-televised football match (see Figure 9-10). Some of this is so-called "spinning reserve" where a certain amount of generating capacity is operating at partial load (or even zero load). This has a potential impact on efficiency. Sometimes the reverse happens: an event triggers a sudden drop in demand (see Figure 9-11); this again reduces efficiency.

生。这意味着我们必须维持一定的发电量储备，以满足可能发生的巨大的需求波动，例如在一个重要的全国电视直播的足球比赛半场休息期间，所有人都接上电热水壶烧水（图 9-10）。这些有时被称为所谓的“运转储备”，即发电量中的一部分在部分负载（或者甚至为零负载）下运行。这对发电效率将有潜在的影响。有时情况则正相反。某个事件触发需求的突然下降（图 9-11），这又降低了发电效率。

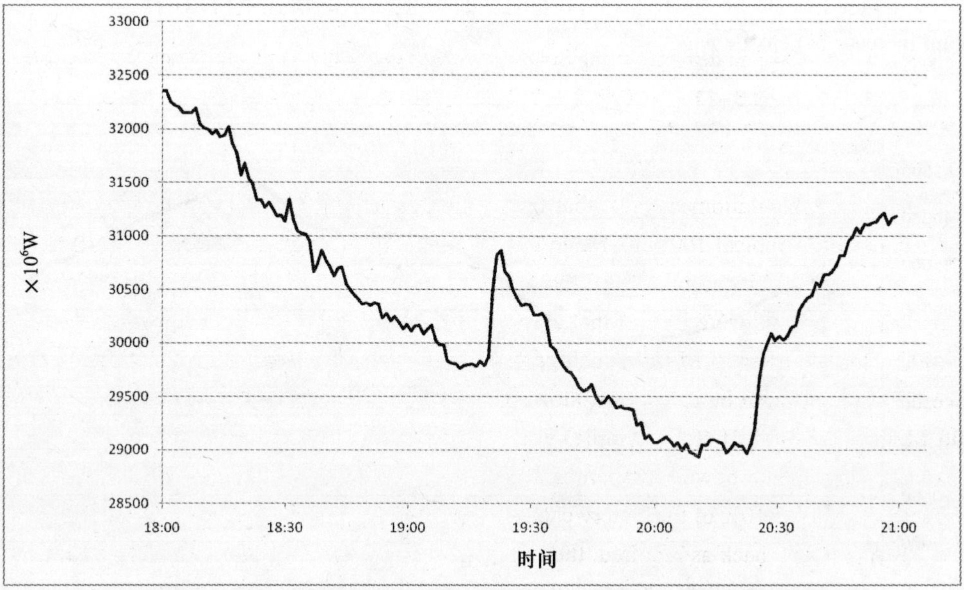

Figure 9–10 Half time surge 12 June 2010 - Data for Figure 9-10 and Figure 9-11courtesy Energy Requirements, Network Operations, National Grid

图 9–10 2010 年 6 月 12 日半场休息时的用电高峰（图 9-10 和图 9-11 的数据由国家电网网络运营部的能源需求室提供）

Most cars spend most of the time parked. The batteries in a fleet of parked EVs could (assuming they were plugged in and had the right electronics) be used as a huge buffer for smoothing out such peaks and troughs. This is sometimes referred to as "vehicle-to-grid" or "V2G" .

大多数汽车在大部分的时间都停着。一队停放着的电动汽车的电池可以作为一个巨大的缓冲器，被用来平滑波峰和波谷（假设它们被插入充电并有适当的电子设备），这有时被称为“汽车电网”或“V2G”。

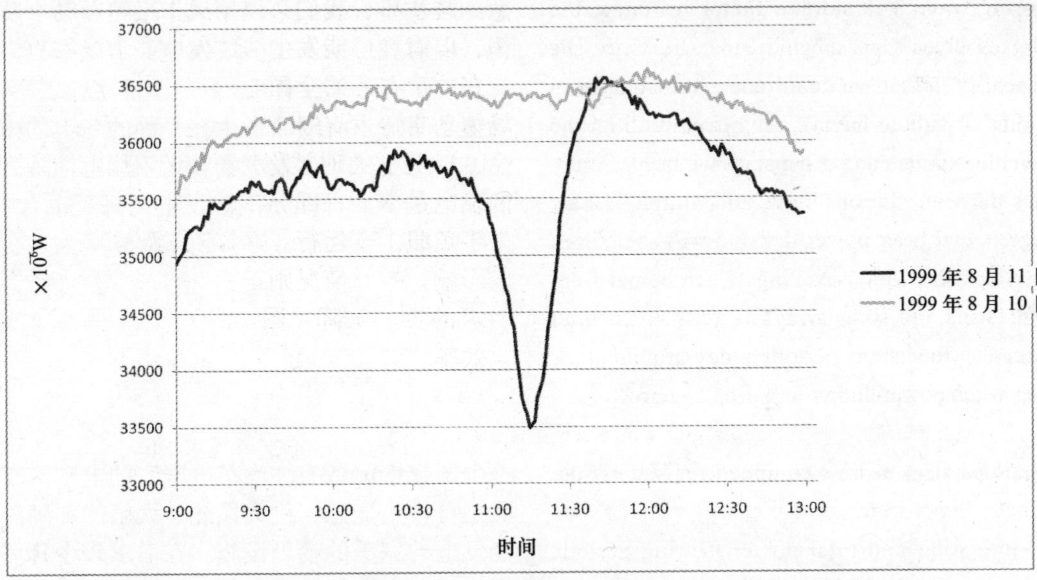

Figure 9–11 Drop in demand during Solar eclipse (August 1999) compared with previous day

图 9–11 1999 年 8 月日食期间的用电需求较前日下降

Order-of-magnitude calculations suggest that this could be significant. A typical 100 mile range EV might have a battery capacity around 25 kW-hours. If 40% of cars on the road were EVs of that class, that would be a little over 10 Million such cars. They would between them be capable of storing 250,000 Megawatt-hours. If (for example) contracts existed between the power companies and the EV owners that up to 10% of the battery capacity could be "borrowed" back as required, then up to 25 GW hours would be available. This would be more than enough to handle half-time surges.

数量级上的计算表明这种缓冲效果可能是显著的。一个典型的 160km 行驶里程的电动汽车所具有的电池容量约为 25kW•h。如果 40% 在路上的汽车都是那类电动汽车，则说明（在英国）将有超过 1 千万辆这样的车。在它们之间将能够存储 2500 亿 W•h 的电能。如果（例如）在电力公司和电动汽车业主间有这样的合同，即高达 10% 的电池容量可按要求被“借”回来，则可用的能量将高达 250 亿 W•h。这将足以处理半场休息时间的电力激增。

If 80% of Britain's cars were EVs, and if battery advances meant that most cars had 75 kW-hour packs then 150 GW hours could in theory be made available. To put that in perspective, that would be sufficient to run the entire country with every power station shut down for between 1.5 and 2.5 hours (in average 112 minutes) depending upon the time of day. The picture becomes even more

如果英国 80% 的汽车是电动汽车，且电池的进展意味着大多数汽车具有 75kW•h 的电池组,那么理论上可以提供1500亿 W•h 的电力。从广义的角度上看，当所有的电站都关闭时，根据不同的时间段，这些电力将足以为整个英国供电 1.5~2.5h（平均值为 112min）。当您开始考虑可再生能源，如风能、太阳能、潮汐能等时，前景将变得更加光明。可

enticing when you start to factor in renewable energy sources such as wind, solar, tidal etc. The sad reality is that we could cover the country in windmills without having any effect at all on the conventional generating capacity we need. Sometimes the wind doesn't blow, and Murphy's Law suggests that peak power demand will sometimes occur on calm winter evenings when output from wind farms and solar arrays is zero. Even tidal power has four short periods a day around slack water when power output will drop to zero.

悲的现实是，我们可以用风车来覆盖整个英国，但对我们所需的传统发电能力丝毫也没有影响。有时并没有风，并且墨菲定律表明，峰值功率需求有时会发生在平静的冬天的夜晚，以至于从风力发电场和太阳能电池阵列的输出是零。即使是潮汐发电，每天也有4个平潮期，导致输出功率下降为零。

A national fleet of EVs equipped for V2G is the perfect adjunct to renewable energy sources such as wind, solar and tidal power. During periods of slack demand and high power availability, the excess energy can be used to charge vehicle batteries. When the wind dies down and demand goes up, power can be borrowed back from those same vehicle batteries.

一个国家中配备有“汽车电网”的电动汽车队是可再生能源，例如风能、太阳能和潮汐能发电的完美的辅助设施。在需求较少且可用电能较多期间，多余的电能可用于对车辆电池的充电。当风力消失且需求上升时，电力可以从那些汽车的电池中借用。

➤ The negatives

➤ 不利因素

Those are all the positive benefits of EVs and they are an impressive list. So what are the negatives? Surely battery powered vehicles have their drawbacks?

这些都是电动汽车的正面效益，它们都是令人印象深刻的。那么，负面因素是什么？电池供电的电动汽车真的有缺点吗？

Well yes – their key deficiency is the limited power that can be stored in today's batteries. Pure electric vehicles will in the near future have limited range, limited carrying capacity and a high price.

呃，有的。它们的主要不足之处在于当今的电池只能存储有限的电力。在不久的将来，纯电动汽车将只有有限的行程里程、有限的承载能力以及高的价格。

Hybrids have little or no range limitation, but suffer from the implicit drawback of having two of everything: an electric motor and an IC engine, a fuel tank and a battery, a fuel injection system and a controller, a battery charger and a fuel filler cap, a fuel gauge and a Depth of Discharge indicator. This can only make them heavier and more

混合动力电动汽车只有很少或根本没有行程里程的限制，但其明显的缺点是所有零部件都要两套：一个电动机和一个内燃机、一个燃油箱和一个电池组、一个燃油喷射器和一个控制器、一个电池充电器和一个油箱盖、一个油位计和一个放电深度指示器。这只能使它们比传统汽车或纯电动汽车更重、更贵。

expensive than either a conventional car or a pure EV. This is not unknown however. Modern sailing vessels inevitably have engines as well as sails. Aircraft have wheel brakes and steering as well as flight controls. Most submarines use diesel power on the surface and battery power submerged.

但这并非没有先例：现代帆船必须要有发动机和船帆；飞机具有机轮刹车和转向以及飞行控制；大多数潜艇在水面上使用柴油动力，在水底时则用电池做动力。

It is also worth considering the impact on our economic infrastructure. The currently-dominant vehicle manufacturers have been slowly refining IC drivetrains for a hundred years. If EVs take over from IC engined vehicles then all that experience, all those patents, all that commercial advantage, become worthless. The risk for the big motor manufacturers is that in the upheaval caused by EVs they will lose out to newcomers in the way that the dominant manufacturers of mechanical watches lost out to new electronic watch brands in the 1970's. The potential impact on western societies in particular could be drastic.

电动汽车对我们经济基础设施的影响也是值得考虑的。目前占主导地位的汽车制造商已经在内燃机驱动系统方面慢慢地完善了一百多年。如果电动汽车取代了内燃机汽车，那么所有的经验、所有的专利、所有的商业优势都将变得一文不值。大汽车制造商所面临的风险是，在由电动汽车所造成的动荡中，对于新的制造商它们将失去优势。这与1970年代机械手表制造商在与新的电子手表品牌对阵中失去主导地位的经历相似，尤其对西方社会的潜在影响可能是非常巨大的。

EVs need far less maintenance than IC engined vehicles. A major move to such vehicles would put half the world's car maintenance facilities out of business and make half the world's motor mechanics unemployed. For governments, a big risk is the loss of tax revenue. Road transport fuel is easy to tax separately because it only has one use, and it is a major taxation revenue stream. Electricity is a core component of our commercial and domestic energy infrastructure and taxing electricity used in road transport would be next to impossible.

比起内燃机汽车，电动汽车只要较少的维护。大举使用这种汽车将使世界上一半的汽车维修业无事可做，并使世界上一半的汽车技工失业。对政府而言，一个很大的风险是税收的损失。道路运输燃料很容易分开收税，因为它只有一个用途，而且这是一个很大的税收来源。电力是商业和住宅能源基础设施的核心组成部分，对道路运输用电进行征税几乎是不可能的。

The commercial interests of the oil companies and oil – dependent economies are too obvious to elaborate. No one in commercial life likes to see a major threat to one of their major revenue streams. There are many other areas of commercial life from oil refining to commercial vehicle production that would be affected to some degree.

石油企业和石油依赖型经济的商业利益所受的影响太过明显而不需详述。在商业生活中没有人愿意看到对其主要收入来源之一的重大威胁。从石油提炼到商用车的生产等商业生活的诸多其他领域也将受到一定的影响。

➢ Resource consumption by EVs

It is sometimes said (or implied by innuendo) that the widespread adoption of electric vehicles would merely shift the problem of resource consumption from one commodity (oil) to another (raw materials for batteries).

There is some truth and some error in this. Broadly speaking there is not enough lead in the world to support universal adoption of EVs powered by lead-acid batteries. Nickel and cadmium stocks are likewise limited, meaning that nickel cadmium or nickel metal hydride batteries are probably never going to dominate if there is a wholesale move to EVs. Cobalt for lithium cobalt batteries is also in short supply.

There is however enough lithium. One 1999 paper[1] concluded that a couple of lithium ion chemistries looked practicable for 2 billion EVs or more.

Electric vehicles have the potential to make our urban areas quieter, pleasanter and healthier places. Widespread adoption of EVs would reduce our wanton consumption of a precious resource that was given to all generations, not just ours. EVs do not steal food from the dinner tables of the world's poorest people.

There is however another good reasons to adopt them. They are more fun. People who drive EVs mostly wouldn't go back to IC engines if you paid them. EVs are in a different league when it comes to low end torque, and it is low end torque which makes a car feel responsive on the road. Travelling

1 "Large-scale Electric-vehicle Battery. Systems: Long-term Metal Resource. Constraints"by B. A. Andersson and I. Råde.

➢ 电动汽车消耗的资源

有时人们会说（或含沙射影地暗示），电动汽车的广泛使用只是将资源消耗的问题从一种商品（石油）转向另一种（电池原材料）。

这有一定的道理也有一些错误。概括地说，世界上的铅存储量远远不够支承普遍使用由铅酸电池提供动力的电动汽车。镍和镉的存储量也同样有限，这意味着如果电动汽车批量生产的话，镍镉或镍氢电池可能永远不会占主导地位。钴酸锂电池中所用的钴也将供不应求。

但锂是足够的。一篇 1999 年的论文[⊖]作出的结论表明，锂离子化学看起来可为 20 亿辆或更多的电动汽车使用。

电动汽车有可能使我们的城市变成一个更安静、更舒心、更健康的地方。电动汽车的广泛采用将减少我们肆意消费那些为世世代代而不只是为我们准备的宝贵资源。电动汽车不会从餐桌上去偷窃世界上最贫穷人的食物。

还有另一个很好的采纳它们的理由——它们更有趣。如果付得起的话，驾驶过电动汽车的人多数不会再驾驶内燃机汽车。在低速转矩方面电动汽车具有不同的体验，而正是低速时的高转矩使得汽车在路上有很好的响应。在一个晴朗的晚上开一辆敞篷的电动跑

⊖ B. A. 安德森和 I. 拉德，"大型电动汽车电池系统：长期的金属资源限制"。

in an open-topped electric sports car on a fine evening is a remarkable experience: surges of power accompanied by nothing more than a bit more wind noise.

车旅行是一个令人心旷神怡的体验——强劲的动力，伴随着仅有风吹过的声音。

➢ A final parable

Let me finish with a cautionary tale from a different era and a different domain. The piston engined Hawker Tempest and the jet engine Gloster Meteor entered RAF (Royal Air Force) service in 1944 within a few months of each other. The Hawker Tempest was one of the last of an illustrious line of piston engined fighters powered by huge engines honed by years of war. The Meteor was the first of the new breed of jet engined fighters. With a top speed a little over 430 m.p.h, the piston-engined Tempest was around 20 m.p.h. faster than the contemporary jet engined Mk I Meteor (Figure 9-12).

➢ 最后一个比喻

让我用一个来自不同时代和不同领域的警世故事作为本书的结束。1944 年在短短几个月内由活塞发动机驱动的霍克风暴和由喷气发动机驱动的格罗斯特流星战斗机分别在英国皇家空军服役。霍克风暴是一个杰出的、经过了多年战争磨炼的、由巨大的活塞发动机作动力的、最后的几架战斗机之一。流星雨则是第一架由喷气发动机作动力的战斗机的新品种。由活塞发动机作动力的风暴的最高速度略高于 690km/h，比同时代的喷气发动机 Mk I 型流星高出 30km/h 左右（图 9-12）。

Figure 9–12 Piston engined Tempest (left) and jet engined Meteor (right). The Tempest was 20 m.p.h.faster than the Mk 1 Meteor (Tempest photo courtesyof Gerald Trevor Roberts, Meteor photo courtesy of Nicholas Foss)

图 9–12 由活塞发动机供能的“风暴”（左）及由喷气发动机供能的“流星”（右）。“风暴”的速度比 Mk 1 流星每小时快 20mile（“风暴”的照片由杰拉尔德 • 特雷弗 • 罗伯茨提供，“流星”的照片由尼古拉斯 • 福斯提供）

Anyone looking at those numbers would have wondered why the RAF bothered with jet engined fighters. 18 months later they would have had their answer: a Meteor took the world air speed record at over 600 m.p.h: 80 m.p.h. faster than the current air speed record for piston engined aircraft.

看到这些数字的人们也许会想，为什么英国皇家空军要费那么大的劲儿去用喷气发动机的战斗机呢。18 个月后，它们就得到了答案。“流星”用超过 960km/h 的速度创造了世界航空领域的速度纪录，它比当时活塞发动机飞机的速度纪录高出了 130km/h。

Any new technology tends to start off at a disadvantage when compared with the incumbent technology. It happened with the jet engine and it happened with digital watches: and who can now credit that the earliest pocket calculators weighed half a kg and cost the equivalent of £1000 in today's money?

任何新的技术在开始时与现有的技术相比往往都处于劣势。这在喷气发动机上发生过，在数字手表上也发生过。现在谁会相信最早的袖珍计算器重达 0.5kg，且其价格相当于现今的 1 万元人民币呢?

When it comes to EVs we have not seen anything yet. We are still at the Mk1 Meteor stage of development. The first jet engines were bulky, temperamental, unreliable and had short service lives. Current EVs have poor range. Batteries are expensive, bulky and need careful management. All these problems will go away just as they went away for jet fighters in the first few years of the jet age.

对于电动汽车我们还没有看到任何的迹象。我们仍然在 Mk1 流星的发展阶段。第一个喷气发动机体积庞大、令人捉摸不定、不可靠、寿命短。目前的电动汽车行驶里程短、电池价格昂贵、体积庞大、需要仔细地管理。正像喷气式战斗机在喷气机时代最初几年所经历的那样，但所有这些问题都会迎刃而解。

If EVs become mainstream they will make piston-engined cars obsolete just as jet fighters rendered piston-engined fighters obsolete. Piston-engined cars won't disappear altogether – enthusiasts will still run them as a weekend hobby, just as enthusiasts still fly old Mustangs, Spitfires, Bearcats and Tempests: but no one will use them for daily transport.

如果电动汽车成为主流，就像当年喷气式战斗机使得活塞发动机式战斗机变得过时一样，它们也将使活塞式发动机汽车变得过时。但活塞式发动机汽车不会完全消失，它们的爱好者们仍然会在周末开一开，就像现在还有爱好者在驾驶老式的野马、喷火、斗士和风暴战斗机一样，但没有人会将它们作为日常交通工具。

10 Selected Bibliography
参考书目选编

I've mentioned a number of papers in the text and included data about them as footnotes. Here are a number of books for further reading. I've included both the good stuff and also some that looked interesting but which I cannot recommend. Apologies to any authors who feel misrepresented. Works are listed in alphabetical order by first author. The comments are all mine, although they have in most cases been previously published elsewhere.

我在本书中提到过好几篇论文并作为脚注使用了那里的数据。下面是一些可供进一步阅读的书籍。我罗列了一些好的书目，也有一些看上去很有意思的书我不能推荐。如果任何作者觉得我曲解了他们，我在此表示道歉。以下书名按第一作者的字母顺序列出。虽然在大多数情况下它们在其他地方出现过，但这些评论都是我做出的。

➢ Good

➢ 好的参考书目

Owning an Electric Car: Discover the Practicalities of Owning and Using Electric Cars- for Business or Leisure

by: Boxwell, Michael Date: 2010 ISBN: 1907215107

Published by: Code Green Publishing, Paperback, 200 pages

拥有一辆电动汽车：作为商务或休闲拥有和使用电动汽车之实用性的探索

作者:迈克尔·波科斯维尔,出版日期:2010年,ISBN：1907215107

出版人：绿色代码出版社，平装，200页

This book deals with owning and operating an EV. The author speaks with authority on a topic he clearly knows well and has researched carefully. He writes lucidly and objectively, marshalling facts and letting the reader draw his or her own conclusions. What more could one ask?

这本书涉及拥有和使用一辆电动汽车。作者以权威的口吻阐述这一他清楚地知道并仔细研究过的话题。他以清晰而客观的方式进行写作，罗列出事实并让读者做出他们自己的结论。人们还能有什么苛求的呢?

The book does not go into much detail about different EV technologies, but that is not what it is about. There are other books for that. If (like me) you react badly to the word "green", but care about your grandchildren's energy supplies, the section on Electric Cars and the environment is worth the price of the book even if you are a petrol head.

这本书没有对不同的电动汽车技术进行详细讲述，但阐述这些技术并不是本书的目的，因为有其他的书籍涉及这些技术。如果您(像我一样)觉得"绿色"这个词不好，但出于关心子孙的能源供应的目的，即便您偏向于使用汽油机汽车，该书的电动汽车和环境这部分也使得这本书物有所值。

Bottled Lightning: Superbatteries, Electric Cars, and the New Lithium Economy

by: Fletcher, Seth Date: 2011 ISBN: 809030535

Published by: Hill and Wang, Hardcover, 272 pages

Excellent. The author is a science reporter and this book is both an easy read and also informative and well researched (it was recommended to me by an academic, a Fellow of the Royal Society which says it all really). It covers the history of Lithium cells and puts flesh on the dry bones of Lithium supply. A nice choice of title too!

瓶装闪电：超级蓄电池、电动汽车及新的锂经济

作者：赛斯·弗莱彻，出版日期：2011 年，ISBN：809030535

出版人：希尔和王出版社，精装，272 页

该书很优秀。作者是一名科学记者，这本书既容易被看懂又含有丰富信息和深入的研究（他是一名学者，一个英国皇家学会的院士推荐给我的。这足以说明一切）。它涵盖了锂电池的历史，并将锂的供应描述得有血有肉。标题的选择也不错！

Electric Motors & Drives

by: Hughes, Austin Date: 2005 ISBN: 750647183

Published by: Newnes, Edition: 3nd, Paperback, 384 pages

This book is brilliant. It isn't stylish, it's not lavishly illustrated, It isn't even a riveting read. It is, however, plain old fashioned lucid. Hughes was an academic, and if he lectured as well as he writes, his students understand electric motors.

He also speaks with authority. The diagrams are small, mostly simple black-and-white drawings, but they fit in with the text. By far the best book I've read in this subject area for a while.

电动机和驱动器

作者：奥斯汀·休斯，出版日期：2005 年，ISBN：750647183

出版人：纽纳斯出版社，版本：第三版，平装，384 页

这本书好极了。它并不时尚，也没有华丽的说明，它甚至读起来不够顺畅。然而，它有一种平白的老式清晰。休斯是一名学者，如果他的讲课像他的写作那样好，他的学生肯定能理解电动机。

他也是以权威的口吻在阐述。插图较小，且大多数是简单的黑白图形，但它们很适合于本书。本书是我这一段时间以来在本学科领域中读过的最好的一本。

Modern electric, hybrid electric, and fuel cell vehicles: fundamentals, theory, and design

by: Ehsani, Mehrdad Date: 2004 ISBN: 849331544

Published by: Boca Raton, FL : CRC Press

This book is just what it says on the tin - fundamentals, theory and design. It is quite well laid out, explained and written. It covers (among other things) transmis-

现代电动、混合动力和燃料电池车：基本原理、理论和设计

作者：迈赫达德·艾莎妮，出版日期：2004 年，ISBN：849331544

出版人：佛罗里达州博卡拉顿 CRC 出版社

这本书正如它在封面所说的那样——基本原理、理论和设计。它的排版、说明和书写都很好。除其他议题外它包括了变速器的拓扑

sion topologies, motors, batteries, controllers and fuel cells. The first section (essentially generalised tree-hugging) is a bit of an aberration and may irritate those who are uncertain about anthropogenic global warming

Witness to Grace

by: John B. Goodenough Date: 2008 ISBN: 1604747676

This is the autobiography of one of the most important (and maybe most under-rated) scientists of the late 20th/early 21st century. John Goodenough invented the lithium-cobalt battery, and a member of his team invented the Lithium iron phosphate battery. He was also one of the key figures in the development of solid-state memory, without which we would have no PCs He was for many years a professor at Oxford and in his late eighties was still professor of mechanical engineering and materials science at the University of Texas at Austin.

The book itself is fairly short: an eclectic description of a personal, scientific and spiritual pilgrimage. Reflections on biblical verses rub shoulders with passages about itinerant electrons and transition metal oxides. Fortunately you don't have to understand either to profit from the book. There are vignettes, brief but fascinating, about co-operation with scientists in many countries including the cold war Soviet bloc.

➢ Middling

Battery Management Systems for Large Lithium Ion Battery Packs

by: Andrea, Davide Date: 2010 ISBN: 1608071049

Published by: Artech House (2010), Edition: 1, Hardcover, 300 pages

结构、电动机、电池、控制器和燃料电池。第一部分（主要从广义环保角度）有些畸形，并可能会激怒那些不相信人类活动会导致全球变暖的人们。

见证优雅

作者：约翰·B·古德诺夫，出版日期：2008 年，ISBN：1604747676

这是一本 20 世纪后期到 21 世纪初期最重要的（也可能是最被低估的）科学家之一的自传。约翰·古德诺夫发明了锂钴电池，并且他的团队的一名成员发明了磷酸铁锂电池。他也是在开发固态存储器方面的关键人物之一。没有固态存储器我们就没有电脑。他曾任牛津大学教授多年，他 80 多岁时还是德克萨斯大学奥斯汀分校的机械工程和材料科学教授。

该书本身相当短。它从个人的、科学的和精神追求的方面进行叙述，视角广，不拘一格。对圣经经文的思考反映在关于游动电子和过渡金属氧化物段落的描述中。所幸的是，为从本书中获益，您不必要了解这些。书中有许多简洁却引人入胜的小插曲，提到与许多国家，包括前苏联的科学家合作的经历。

➢ 中等用处的参考书目

大型锂离子电池组的电池管理系统

作者：达维德·安德烈，出版日期：2010 年，ISBN：1608071049

出版人：艺达大厦出版社（2010 年），版本：第 1 版，精装，300 页

There is a school of thought that BMS systems do more harm than good. This book is an authoritative presentation of the "pro" camp from someone who builds BMS systems for a living, and is useful for anyone wants to understand both sides of the argument.

有一个流派认为电池管理系统弊大于利。这是一本权威介绍“正方”阵营的、以建立电池管理系统为生者的代表作，对任何想要了解双方观点的人也是有用的。

A good grasp of school-level physics is helpful for readers of this book. For sections of it you also need some familiarity with the jargon of modern electronics - MOSFETS, ASICs, Multiplexers and the rest - but the book still has value if you skip those bits. To the author's credit he doesn't big up his own products, and uses plenty of examples of competitive devices. He also to his credit goes into some details of precautions to take when wiring up circuits, and give an example of a converted Prius, burned out for lack of a washer on a battery connection.

读者若对高中物理有很好的把握将有助于对本书的理解。对于这本书的某些章节，您还需要熟悉一些现代电子技术的术语——MOSFET（金属氧化物半导体场效应晶体管）、ASIC（专用集成电路）、多路复用器及其他。但如果您跳过那些章节，这本书仍然具有价值。以该书作者的信用，他并没有吹捧他自己的产品，而是使用了大量竞争对手的设备的例子。他还以他的信用详述了在电路布线时必须采取的一些预防措施的细节，并举了一个改装过的普锐斯的例子，由于在电池的连接处没有垫圈而烧毁。

The book has in my view three weaknesses. Firstly the big question with Lithium Ion battery packs is the extent to which individual cells in a pack drift apart in capacity and state of charge. There is published test evidence of this with AGM (a form of valve regulated lead acid) batteries, but the author presents no hard documentary evidence to confirm that Lithium chemistry cells behave the same way. Secondly his arguments for top-balancing rather than bottom balancing are rather shaky. Thirdly, it is an expensive book.

我认为这本书有三个弱点。首先对锂离子电池组而言，最大的问题是单个电池单元在何种程度上对其容量和荷电状态的漂移。AGM（某种形式的阀控式密封铅酸）电池的测试结果已经公布于众，但该书的作者并没有可靠的证据证明锂化学电池具有相同的行为方式。其次，他对顶部平衡而不是底部平衡的论述是很不可靠的。第三，这本书很贵。

Build Your Own Electric Vehicle

by: Brant, Bob Date: 1993 ISBN: 830642315

Published by: McGraw-Hill/TAB Electronics (1993), Edition: 1, Paperback, 310 pages

建造您自己的电动汽车

作者：鲍勃·勃兰特，出版日期：1993 年，ISBN：830642315

出版人：麦格劳 - 希尔 /TAB 电子学出版社（1993 年），版本：第一版，平装，310 页

This review covers the 1993 edition. Seth Leitman's update is reviewed below

这里的评论仅对 1993 年的版本。对于赛斯·莱特曼更新版的评论见下。

The book is mixed - good in parts, not so good in others. I found the explanation of controllers very useful. The stuff about EVs and the environment was a bit tedious. The whole book naturally suffered from being a bit dated but much of it was still relevant (depressing how little real progress has been made in the last 19 years).

这本书有好有坏，一部分很好，而其他部分则不是那么好。我发现它对控制器的描述非常有用。有关电动汽车和环境的部分则有点乏味。整本书自然显得有点过时，但它的大部分仍然是有用的（令人郁闷的是在过去 19 年中已经取得的真正进展是如此之少）。

Electric Motors - Workshop Practice Series

by: Cox, Jim Date: 2007 ISBN: 1854862464
Published by: Trans-Atlantic Publications, Inc., Edition: 2nd, Paperback, 134 pages

电动机 - 车间实践系列

作者：吉姆•考克斯，出版日期：2007 年，ISBN：1854862464
出版人：跨大西洋出版公司，版本：第二版，平装，134 页

The good bits: the author writes with authority on a subject that he clearly knows well. The book seems well organised and is generally well written and illustrated clearly.

本书的优点是作者以权威的口吻描述他显然很熟悉的主题。这本书组织得很不错，总的说来写得很好并且解释得很清楚。

The not-so-good: the book is a little bit limited in its scope, with all the examples being small motors. You won't find the kind of motor used in the Tesla for example. I'd have liked to have seen a bit more on brushless DC motors. Also (a minor carp) some of the photographs were a bit dark and a bit small. Whether you find the book useful probably depends on what you are looking for and what else you have read. If you run a small machine shop, I guess it would be ideal. I'm glad I read it but I probably won't read it twice.

不太好的方面是，本书在论题上有点受限，所有的例子都是小型电动机。例如，您找不到像应用于特斯拉电动车那样的电动机。我更愿意看到对无刷直流电动机的篇幅更大一些。另外，（很小的不足）有些照片有点暗，有点小。这本书好不好可能取决于您需要什么，以及您还读过其他什么书籍。如果您正在经营一个小型的机械加工车间，我认为这本书是很理想的。我很高兴我读了它，但我可能不会再读第二遍了。

Lightweight Electric/Hybrid Vehicle Design (Automotive Engineering)

by: Fenton, John Date: 2001 ISBN: 750650923
Published by: Butterworth-Heinemann, Perfect Paperback, 320 pages

轻便的电动 / 混合动力汽车的设计（汽车工程）

作者：约翰•芬顿，出版日期：2001 年，ISBN：750650923
出版人：巴特沃思 - 海涅曼出版社，完美平装，320 页

This is a highly academic work. If you don't have an engineering degree or equivalent, don't bother.

这是一本学术性很强的著作。如果您没有一个工程学位或同等学历就不要去读它了。坦

Even at that, the structure is, frankly, muddled. The diagrams are poorly labelled and, one suspects, sometimes chosen for availability rather than to serve the flow of the narrative. Concepts and organisations pop up at random. For example PNGV is mentioned on page 61, but not explained to p98.

率地说，即便如此，该书的结构是有点乱的。插图的标记很差，并且令人怀疑有时插图的选择是根据该图能否被方便地找到，而不是服务于文中的叙述。各种概念和组织随机地被列出。例如书中的第 61 页提到 PNGV（新生代汽车联盟），但直到第 98 页才对此做出解释。

Most of the last 75 pages relate to vehicle structures and suspension for efficiency that apply to any vehicle; not just electric ones. Most of the references and recommendations for further reading date from the mid nineties or earlier. The only redeeming feature is that the authors clearly know their stuff.

最后 75 页中的大部分涉及车辆结构和防震系统的效率，它们可用于任何汽车，而不仅仅是电动汽车。大多数的参考文献和进一步的阅读材料都是 90 年代中期或更早的。唯一可取之处是作者对他们自己所写的内容很熟悉。

Electric Motors and Control Techniques

by: Gottlieb, Irving Date: 1994 ISBN: 70240124

Published by: McGraw-Hill/TAB Electronics, Edition: 2, Paperback, 304 pages

电动机及其控制技术

作者：欧文•戈特利布，出版日期：1994 年，ISBN：70240124

出版人：麦格劳 - 希尔 /TAB 电子学出版社，版本：第二版，平装，304 页

This book is in many ways a good effort. It is detailed and explores some unusual motor configurations. The first third is about various designs of electric motor and most of the rest is about controllers, with a shortish section at the end about electric vehicles and discussion of hyperflywheels, cold fusion and the like.

这本书在很多方面都尽了力，很详细，并探讨了一些不寻常的电动机配置。本书的前三分之一是关于电动机的各种设计，其余大部分是关于控制器的，结尾有一小部分是有关电动汽车的，并讨论了超级飞轮和冷聚变等。

The main problem for me was that it was dated. There was no mention of IGBTs for example and in the (brief) discussion of Electric Vehicle batteries, no mention of Nickel metal-hydride batteries. Lithium batteries were only mentioned as little more than a research project. The other thing I struggled with was that the text was poor at explaining principles: a few paragraphs of description, then it would slap a circuit diagram in front of you.

我的主要问题是这本书的写作时间。例如它没有提及 IGBT（绝缘栅双极晶体管），并且在（简要）讨论电动汽车的电池时没有提到镍金属氢化物电池。锂离子电池只作为一个研究项目被稍稍提到。让我觉得费力的另一个问题是该书解释原理部分的文字较差，在几段的描述之后摆在您面前的往往会是一个电路图。

21st Century Hybrid Car and Hybrid Electric Vehicle Technology Assessment, Report for the Department of Energy

by: Government, U.S. Date: 2005

ISBN: 142200032X

Published by: Progressive Management, Ringbound, 138 pages

21世纪混合动力汽车和混合电动汽车技术的评估，美国能源部的报告

作者：美国政府，出版日期：2005年，ISBN：142200032X

出版人：渐进式管理出版社，环装订成册，138页

This work is a cross between an article and an academic paper. It is quite readable. It's based wholly on a series of simulations using the ADVISOR package. Despite its date, the content is a little dated though. NiMh batteries are assumed. Also the baseline comparison conventional vehicles are US mid-sized petrol vehicles. Comparison with a European diesel would have yielded different results. They dismiss out of hand the idea of a series hybrid with an engine sized for average power requirements - which is close to what the PML Flightlink Mini has already demonstrated.

这份报告介于一般性文章和学术论文之间。它具有很好的可读性。它完全根据ADVISOR软件包的一系列模拟来评估。由于出版的时间较早，内容有点过时了。镍氢电池在报告中也被提到。传统汽车的比较基准是美国的中型汽油车。若与欧洲柴油车相比将会有不同的结果。他们摒弃了平均功率需求时串联混合动力的想法，这与PML Flightlink（译注：PML Flightlink是英国汉普郡一家具有50年历史的、专门从事设计和制造扁平式电动机的公司）的迷你车已展示的观点相同。

There is an interesting discussion of "grid-connected" (plug in) hybrids. They investigate a hybrid configuration with an IC engine sized to handle gradeability (20 minutes up 6.5% grade at 55mph), plus Electric Motor sized for acceleration. This is a timely reminder of the careful trade-offs in specifying engine and motorsizes.

该报告对“电网连接”（插入式）混合动力汽车有一个有趣的讨论。他们研究了一种混合动力的配置，该配置由一个能用来处理爬坡（以88km/h的速度在坡度为6.5%的坡上持续20min）的内燃机和一个能用来加速的电动机所组成。这项研究对于在确定发动机和电动机的大小时进行仔细权衡是很有用的。

Propulsion systems for hybrid vehicles

by: Miller, John M. Date: 2004

ISBN: 863413366

Published by: London : Institution of Electrical Engineers.

混合动力汽车的驱动系统

作者：约翰•M•米勒，出版日期：2004年，ISBN：863413366

出版人：伦敦：英国电气工程师学会出版社

This is a very detailed and quite highly mathematical coverage of hybrid architectures, motors, batteries, controllers etc. The strength of this book is

本书非常详细地了介绍混合动力汽车的体系结构、电动机、电池、控制器等，但需要相当高深的数学知识。这本书的强项是其权威性、仔

its authoritative and carefully-researched content and good references. Its weakness is that it does not explain many of the concepts and terms that it uses. This is a book which will send the beginner to sleep but should deepen the knowledge of readers who are already familiar with the content.

细研究过的内容及良好的参考文献。缺点是它并没有解释很多它用过的概念和术语。这是一本会令初学者打瞌睡的书，但对那些已经熟悉本书内容的读者则可深化他们的知识。

In summary, a book for experts only.

总之，本书仅适用于专家。

The complete idiot's guide to hybrid and alternative fuel vehicles

by: Nerad, Jack R. Date: 2007
ISBN: 9781592576357
Published by: New York, N.Y. : Alpha Books, c2007.

混合动力和可替代燃料汽车的完整的白痴指南

作者：杰克 •R. Nerad，出版日期：2007 年，
ISBN：9781592576357
出版人：纽约阿尔法图书出版社（2007 年）

This is a survey of then-current options for alternative propulsion cars in the US. It is non-technical (it deals more with behaviour than construction details). The content is quite well-balanced: for example it addresses "green" issues but doesn't assume that the reader is a tree-hugger. Very properly in my view, the author handles man-made global warming as theory rather than fact without requiring the reader to adopt one position or another.

这是当时美国关于可替代动力汽车的一项调查。它不涉及技术（它更多地涉及行为而不是结构上的细节）。其内容是相当均衡的，例如它谈到"绿色"问题，但并不假定读者是环保主义者。作者将人为的全球变暖问题作为理论，而不是事实来处理，它并不要求读者去赞同一方或另一方的观点。这在我看来是非常恰当的。

It covers hybrids, EVs (briefly), flex fuel, displacement on demand, diesels (old news for Europeans but less common in the US), autogas and hydrogen. The book is an easy read: clearly written, nicely laid out and with lots of space on the page.

它涵盖了混合动力电动汽车（简要地）、柔性燃料、按需换置、柴油车（对欧洲人而言是旧闻但在美国并不常见）、燃气汽车和氢燃料汽车。这是一本易读的书。它叙述清楚、布局合理且在页面上有大量的可用空间。

Electrical Contacts: Principles and Applications (Electrical and Computer Engineering)

by: Slade, Paul G. Date: 1999 ISBN: 824719344
Published by: CRC, Edition: 1, Hardcover, 1104 pages

电气接触：原理与应用（电气与计算机工程）

作者：保罗 •G• 斯莱德，出版日期：1999 年，
ISBN：824719344
出版人：伦敦 CRC 出版社，版本：第 1 版，精装，1104 页

This is a serious academic work of over 1000

这是一本严肃的学术著作，页数超过 1000。

pages and covers a range of topics in detail from the mechanical and electrical issues in connector design to arcing in high-current switches. There is a lot of detailed information on the behaviour of different kinds of materials and platings. The book introduced me to the idea of 'fretting' (the build up of insulating oxides in a connector resulting from wear under vibration) and discusses the benefits of using lubricants on connectors: although the discussion is fairly academic for the general user. There is a discussion of brush design relevant to DC motors with a reminder of the trade off between electrical efficiency and brush life.

它详细讨论了一系列主题，涵盖了从连接器设计中的机械和电气问题到大电流开关中的电弧，提供了很多不同材料和镀层特性的详细信息。本书让我了解到了“微振磨损”（在连接器上由于振动产生的磨损而导致绝缘氧化物的堆积）的概念，并讨论了在连接器上使用润滑剂的好处。但对于一般用户而言，这种讨论是相当学术性的。书中对直流电动机中电刷的设计进行了讨论，并就电气设备的效率和电刷的寿命之间的权衡做出了提醒。

➢ Limited usefulness

➢ 用处有限的参考书目

Electric and hybrid vehicles : design fundamentals

by: Husain, Iqbal Date: 2003

ISBN: 849314666

Published by: London : CRC Press

电动和混合动力汽车：设计基础

作者:伊克巴尔•侯赛因，出版日期:2003 年，

ISBN：849314666

出版人：伦敦 CRC 出版社

Despite its title, this book is emphatically not for someone trying to understand the basics of EVs and HEVs. The qualitative descriptions are thin. A good example is the explanation of Peukert's number on page 68/69. This is almost wholly mathematical with no hint of its significance (a high Peukert number is an issue in an EV battery because it means the battery won't perform as well as expected at the high discharge rates used).

尽管书名是这样写的，但这本书的重点不是针对那些试图了解电动汽车和混合动力汽车基本知识的人。这本书在定性描述方面具有不足。一个很好的例子是 68~69 页处对帕克特数的解释。这几乎全是数学，没有一丝含义方面的解析（一个高的帕克特数字对电动汽车的电池是个问题，因为这意味着在高放电倍率时电池的性能将不如预期的那么好）。

Even at a qualitative level I did not have a great deal of confidence in the book. The coverage of engine and motor sizing for an hybrids in the final chapter seemed to me to be less incisive than I have encountered elsewhere, and possibly mistaken

即使在定性方面我对这本书也没有很大的信心。在我看来最后一章中关于为混合动力汽车确定发动机和电动机大小的内容不如我在其他地方看到不那么清晰，并且可能有误。

Novel cathodic materials for rechargeable Lithium batteries

by: Koltypin, Maxim Date: 2011

ISBN: 3639356993

Published by: VDM Verlag Dr. Muller, Paperback, 64 pages

This book has little useful content. It looks suspiciously like recycled material from the author's PhD thesis from 2006 which makes it an historical text in this field.

可充电锂电池的新型阴极材料

作者：马克西姆•科尔太平，出版日期：2011年，ISBN：3639356993

出版人：VDM出版社穆勒博士，平装，64页

本书没什么有用的内容。它看起来像作者2006年博士论文的废物再利用，这使得它像这个领域中的一个历史文本。

Build Your Own Electric Vehicle

by: Leitman, Seth Date: 2008 ISBN: 71543732

Published by: McGraw-Hill Professional, Edition: 2, Paperback, 327 pages

This is Leitman's update of Bob Brant's original 1993 book (see above).Like the original book it suffered from excessive tree-hugging. I read the book for an insight into electric vehicles, not a rehash of material from the International Panel on Climate Change. Given its date, I was surprised that there was not more discussion of Lithium batteries and AC drives.

Also, do not expect a lot of detail on the actual process of conversion. There was just one chapter on this and it was quite general - not clearly based on a single conversion exercise, and certainly nothing like detailed step-by-step instructions.Even the theory chapters were a bit shallow and lacking both clarity and authority. If you were expecting to come away with a clear understanding of the difference between a wound-rotor and a squirrel cage motor, or the pluses and minuses of different Lithium chemistries, you would be disappointed.

建造您自己的电动汽车

作者：赛斯•莱特曼，出版日期：2008，ISBN：71543732

出版人：麦格劳-希尔专业出版社，版本：第二版，平装，327页

这是莱特曼对鲍勃•勃兰特1993年那本书（见上文）的更新版。与原书相同，本书也过分强调环保。我读本书的目的是为了深入了解电动汽车，而不是那些来自国际气候变化专门委员会的老调重弹的材料。鉴于它出版的日期，我很惊讶它为什么不对锂离子电池和交流驱动做更多的讨论。

另外，您别指望在电动汽车的实际转换过程中会有更多的细节。只有一章是关于这方面的并且还是很笼统的，显然不是基于单一的转换经验，肯定也没有详细的一步一步的指导。即使是关于理论部分的章节也有点浅，缺乏清晰与权威性。如果您指望对绕线转子与笼式电动机之间的差异，或对不同锂化学电池的优缺点有清楚的认识，您会感到失望的。

Build Your Own Plug-In Hybrid Electric Vehicle (Tab Green Guru Guides)

by: Leitman, Seth   Date: 2009 629.229

ISBN: 71614737

Published by: McGraw-Hill/TAB Electronics, Edition: 1, Paperback, 320 pages

This book is riddled with basic misunderstandings (e.g. lack of clarity about the distinction between torque and power). One graph for example purports to show the power output of series DC motors but uses a typical torque curve instead, showing power as a maximum at zero r.p.m. (a mathematical impossibility) This is like finding a book on climate confusing heat and temperature: it undermines any confidence in anything else the author says. The text was poorly structured both in terms of the flow of the topics and the depth at which they were tackled: you would read a page of general description then turn the page to find a circuit diagram from a Prius.

Finally I found the environmental finger-wagging irritating: I bought the book wanting to understand more about the engineering of hybrids and the environmental bits struck me as both inappropriate and partisan.

构建您自己的插电式混合动力电动汽车（TAB 绿色宗师指南）

作者：赛斯·莱特曼，出版日期：2009，

ISBN：71614737

出版人：麦格劳 - 希尔 TAB 电子学出版社，版本：第一版，平装，320 页

这本书有许多基本的错误（例如，对扭矩和功率之间的区别缺乏清楚的认识）。例如有一个曲线试图显示串励直流电动机的功率输出，但用的是一个典型的转矩曲线。它表示在零转速的情况下功率最大（这在数学上是不可能的）。这就像在一本关于气候的书中混搅了热量和温度一样。这就降低了对作者在本书其他地方所说是否正确的信心。在论题的组织和它们被处理的深度方面，本书的结构都是不好的。您可能会看到某页是个一般的描述，但翻到新的一页时它却是普锐斯的电路图。

最后，我发现本书对环境的“指手划脚”令人不舒服。我买这本书的目的是想多了解些关于混合动力车的工程，但它对环境的描述给我的印象是不适当的而且是有偏见的。

The Electric Car: Development and Future of Battery, Hybrid and Fuel-Cell Cars (Iee Power & Energy Series, 38)

by: Westbrook, Michael H.   Date: 2001

ISBN: 852960131

Published by: Institution Electrical Engineers, Edition: 1st, Hardcover, 224 pages

This is a review of battery electric vehicles, which also covers fuel cell and hybrid cars. By the time I read it (2008), it was already a little dated, with some predictions looking mildly quaint. The style is a bit dry and much of it is not well explained. Don't bother unless you are happy about the distinction between (say) Watts and Watt-hours.

电动汽车：电池的发展和未来，混合动力和燃料电池汽车（IEE 电力和能源系列，38）

作者：迈克尔 •H• 威斯布鲁克，出版日期：2001 年，ISBN：852960131

出版人：英国电气工程师学会，版本：第 1 版，精装，224 页

这是一本对电池电动汽车进行评论的书籍，它也包括燃料电池和混合动力汽车。2008 年我读到它时，它已经有点过时了，有些预测也有点过时。其风格有点乏味，且许多内容并没有进行很好的阐述。除非您对（例如）瓦和瓦时的区别是清楚的，否则别碰它。

附录 Appendix Conversion of Commonly Used Imperial Units 常用英制单位换算表

英制单位多而复杂，除了一些最常用的以外，其他的单位大多数英国人也分不清楚。因此，本附录中只列出一些较常用的单位换算，对于那些不太常用的单位则不在本附录中列出。

1. 长度单位

1 mile（英里，哩）=1.609344 km（千米）=1760 yards（码）=5280 feet（英尺）

1 nautical mile（海里）=1852 metres（米）

1 furlong（浪）=220 yards（码）=201.17 metres（米）

1 fathom（英寻）=2 yards（码）=1.8288 metres（米）

1 yard（码）=0.9144 metres（米）=3 feet（英尺）

1 foot（英尺 ft, 复数为 feet）=30.48 centimetres（厘米）=12 inches（英寸）

1 inch（英寸）=2.54 centimetres（厘米）

1 inch（英寸）=1000 milliinches（英丝）

注：在英制单位里其实没有英分和英丝这种单位，1 英寸以下的长度，通常用英寸的分数来表示，如 1/2、1/4、1/8、1/16、1/32、1/64 英寸等。

2. 面积单位

1 square mile（平方英里）=640 acres（英亩）=259 hectares（公顷）

1 acre（英亩）=4840 square yards（平方码）=1/640 square mile（平方英里）

1 square foot（平方英尺）=144 square inches（平方英寸）=9.29 square decimetres（平方分米）

1 square yard（平方码）=9 square feet（平方英尺）=0.836 square metre（平方米）

3. 体积单位

1 cubic inch（立方英寸）=16.4 cubic centimetres（立方厘米）

1 cubic foot（立方英尺）=1728 cubic inches（立方英寸）=0.0283 cubic metre（立方米）

1 cubic yard（立方码）=27 cubic feet（立方英尺）=0.765 cubic metre（立方米）

4. 容积单位

1 US gallon（美加仑）=3.785 Litre（升）=4 US quarts（美夸脱）

1 US quart（美夸脱）=0.946 Litre（升）=2 US pints（美品脱）

1 US pint（美品脱）=0.473 Litre（升）=16 US fluid ounces（美液盎司）

1 US fluid ounce（美液盎司）=0.029 Litre（升）

1 UK gallon（英加仑）=4 UK quarts（英夸脱）=8 UK pints（英品脱）=4.546 Litre（升）

1 UK quart（英夸脱）=1.137 Litre（升）=2 UK pints（英品脱）

1 UK pint（英品脱）=0.5683 Litre（升）=20 UK fluid ounces（英液盎司）

1 UK fluid ounce（英液盎司）=28.4131 millilitre（毫升）

1 UK fluid dram（英液打兰）=3.552 millilitre（毫升）

5. 重量单位

1 ton（英吨，长吨）=1016 kg（千克）=20 hundredweights（英担）= 2240 pounds（磅）

注意：在英语中米制的吨叫 tonne，1 tonne（公吨）= 1000 kilograms（千克）。

1 short ton（美吨，短吨）=907 kilograms（千克）= 2000 pounds（磅）

1 hundredweight（英担）=50.8 kilograms（千克）=8 stones（英石）

1 stone（英石）=14 pounds（磅）=6.356 ki-

lograms（千克）

1 pound（磅）=16 ounces（盎司，常衡）=12 ounces（盎司，金衡、药衡）

1 pound（磅，常衡）=1.215 pound（磅，药衡、金衡）= 0.4536 kilogram（千克）

1 ounce（盎司）=28.3495 grams（克，常衡）=31.1035 grams（克，药衡、金衡）=437 grains（格令）

1 grain（格令）=64.8 milligrams（毫克）

6. 温度单位

华氏度 = 摄氏度 ×9 ÷ 5+32= 摄氏度 ×1.8+32

7. 货币单位

1 pound（英镑，GBP）=100 pence（便士）= 10 Chinese Yuan（元，人民币）= 1.5 US Dollar（美元）= 1.2 Euro（欧元）= 140 Japanese Yen（日元）

注：由于货币的兑换率每分每秒都在变，以上只给出本书翻译时的近似值。